Pro Ajax and the .NET 2.0 Platform

Daniel Woolston

Pro Ajax and the .NET 2.0 Platform

Copyright © 2006 by Daniel Woolston

ISBN-13 (pbk): 978-1-59059-670-8

ISBN-10 (pbk): 1-59059-670-6

Printed and bound in the United States of America 9 8 7 6 5 4 3 2 1

Lead Editor: Matthew Moodie
Technical Reviewer: Nick McCollum
Editorial Board: Steve Anglin, Ewan Buckingham, Gary Cornell, Jason Gilmore, Jonathan Gennick, Jonathan Hassell, James Huddleston, Chris Mills, Matthew Moodie, Dominic Shakeshaft, Jim Sumser, Keir Thomas, Matt Wade
Project Manager: Julie M. Smith
Copy Edit Manager: Nicole LeClerc
Copy Editor: Ami Knox
Assistant Production Director: Kari Brooks-Copony
Senior Production Editor: Laura Cheu
Compositor: Linda Weidemann, Wolf Creek Press
Proofreader: April Eddy
Indexer: Broccoli Information Management
Artist: April Milne
Cover Designer: Kurt Krames
Manufacturing Director: Tom Debolski

Distributed to the book trade worldwide by Springer-Verlag New York, Inc., 233 Spring Street, 6th Floor, New York, NY 10013. Phone 1-800-SPRINGER, fax 201-348-4505, e-mail orders-ny@springer-sbm.com, or visit http://www.springeronline.com.

For information on translations, please contact Apress directly at 2560 Ninth Street, Suite 219, Berkeley, CA 94710. Phone 510-549-5930, fax 510-549-5939, e-mail info@apress.com, or visit http://www.apress.com.

The source code for this book is available to readers at http://www.apress.com in the Source Code section.

For Terry and Cathy Woolston.
This book is a testament to the perseverance and faith
that you have had throughout the years.
Thank you.

Contents at a Glance

PART 1 ■ ■ ■ Ajax Concepts

PART 2 ■ ■ ■ Ajax Components

PART 3 ■ ■ ■ Concept to Code

PART 4 ■■■ Security and Performance

PART 5 ■■■ Moving Forward

Contents

PART 1 ■■■ Ajax Concepts

PART 2 ▪▪▪ Ajax Components

PART 3 ■■■ Concept to Code

PART 4 ■■■ Security and Performance

PART 5 ■ ■ ■ Moving Forward

About the Author

DANIEL WOOLSTON is a software engineer from the Grand Rapids, Michigan area. Daniel's software journey began in the late 1980s with the infamous Sinclair ZX80. His current ambitions involve developing next-generation .NET web applications utilizing the latest technologies and beyond. His work efforts have branched from Fortune 500 enterprise application development to pattern-driven project implementations on various corporate levels. He has years of experience in designing and distributing JavaScript/.NET components as well as numerous VB/VB .NET/C# development projects. When he's not cutting through code, he can usually be found in his makeshift mad-scientist basement lab building robots, one of which was recently featured in a national robotics magazine.

About the Technical Reviewer

 **NICK MCCOLLUM** has over 18 years of experience designing and developing enterprise applications on a variety of platforms. He is a principal consultant for NuSoft Solutions, Inc., and for the past year has been the architect and lead developer for Spout (www.spout.com). In addition to this publication, Nick has acted as a technical reviewer for *C# COM+ Programming* by Derek Beyer (Hungry Minds, 2001). He is a Microsoft Certified Solution Developer and was recently named one of the first Community Server MVPs by Telligent Software. In his free time, Nick coaches youth basketball and soccer and is a frequent presenter at Microsoft events and .NET user group meetings in the West Michigan area.

Acknowledgments

This book is barely the work of one man. So many people have shaped and contributed to the work as a whole that I will find it difficult to name them all. But if I miss anyone, it is an oversight and not a lack of gratitude.

First and foremost, I must thank Gary Cornell and Ewan Buckingham for making the book a reality. I can't imagine writing for anyone else. Thank you for your spontaneous words of encouragement and leadership on this project.

I also must give a special thanks to Nick McCollum for his enduring patience during the technical editing phase of the project. Without Nick's encouragement and mentoring, this would have been a hard book to write.

Thank you to the Apress team for your continuous and positive efforts: Laura Cheu, Matthew Moodie, Ami Knox, and Tina Nielsen. A special thanks to Julie Smith, who always seemed to know when I was in need of encouragement and was ready to help at a moment's notice.

I'd also like to express my undying gratitude to the NuSoft Solutions team. Your desire to be the best in the industry has certainly brought out the best in me. Thanks to all: Brian Anderson, Jim Becher, Aaron Kamphuis, Kevin Schultz, Rick Krause, Ted Walker, Mike Perry, CS Tang, Bruce Abernethy, Jack Leung, Bruce Benson, Keith Brophy, Dale Mansour, and Bob Kreha.

Thanks also to Adrian Pavelescu, Ryan Smallegan, and Stacy Rood for their words of encouragement and for helping me keep things in perspective.

I also need to say a special thanks to the founding members of Spout: Rick DeVos, Daryn Kuipers, Dave DeBoer, Paul Moore, and Bill Holsinger-Robinson. Without your vision and faith in cutting-edge web technology, this book would not have been possible.

Lastly, I must offer up an endless supply of appreciation and respect to Michelle, Aymee, and Michael Woolston. You have graciously given up a daddy and a husband for most of the year so that I could accomplish a long-standing goal. And now that I've finished the book, I find that the greatest achievement was not the book itself, but the encouragement and patience that you've given me for the last few months. Thank you so much!

Introduction

It's been well over a year since I first began working with the team over at Spout (www.spout.com). In the course of that year, I've been professionally challenged by the sheer amount of cutting-edge work that I have been asked to develop. I can still remember Brian Anderson (NuSoft Solutions) coming to Nick McCollum and me with a few sheets of paper detailing a new third-party web tool that we should take a look at. The design documents were a brief listing of the sample code for Ajax.NET by Michael Schwarz. Not only had Michael built an awesome library, but he had done so for free. Nick and I embraced the library without hesitation. Admittedly, we overused the library at first. We Ajax'd the site to its fullest extent. Need a user control built? Use Ajax! At least that is how it felt at first. We were truly excited (and remain so today) about the possibilities of Ajax and where it would lead our project. I want to share this excitement with you.

An Overview of This Book

I want to deal with the world of Ajax to its finest detail. In order to do that, we'll need to discuss where Ajax came from, what it comprises, and how we can implement modern third-party Ajax libraries. The technology is ever changing, and I encourage you to visit the various author sites found throughout the book so that you may stay up to date. Many of the chapters have real-world application, and you may find yourself coming back to the book as a reference for future projects. I would also encourage you to blog about your work and the obstacles you overcome. Had Peter Bromberg (http://petesbloggerama.blogspot.com) not taken the time to blog about his Ajax application, this book may have taken an entirely different course. Or perhaps never have been written at all. As you find the knowledge, share the knowledge. This book will help get you started.

- Chapter 1 will discuss briefly the history of DHTML and Ajax in general. You'll get a chance to look at some real-world examples of Ajax at work, so that you can get an idea of where the industry is leading with dynamic web development.

- Chapter 2 will be a short primer on the JavaScript language. A majority of the scripting concepts that will be used throughout the book are detailed here.

- Chapter 3 is a detailed discussion on the heart of Ajax: the XmlHttpRequest object.

- Chapters 4 and 5 discuss the role of Ajax in an n-tiered environment and the definition of Ajax as it relates to the world of rich clients.

- Chapter 6 is an examination of cascading style sheets and the Document Object Model. The DOM and CSS are two very key components to Ajax, and this chapter is vital to the book as a whole.

- Chapter 7 discusses the existence and details of various other Ajax entities out on the web. Should your future endeavors fall on non-.NET environments, this chapter will help you to seek out a comparative solution.

- Chapter 8 is an in-depth look at Jason Diamond's Anthem library. We'll be using his product in a majority of the sample applications that you'll be working through.

- Chapter 9 takes a cursory look at using Ajax with .NET web services.

- Chapters 10 through 13 are application-building-centric chapters. You'll have an opportunity to build Ajax websites that mimic some of the more popular technologies in the spotlight: tagging, type-ahead, and dynamic mapping.

- Chapter 14 will be an introduction to .NET 2.0 Web Parts and how the dynamic library can work within the constraints of the part.

- Chapters 15 through 19 will deal exclusively with the usage aspect of Ajax. How we design, debug, monitor, and scale the projects that we build will be the key concepts covered.

- Chapter 20 will wrap up the book with a detailed look at Microsoft's Atlas. We'll build a few applications to demonstrate some of the central functionality that the library provides.

Ajax Requirements

I'd like to discuss a few of the various requirements that Ajax may impose upon your development realm.

Browser Support

A key component of Ajax technology is the XmlHttpRequest object, and without it any form of communication with the server would be nearly impossible. It wasn't until Internet Explorer version 5 was released that the XmlHttpRequest capability was available to developers. Unfortunately, it was only functional within the IE browser. However, more and more companies/open source communities are embracing the object, and subsequently the XmlHttpRequest object has become widely compatible with modern browsers:

- Internet Explorer 5.0 and above

- Firefox 1.0 and above

- Safari 1.2 and above

- Opera 7.6 and above

- Konqueror

- Netscape 7.0 and above

JavaScript Enabled

One of the criticisms surrounding Ajax.NET technology is that unilateral support may be interrupted by those users who have disabled JavaScript or ActiveX functionality.

By default, most browsers will allow ActiveX and JavaScript to operate correctly. However, some third-party antivirus and web security software may limit the browser's ability to render Ajax.NET applications. Repairing the settings within Internet Explorer is as simple as modifying the selections under the Security tab of Internet Options.

Development Tools

You bought this book because you're keenly interested in developing Ajax.NET applications within the .NET Framework. Our obvious choice for .NET development is the Microsoft Visual Studio product collection. While this book centers primarily on ASP.NET 2.0 and Visual Studio 2005, you can just as easily port a majority (not including the Atlas stuff, of course) of this book to the 2003 edition. The technology is virtually unchanged across the platforms when dealing with the XmlHttpRequest object.

If you do not have Visual Studio 2005, I encourage you to visit the Microsoft site and download the (currently) free version of Visual Web Developer 2005 (VWD). It's an awesome application, and you can't beat the price.

VWD can definitely get you started on the ASP.NET 2.0 road, but ultimately you'll want to pick up the Visual Studio package. VWD is lacking in some core components that you'll definitely need long term:

- No mobile device support

- Missing full MSDN help file

- No Class Designer

- Lack of deployment tools

- No source code control

These are just a few of the differences between the two products, but they're enough to justify purchasing the full product later.

Programming Languages

Once you've installed a development tool, you'll want to decide on the language in which you'll develop. The code within this book is listed in C#, but can be easily ported over to Visual Basic .NET. I won't editorialize the ongoing debate on which is better. I will say that I was in total agreement with something that Rocky Lhotka said at a .NET users group meeting: "If you're not learning and using both, then you're selling yourself short." Well put, Rocky!

Ajax.NET Library

As Ajax grows in popularity, so does the volume of Ajax.NET interface libraries available across the web. Essentially these libraries take the complexity out of utilizing XmlHttpRequest and render simple methods for client- and server-side usage. You could, of course, skip the implementation of an Ajax.NET library and code the XmlHttpRequest processes yourself. However, as many developers have said, "Why reinvent the wheel?"

There are many libraries out there, as I've said before, but two stand out from the rest:

- *Michael Schwarz's Ajax.NET Professional* (http://weblogs.asp.net/mschwarz/): A popular and effective toolset. It's updated and supported by Michael and a newly established Google group (http://groups.google.com/group/ajaxpro). Keep in mind that this library makes use of HTTPHandlers and for some that could create some issues. I've had the opportunity to use this on a work-related project (www.spout.com) and was quite pleased with its transparent ability to "just work."

- *Jason Diamond's Anthem.NET* (http://jason.diamond.name/weblog/): Formerly referred to as *My Ajax.NET*, Jason's class library is compact and does not use HTTPHandlers. It's a single class file that can be implemented seamlessly into any ASP.NET project. This book will make use of this particular library, simply for its conciseness and ease of learning.

The Source Code for This Book

If you travel over to the Apress website (www.apress.com), you'll find the sample applications for each of the corresponding chapters. Click the Source Code link and search for *Pro Ajax and the .NET 2.0 Platform*. You'll find that the code has been organized in chapter format for easy location and execution.

Summary

I'm confident that working through the examples and illustrations contained within will leave you well prepared for some really cool development work. It truly is an exciting time in the web development world, and I hope that your journey through it is as fascinating as mine has been.

Thank you for buying the book! I hope it's as much fun to read as it was to write!

PART 1

■ ■ ■

Ajax Concepts

Everyone has an opinion on what constitutes Ajax technology. The term *Ajax*, coined by Jesse James Garrett of Adaptive Path, is actually an acronym for Asynchronous JavaScript And XML. However, for some, simply modifying a web page through CSS categorically indicates Ajax in use. Some say that Ajax is simply HTML with an inherent ability to avoid postbacks. Others would passionately argue that Ajax technology is the explicit access of server-side code from within the context of client-side scripts. So who's correct? Everyone! Ajax is a collaboration of technologies rather than a rigid enforcement of a particular tool or methodology. Ajax for the .NET Framework, an implementation of Ajax for the ASP.NET platform, marries CSS, HTML, JavaScript, and the .NET Framework to produce dynamic web content. However, this collaborative effort was not born in a day. It may surprise many to find out how this "new" technology has surfaced as a powerhouse of dynamic web content. Before we jump into coding and conventions, let's take a look at the relatively short history of web development.

CHAPTER 1

History and Revival of Ajax

The history of Ajax is not a solitary account of one particular technology. It's more of an analysis of web development as a whole. To appreciate the whole, we must look at the individual parts and how they came to be. And how they came to be is a bizarre and often surprising tale of corporate warfare and heroic deeds by developers of an age gone by.

OK, so maybe the age isn't that far gone, but at the current pace of Internet progress, it often seems that we should be reviewing in terms of decades as opposed to years. Those of us who have been with the software world for more than 10 years typically quantify the motion of the web in terms of technical checkpoints. I personally have a few defining moments that shape my perception of where the web has been recently. First and foremost was the BBS systems of the eighties. Sure, it was all text based, menu driven, and almost exclusively the stomping grounds of nerds, but it was innovative, and nearly anyone associated with it could visualize the coming communication storm that was brewing on the horizon of computer science.

Secondly, I think of the web in terms of browser purchase versus browser free-ness (I know, free-ness isn't officially part of the English language, but it's a cool descriptor of what Internet Explorer did for those of us who actually paid for Netscape.) You'll read more of the browser war momentarily. Finally, I think of the web in terms of when the web browser became a dynamic container for content. Shifting from static pages that folks like me simply accepted as the end-all of what the web form could be to a real-time interactive vehicle that could mimic Windows desktop applications has revitalized the IT market. Many developers that I've had the pleasure of talking to regarding Ajax have nearly the same perception of the recent explosion of web development and how it seems to resemble closely the dot-com era of the previous decade. It is truly an amazing time to be a software developer riding on the edge of a wave of new Internet capabilities. But how did we get from the ARPANET of the early seventies to this awesome state of the web today? Let's open our history books and start a cursory examination of modern nerd heritage.

The Age of Discovery

1970

Despite what Hollywood and television executives have pumped into your brain via the big screen and the dumb-inducing TV screen, the early seventies was not exclusively a period of drugged-out flower children roaming the countryside. Believe it or not, people actually had jobs. Some of those jobs even centered around technology. It was during this age that the predecessor of the modern Internet was birthed in all its binary glory. The ARPANET (Advanced Research Projects Agency Network) came to life as the end result of J. C. R. Licklider's notion of a "galactic network" of data communication. The first four *nodes* of Arpanet were limited to the west coast of the U.S. as shown in Figure 1-1.

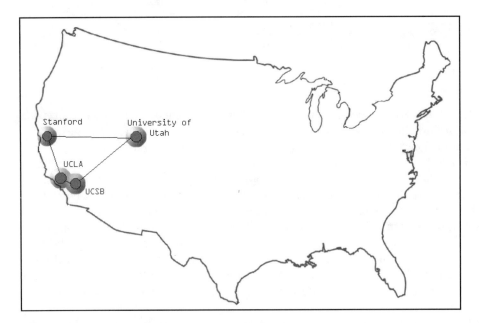

Figure 1-1. *The first four nodes of the ARPANET*

Licklider left the ARPANET project before the implementation of his concepts, but his 1962 series of memos would pave the way for the Internet that you and I use today.

1975

Bill Gates and Paul Allen developed BASIC for the MITS Altair 8800 around this time. Subsequently Microsoft was born.

1979

The first USENET groups joined the technology planet, allowing forum-style conversations on a very large scale. Compuserve became the first company to bring e-mail to the masses. Well into the mid-eighties, they would serve as the largest provider of "online" services. Prior to their competitive battle with AOL, it was typical for users of their "online" service to pay well over $10 an hour for access. However the early nineties brought about ISP pricing wars, and the model shifted from an hourly rate to a monthly fee, which is still the customary means of purchase. Compuserve would later be purchased by AOL in 1997 for a hefty sum of 1.2 billion dollars.

1991

It is generally accepted that the *Internet* was officially born in 1991 when CERN released World Wide Web software. Commercial restrictions on the Internet were then lifted, paving the way for corporate portal opportunities. By 1992, the web would grow to well over one million hosts.

The Age of Implementation

1993

NSF-funded National Center for Supercomputing Applications released Mozilla, the first graphics-based browser for the web. A Windows version of the AOL service hit the streets, bringing with it a multitude of the "general public," whereas previously the web was primarily a domain filled with nerds, scientists, and hobbyists all using text-based browser applications. Mozilla's support of inline images brought an entirely new dimension to the web. The explosion of Internet access spread across the world with tremendous fervor. Most historians would point to this year as the phase at which the web went "BOOM!"

1994

The Netscape 1 browser hit the web and quickly took over as the tool of choice for many. It was a much needed improvement over the Mozilla application, supporting multiple TCP/IP connections as well client-side cookies. The browser was not free, and the general public accepted the fact that they would have to purchase the product for access to the web. I can remember a friend telling me, "If you want to access music, you need to purchase a radio. If you want to get to the Internet, you buy Netscape." However, Netscape was kind enough to release free versions to students, teachers, and various targeted organizations. This marketing ploy helped spread the browser's dominance significantly. By 1996, further revisions of the application would build on a community-driven feature set. Versions 2 and 3 would introduce frames, JavaScript, and mouseovers.

The Age of War

1995

Microsoft was, indisputably, late to the Internet party. However, they were able to recover and implement rather quickly. Their first foray into the browser skirmish was, unfortunately, lacking in features. Internet Explorer versions 1 and 2 are generally skipped over when assessing the seriousness of Microsoft's attempt at swapping blows with Netscape. As you can see from Figure 1-2, browser capabilities were certainly lacking.

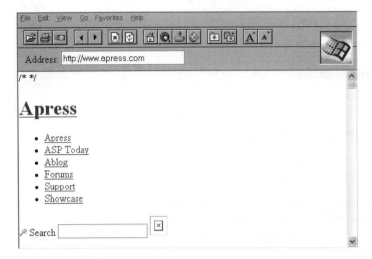

Figure 1-2. *The Apress website through the eyes of IE 2.0*

1996

With nearly 40 million users spread across 150 countries, the web became a corporate necessity as well as a huge social portal. Companies scrambled to establish a presence on the web. E-commerce was responsible for nearly one billion dollars trading hands via the web. A flood of development tools began to surface as software powerhouses started to introduce their own implementation of server-side technologies. Sun's Java and Microsoft's Active Server Pages would lay the foundation for core programming and change the shape of the industry by bringing a multitude of client/server developers to the Internet platform. On the client side, Microsoft fully embraced the web with its release of IE version 3. This was the first version to adopt support for Cascading Style Sheets (CSS), which up until this time was a relatively unknown technique. What it lacked in feature set, as compared to Netscape's version 3, it made up for in being free to the public. Netscape still commanded a large share of the browser market, simply because of name association. That would change soon.

1997

It wasn't until 1997 that the browser war really became ugly. And by ugly, I mean that Netscape and Microsoft began to run with their own perception of what technologies should be brought to the web and how they should be built within the script. The W3C had published CSS specifications; however, the interpretation of the standard differed greatly between the two application giants. Both parties would have agreed to the idea that CSS by itself was somewhat lame, and that dynamically modifying CSS content from within the browser is where the true power would be. DHTML, which was built and pushed off to the developer community, would enable modification of CSS through JavaScript code; however, both camps were extending JavaScript without regard to the other's efforts. Consequently, two implementations of DHTML forced developers to support both for true user compatibility. Where Microsoft truly succeeded in the DHTML battle was their built-in ability to "repaint" the web form upon modification. If content within a CSS element was modified or deleted, the page would redraw itself without postback, allowing the page to shrink to fit. Regrettably, Netscape was unable to implement this feature in time, and the lack of Document Object Model (DOM) standards was beginning to take its toll on developers. When Netscape 4 and Internet Explorer 4 were released in 1997, the market share for Netscape had begun to shift. Microsoft could well afford to pump the browser out to the web community for free, while Netscape had few options within their business model to account for a competitor that willingly gave away their product. Figure 1-3 demonstrates the rapid rate at which Internet Explorer would dominate the browser environment.

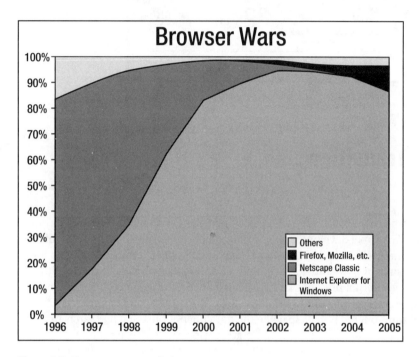

Figure 1-3. *Browser war statistics*

1998

Microsoft launched a web version of Outlook, which by definition is an Ajax application. It would grow in popularity, exceeding 80 million users.

1999

With the release of Internet Explorer 5 (as shown in Figure 1-4), the dominance of Microsoft in the browser market was solidified, and for good reason. Netscape's Navigator was showing more and more bugs, while IE 5 began to lock down more and more features. IE was the first browser to support a good chunk of the W3C Document Object Model standard. The CSS support exceeded anything Netscape had produced to this point. The largest contribution that version 5 made to the world of web application development was the invention and inclusion of the XMLHttpRequest object. Delivered as an ActiveX object, the inclusion of this new tool enabled client-side script to access server-side components. However, one major drawback prohibited widespread adoption of XMLHttpRequest—only Internet Explorer version 5 maintained support for this object, and the script execution of this web apparatus was confusing at best to many web developers. Although it was ultimately the birth of Ajax, it proved to be a technology that would go unnoticed and dormant for years.

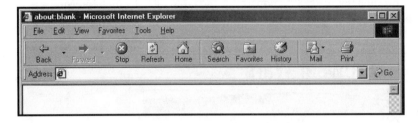

Figure 1-4. *Internet Explorer version 5 toolbar*

The Age of Transition

2000

Internet spending, by the year 2000, had reached all-time highs. Companies were shelling out huge amounts of cash to propel development of various retail and portal applications. While technological developments had grown somewhat stagnant, the sheer volume of demand for site presence was certainly overwhelming. Corporations around the world were sparing little expense in making their Internet presence known. For instance, during the 2000 Super Bowl game, companies were each dishing out two million dollars for a 30-second commercial spot. The massive expenditures offered little help when the dot-com bubble burst on March 10, 2000. There were many contributing factors to the market-wide crash of tech spending. Notable were the findings in the Microsoft Antitrust case that indicated the company was indeed a monopoly and delivered a blow that dropped the NASDAQ indexes into a downward spiral.

Many speculate that the Y2K scare had left many companies with bloated staffing and hardware that needed to be pared down to a manageable and profitable size. Substantial downsizings shook the developer realm as investment capital ceased to flow. Very little effort was poured into browser or DHTML development for a significant amount of time. With Microsoft firmly established as the browser of choice for millions, there was little reason to stretch the limits of browser abilities. Developers spent more time dealing with content issues rather than presentation facilities.

2001

IE version 6 (see Figure 1-5) was released just before the unveiling of the Windows XP operating system. A few DHTML improvements were added as well as improved support for DOM and CSS specifications.

Figure 1-5. *Internet Explorer version 6 (sp2) browser*

The Age of Experimentation

2002–2004

DHTML took a back seat for a few years. Developers across the world formulated their own concepts of what constituted a "dynamic" website. Flash, JavaScript, and IFrame hacks appeared in numerous quantities across the web. Microsoft shifted gears in browser development as they delivered the .NET Framework to the world in 2002. ASP.NET presented an awesome opportunity to programmers to work within the common language runtime environment. It also brought a lot of Windows application developers to the world of Internet development by introducing a control- and component-based structure that was similar to the user interfaces they had previously constructed for installable applications.

It was during this "Age of Experimentation" that the folks at Google began to release some very interesting products. First and foremost was the release of their invitation-only e-mail service—Gmail (see Figure 1-6). Although it was issued forth as beta software, it brought to the world a large-scale realization of Ajax concepts.

Ludicorp, a Canadian gaming company, developed FlickrLive to use as a photo sharing tool for their web-based role playing game. FlickrLive would later evolve into Flickr (see Figure 1-7), overshadowing and eventually eliminating the background gaming direction. They were later purchased by Yahoo as the Internet giant sought to add to their toolset of community-building applications. Flickr, although a relatively simple site (they must have attended the Google school of web design), would make heavy use of Ajax technology. Introductions were made as well for a mass tagging functionality that would go on to lead the industry as a role model for social content classification.

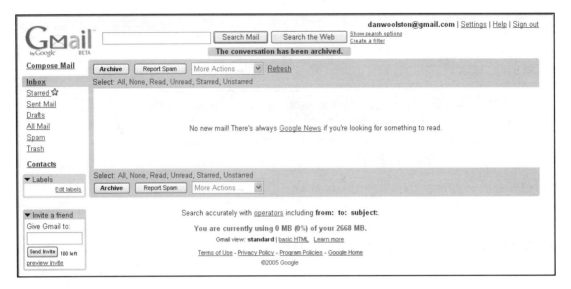

Figure 1-6. *Google's Gmail e-mail web portal*

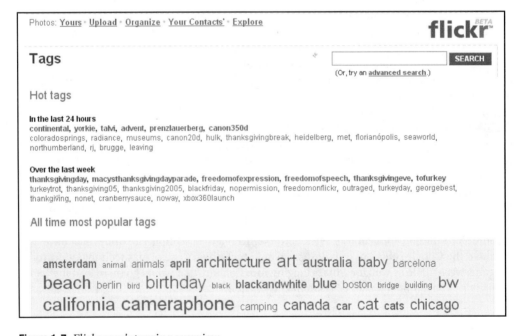

Figure 1-7. *Flickr.com's tagging overview*

2005

In my opinion, 2005 was when Ajax truly took center stage as a tool worth using. Here again, it was Google that garnered the world's attention for next-generation applications. The beta release of Google Suggest snuck onto the web without much celebration or clamor from the folks at Google Labs at the tail end of 2004, but it wasn't until 2005 that the general public took note. The Suggest application is similar to the typical Google search page with a unique twist. In the user's textbox, as the user enters query parameters, the Ajax client-side script is hitting the index on the server to bring back matching results for what has been typed up to that point. So if you were to type "micr", the application would pop up a drop-down list below the textbox and "autocomplete" some possible results for you. The result set that is returned to the client is cached, so that if a user presses the Backspace key, the client will simply call up the previously held results and redisplay them rather than making another hit to the database. It's an awesome and simplified use of the Ajax toolset, developed primarily by Kevin Gibbs on a part-time basis. Google has acknowledged the fact that most developers like to work on side projects as a means of keeping up to date with emerging technology or as a diversion from their daily build process. The company allows their employees to spend 20 percent of their work week involved with said side projects. Out of that accommodation, Google Suggest was born. Figure 1-8 demonstrates a search in action.

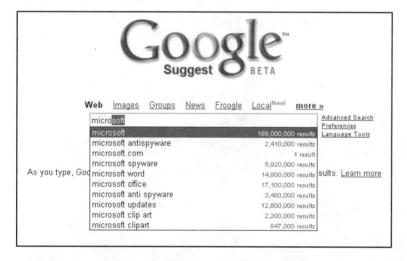

Figure 1-8. *Google Suggest in action*

With two prominent Ajax releases, the world began to recognize that Ajax-enabled sites were beginning to take root in the world of web possibilities. I found the media reaction to the Ajax storm amusing. In an article released to the web in October 2005, CNN.com boldly proclaimed, "Web-based software challenges Windows," and detailed how the "quiet revolution" was quite possibly bad luck for Microsoft. The inference drawn was that dynamic Internet content could possibly eliminate the need for installable applications. I don't really hold to that conclusion. I thought then (and still do) it would offer some competitive edge for various online vendors, but a full-fledged replacement for Office apps remains a long way out even today. And with Microsoft joining the party with their own Ajax library (more on this in

Chapter 20), it's hard to fathom the idea that Bill Gates and Friends would see Ajax as a threat to their application longevity. The *Wall Street Journal* broadcast, "New Web-based Technology Draws Applications, Investors." I'm not sure where they came up with the "new" terminology as an appropriate description for Ajax, since the technology was born years ago. Even *Popular Mechanics* (http://www.popularmechanics.com) jumped into the marketing pool, declaring it one of the "Must-Know Technologies of 2006." The articles, as a whole, tended to agree that it was Google that kick-started the revival of DHTML and Ajax. Google had broken the ice with Gmail and Suggest, and next they dropped the Google Maps bomb on the Internet community. The rookie site (http://maps.google.com) used Ajax to allow users the ability to simply drag a map around within the browser, zooming in or out for refined detail. As the user seeks an area that exists outside the browser, the client-side script hits the server, grabs the new map graphics, and pushes it back to the web page—all without postback and interruptions to the user experience. And just because a dragging map wasn't quite cool enough, they threw in satellite imagery (as shown in Figure 1-9). By now, who hasn't spent hours finding their house, workplace, and national landmarks?

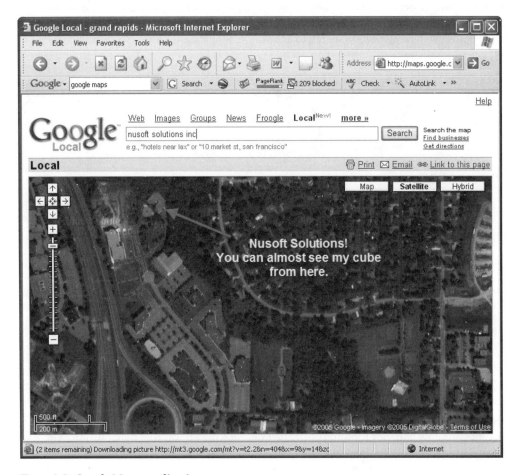

Figure 1-9. *Google Maps application*

ONLINE MAPPING

Many other virtual mapping applications will begin to surface, some better than others. One in particular that I feel I should mention is Flickrmap (`http://www.flickrmap.com`). This particular application is an extension of the aforementioned Flickr photo site. A drag-and-drop map is overlayed with various "pushpins" that, when hovered over, pop up a small image stored in Flickr that is particular to the area that you have selected. Figure 1-10 demonstrates the site, but be warned, it's still very much a beta application (as of this writing), and I'm sure the team at Flickr is hard at work developing a much more stable page.

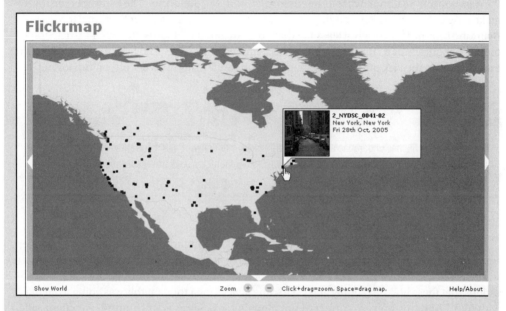

Figure 1-10. *Flickrmap with pop-up Flickr image*

While the cool factor of these rapidly appearing websites has yet to wear off even now, many ASP.NET developers had begun to feel left out of the revolution. A majority of the sites were being built with client-side JavaScript and Java on the server. A few would branch out here and there, but nothing on an enterprise or global level. The primary reason for this was that the XMLHttpRequest object was difficult to wield for many developers. What the community really needed was an interface of sorts that would take care of a majority of the typical tasks associated with creating and accessing an asynchronous path to the server. A few frameworks began to dot the web, but here again, they were associated with other development languages. During the spring and summer of 2005, two serious contenders emerged from the community, both of them open source and freely available to developers.

First and foremost was Michael Schwarz's Ajax library. His library would give ASP.NET developers easy access to the server side by implementing his class library as a structured tool.

TRY IT!

Michael Schwarz has published his library for general public use. You can find his site, which has many informative articles and illustrations, at `http://weblogs.asp.net/mschwarz/`.
You'll find that Michael updates his site and software quite frequently. Definitely a must-have bookmark.

Second, and perhaps my favorite, is Jason Diamond's Anthem library. He has implemented the Ajax concept in a somewhat different format from Mr. Schwarz's. The Schwarz construct makes use of HTTPHandlers, adding bulk and difficulty to your web application. However, Diamond's Anthem is simply a class file that you can either include within your Visual Studio project or compile as a DLL and reference as a named entity. I've used both and am happy with each; however, the lack of HTTPHandling brings Jason Diamond's work out on top for me.

TRY THIS ONE TOO!

Diamond's class file has undergone a few iterations, much like Schwarz's. His current version (as of this writing) has experienced a name change from MyAjax to Anthem. It also is freely available at `http://jason.diamond.name/weblog/`.

With the advent of a community-driven supply of Ajax libraries, .NET developers no longer have to scramble to implement decent interactive websites inside of a Visual Studio solution. You might already be thinking to yourself, "But wait a minute! I'm looking through the sample applications that these libraries supply and I see some JavaScript. I thought this was going to change with Ajax." And, yes, you are correct in noticing that JavaScript is still around. For client-side scripting, it's a clean and universal way of doing things. And to be honest with you, if you're coding in the .NET Framework either through Visual Basic .NET or C#, you will have an absolutely easy time picking up JavaScript if you've never worked with it before. I've yet to talk to a Microsoft products programmer who's claimed that JavaScript was a tough transition for them. I'll cover JavaScript in a later chapter so that you'll have the basic scripting skills to get a head start on the client-side coding.

Summary

In this chapter, we've taken an in-depth look at the evolution of DHTML into Ajax and some of the major corporate contributions as well. It's only been a few short years, but within this minor timeframe, so much has transpired. We've gone from simple text messages sent back and forth from a few nodes on the ARPANET to a multimillion-user network. We've witnessed applications grow from simple line-mode browsing pumping out simple text data to dynamic web interfaces that have put virtually every aspect of life before our eyes. It's an exciting time to be involved with software development!

In the next chapter, we'll dive right into JavaScript as we take our first step towards Ajax coding.

CHAPTER 2

■ ■ ■

Introducing JavaScript

One of the key components of Ajax.NET, as I'm sure you've already surmised, is the JavaScript programming language. JavaScript provides the client-side programming platform that Ajax has come to depend on. If you're one of those developers who have had little JavaScript exposure, this chapter will introduce you to this scripting language: I'll show you the introductory syntax needed to survive in a web application project. If you're a seasoned JavaScript veteran, however, you may find your time better spent by simply browsing the chapter and moving on to the next.

First and foremost: JavaScript is **NOT** Java! They have very little in common, semantically speaking. The language was created by Netscape developer Brendan Eich under the names *Mocha*, *LiveScript*, and later *JavaScript*. Even from its first browser introduction (Netscape 2.0, 1995), the name has caused great confusion among developers. And with the great and ongoing "Sun versus Microsoft" development platform war, many .NET developers have tried at all costs to avoid JavaScript, assuming that it was an extension of Java. I was one such developer. For years I avoided JavaScript, not knowing that the language syntax was actually closer to the C/C++ background that I had become accustomed to.

I feel comfortable in stating that C# developers should have a pretty easy time with the inclusion of JavaScript in their web development projects. It's been my experience that a majority of the problems that programmers associate with JavaScript are typically **NOT** JavaScript issues; instead, it tends to be CSS and DOM element issues that frustrate developers, which they unwittingly associate with JavaScript. I'll cover CSS and DOM in Chapter 6, but for now you need to gain a solid foundation of core client-side coding.

HTML Presence

So when we talk about including JavaScript code on our web page, what exactly does that mean? Chances are you've had some exposure to ASP.NET. So something like the following should not surprise you:

```
<%@ Page Language="C#" AutoEventWireup="true"
CodeFile="Default.aspx.cs" Inherits="_Default" %>
<!DOCTYPE html PUBLIC
"-//W3C//DTD XHTML 1.0 Transitional//EN"
"http://www.w3.org/TR/xhtml1/DTD/xhtml1-transitional.dtd">
<html xmlns="http://www.w3.org/1999/xhtml" >
```

```
<head runat="server">
    <title>My HTML Page</title>
</head>
<body>
    <form id="frmDefault" runat="server">
    <div>
     // Our code begins here:
 Enter Your Name:<br />
    <asp:TextBox ID="txtName" runat="server"></asp:TextBox>
    </div>
    </form>
</body>
</html>
```

Executing the preceding code will produce an application like the one shown in Figure 2-1.

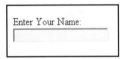

Figure 2-1. *Simple HTML application*

This is an incredibly simple application, but I'm showing you this to demonstrate that HTML, as you may already know, is a *tags*-based markup language. JavaScript, to successfully run in an HTML environment, must adhere to that same pattern. To illustrate this, let's throw a simple alert box into our cool application, nested appropriately within the necessary tags.

COMMENTING YOUR CODE

We all hate inheriting code from someone/somewhere else that has never been commented. So break the cycle by commenting everything you build, including your JavaScript. To add a comment to your JS code, follow the same pattern as C#.

Using // to start a line-by-line code comment:

```
// Our code begins here:
```

Using /* and */ to start and end a comment block:

```
/*

        My code is awesome!
        code comments make people happy!
    */
```

We must first add our required HTML <script> tags that let the compiler know that we're about to include JavaScript code within our page:

```
<body>
```

```
<script type="text/javascript" language="javascript">
</script>
```

```
    <form id="frmDefault" runat-"server">
    <div>
    Enter Your Name:<br />
    <asp:TextBox ID="txtName" runat="server"></asp:TextBox>
    </div>
    </form>
</body>
```

This code has the added inline declaration of a JavaScript code block. We use the <script> tag with the appropriate attributes set to indicate that we are indeed using a text type as well as the "javascript" language. We end with the required closing </script> tag. However, we have no JavaScript code within our tags, so let's add a simple alert (a JavaScript message box) to our code:

```
<script type="text/javascript" language="javascript">
    alert("Welcome to the world of JavaScript!");
</script>
```

Running this short web application will display a dialog box, as shown in Figure 2-2.

Figure 2-2. *Simple JavaScript execution*

Declaring your JavaScript HTML tags gives you the room to grow your code, and it's imperative that you keep your scripting within the tags. Otherwise, bad things may happen. For instance, you'll find that your page may run up to a certain point and then fail. The page will be compiled up to the point of error and then delivered. This can create an enormous debugging headache as you dig through code, only to find that you've coded outside of the tags.

Now, if you're like many .NET developers, you have this Microsoft-embedded desire to separate your code from your HTML. Some of us have grown so used to "code-behind" files that we envision and demand that other facets of development should follow that same methodology. Can we apply that to JavaScript coding? Yes. And it's relatively easy.

Create a new WebSite project in Visual Studio 2005, naming it ExternalJS.

Once your site has loaded, you'll need to right-click the site and choose Add New Item. This brings up the Templates dialog box shown in Figure 2-3.

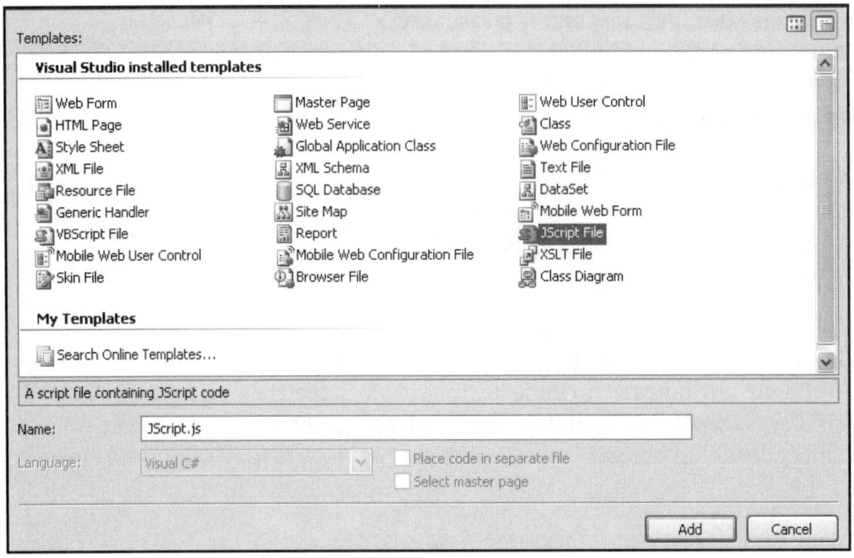

Figure 2-3. *Adding JavaScript file*

On the Templates dialog box, select JScript File from the list of Visual Studio–installed templates. Enter **JScript.js** in the name textbox and click the Add button.

Inside of your new JavaScript file, add the following code:

```
alert("Welcome to External JavaScript!");
```

After saving the added code to the .js file, shift your attention to the previous HTML code and modify it to reflect the following change:

```
<body>
    <script type="text/javascript" language="javascript"
        src="JScript.js"></script>
    <form id="frmDefault" runat="server">
    <div>
    Enter Your Name:<br />
    <asp:TextBox ID="txtName" runat="server"></asp:TextBox>
    </div>
    </form>
</body>
```

What we've done is modify the <script> tag and added the src attribute to refer to our external JavaScript file. When the page is compiled, the .js file will be placed inline and will execute as if it were included in the actual HTML, as you can see in Figure 2-4. It's a nice way to keep things tidy and maintainable.

Figure 2-4. *External JavaScript execution*

Scripting Load Cycle

Much like the ASP.NET page cycle has a patterned page load cycle, JavaScript can execute script at established points in time:

- During document load

- After document load

- When called by other JavaScript statements

Where you locate the script in your HTML will determine at which of the preceding stages the code will execute.

During Document Load

The JavaScript shown in the following code will be executed as the page is rendered in the users browser. As the page is "painted," the embedded events will trigger in the order that they are listed within the tags.

```
<html xmlns="http://www.w3.org/1999/xhtml" >
<head runat="server">
    <title>My HTML Page</title>
</head>
<body>
    <h1>During load script execution</h1>
        <script type="text/javascript" language="javascript">
            alert("executing during page load.");
        </script>
    <h1>alert has executed!</h1>
    <form id="frmDefault" runat="server">
    <div>
    </div>
    </form>
</body>
</html>
```

Including this HTML into an .aspx page and running it will produce the results shown in Figure 2-5.

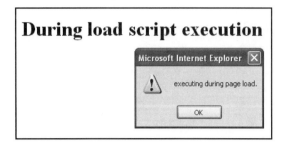

Figure 2-5. *JavaScript during page load*

As you can see in Figure 2-5, the alert has "interrupted" page flow as it waits for the user to click OK. Because we are running the script tags "on the fly," the client-side code will render as the server processes the HTML tags. By placing our JavaScript in the midst of other HTML elements, we ensure that it will execute as the page processes. Notice that the second <h1> tag has yet to be written to the browser. Clicking OK will, as expected, allow page processing to continue, as the message in Figure 2-6 indicates.

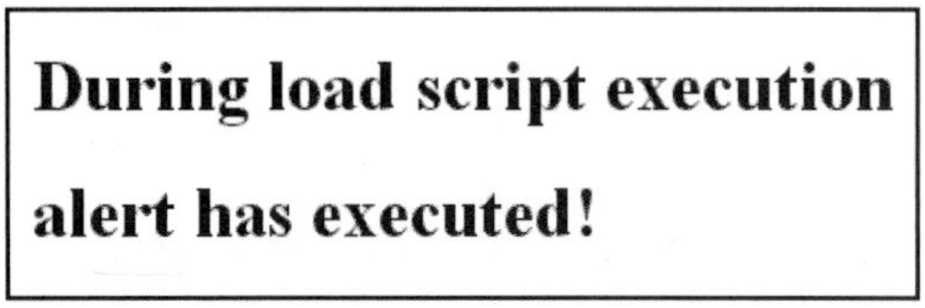

During load script execution
alert has executed!

Figure 2-6. *The completed page cycle*

After Document Load

If you have a need to run the script tags after the document has loaded, you'll have to implement the <body> tag's onload() function. This particular event will fire after the page has completed its load cycle. We'll need to call a JavaScript function (discussed in the upcoming "Functions" section) from within this event handler, as shown in the following:

```
<html xmlns="http://www.w3.org/1999/xhtml" >
<head runat="server">
    <title>My HTML Page</title>
</head>
<script type="text/javascript" language="javascript">

    function alldone()
    {
        alert("all done!");
    }
```

```
</script>
<body onload="alldone();">
    <h1>After load script execution</h1>
    <h1>Final line...almost done!</h1>
    <form id="frmDefault" runat="server">
    <div>
    </div>
    </form>
</body>
</html>
```

We've moved the <script> tag (and the subsequent function) outside of the HTML <body> region. You should also notice that we've added event-handling code to the <body> tag. Running this within an .aspx page will display the <h1> tag information and then wrap it up by popping up the alert box shown in Figure 2-7.

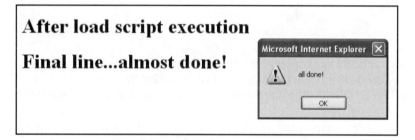

Figure 2-7. *After load execution of JavaScript*

When Called by Other JavaScript Statements

The third and final scenario where JavaScript code executes is when a JavaScript function refers to another JavaScript function:

```
<html xmlns="http://www.w3.org/1999/xhtml" >
<head runat="server">
    <title>My HTML Page</title>
<script type="text/javascript" language="javascript">

    function sayhello()
    {
        alert("Hi There");
    }
```

```
    function alldone()
    {
        alert("All Done!");
    }
</script>
</head>
<body onload="alldone();">
<script type="text/javascript" language="javascript">
    sayhello();
</script>

    <h1>Function call script execution</h1>
    <h1>Final line...almost done!</h1>
    <form id="frmDefault" runat="server">
    <div>
    </div>
    </form>
</body>
</html>
```

In this code section we have two script blocks. The first, inside of the <head> tags, has our two functions (alldone() and sayhello()) that will be called as needed. The second <script> tag makes a call to the sayhello() function. Even though they are separated within the HTML, access is still available.

It's very easy to place script inappropriately and find yourself banging your head against the wall in frustration because of JavaScript debugging. If you keep the page flow in the back of your mind when you're dropping <script> tags onto your HTML, then you should be fine.

Variables

Declaring variables in JavaScript is quite simple. JavaScript variables are open-ended objects and have very few requirements for instantiation. Declaring a variable is as simple as assigning a value to the variable name or declaring it with a var statement:

```
// by declaration:
var myname = "John Doe";

// by assignment:
mynickname = "Johnny";
```

Initializing numerical variables uses the same syntax:

```
    var currentcount = 0;
    currentcount ++;
```

This code will initialize currentcount as a numeric variable with the initial setting of zero and then increment the value by one.

Boolean values are declared as you would expect:

```
    var myswitch = false;
```

Concatenating and Adding

If we want to concatenate two strings, we use the overloaded + operator:

```
var firstname = "John";
var lastname = "Doe";
var fullname = firstname + " " + lastname;

// produces: "John Doe"
```

Adding two numbers uses the same overloaded + operator:

```
var x = 2;
var y = 3;
var total = x + y;

// produces: total = 5;
```

This syntax is not complicated and, for the most part, adheres to what we generally expect from most scripting languages.

Variable Scope

Variables that are declared outside of functions (discussed next) are considered to be global and accessible to all JavaScript functions within the current web page.

Variables that are declared within functions are only accessible within the scope of the current function.

Control Structures

Conditional data manipulation in JavaScript is identical to most modern language syntax. Handling the if/else switch bears a striking resemblance to C#:

```
if(condition)
{
    Statement(s);
}
else
{
    Statements(s);
}
```

The usage of this syntax should be quite familiar already:

```
var a =1;
var b=2;
if(a == b)
```

```
{
      a++;
}
else
{
      a = b;
}
```

Another conditional operator that can also make for smaller code is the *ternary operator*. It does have the drawback of being somewhat difficult to casually browse. One of the biggest complaints that newer developers have with this particular operator is not that they can't understand it, but that it forces them to pause when attempting to just scan through code. Using it is a personal thing, in that it accomplishes the same process as using the `if`/`else` structure:

```
(condition) ? statement1: statement2;
```

Statement 1 will execute if the preceding condition is determined to be true. Subsequently, Statement 2 will run on a false condition. In the following code sample, we compare the variables a and b. If a is equal to b, we'll increment a by one. Should a not equal b, we simple assign a to be equal to b.

```
(a == b) ? a++ : a=b;
```

If we code the preceding line in the typical `if`/`else` notation, it appears as shown here:

```
if(a == b)
{
      a++;
}
else
{
      a = b;
}
```

Looping and Iteration

It is highly likely that you will need to do some level of iterative data processing. You have at your disposal a variety of tools that do just that:

- `while` loops
- `do/while` loops
- `for` loops

while Loops

A while loop will execute the bracketed statements only while the conditional expression is true.

```
while(condition)
{
        statements;
}
```

The following code demonstrates this concept:

```
<script type="text/javascript" language="javascript">
    var a=1;
    var b=1;
    while(a==b)
    {
        b++;
    }
</script>
```

Because a initially equals b, the incremental (b++) statement will run. However, after modifying that variable, the conditional statement will no longer be true, and the statement that increments b will be skipped. Also, if the condition is initially false, the code block will never execute. The following is an example of this:

```
<script type="text/javascript" language="javascript">
    var a=1;
    var b=2;
    while(a==b)
    {
        b++;
    }
</script>
```

The variable b will remain at 2 because it is never incremented. In other words, the a==b test fails the first time.

do/while Loops

When you use a do/while loop, the conditional expression is evaluated after an initial execution of the code block.

```
do
{
        statements;
} while (condition);
```

Here again, code in practice shows the syntax in action:

```
<script type="text/javascript" language="javascript">
    var a=1;
    var b=2;
    do
    {
        b++;
    } while (a==b);
</script>
```

The b++ statement will run only once because the value of b is not equal to a and the condition will evaluate to false. Because we are checking the true/false condition following the statement block, we're assured of at least one full execution of the bracketed code.

for Loops

The structure of the for loop is different from that of the other iteration loops, but the methodology of using it is the same. A section of code is executed until a specified condition is met:

```
<script type="text/javascript" language="javascript">
    var max = 10;
    var a = 0;
    for(var i = 1; i <=max; i++)
    {
        a=i;
    }
    alert(a);
</script>
```

The preceding for loop initializes a variable, i, and checks to see whether i is less than or equal to the max. If the value is less than or equal to max, the statement code is executed. Following execution of the bracketed code, the value of i is incremented. When the max has been exceeded, the code terminates and falls through to the next available statement, as shown in Figure 2-8.

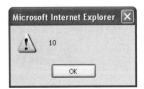

Figure 2-8. *Execution of the for loop*

Switch Statements

I don't know if you've ever had the displeasure of inheriting code from someone who believes whole-heartedly in nested if statements rather than switch statements. I have had the honor of spending hours trying to decipher someone else's intentions, even going so far as printing out their code and drawing colored boxes around individual if/then blocks to differentiate them from the other 40-to-50 parent statements.

switch statements, when used properly, can help improve code execution and readability. Often, if statements do not provide the proper execution channels that a switch can. The basic premise of the statement is that a condition may have a variety of branches that result from examination of the condition itself. For instance, a distant relative calls to say that they're going to be in your hometown this weekend and would love to stop for the night. You agree, hang up, and suddenly realize that you forgot to ask how many family members would be invading soon. A mental decision-making process begins to kick in as you make preparations:

```
switch (condition = "How Many People Are Invading")
{
case "One" :
      "Only prepare the couch. The relative is alone; hooray!"
      break;
case "Two" :
      "Prepare the guest room bed.
       There will be two, hopefully they
       can share the room."
      break;
case "Three" :
      "Do some shopping. Food will probably be needed."
      break;
case "Four" :
      "Stock up on shopping, provide entertainment and purchase some Tylenol."
      break;
default :
      "Oh no...It's not one through four. That can't be good. Run away!"
}
```

As we can see, based on what our condition is, we select the appropriate results and perform a unique operation based on that. Let's translate this mental analysis into code. Drop the following onto an .aspx page and run the site:

```
<%@ Page Language="C#" AutoEventWireup="true"
CodeFile="Default.aspx.cs" Inherits="_Default" %>
<!DOCTYPE html PUBLIC "-//W3C//DTD XHTML 1.0 Transitional//EN"
"http://www.w3.org/TR/xhtml1/DTD/xhtml1-transitional.dtd">
<html xmlns="http://www.w3.org/1999/xhtml" >
<head runat="server">
    <title>My HTML Page</title>
</head>
```

```
<body>
<script type="text/javascript" language="javascript">
    var peoplevisiting = 3;
    var plans = "Not sure";

    switch(peoplevisiting)
    {
        case 1 :
            plans = "Prepare the couch.";
            break;
        case 2 :
            plans = "Prepare the guest room.";
            break;
        case 3 :
            plans = "Buy extra groceries.";
            break;
        case 4 :
            plans = "Buy Tylenol. You'll need it.";
            break;
        default:
            plans = "Uh oh. This can't be good.";
    }
    alert(plans);
</script>
    <form id="frmDefault" runat="server">
    <div>
    </div>
    </form>
</body>
</html>
```

What will pop up, as expected, is an alert box like the one in Figure 2-9, letting you know that you should "Buy extra groceries."

Figure 2-9. *Impending visitor warning*

We've obviously hit the code block for case 3. You'll notice a few things about the individual case blocks. First, the break statement has been included within the first four cases. This enables the page execution to "jump out" of the switch statement once this particular case has been handled. You'll also find a default declaration at the tail end of the select statement. If none of the previous cases have been met, then by default the code within this section will run, and the switch statement will then exit.

Functions

A JavaScript function is the workhorse of the scripting language. It is where we'll place a majority of our client-side functionality. And one very important consideration that you must understand about functions is that they are, at their core, objects. We'll look at the object-based functionality in a moment, but first let's catch up on basic implementation. We declare one as follows:

```
function sayhello()
{
alert("Hi there!");
}
```

We can also supply parameters:

```
function sayhello(name)
{
alert("Hi there " + name + "!");
}
```

Of course, we'll need to call our function from within a JavaScript <script> tag:

```
sayhello("Joe");
```

Here's our completed script:

```
<script type="text/javascript" language="javascript">

    function sayhello(name)
    {
        alert("Hi there " + name + "!");
    }
    // now let's call that function:
    sayhello("Joe");

</script>
```

Figure 2-10 proudly displays our results as expected.

Figure 2-10. *Simple function call*

Returning Values

Functions can also return values by implementing the `return` statement from within the function call. Unlike C#, you do not need to declare the return value in the function header:

```
function addthis(firstnumber, secondnumber)
{
    return firstnumber + secondnumber;
}
var total = addthis(4, 3);
alert(total);
```

As you would most certainly guess, an alert box will pop up and display our total, "7".

JavaScript functions have a versatility that many have come to take for granted. Their open and dynamic nature can help you move and process a variety of data. Later, in Chapter 6, we'll take a look at passing page controls as parameters into JavaScript functions for CSS and DOM manipulation.

Arrays

One of the key components of client-side programming in the Ajax world is the use of arrays. As you'll find later, passing data back to the client in the form of an array can be especially beneficial when you have to parse the data in JavaScript. Working with arrays can be a bit tricky, but you'll see the various idiosyncrasies here.

One of the best features (though some would argue against its use) of JavaScript arrays is the ability to house varying data types in the array elements. If you want to store a string in the first element and an object in the second, it is totally acceptable. A bit awkward for some developers to grow comfortable with, but it does have some practical application.

Creating an Array

You'll use a single variable to house your array, but be aware that when you "look under the hood," you will find that arrays are still just objects. And as such you will be using the `new` keyword when instantiating them:

```
<script type="text/javascript" language="javascript">
    var newarray = new Array;
    newarray[0] = "Bob";
    newarray[1] = "Joe";
</script>
```

Notice that we haven't actually declared the initial element amounts in the variable. Most of us are used to declaring our variables with a set amount: `var newarray = new Array(2)`. The JavaScript language is very forgiving on array syntax. We can choose to use starting element counts or we can set up an "empty" parameter and add the individual items as needed.

As discussed before, arrays can contain a variety of data types:

```
<%@ Page Language="C#" AutoEventWireup="true"
CodeFile="Default.aspx.cs" Inherits="_Default" %>
<!DOCTYPE html PUBLIC "-//W3C//DTD XHTML 1.0 Transitional//EN"
"http://www.w3.org/TR/xhtml1/DTD/xhtml1-transitional.dtd">
<html xmlns="http://www.w3.org/1999/xhtml" >
<head runat="server">
    <title>My HTML Page</title>
</head>
<body>
<script type="text/javascript" language="javascript">
   var newarray = new Array;
   var address = new Array(2);

   address[0] = "101 Nowhere Lane";
   address[1] = "United States";

   newarray[0] = "Bob";
   newarray[1] = address;

   newarray[2] = 45;

   alert (newarray[0] + ": " + newarray[1][0] + ". Fees: $" + (newarray[2] + 3));
</script>
    <form id="frmDefault" runat="server">
    <div>
    </div>
    </form>
</body>
</html>
```

If you drop the preceding code into an .aspx page and run it, you will receive the appropriate response, as shown in Figure 2-11.

Figure 2-11. *Varied array elements at work*

What we've demonstrated in this sample is that the array object is capable of holding a multitude of data types. We're storing a string in newarray[0] and an address array in newarray[1]. And to show that the variable type in newarray[2] is really numeric, we add a value to it while displaying it in the alert box.

Iterating through an array is easily accomplished by changing the element index:

```
<script type="text/javascript" language="javascript">
    var newarray = new Array;
    newarray[0] = "Joe";
    newarray[1] = "Bob";
    newarray[2] = "Don";

    for(var i=0; i<newarray.length; i++)
    {
        document.write("newarray element #" + i + " = " + newarray[i] + "<br>");
    }
</script>
```

If we add this code to a new web page and run it, we'll have the results as shown in Figure 2-12.

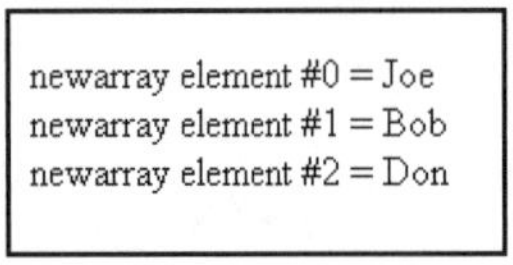

```
newarray element #0 = Joe
newarray element #1 = Bob
newarray element #2 = Don
```

Figure 2-12. *Array iteration*

Because all arrays have a length, we're able to establish the boundaries of the for loop and iterate through the individual array items by calling them out according to their index.

Objects

JavaScript has many object types, namely Boolean, Date, Function, Array, Math, Number, RegExp, String, and Object. It is this last object type that we want to concentrate on. The custom object in JavaScript is of type Object and can be instantiated with the new keyword:

```
var myObject = new Object();
```

But the fun doesn't stop there. We can also declare our object variables by simply initializing them:

```
var myObject = {};
```

or

```
var myObject = {'attribute1' : 'Joe', 'attribute2' : 'U.S.A.'};
```

Objects can take advantage of what are commonly known as *constructor functions*. This will allow you to create multiple instances of the same object:

```
<script type="text/javascript" language="javascript">
    function person(name, country)
    {
        this.name = name;
        this.country = country;
    }

    var theauthor = new person('Daniel', 'U.S.A.');
    var thereader = new person('Joe', 'Germany');

    alert (theauthor.name + " : " + theauthor.country);
    alert (thereader.name + " : " + thereader.country);

</script>
```

In this example, we create a person object through the use of the constructor function. A pair of instances is created and the appropriate information is assigned through the object constructor:

```
var theauthor = new person('Daniel', 'U.S.A.');
```

Like most object-oriented programming languages, JavaScript objects have properties and methods (functions in JavaScript) as well. As you would expect with JavaScript, you may either declare them from the beginning or add them later.

Declaring Properties

We've already seen how to add properties in the constructor:

```
function person(name, country)
{
    this.name = name;
    this.country = country;
}
```

You can also add properties dynamically:

```
<script type="text/javascript" language="javascript">
    function person(name, country)
    {
        this.name = name;
        this.country = country;
    }

    var theauthor = new person('Daniel', 'U.S.A.');
    var thereader = new person('Joe', 'Germany');
```

```
    theauthor.hobbies = "robotics";

    alert (theauthor.name + " : " + theauthor.hobbies);
    alert (thereader.name + " : " + thereader.country);
```

</script>

The property hobbies is added after instantiation, and fortunately nothing blows up. This can really come in handy when you're dealing with dynamically changing data.

Declaring Functions

Functions maintain the same methodology as properties when being added to the object. You can either declare them within the object constructor or individually, after initialization.

Here we declare the sayHello() function in the constructor:

```
<script type="text/javascript" language="javascript">
    function person(name, country)
    {
        this.name = name;
        this.country = country;
        this.sayHello = function() { alert(this.name + " says: 'Hello.'"); };
    }

    var theauthor = new person('Daniel', 'U.S.A.');
    var thereader = new person('Joe', 'Germany');

    theauthor.sayHello();
    thereader.sayHello();
</script>
```

If we want to add an object function dynamically, we would follow the same pattern as before:

```
<script type="text/javascript" language="javascript">
    function person(name, country)
    {
        this.name = name;
        this.country = country;
        this.sayHello = function() { alert(this.name + " says: 'Hello.'"); };
    }

    var theauthor = new person('Daniel', 'U.S.A.');
    var thereader = new person('Joe', 'Germany');

    thereader.sayGoodbye = function() {alert(this.name + " says 'Goodbye!'"); };
```

```
  theauthor.sayHello();
  thereader.sayHello();
  thereader.sayGoodbye();
</script>
```

Adding the script to a web page and running it will trigger a series of three alert boxes with the appropriate dialog, as you can see in Figure 2-13.

Figure 2-13. *Object communication series*

You should keep in mind that dynamically added functions are viable only for the instantiated object. Referring to the preceding code, if you attempted to call

```
theauthor.sayGoodbye();
```

you would be met with much resistance by the browser. Because you've only added that particular function to `thereader`, your access path is limited to that particular object. The function was added to an instance of `person` and is, therefore, applicable to that instance only. Attempting to call the function from another instance would cause an error, as shown in Figure 2-14.

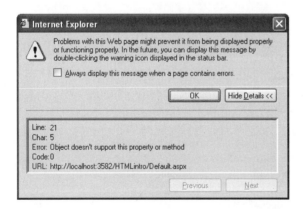

Figure 2-14. *Accessing dynamic method in base class*

If you need actions performed on the object, it is best to keep them within the constructor to avoid confusion and ugly error screens as shown.

Objects can be passed as function parameters as well, enabling you to practice good object-oriented programming techniques even on the client side. Create a new website and add the following code to an `.aspx` page:

```
<%@ Page Language="C#" AutoEventWireup="true"
CodeFile="Default.aspx.cs" Inherits="_Default" %>
<!DOCTYPE html PUBLIC "-//W3C//DTD XHTML 1.0 Transitional//EN"
"http://www.w3.org/TR/xhtml1/DTD/xhtml1-transitional.dtd">
<html xmlns="http://www.w3.org/1999/xhtml" >
<head runat="server">
    <title>My HTML Page</title>
</head>
<body>
    <script type="text/javascript" language="javascript">
        function person(name, country)
        {
            this.name = name;
            this.country = country;
        }
    </script>

    <form id="frmDefault" runat="server">
    <div>
    <script type="text/javascript" language="javascript">
        function sayHello(objPerson)
        {
            return "Hello " + objPerson.name;
        }

    </script>
    <h1>Object Communication</h1>

    <script type="text/javascript" language="javascript">

        var theauthor = new person('Daniel', 'U.S.A.');

        document.write( sayHello(theauthor) );

    </script>

    <h1>Response:</h1>

    <script type="text/javascript" language="javascript">

        var thereader = new person('Joe', 'Germany');

        document.write( sayHello (thereader) );

    </script>
```

```
        </div>
        </form>
</body>
</html>
```

Running the code will render the web page shown in Figure 2-15.

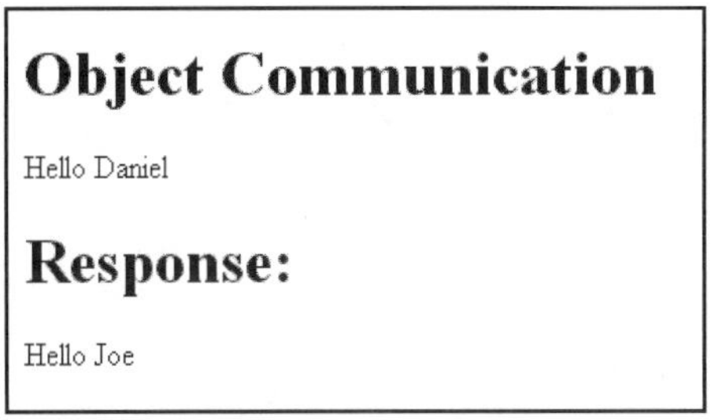

Object Communication

Hello Daniel

Response:

Hello Joe

Figure 2-15. *Passing objects as parameters*

We've created four separate `<script>` blocks to illustrate the ability that we have to create
the initial constructor object and then pass those instantiated blocks into our `sayHello` function. There is much more functionality available when using objects, and this chapter is not the
venue for such an in-depth conversation. We only want to touch on the initial issues involved
with creating our awesome object classes. I encourage you to pick up a full-fledged JavaScript
title or do some intense research on the web.

Error Handling

Let's face it, bad things happen in code execution, and some of it isn't necessarily "bad coding"
but environmental issues. For instance, you could write an awesome web portal that talks to
a Microsoft SQL Server database on the backend. You've meticulously debugged and reviewed
your code and are confident that your application will never crash. You run the thing for the
first time and "Blammo!"—it crashes, much to your dismay. Further investigation reveals that
your DBA has taken the server down for maintenance without notifying you first. Fortunately,
we have structured error handling through the use of `try`/`catch`/`finally` blocks.

Most .NET developers will be right at home with this particular concept, as they have
used it before for server-side programming. The basic premise is the same. We attempt to
execute code in the `try` block, handle exceptions in the `catch` block, and wrap things up in
the `finally` block:

```
<%@ Page Language="C#" AutoEventWireup="true"
CodeFile="Default.aspx.cs" Inherits="_Default" %>
<!DOCTYPE html PUBLIC "-//W3C//DTD XHTML 1.0 Transitional//EN"
"http://www.w3.org/TR/xhtml1/DTD/xhtml1-transitional.dtd">
<html xmlns="http://www.w3.org/1999/xhtml" >
```

```
<head runat="server">
    <title>My HTML Page</title>
</head>
<body>
    <script type="text/javascript" language="javascript">
        function person(name, country)
        {
            this.name = name;
            this.country = country;
        }
    </script>

    <form id="frmDefault" runat="server">
    <div>
    <script type="text/javascript" language="javascript">
        function sayHello(objPerson)
        {
            return "Hello " + objPerson.name;
        }

    </script>
    <h1>Structured Error Handling</h1>
    <br />
    <script type="text/javascript" language="javascript">

        var theauthor = new person('Daniel', 'U.S.A.');

        try
        {
            document.write( sayHowdy(theauthor) );
        }
        catch(error)
        {
            document.write ("Error: " + error.value + "<br>");
        }
        finally
        {
            document.write("Hit the Finally block.");
        }
    </script>
    </div>
    </form>
</body>
</html>
```

A keen eye will spot that we have included an error in the try block (on purpose even).
We're attempting to call a function that does not exist, sayHowdy().

When we run the application, notice that it does not "crash." It completes the run because we've handled the error gracefully, as shown in Figure 2-16.

Structured Error Handling

Error: undefined
Hit the Finally block.

Figure 2-16. *Error handling at work*

Notice that the `finally` block code was also executed. Typically, however, most developers do not use the `finally` section, and it is not strictly required by JavaScript for proper execution. If you do choose to use it, remember that the code within its midst will always execute, regardless of the success or failure of the `try` block.

Summary

This chapter focused solely on the introductory knowledge necessary to implement Ajax. It is purely introductory, however. You will find that a good solid foundation of JavaScript coding skills will go a long way in your web development projects. Fortunately, JavaScript has evolved in much the same way as Microsoft programming products. There's a consistent effort to push for a proper object-oriented platform, and it is beginning to show. With modern browsers taking advantage of JavaScript as the client-side code of choice, you can rest assured that the language will be around for a while.

In the next chapter, you'll put your JavaScript skills to task as we dive into the heart of Ajax and take our first look at the `XmlHttpRequest` object.

CHAPTER 3

■■■

The XmlHttpRequest Object

In the first two chapters, we took an in-depth look at the brief history of web development. You had an opportunity to see some real-world examples of how Ajax is helping to change the face of the Internet. I also gave you an introductory look at JavaScript, preparing you for the code ahead. So without further hesitation, let's press the pedal down and get this technology bus moving.

As we've briefly discussed before, the XmlHttpRequest (XHR) object is the heart of the Ajax machine. Without it, you're back to static, boring old HTML sites. So before we move on to cool dynamic content, you must first understand the XmlHttpRequest process. We'll take a look at the basic syntax of creating the object, sending a request to the server side of things, and then processing the results back on the client. And you'll be pleasantly surprised by how easy it is.

Before you really jump into the XmlHttpRequest object, it's essential that you understand how the "normal" page postback process works. Then, I'll show you how to circumvent that procedure and get to the server side without following the normal flow of things. In Figure 3-1, you'll find a typical "page cycle" diagram. You'll benefit greatly from a grasp of the individual steps involved, so we'll discuss each of them in the upcoming sections.

When a user's browser submits a request to your web server, the initial request passes into the server and is subsequently handed off to the `aspnet_isapi.dll` for processing. The process follows through various HTTP modules and ASP.NET file security, and restores any session state that might be lingering about. After all of that is said and done, the real fun begins. The page request finally hits the HTTP handler and the inclusive `ProcessRequest()` method is called. This is where the page cycle magic happens.

Refer to Figure 3-1 for visual representation of the following page cycle descriptions.

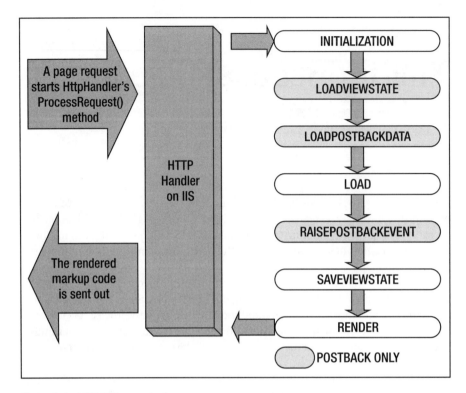

Figure 3-1. *ASP.NET page cycle*

Initialization

The page object has been instantiated and during this phase the Init event will trigger for the page and associated controls.

LOADVIEWSTATE

You'll only ever hit this phase during a postback. It is a pretty self-explanatory phase, as the page and control viewstates are restored to their appropriate values.

LOADPOSTBACKDATA

Here again, this is a postback-only phase and is responsible for helping controls that inherit from IPostBackDataHandler regain data that has been posted back.

LOAD

OK, you should already know this stage. This is the page's Load event that you've become quite accustomed to by now. Viewstate and posted back data has been properly loaded and assigned by the time this event has fired.

RAISEPOSTBACKEVENT

During this postback-only event, you'll have individual control events that will trigger and look for posted-back data. For instance, you may have a textbox with modified data and the TextChanged event would fire during this phase of the page cycle.

SAVEVIEWSTATE

The new page viewstate is assembled, and during the render phase, it will be parsed as a hidden field value.

Render

This is the final stop on the page cycle and is responsible for generating the markup that will be delivered back to the user's browser. The page controls will be asked to call their RenderControl() method to emit the necessary HTML for inclusion in the final page.

We discuss the page life cycle in the context of Ajax development so that you can appreciate that when you're bypassing typical IIS actions for server interaction, you're really avoiding a **LOT** of overhead.

Ajax calls can be made asynchronously or synchronously, depending on your application requirements. Either way, both avoid the typical postback trap. When using a majority of the preexisting Ajax-oriented libraries that are available across the web, you'll find that the same pattern exists when examining a generalized data-retrieval process. Figure 3-2 demonstrates a typical Ajax call.

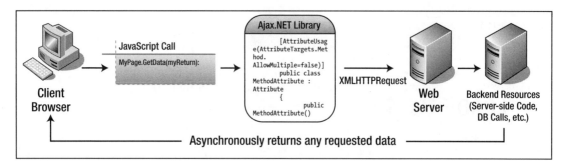

Figure 3-2. *Ajax operation cycle*

At the heart of all this interaction is the XmlHttpRequest object. It is the primary driver for most things Ajax, and it's in your best interest to fully understand what the object does for you when using this technology.

As you may recall from the first chapter, Microsoft released the XmlHttpRequest as an ActiveX object to facilitate the transfer of data in the soon-to-be popular XML format. However, browser support for the object was pretty lame on non-IE platforms, so the tool never really took off. Today, there is widespread support for XHR activity. This is a good news/bad news situation though. The good news is that modern Mozilla spin-offs (i.e., Netscape and

Firefox) and IE are ready and able to handle asynchronous Ajax action. The bad news is that the ActiveX object is instantiated differently for different target browsers. Let's take a look at implementing the XmlHttpRequest on a web page and the function necessary to make the asynchronous process available for further work.

In Internet Explorer, the object is created with JavaScript on the HTML page as

```
var req = new ActiveXObject("Microsoft.XMLHTTP")
```

For the Mozilla and Safari browsers, a slightly different approach is required, in that the XmlHttpRequest is a built-in native object for those applications. Creating the object for use on this browser type uses the following call:

```
var req = new XmlHttpRequest();
```

Obviously, with Mozilla market share rising and continued use of Apple's Safari, you'll need to support these browsers for web-facing projects. A typical JavaScript function for creating a multibrowser XmlHttpRequest variable would look something like the following:

```
<script type="text/javascript" language="javascript">
var xmlhttp = false;

function getHTTPRequestObject()
{
    try
    {
        // try legacy object first
        xmlhttp = new ActiveXObject("Msxml2.XMLHTTP");
    }
    catch(e)
    {
        try
        {
            // try IE implementation now
            xmlhttp = new ActiveXObject("Microsoft.XMLHTTP");
        }
        catch(E)
        {
            xmlhttp = false;
        }
    }
    if(!xmlhttp && typeof XmlHttpRequest!= 'undefined')
    {
        // we must be using a Mozilla-based browser
        // so create a native request object now
        xmlhttp = new XmlHttpRequest();
    }
}
</script>
```

Asynchronous Resource Retrieval

What we've done with the preceding JavaScript function is created a "globally" accessible function that can be made from anywhere in the page when an XmlHttpRequest object is required. You'll notice that we attempt to create an object as appropriate for the browser type making the request. Through the use of the try...catch fall-through, we will eventually end up with the appropriate object for our browser type.

You can see for yourself that this methodology will actually work by following these steps:

1. In Visual Studio 2005, create a new WebSite project with C# as your language of choice.

2. Change your .aspx HTML code to resemble the following:

```
<%@ Page Language="C#" AutoEventWireup="true"
CodeFile="Default.aspx.cs" Inherits="_Default" %>

<!DOCTYPE html PUBLIC "-//W3C//DTD XHTML 1.0 Transitional//EN"
"http://www.w3.org/TR/xhtml1/DTD/xhtml1-transitional.dtd">

<html xmlns="http://www.w3.org/1999/xhtml" >
<script type="text/javascript" language="javascript">
var xmlhttp = false;

getHTTPRequestObject();

if(xmlhttp)
{
    xmlhttp.open("GET", "TextFile.txt", true);
    xmlhttp.onreadystatechange = function()
       {
         if(xmlhttp.readyState == 4)
         {
             alert(xmlhttp.responseText);
         }
       }
       xmlhttp.send(null);
}

function getHTTPRequestObject()
{
    try
    {
        // Try legacy object first
        xmlhttp = new ActiveXObject("Msxml2.XMLHTTP");
    }
    catch(e)
    {
        try
```

```
        {
            // Try IE implementation now
            xmlhttp = new ActiveXObject("Microsoft.XMLHTTP");
        }
        catch(E)
        {
            xmlhttp = false;
        }
    }
    if(!xmlhttp && typeof XmlHttpRequest!= 'undefined')
    {
        // We must be using a Mozilla-based browser
        // so create a native request object now
        xmlhttp = new XmlHttpRequest();
    }
}
</script>


<head runat="server">
    <title>Untitled Page</title>
</head>
<body>
    <form id="form1" runat="server">
    <div>
        XmlHttpRequest hard at work!
    </div>
    </form>
</body>
</html>
```

Don't run the project quite yet! You should take note of a few additions to the function call that we discussed earlier. We're first calling and instantiating our xmlhttp object:

```
getHTTPRequestObject();
```

With that out of the way, we're free to actually use the object now:

```
xmlhttp.open("GET", "TextFile.txt", true);
xmlhttp.onreadystatechange = function()
    {
      if(xmlhttp.readyState == 4)
      {
          alert(xmlhttp.responseText);
      }
    }
  xmlhttp.send(null);
```

We're requesting, through the use of our object's open/GET method, information from the TextFile.txt that you haven't yet added to the current site. Let's do that now so that we can see what exactly transpires during runtime:

3. In Visual Studio 2005, right-click the Solution Explorer's WebSite name and choose Add New Item from the context menu.

4. Select Text File from the list of available templates and accept the default filename, as shown in Figure 3-3.

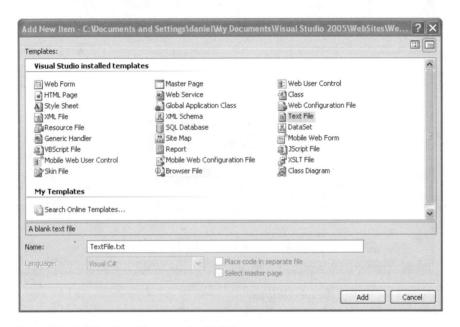

Figure 3-3. *Adding TextFile.txt to the WebSite*

5. Click Add when you're done.

Your site should appear as shown in Figure 3-4.

Figure 3-4. *WebSite files*

6. Open your text file and type some text in the editor:

```
Hello World!
```

7. Save your work and start the application. You'll be prompted to add a `web.config` file, which you'll need to do.

8. Accept the defaults, adding the file with debugging on, and click OK. After a short moment of compile time, a new browser window will open up, and you should be met by an alert box, letting you know that you've successfully retrieved data from an external source, as shown in Figure 3-5.

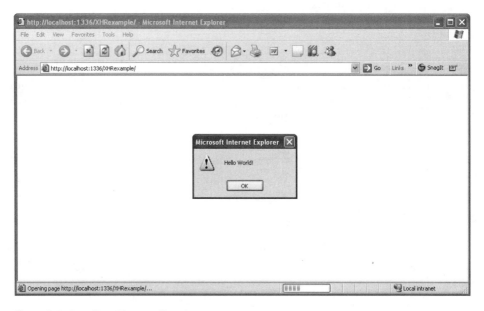

Figure 3-5. *Our first Ajax application*

OK, so maybe it's not a cutting-edge application, but it's a start! Now that you've had a chance to see the application in action, you should understand the XmlHttpRequest methods that we took advantage of.

Our first call consists of an HTTP GET of the destination object, which in our situation is a text file:

```
xmlhttp.open("GET", "TextFile.txt", true);
```

The third parameter in our method is a Boolean value indicating whether or not an asynchronous call should be made. Changing this value to `false` would cause the function to basically wait for the returning data. This could also cause the browser to hang if you have network connection issues.

HTTP GET AND POST

- HTTP GET: Parameters are parsed as name-value pairs and then appended to the URL.

- HTTP POST: Parameters are parsed as name-value pairs and then built into the message body.

The open() method also accepts a fourth and fifth parameter (username and password for secured situations), but we'll not be using those within the context of this example.

The second XmlHttpRequest call that we want to take note of is as follows:

```
xmlhttp.onreadystatechange = function()
    {
     if(xmlhttp.readyState == 4)
     {
          alert(xmlhttp.responseText);
     }
    }
```

The vital portion of this call is the onreadystatechange() method. This interesting, but small, function allows the client side to monitor the current state of the asynchronous call. If the state of the XmlHttpRequest call process changes, this event will be triggered, and any assigned function will be called. In our case, we've created an inline function to be run on the aforementioned trigger. Within that function, we identify exactly what the readyState that we've been monitoring has been changed to and determine our next course of action. There are five possible values for this state:

- 0 = Uninitialized

- 1 = Loading

- 2 = Loaded

- 3 = Interactive

- 4 = Complete

Of interest to us is the complete value, 4. This status indicates that our request has made the complete trip.

But what happens if our destination isn't there? It's possible that a network issue could disrupt the chain of events. Let's re-create a similar situation by renaming our text file to TextFile2.txt and then running the application. We're seeking out a resource that does not exist, and the application will render a message with a certain ugliness, as shown in Figure 3-6.

```
<span><H1>Server Error in '/XHRexample' Application. <hr width=100% size=1 color=silver></H1>

<h2> <i>The resource cannot be found. </i> </h2></span>

<font face="Arial, Helvetica, Geneva, SunSans-Regular, sans-serif ">

    <b> Description: </b>HTTP 404. The resource you are looking for (or one of its dependencies) could have been removed, had its name changed, or is temporarily unavailable.
 Please review the following URL and make sure that it is spelled correctly.
    <br> <br>

    <b> Requested URL: </b>/XHRexample/TextFile2.txt<br><br>
```

Figure 3-6. *Application crash*

Of particular interest is the "Description" portion of the returned XML dump. You'll notice that the error is an HTTP 404, which as you probably already know, is "resource not found." Because we're essentially dealing with a request/response environment, we'll be able to identify and handle these errors as we would with any other HTML request.

Since we are only interested in working with a successful retrieval process, we need to handle an XmlHttpRequest **state** of 4 (indicating complete) as well as an HTTP **status** of 200. Let's take a look at some sample code that will do just that:

```
xmlhttp.onreadystatechange = function()
    {
    if(xmlhttp.readyState == 4)
    {
            if(xmlhttp.status == 200)
            {
               alert(xmlhttp.responseText);
            }
            else
            {
    alert("oops...somethings wrong!");
}
 }
      }
```

As you can see in this code, the only modification that was necessary was the inclusion of the status-filtering if statement. Any status other than a successful 200 will kick off an alert to the user, notifying them that there is something wrong with the object that has been requested. Obviously this is a very generic method of handling a response, in that you would typically want to take corrective measures based on the appropriate error code.

Header Requests

The XmlHttpRequest object is capable of so much more than just talking to a local text file. One method that has seen widespread implementation across the web is the HEAD request that could allow a browser to check the last-modified date of a URL.

To achieve the message shown in Figure 3-7, we must once again refactor our code:

```
if(xmlhttp)
{
    xmlhttp.open("HEAD", "http://www.cnn.com", true);
    xmlhttp.onreadystatechange = function()
        {
        if(xmlhttp.readyState == 4)
        {
            if(xmlhttp.status == 200)
            {
                alert("Last modified on: " + xmlhttp.getResponseHeader("Last-
    Modified"));
            }
        }
        }
    xmlhttp.send(null);
}
```

Figure 3-7. *URL's last-modified date*

We've replaced the GET parameter with HEAD so that we will only be retrieving the HTTP headers of the web resource. Also notice that we'll be accessing the getResponseHeader() method of the instantiated object and returning the last-modified date of the page to the user, which is contained in the Last-Modified HTTP header.

Should you find a need to return all of the response headers, you could simply replace the named getResponseHeader() with the generic getAllResponseHeaders():

```
if(xmlhttp.status == 200)
   {
       alert(xmlhttp.getAllResponseHeaders());
   }
```

Running the site with the preceding code will return results as shown in Figure 3-8.

Figure 3-8. *Retrieving all response headers from the page*

Examining these response headers, you can likely surmise that all of the headers could be retrieved individually with the aforementioned `getResponseHeader()` method by simply passing in the header title as a parameter.

Before we move on to more XmlHttpRequest functionality, Table 3-1 presents a quick summary of the overall capabilities that have been made available to us.

Table 3-1. *Common XmlHttpRequest Methods*

Method	Description
`abort()`	Cancels the current HTTP request.
`getAllResponseHeaders()`	Retrieves values for all HTTP headers.
`getResponseHeader()`	Retrieves specified value of HTTP header.
`open()`	Initializes request object with method, URL, and security information.
`send()`	Sends the HTTP request to the HTTP server and receives response.
`setRequestHeader()`	HTTP header name is set.

We've already utilized a few of these methods, and we've also monitored a few of the common properties, which are listed in Table 3-2.

Table 3-2. *Common XmlHttpRequest Properties*

Property	Description	Read/Write
`onreadystatechange`	Identifies the event handler that is to be used when the `readystate` property has changed	Read/Write
`readyState`	The current state of the request	Read-only
`responseBody`	One of the many ways in which the HTTP response can be returned	Read-only
`responseStream`	One of the many ways in which the HTTP response can be returned	Read-only
`responseText`	The response body in string format	Read-only
`responseXML`	The response body in XML format	Read-only
`status`	The status code returned by the request	Read-only
`statusText`	Text for the corresponding response status	Read-only

Retrieving XML Data

So far we have worked with some pretty common HTTP functionality, but you'll notice from Table 3-2 that we also have access to a `responseXML` property. If our request object is seeking out and returning a well-formed XML file, we'll be able to parse and manipulate the results stored in this particular property.

Let's build a small XML file reader so that we can see this in action for ourselves.

1. Start a new WebSite project in Visual Studio 2005 and name it XMLFile.

2. Right-click `Default.aspx` and delete the file.

3. Right-click the root site folder and choose Add New Item.

4. Select Web Form and name your file GetXML.aspx.

Since we intend to make use of an XML file, let's go ahead and add that now:

5. Right-click the site root folder and choose Add New Item.

6. Select XML File and accept the default filename.

You'll need to populate the XML file with some sample data:

```
<?xml version="1.0" encoding="utf-8" ?>
<messages>
    <message>
        Hello!
    </message>
</messages>
```

Having entered that into our file and saved it, let's switch back to our .aspx file. You'll need to modify the HTML code to match the following:

```
<%@ Page Language="C#" AutoEventWireup="true"
CodeFile="GetXML.aspx.cs" Inherits="GetXML" %>
<!DOCTYPE html PUBLIC "-//W3C//DTD XHTML 1.0 Transitional//EN"
"http://www.w3.org/TR/xhtml1/DTD/xhtml1-transitional.dtd">
<html xmlns="http://www.w3.org/1999/xhtml" >
<head id="Head1" runat="server">
    <title>XML Reader</title>
</head>
<script type="text/javascript" language="javascript">

var xmlhttp = false;

getHTTPRequestObject();

function getHTTPRequestObject()
{
    try
    {
        // Try legacy object first
        xmlhttp = new ActiveXObject("Msxml2.XMLHTTP");
    }
    catch(e)
    {
        try
        {
            // Try IE implementation now
            xmlhttp = new ActiveXObject("Microsoft.XMLHTTP");
        }
        catch(E)
```

```
        {
            xmlhttp = false;
        }
    }
    if(!xmlhttp && typeof XmlHttpRequest!= 'undefined')
    {
        // We must be using a Mozilla-based browser
        // so create a native request object now
        xmlhttp = new XmlHttpRequest();
    }
}

function trimString (str)
{
  str = this != window? this : str;
  return str.replace(/^\s+/g, '').replace(/\s+$/g, '');
}

function callback()
{
        if(xmlhttp.readyState == 4)
        {
            if(xmlhttp.status == 200)
            {
                var xmlresponse = xmlhttp.responseXML.documentElement;
                var textresponse = xmlhttp.responseText;
                var finddiv = document.getElementById("divResponse");
                finddiv.innerText = textresponse;
                alert(trimString(xmlresponse.getElementsByTagName
                ("message")[0].firstChild
.data));
            }
        }
}

function btnClick()
{
    xmlhttp.open("GET", "XMLFile.xml", true);
    xmlhttp.onreadystatechange = callback;
    xmlhttp.send(null);
}
</script>
```

```
<body>
    <form id="form1" runat="server">
        <input id="btnGetXML" type="button" value="Get XML" onclick="btnClick();" />
        <div id="divResponse"></div>
    </form>
</body>
</html>
```

We now have all of the structure in place. Your site should look similar to Figure 3-9.

Figure 3-9. *XML file reader site files*

It's time to run the application to check our results. Once again, you'll be prompted to add a web.config to the site. Accept the defaults and wait for the application to load. Go ahead and click the Get XML button and watch in amazement as our XmlHttpRequest loads and displays our complex data structure, as shown in Figure 3-10.

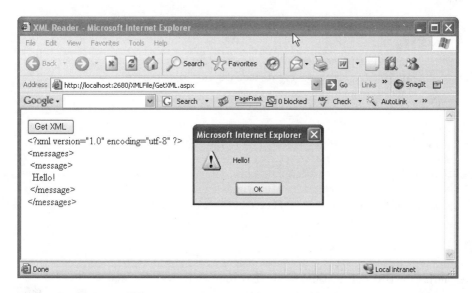

Figure 3-10. *XML greetings*

OK, so maybe it's not that complex. Let's take a look at what we've added in functionality versus our last demo application:

```
if(xmlhttp.status == 200)
{
    var xmlresponse = xmlhttp.responseXML.documentElement;
    var textresponse = xmlhttp.responseText;
    var finddiv = document.getElementById("divResponse");
    finddiv.innerText = textresponse;
    alert(trimString(xmlresponse.getElementsByTagName
    ("message")[0].firstChild.data));
}
```

We are using both of the response properties in the callback function. For a visual representation of the incoming XML file, we simply dump the HTTP response text out to our div tag. And to prove that we're really working with a live XML file, we obtain and display a nested XML child node from within the responseXML document. As you sift through the code of this small program, you can begin to visualize other web-enabled applications that could be quickly built, given the prevalence of XML and RSS feeds on the web. For instance, just for fun, let's modify this last example to actually hit the web and bring back some data across the wire.

Modify your callback() and btnClick() functions as shown:

```
function callback()
{
    if(xmlhttp.readyState == 4)
    {
        if(xmlhttp.status == 200)
        {
            var textresponse = xmlhttp.responseText;
            var finddiv = document.getElementById("divResponse");
            finddiv.innerText = textresponse;
        }
    }
}


function btnClick()
{
    xmlhttp.open("GET", "http://rss.netflix.com/NewReleasesRSS", true);
    xmlhttp.onreadystatechange = callback;
    xmlhttp.send(null);
}
```

We're altering the URL of the open() method to point at the RSS feed that Netflix (http://www.netflix.com) supplies to the public. We'll have access to the "New Release" XML stream, and we'll promptly display that information within the inner HTML of our form's div tag. Also notice that the responseXML and alert code have been removed for this example, as they are unnecessary for this demonstration.

Once you've made the changes to this small amount of code, run the application and click the Get XML button once again (see Figure 3-11).

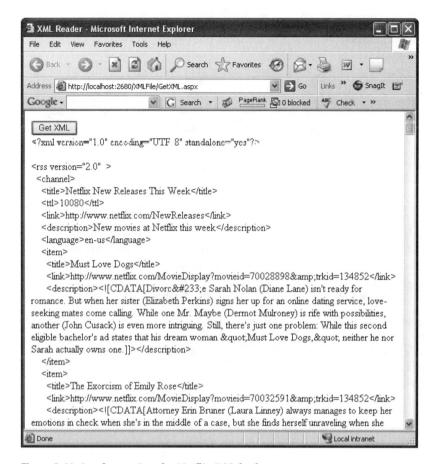

Figure 3-11. *Implementing the Netflix RSS feed*

Obviously your results will vary, as my "New Releases" won't be so new by the time this book has hit the shelves. But this figure helps to demonstrate that our XmlHttpRequest and JavaScript process can not only manipulate and display local data, but also dynamic content from the web as well. And it does it all asynchronously and without interruption to the user's interactive experience.

We've managed to interact with XML, and that's a great start. But the technology road doesn't simply stop with XML messages. While it is the most publicized and distributed means of structured data transfer, other options are made available to web developers. One such means is JavaScript Object Notation (JSON).

Introducing JSON

JavaScript Object Notation (http://www.json.org) is a technology that has crept beneath the radar for quite some time. What is really amazing about JSON is that it can be faster and more efficient than XML for client-side scripting. Yahoo web services provides JSON output as an alternative to XML data retrieval. Yahoo is even so kind as to provide an in-depth analysis of this interaction at `http://developer.yahoo.net/common/json.html`. As you can see from Figure 3-12, JSON works in much the same way that XML does.

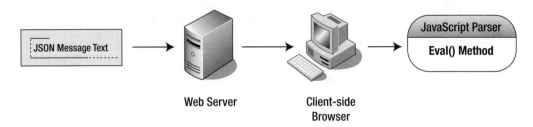

JSON Message Text → Web Server → Client-side Browser → JavaScript Parser / Eval() Method

Figure 3-12. *JSON file usage*

We start out with a JSON file and serve it up to the client's browser. Within the JavaScript we will be calling the eval() method, which will parse the message and render the appropriate data structure. Let's take a look at this process and the JSON text.

The following is a sample XML file detailing a simple data layout:

```
<results total_computers = "2">
  <computer>
        <Manufacturer>Dell</Manufacturer>
        <Model>Latitude</Model>
        <Price>1650</Price>
  </computer>
  <computer>
        <Manufacturer>Dell</Manufacturer>
        <Model>Inspiron</Model>
        <Price>1850</Price>
  </computer>
</results>
```

This same set of data converted to a JSON file would read as follows:

```
{"Results": {
        "total_computers": "2",
        "computer": [
          {
            "Manufacturer":"Dell",
            "Model":"Latitude",
            "Price":"1650"
          },
          {
            "Manufacturer":"Dell",
            "Model":"Inspiron",
            "Price":"1850"
          }
                ]
            }
}
```

The information is the same, but they are differentiated by their syntax and descriptors. To understand the file layout, we must first understand the underlying notation.

JSON descriptors contain these general elements:

- *Objects*: They begin and end with braces ({ }).

- *Object members*: They're name-value pairs, separated by a colon (:). Multiple object members are separated by a comma (,).

- *Arrays*: They begin and end with braces ([ ]), and their corresponding values are separated by a comma (,).

- *Values*: They could be strings, numbers, objects, arrays, or literal values (true, false, or null).

- *Strings*: They're surrounded by double quotes and should contain Unicode characters or backslash escape characters.

There are some things that you'll want to bear in mind when you're comparing or converting XML to JSON:

- You'll want to have at least one top-level object that will represent the response. In our previous data sample, we named our top-level object Results.

- Nested complex XML elements become nested objects.

- XML attributes will convert to name-value pairs.

- Simple XML elements will become name-value pairs.

- Repeated elements (computer from our data example) will become arrays.

Now that we know the file structure, let's put that knowledge to use by actually parsing a JSON file and making use of the rendered object.

1. Create a new WebSite project and name it JSONFile.

2. Rename the Default.aspx file to GetJSON.aspx.

3. You'll need to add a JSON.txt file in much the same fashion as you did with the previous XML file. Right-click the WebSite, select Add New Item, and select Text File.

4. Save the text file as JSON.txt.

5. Within JSON.txt, add the following text and then save all of the site files:

```
{"Results": {
      "total_computers": "2",
      "computer": [
        {
          "Manufacturer":"Dell",
          "Model":"Latitude",
          "Price":"1650"
        },
```

```
        {
          "Manufacturer":"Dell",
          "Model":"Inspiron",
          "Price":"1850"
        }
              ]
        }
  }
```

Your WebSite file structure should resemble Figure 3-13.

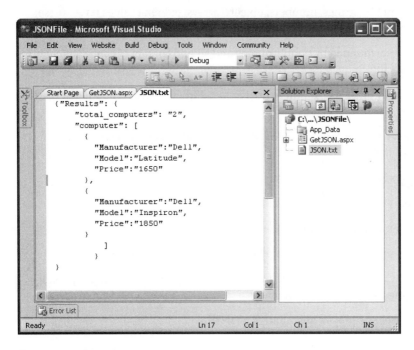

Figure 3-13. *JSON site structure*

As before, the web.config file will be added when we run the site for the first time.

We now need to add the appropriate code to the .aspx file (HTML source view). Much of the code can be copied and pasted from the previous XML sample application. Ultimately your .aspx code should be as follows:

```
<%@ Page Language="C#" AutoEventWireup="true"
CodeFile="GetJSON.aspx.cs" Inherits="GetJSON" %>
<!DOCTYPE html PUBLIC "-//W3C//DTD XHTML 1.0 Transitional//EN"
"http://www.w3.org/TR/xhtml1/DTD/xhtml1-transitional.dtd">
<html xmlns="http://www.w3.org/1999/xhtml" >
<head id="Head1" runat="server">
    <title>JSON Reader</title>
```

```
</head>
<script type="text/javascript" language="javascript">
var xmlhttp = false;

getHTTPRequestObject();

function getHTTPRequestObject()
{
    try
    {
        // Try legacy object first
        xmlhttp = new ActiveXObject("Msxml2.XMLHTTP");
    }
    catch(e)
    {
        try
        {
            // Try IE implementation now
            xmlhttp = new ActiveXObject("Microsoft.XMLHTTP");
        }
        catch(E)
        {
            xmlhttp = false;
        }
    }
    if(!xmlhttp && typeof XmlHttpRequest!= 'undefined')
    {
        // We must be using a Mozilla-based browser
        // so create a native request object now
        xmlhttp = new XmlHttpRequest();
    }
}

function callback()
{
        if(xmlhttp.readyState == 4)
        {
            if(xmlhttp.status == 200)
            {
              // Convert our JSON text into JavaScript Object
              eval("var objResults =" + xmlhttp.responseText);

              var displaytext = "";
              // Iterate through the computer object array
              // parsing each property into the string that
              // we'll dump into the DIV's inner HTML property
```

```
        for (var i=0; i < objResults.Results.computer.length; i++)
        {
          displaytext += objResults.Results.computer[i].Manufacturer + " " +
              objResults.Results.computer[i].Model + ": $" +
              objResults.Results.computer[i].Price + "<br>";
        }
          var finddiv = document.getElementById("divResponse");
          finddiv.innerHTML = displaytext;
      }
    }
}

function btnClick()
{
    // Retrieve the JSON text from the local file.
    xmlhttp.open("GET", "JSON.txt", true);
    xmlhttp.onreadystatechange = callback;
    xmlhttp.send(null);
}
</script>

<body>
    <form id="form1" runat="server">
        <input id="btnGetJSON" type="button"
         value="Get JSON" onclick="btnClick();" />
        <div id="divResponse"></div>
    </form>
</body>
</html>
```

After entering the code or downloading the sample project, running it will display a simple Get JSON button. As we did with the Get XML project, clicking the button will use the XmlHttpRequest object to dynamically retrieve our file. The results are parsed and pumped back out to the user's browser, as shown in Figure 3-14.

Figure 3-14. *JSON retrieved*

In this sample application, there are two primary differences that separate it from the XML application from the earlier portion of the chapter.

The button click event calls the JSON.txt file:

```
xmlhttp.open("GET", "JSON.txt", true);
```

And the callback() function has been modified to include the JSON parsing. Of particular interest to us is the eval() statement:

```
eval("var objResults =" + xmlhttp.responseText);
```

This is where the JSON magic really happens. The JavaScript eval() statement is responsible for taking the incoming response text and rendering it as the object that it was destined to become. This "magical" rendering of the text is simply a JavaScript interpretation method for the text passed into it as a parameter. To understand this process, we must first understand that the JavaScript eval() statement will render the incoming text in its literal sense. For instance, in JavaScript, to declare an array with literal script, you would write

```
var myStates = ["Michigan", "California", "New York"];
```

The preceding statement is declared in its literal sense with square brackets ([ ]) declaring that the enclosed text is an array and should be treated and used as such:

```
alert(myStates[0]);  // Would output "Michigan"
alert(myStates[1]);  // Would output "California"
alert(myStates[2]);  // Would output "New York"
```

The same process of interpretation holds true for JavaScript objects. They too can be declared, on the fly, with literal coding:

```
var myCustomer = {
                  "Name" : "John Doe",
                  "State" : "Michigan"
                 };
```

This particular object has been declared with two Name/Value properties that we can access in much the same way as typical OOP syntax:

```
alert(myCustomer.Name);  // Would output "John Doe"
alert(myCustomer.State);  // Would output "Michigan"
```

As you can see, the primary difference between the array literal and the object literal is the use of curly braces versus the square brackets. The object also is composed of Name/Value pairs of whatever data type you desire.

So now when our code assigns text to the objResults variable and sends it to the eval() statement, we're essentially saying to JavaScript, "Take this text and treat it as a literal declarative statement." If the output of that process happens to be an object, then the eval() statement will have helped the JSON text make the transition from a textual representation of an object to the real-world JavaScript object type.

A NOTE ON EVAL()

When using the JSON `eval()` function in a web-facing environment, you should be aware of potential security risks when parsing raw code. The `eval()` function will compile anything fed to it without security validation or structural integrity. If you're accessing JSON data from within your own organization (databases, files, etc.), it's not an issue. However, retrieving data from a third-party site could leave you open to a cross-site scripting attack. Many JSON developers prefer to channel the incoming JSON data through an external third-party parsing utility. You can find a variety of those, for free, at `http://www.json.org`.

We assign this rendered object to the variable `objResults` and, as you'll see in the next step, we iterate through the object's properties with OOP-like access to the properties:

```
for (var i=0; i < objResults.Results.computer.length; i++)
    {
        displaytext += objResults.Results.computer[i].Manufacturer + " " +
        objResults.Results.computer[i].Model + ": $" +
        objResults.Results.computer[i].Price + "<br>";
    }
```

Not at all a terribly difficult technology to work with, but it can be a powerful tool when used appropriately. JSON has the advantage of being very lightweight versus its XML counterpart. And a JSON parser is, as you've seen here, simply started with the JavaScript `eval()` function.

Summary

You've been introduced to the XmlHttpRequest object as well as a few of the data formats that you can pass, inherently, through the dynamic process. Many developers will admit that XML is a powerful tool, but as you've seen, it's not the **ONLY** tool available. I've brought JSON into the context of this book because there are a few Ajax libraries that rely heavily on JavaScript Object Notation as the carrier of choice for their asynchronous data. Given a chance, you may find yourself using the tool with other non-Ajax development projects.

In the next chapter, we'll take a look at the impact that Ajax has had on n-tier development structures. I'll suggest a "means to an end" for ensuring that your application structures maintain established patterns, while implementing asynchronous technologies.

■ ■ ■

CHAPTER 4

N-Tier and Ajax

One of the few negative conversations that I've had concerning implementations of Ajax centers primarily on the perceived erosion of n-tier programming. Many architects and coders feel that client-side coding should have a certain level of restraint and guidelines built into what is commonly known as the *presentation layer*. While a set of standards and guidelines has yet to garner any kind of industry-wide approval, it is possible to set some level of standard for your projects. The fact that Ajax has the capability to destroy business and data layers doesn't necessarily mean that you should. Many of us have been witness to such nightmares as finding data access layers dynamically built into the web page. That is so bad on so many levels, and I'm sure that you can guess why. I still have a special pet peeve that twitches every time I find dynamic SQL in a web page.

What this chapter will attempt to accomplish is to demonstrate how Ajax can fit into a structured application framework. We'll examine the guidelines that commonly define n-tier development, and I'll also introduce you to a project setup that has worked successfully for me. We'll code out presentation, business, and data layers that will keep well within the bounds of common practices and patterns.

What Is N-Tier?

The literal meaning of a tier is often translated as an individual row, layer, or level that is ranked or arranged one on top of another. Therefore, n-tier as compared to the singular version comes to mean a set of *N* number of tiers. Imagine the corporate structure in Figure 4-1 as it relates to you.

So there you are, at the bottom of the pile. You have recently noticed that some funny things are going on with the company and mention to your coworker (also at the bottom of the pile) that "somebody ought to say something." To which your associate replies, "Well, tell it to Mr. Moneybags, the owner." Great idea! However, if your organization is similar to many others, you just don't walk into the owner's office (the one with the magnificent corner view) and offload what is on your mind. After the awkward moment of silence, his secretary would undoubtedly introduce you to the majesty of the mail room: your new home for the next few years.

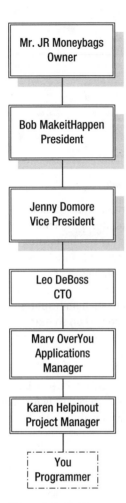

Figure 4-1. *Corporate n-tier structure*

Hopefully, it would never come to that. Hopefully, your coworker would also remind you that you'll need to follow "the proper chain of command." So you first need to bring your issues to the attention of Karen, your project manager. She in turn takes it up with her boss, who takes your cause to heart and discusses it at the next corporate vision assessment meeting. Your idea has taken on a life of its own and inspires the president to discuss the revolutionary process with the owner at the next shareholders' gathering. Mr. Moneybags loves it! He immediately institutes it as solid company policy and calls his peers to tell them of this extraordinary methodology that he's worked long and hard on, leaving your name unmentioned. Oh well. You can't win them all. But the moral of the story is that the structure exists for a reason. Perhaps your owner is overwhelmed by requests on a daily basis, and an open door policy has rendered his schedule useless. By filtering visits to a minimum amount of traffic, each individual in the chain is able to perform and address situations in their own unique way. And software development is no exception. Much like the corporate structure, application framework structure exists in a similar fashion. Following the chain of command becomes a necessity if you want to reap the benefits of the n-tier approach.

Most application architecture guides follow a simple yet universal pattern when describing n-tier application patterns. Figure 4-2 demonstrates a generic template that illustrates how our corporate example mirrors that of tiered software development.

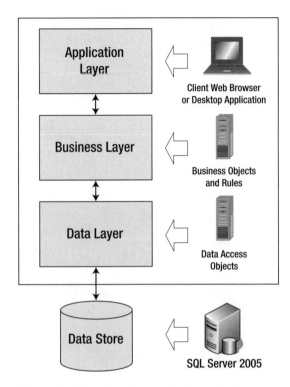

Figure 4-2. *Typical n-tier application structure*

OK, so that is one fancy diagram, but what does it mean? Without being entirely verbose, let's try to describe this process as it would relate to a simple web application built in ASP.NET. As the application is built, it will begin to shape the application structure in Figure 4-2 into a customized representation of the n-tier application as shown in Figure 4-3.

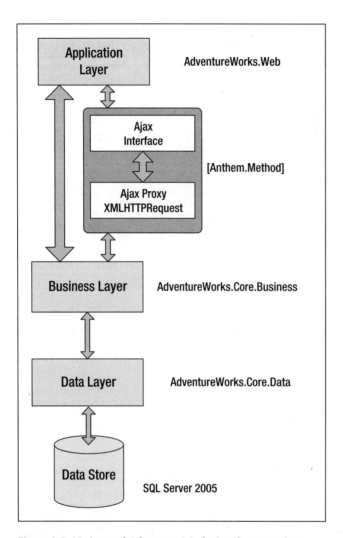

Figure 4-3. *N-tier and AdventureWorks implementation*

Application Layer

Most web pages are designed and hosted to accomplish a particular task. That task could involve anything from retail sales to simple picture galleries of the grandkids. For this particular example, we'll suppose that we're working on a store site responsible for selling t-shirts to the world. Aside from displaying the product on the web page, we'll need to also include the standard Add To Cart button, as you see in Figure 4-4.

Figure 4-4. *Sample retail application*

Our Add To Cart button will have a server-side click event handler that will have the responsibility of converting the user's request into a usable transaction:

```
protected void btnAddToCart_Click(object sender, EventArgs e)
{
    ShoppingCart.AddToCart('1513345', 'Ajax Rocks');
}
```

In the preceding function, we're passing the presentation layer request off to a class method, ShoppingCart.AddToCart(). This particular method resides quite peacefully in the next tier of our chain of command, the business layer.

Business Layer

Objects and rules in this realm are responsible for responding to presentation layer requests and enforcing business entity constraints. For instance, our class can provide the presentation layer with the ability to access back-end processes. Take a look at the following class and you'll find two methods that provide the aforementioned functionality, AddToCart and GetQuantity:

```
using System;
using System.Data;
using System.Configuration;
using System.Web;
using System.Web.Security;
using System.Web.UI;
using System.Web.UI.WebControls;
using System.Web.UI.WebControls.WebParts;
using System.Web.UI.HtmlControls;
```

```
public class ShoppingCart
{
      public ShoppingCart()
      {
      }

    private string _productid = 0;
    public string ProductID
    {
       get { return _productid; }
       set { _productid = value; }
    }

    private int _quantity = 0;
    public int Quantity
    {
       get { return _quantity; }
       set { _quantity = value; }
    }

    public static void AddToCart(string productid, string description)
    {
       ShoppingCartData.AddToCart(productid, description);
    }

    public static int GetQuantity(string productid)
    {
       return ShoppingCartData.GetQuantity(productid);
    }

}
```

This class represents our business layer in its entirety. You'll notice that there really doesn't seem to be much in the way of coding within the methods. Because of the growing trend that dictates core business rules can be maintained and distributed from the safety of database stored procedures, you'll find that business layers have a tendency to be rather transparent when combined with an associative data layer, as was the case with our ShoppingCart (business layer) communicating with ShoppingCartData (data layer).

Data Layer

As you may expect, the data layer has the primary task of providing access to the underlying database application. Why do we separate the data layer from the business layer? Wouldn't it make sense to simply include our stored procedure calls from within the business class? For short-term coding, sure, you could combine the two. And very simple applications always tempt you to include the calls in the business layer. Avoiding this temptation means that when your application grows, you are in a good position. Imagine that your company switches from an Oracle database to Microsoft SQL Server. Your DBA scrambles to rewrite all of the stored procedures so that they implement the same functionality, but on a different platform. Had you combined the data layer within the business tier, you would most likely find yourself with a considerable amount of refactoring.

Without getting too in depth on the specifics of the data layer (we'll be doing that later in the chapter), just be aware that this distinct layer is responsible for connecting the business layer to the data source:

```
using System;
using System.Data;
using System.Configuration;
using System.Web;
using System.Web.Security;
using System.Web.UI;
using System.Web.UI.WebControls;
using System.Web.UI.WebControls.WebParts;
using System.Web.UI.HtmlControls;
using System.Data.SqlClient;

public class ShoppingCartData
{
    public ShoppingCartData()
    {
    }

    public static objProduct GetProductPrice(string productid)
    {
        SqlConnection conn = null;
        SqlDataReader rdr = null;

        try
        {
            conn = new SqlConnection("Server=(local);
DataBase=MyDatabase;Integrated Security=SSPI");
            conn.Open();
            SqlCommand cmd = new SqlCommand("My Special Proc Name", conn);
            cmd.CommandType = CommandType.StoredProcedure;

            rdr = cmd.ExecuteReader();

            while (rdr.Read())
            {
                // Fill the business object with the reader results.
            }
        }
        finally
        {
            // Clean up coding
        }
    }
}
```

ENTERPRISE LIBRARY

Microsoft's Enterprise Library can be an incredible time saver and is definitely worth a look. Microsoft now has a release available for Visual Studio 2005. This is one of those tools that developers either love or hate. Personally, I'm a big fan of anything that cuts down on the amount of coding that I must do. Check it out for yourself at `http://msdn.microsoft.com/practices/vs2005`.

One of the main benefits of having a set-aside class for data access is that it helps you account for data source modifications. It is likely that you'll either be using a SQL helper class or perhaps Enterprise Library 2.0 for data access, and those particular methods would find their residence in this tier. I'll shed more light on these tiers as I demonstrate them with this chapter's sample application.

Data Store

Our database server lies at the bottom of the chain, but it certainly is not the lowest in importance. Here is where our stored procedures, tables, and much-acclaimed data reside. The data layer will communicate directly with the store; whether it be by OLEDB, ODBC, or other connection method, all calls end here. The server processes the requests, updates the appropriate information, and sends the process back up the chain of command.

The Place for Ajax

So where does Ajax fit into this grandiose scheme of things? Can we really implement something as dynamic into a structured environment? Let's first take what we've discussed about Ajax communication so far and how we can slot it into our diagram. We know that our user interface will be communicating via XmlHttpRequest coding. And we're relatively sure that our Ajax library will provide us with an interface appropriate for such communication. So let's plug that into a revised edition of our previous n-tier structure, shown in Figure 4-5.

We must make a conscious decision that, if we really are going to implement n-tier, Ajax must adhere to the same constraints that we would generally apply to other levels of coding. Our Ajax library should bear the burden of communicating with the business layer for all of the dynamic interface requests.

I've seen various sample applications where the developer makes database calls from the tail end of the Ajax request. There isn't anything inherently wrong with that, aside from the fact that it deviates from proper n-tier architecture. With n-tier, I've found that it is an all-or-none proposition. Imagine that you slacked off on a particular business object and dropped some SQL code in there. A few months go by and the DBA calls and says that the company just got a great deal on Oracle and that the migration will begin soon. You modify the data layer and fire up the application only to find that some of the pages aren't loading correctly. Unfortunately, the cut corners are now starting to compound the problem exponentially. Sticking to the playbook will ultimately pay off in time saved and ease of maintainability.

All of this theory looks really awesome on paper, but it is better demonstrated. The sample application for this chapter illustrates the basics tenets of n-tier and Ajax. We'll take a look at a possible website file structure that will help to segregate the tiers appropriately.

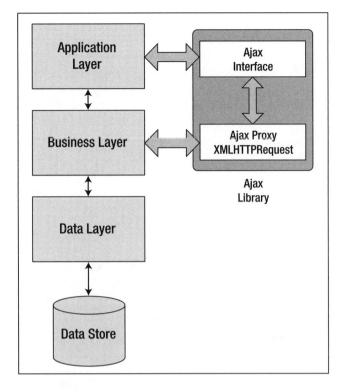

Figure 4-5. *Ajax and n-tier structure*

Sample N-Tier Application

If you haven't already, jump out to the web and snag the download for this book at the Apress Source Code web page (http://www.apress.com/book/download.html). The application implements a Google Suggest–like control (discussed in Chapter 11) and utilizes the AdventureWorks database. If you don't already have the database, Microsoft has packaged the install for it as an MSI and made it available across the web. The primary purpose of this application is not to concentrate on the coding value, but rather the structure of the Solution.

Let's first take a look at the overall Solution as it appears in the Explorer (see Figure 4-6).

We have two projects and a website within the confines of our Solution file. The website consists of three web pages that we'll use as our application layer. The only n-tier component not represented in this particular Solution is, of course, the AdventureWorks database. We could have easily added a Database project to the Solution, but for now we'll just accept that our SQL Server database is in fact the data store.

We also have, added as a reference, the Ajax utility Anthem.dll that will facilitate our dynamic calls. We'll look at it in depth later on in Chapter 8. For now, we'll just put it to work.

Without diving too deeply into the coding for this Solution, let's take a look at our n-tier setup using sample code from each of the individual projects to illustrate a possible methodology behind the concept.

Figure 4-6. *AdventureWorks application structure*

Presentation Layer

One of the first steps that I generally take when designing an application is to establish a name-space that makes sense for the particular solution. You may choose to use either a company name, corporate division, or perhaps, as we have, the name of the application itself. We're using AdventureWorks as our namespace, and you'll find that all of the project files have been named with that associative name.

AdventureWorks.Web is an ASP.NET 2.0 website that has three pages with limited function-ality. This particular project represents the n-tier presentation layer. The tier comprises not only the visual component of the .aspx page, but also the code behind the .cs file. We'll be using Ajax within the confines of this layer, specifically inside of SearchPage.aspx.

Another key component of the overall structure that we'll be demonstrating is the use of a transitional tool known as the Utility class library. Before we take a look at AdventureWorks.Utility, let's first understand the makeup of our presentation layer by running the application and getting a feel for what the pages represent. If Default.aspx, shown in Figure 4-7, has not been set as the startup page, then you'll want to set that now.

If you click the Search Stores link, you'll be taken directly to SearchPage.aspx, shown in Figure 4-8.

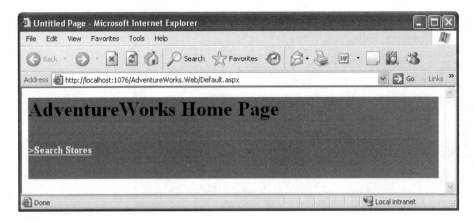

Figure 4-7. *Default.aspx*

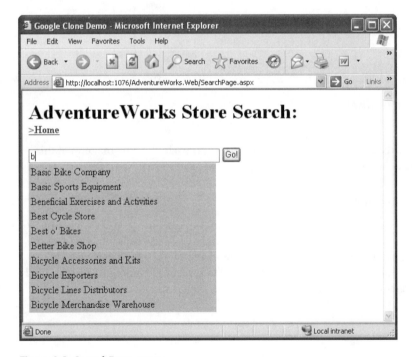

Figure 4-8. *SearchPage.aspx*

We'll discuss this page in a moment, but for now simply try out the Suggest textbox and then click an entry. After you've selected a search result, click the Go button, and you'll be sent to DestinationPage.aspx, shown in Figure 4-9. This page will be the end of the road for our presentation layer and will do nothing more than display the selected results that were passed in as a parameter.

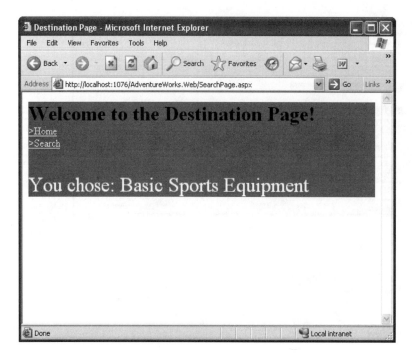

Figure 4-9. *DestinationPage.aspx*

Now that we've had a chance to view the website, let's take a look at the makeup of this particular n-tier layer.

Components of the Presentation Layer

We'll be taking a much more in-depth look at the usage of the Ajax library in Chapter 8, but for now you should understand that just because Ajax can make database calls straight from the presentation layer does not necessarily mean that it should.

Within SearchPage.aspx, we have an Anthem.Method (a server-side function) that is called dynamically from a client-side JavaScript method. Here is the JavaScript call:

```
function LoadResults(searchterm)
{
        if (searchterm.length == 0)
        {
                // If the input box is empty, let's dump all the rows
                // from the results table
                ClearResults();
                HideDiv("searchresults");
                return;
        }
```

```
    // Fetch results from server side.
    // This is our actual Ajax call
    My.Page.RetrieveRows(searchterm, LoadResultsCallback);

}
```

Now the server-side call:

```
[Anthem.Method]
public StoreCollection RetrieveRows(string searchterm)
{
    // Call the business layer
    return Store.GetStoreNames(searchterm);
}
```

Our server-side Ajax call, RetrieveRows(), does nothing more than call our business-layer object Store. Don't dwell on the Ajax code for the moment, we'll come back to that later in the book.

Another interesting aspect of the presentation layer is how we assign the NavigateUrl of our hyperlink controls. We're actually calling a method of our utility object that determines the correct URL for us at runtime. It is also responsible for delivering page parameters as the system passes data from one page to another.

AdventureWorks.Utility

This is an interesting, and rarely used, methodology of process handling between web pages. In fact, it wasn't until I began working for Nusoft Solutions (http://www.nusoftsolutions.com) that I was introduced to the functionality of the library. And I have to say that I was immediately hooked. I often wonder how I developed without it. The Utility class really becomes a transitional carrier for data that you would like to carry across page transfers as well as a reference point from which you can gather URLs, parameter names, etc. As we examine the two main classes that make up the library, you'll begin to understand how efficient and easy to use the Utility library really is.

AdventureWorks.Utility.Constants

As its name implies, the Constants class is a warehouse of variable constants. However, don't feel as if it is the only thing that you can park there. If I have a need for site-wide enumerations, I'll drop them in here as well. I find that a majority of my .Constants classes are just that, constants. If we open up the class, we'll find a few variables declared within:

```
using System;
using System.Collections.Generic;
using System.Text;
```

```
namespace AdventureWorks.Utility
{
    public class Constants
    {
        // Query string constants
        public const string STORENAME_PARAM = "storename";

        // URL constants
        // We'll assign our page URLs here for maintainability
        public const string SEARCHPAGE_URL = "SearchPage.aspx";

        public const string HOMEPAGE_URL = "Default.aspx";

        public const string DESTINATIONPAGE_URL = "DestinationPage.aspx";


    }
}
```

It is in our best interest to assign our web page URLs to a site-wide-accessible constant. As most developers know, the likelihood of a page changing its filename is quite possible. And it can be an absolute nightmare repairing links throughout an entire site if you've made the mistake of statically assigning them to the web navigation controls. So park the values here and partner with our other utility class, ProcessControl.

AdventureWorks.Utility.ProcessControl

You'll find that you can place a lot of functionality in this class. It can handle a great deal of page-process tasks, from simple URL lookups to parameter passing and more. For this sample application, we use it to retrieve URLs for other project entities as well as for passing page parameters from the SearchPage.aspx to the DestinationPage.aspx. Let's take a look at the sample file before proceeding:

```
using System;
using System.Collections.Generic;
using System.Text;
using System.Web;

namespace AdventureWorks.Utility
{
    public class ProcessControl
    {
        private static string GetAppPath()
        {
            string AppPath = HttpContext.Current.Request.ApplicationPath;
            if (!AppPath.EndsWith("/"))
            {
                AppPath = AppPath + "/";
            }
```

```
        return AppPath;

    }
    public static string GetSearchPageURL()
    {
        return GetAppPath() + Constants.SEARCHPAGE_URL;
    }

    public static string GetHomePageURL()
    {
        return GetAppPath() + Constants.HOMEPAGE_URL;
    }

    public static string GetDestinationPageURL(string storename)
    {
        System.Text.StringBuilder sbURL = new System.Text.StringBuilder();

        sbURL.Append(GetAppPath());
        sbURL.Append(Constants.DESTINATIONPAGE_URL);
        sbURL.Append("?");
        sbURL.Append(Constants.STORENAME_PARAM);
        sbURL.Append("=");
        sbURL.Append(storename);

        return sbURL.ToString();

    }

    public static string GetStoreName()
    {
        string storename = string.Empty;

        if (HttpContext.Current.Request.QueryString
           [Constants.STORENAME_PARAM] != null)
        {
            storename = HttpContext.Current.Request.QueryString
                    [Constants.STORENAME_PARAM];
        }

        return storename;
    }

    }
}
```

By working hand in hand with the Constants file, we're able to establish an interface for the rest of the site that will allow developers to assign easily modified URLs to web content. For instance, our Default.aspx page has a HyperLink on the page. We don't assign the NavigateUrl property until the page load process. Here's the client-side code:

```
<asp:HyperLink ID="lnkSearch" runat="server"
style="font-size: medium" ForeColor="White">
>Search Stores</asp:HyperLink>
```

And the server-side code:

```
if (!Page.IsPostBack)
{
    lnkSearch.NavigateUrl = ProcessControl.GetSearchPageURL();
}
```

You'll notice that the asp:HyperLink control has not had its NavigateUrl attribute assigned yet. We'll do that with our ProcessControl call. Essentially what is happening behind the scenes on the PageLoad event is that ProcessControl.GetSearchPageUrl() retrieves the page's URL from the constants file, assembles it into a usable link, and returns it to the page process for assignment to the control:

```
private static string GetAppPath()
{
    string AppPath = HttpContext.Current.Request.ApplicationPath;
    if (!AppPath.EndsWith("/"))
    {
        AppPath = AppPath + "/";
    }

    return AppPath;

}
public static string GetSearchPageURL()
{
    return GetAppPath() + Constants.SEARCHPAGE_URL;
}
```

We're building the returnable hyperlink URL with information from the HttpContext object as well as the Constants class. Notice also that the function has been declared as static. This allows us the ability to access the method without an instantiation of the class itself.

Another beneficial aspect of the utility class is our ability to pass parameters to another page by building the URL within the ProcessControl call itself. As you recall, we also store parameter-naming values within our constants file. We do this so that if we ever need to modify our parameter calls, we can do so from the Constants file as well. This technique also allows us to create obscure query string parameter names while still making our code easy to read and maintain. Generating the URL link with the inclusive parameters is as simple as the following method:

```
public static string GetDestinationPageURL(string storename)
{
    System.Text.StringBuilder sbURL = new System.Text.StringBuilder();
```

```
sbURL.Append(GetAppPath());
sbURL.Append(Constants.DESTINATIONPAGE_URL);
sbURL.Append("?");
sbURL.Append(Constants.STORENAME_PARAM);
sbURL.Append("=");
sbURL.Append(storename);

return sbURL.ToString();


}
```

We retrieve our URL and parameter constants and build the URL as we would expect it to be represented in a typical HTTP call. Hopefully you've picked up on the fact that we pass the parameter that we're looking to use on the next page as our function parameter as well (string storename).

So how do we grab the parameter once we've been transferred to the destination page? Let's open up the server-side code for DestinationPage.aspx:

```
using System;
using System.Data;
using System.Configuration;
using System.Collections;
using System.Web;
using System.Web.Security;
using System.Web.UI;
using System.Web.UI.WebControls;
using System.Web.UI.WebControls.WebParts;
using System.Web.UI.HtmlControls;
using AdventureWorks.Utility;

public partial class DestinationPage : System.Web.UI.Page
{
    protected void Page_Load(object sender, EventArgs e)
    {
        if (!Page.IsPostBack)
        {

            // Retrieve parameters
            divStoreInfo.InnerHtml = "You chose: " +
            ProcessControl.GetStoreName();

            // Assign links
            lnkHome.NavigateUrl = ProcessControl.GetHomePageURL();
            lnkSearch.NavigateUrl = ProcessControl.GetSearchPageURL();
        }
    }
}
```

The bold text represents the `ProcessControl` call that fetches our incoming parameter for us:

```
public static string GetStoreName()
{
    string storename = string.Empty;

    if (HttpContext.Current.Request.QueryString
        [Constants.STORENAME_PARAM] != null)
    {

        storename = HttpContext.Current.Request.QueryString
                    [Constants.STORENAME_PARAM];
    }

    return storename;
}
```

The function visits the current `Request` and searches for an existing `QueryString`. If it finds one that matches the constants value of the parameter that we happen to be searching for, it will promptly return it back to the caller.

The `ProcessControl` library can be expanded to meet many needs. I have found that using it to fetch URL information has become an indispensable part of my web coding. I'm pretty sure that if you give it an honest shot, you'll soon find it as vital to your applications as I have.

So far we've discussed the presentation layer as it relates to our Ajax application. As you've likely discovered, the client page has a call into the business layer:

```
return Store.GetStoreNames(searchterm);
```

The server-side coding calls a static business class method and returns the data to the associated Ajax callback function. Our application coding is kept to a minimum because we have made use of the business tier.

Business Layer

I'm a firm believer in business objects. If you haven't yet checked out Rocky Lhotka's book, *Expert C# Business Objects, Second Edition* (Apress, 2006), then you are truly missing a great read. The general concept is that everything can be broken down into business classes that represent the data that you are using, whether it be database tables or custom classes (i.e., a customer class). We can find our business and data tiers inside of the `AdventureWorks.Core` project, as shown in Figure 4-10.

Of interest to us at the moment is the `Business` folder, wherein we've placed our custom objects.

Figure 4-10. *The core*

Store.cs

Because our application centers on the acquisition and display of store information, it makes perfect sense to create a specialized class with properties and methods befitting that unique role. We'll need information stored within that instantiated class that is relevant to store data, as well as methods to fill the class or return information that is associated with this particular object. Let's take a look at the Store class:

```csharp
using System;
using AdventureWorks.Core.Data;
    [Serializable]
        public class Store
        {
            public Store()
            {
                //
                // TODO: Add constructor logic here
                //
            }

            // We only need one property for the purposes of this demo.

            private string _storename = string.Empty;
            /// <summary>
            /// Stores Name
            /// </summary>
            public string Name
            {
                get{return _storename;}
                set{_storename = value;}
            }

            // Object methods

            public static StoreCollection GetStoreNames(string searchterm)
            {
                // Call the data layer
                return StoreData.GetStoreNames(searchterm);
            }
        }
    }
```

If you take a look at the AdventureWorks.sales.store table, you'll see that there is a lot of information that we could easily bring to the site. However, for the sake of simplicity, we'll just narrow that down to using the store Name column. Inside of our business object, we have only one property, Name. Notice that we also have a single object method as well. GetStoreNames() returns a StoreCollection object that we'll fill in our data layer call, StoreData.GetStoreNames(). It's a good idea to include your object's data access calls within the business objects as static calls as well, so as to adhere to a uniform method of calling various retrieval processes.

As you can see, the data access call is relatively transparent and low key, and will typically be so. The code should only concern itself with the actual object call. Any data manipulation should be handled on the data layer before being passed back to the business tier. In this particular example, we're using a StoreCollection as the informational transfer object.

StoreCollection.cs

It is quite possible that we will need to access more than just one store object from within our program. Our immediate solution to that is to implement a custom collection. We could, of course, use Generics as a choice for storage of the serializable class, but for now let's just stick to the collection class:

```
using System;
using System.Collections;
using System.Xml;
```

```
[Serializable]
public class StoreCollection : CollectionBase
{
    public StoreCollection()
    {
    }

    public StoreCollection(Store[] value)
    {
        this.AddRange(value);
    }

    public Store this[int index]
    {
        get { return ((Store)(this.List[index])); }
    }

    public int Add(Store value)
    {
        return this.List.Add(value);
    }

    public void AddRange(Store[] value)
    {
        for (int i = 0; (i < value.Length); i = (i + 1))
        {
            this.Add(value[i]);
        }
    }
}
```

```csharp
public void AddRange(StoreCollection value)
{
    for (int i = 0; (i < value.Count); i = (i + 1))
    {
        this.Add((Store)value.List[i]);
    }
}

public bool Contains(Store value)
{
    return this.List.Contains(value);
}

public void CopyTo(Store[] array, int index)
{
    this.List.CopyTo(array, index);
}

public int IndexOf(Store value)
{
    return this.List.IndexOf(value);
}

public void Insert(int index, Store value)
{
    List.Insert(index, value);
}

public void Remove(Store value)
{
    List.Remove(value);
}

public new StoreEnumerator GetEnumerator()
{
    return new StoreEnumerator(this);
}

public class StoreEnumerator : IEnumerator
{
    private IEnumerator _enumerator;
    private IEnumerable _temp;

    public StoreEnumerator(StoreCollection mappings)
    {
        _temp = ((IEnumerable)(mappings));
        _enumerator = _temp.GetEnumerator();
    }
```

```
        public Store Current
        {
            get { return ((Store)(_enumerator.Current)); }
        }

        object IEnumerator.Current
        {
            get { return _enumerator.Current; }
        }

        public bool MoveNext()
        {
            return _enumerator.MoveNext();
        }

        bool IEnumerator.MoveNext()
        {
            return _enumerator.MoveNext();
        }

        public void Reset()
        {
            _enumerator.Reset();
        }

        void IEnumerator.Reset()
        {
            _enumerator.Reset();
        }
    }
}
```

As I've said before, don't concentrate too hard on the logic involved, as we'll be visiting this code again later when we discuss the Google Suggest clone. If you have worked with collections before, you'll find no surprises in our StoreCollection class. All of the typical add/delete and iteration functions have been prepared for us, but we'll only be using the StoreCollection.Add() method within our data layer.

Data Layer

In the confines of AdventureWorks.Core also lies the data layer, cleverly disguised as AdventureWorks.Core.Data. We have the aforementioned StoreData class that is primarily responsible for retrieving database information and stuffing it into a return object. In our sample site, we use this class to populate a StoreCollection. We achieve those results by querying the database directly:

```csharp
using System;
using System.Collections.Generic;
using System.Text;
using System.Data;
using System.Data.SqlClient;

namespace AdventureWorks.Core.Data
{
    class StoreData
    {
        public static StoreCollection GetStoreNames(string searchterm)
        {
            // You may need to modify this connection string for your environment
            SqlConnection conn = new SqlConnection(
              "Data Source=(local);Initial Catalog=AdventureWorks;Integrated
 Security=SSPI");
            DataTable dtReturn = new DataTable();

            conn.Open();
            SqlCommand cmd = new
             SqlCommand("Select Top 10 Name from Sales.Store
             where Name like @searchterm Order By Name", conn);
            SqlParameter param = new SqlParameter();
            param.ParameterName = "@searchterm";
            searchterm.Trim().Replace("'", "''");
            searchterm += "%";
            param.Value = searchterm;
            cmd.Parameters.Add(param);

            SqlDataAdapter adpt = new SqlDataAdapter(cmd);
            adpt.Fill(dtReturn);

            conn.Close();

            StoreCollection strCollection = new StoreCollection();

            for (int i = 0; i < dtReturn.Rows.Count; i++)
            {
                Store stre = new Store();
                stre.Name = (string)dtReturn.Rows[i]["Name"];
                strCollection.Add(stre);
            }

            // Send the CustomerCollection back to the CallBack function
            return strCollection;
```

```
        }


    }
}
```

`StoreData.GetStoreNames()` takes in a search term and returns a collection of `LIKE` results from the database. The key point here is that we have provided an avenue of access for our business tier to the data store via specialized object calls. One benefit of this methodology is that it gives us the ability to change database providers at will. Should your company decide to modify or altogether change your storage facilities, you'll have a one-stop shop for coding changes here in the data layer.

Data Store

I'm quite sure that this final tier needs no introduction. We have discussed the fact that our sample application makes use of SQL Server 2005 and the `AdventureWorks` database. However, you could just as easily modify the solution to access an Oracle, MySQL, or DB2 database by adjusting your connection strings and customizing the data objects to reflect your current table structures.

Summary

Fitting Ajax into an n-tier structure is manageable and, in my opinion, nearly a requirement. By implementing some constraints in our dynamic library, we have the added benefit of manageability and modification.

We've introduced quite a few preparatory concepts in these first few chapters. Our examination of the coding has been only a cursory one of the Ajax projects that are coming up later in the book. Don't be discouraged by the fact that we skimmed through the Anthem portion of the application. We'll dig deeply into the `Anthem.dll` as I demonstrate exactly how our Ajax library works. Simply using it out of the box is always an option; however, fully understanding the underlying process will benefit you greatly.

In Part 2, we will start an in-depth look at legacy Ajax/DHTML that will set the stage for modern Ajax. We'll take a look at some interesting hacks as well as some CSS and DOM scripts that could boost your dynamic web content up a notch. And we should definitely discuss alternatives to Ajax and how they have may have an impact on your projects. As you will see, Ajax is not the only show on the road, and understanding the competition can only lead to a better understanding of Ajax as a whole.

PART 2

■ ■ ■

Ajax Components

Part 2 will cover what some have called *Ajax core components*, in that, without prior knowledge of these key elements, Ajax development would be incredibly difficult at best. A full-scale investigation into JavaScript, CSS, and the DOM will better prepare you for the transition to typical Ajax development, and so we'll dive into each of those topics accordingly. We'll also take a closer look at some of the Ajax components that have popped onto the scene as Ajax alternatives.

Rich Internet Applications

If you ask two people what a rich Internet application (RIA) is, you'll probably get two entirely different responses. Everyone has a unique view on what defines the technology. I've read a multitude of blogs, white papers, and books on RIAs, and they all seem to have a proprietary take on things. I don't really want to lay down the law on what I feel defines the entire genre. I have, however, taken the liberty of compiling a general consensus that seeks to find common ground on most points involving rich Internet applications.

What It Is Not

Traditional Internet applications followed the established client-server design pattern. A request was made to the server, where all of the page-logic processing took place, and the resultant data was merely passed back to the browser, where it was rendered and displayed to the user. It was nothing more than a generic request/response model. Unfortunately, this particular model forces all of the workload onto the server and very little processing occurs on the client. A Rich Internet Application expands upon the request/response model and seeks to move some of the processing out to those lazy browsers.

What It Could Be

I say "could be" because not everything that is listed here must be present for an application to be considered by some as being a rich client. There are, however, some common requirements for rich Internet applications:

- The application should run from a web browser. Bonus points for cross-browser support!

- The application needs to be capable of client-side logic processing. This contributes to scalability of server-side resources.

- In general, little installation should take place when implementing the application. It is understandable that some third-party controls may be necessary (Flash, Java, etc.).

- Browser-transition logic should be preserved (Back and Forward buttons, for example).

As you can imagine, there are countless other requirements that some impose upon rich clients. However, if you pare it down, you'll be left with the preceding list. I will give you a brief look at each point so that you can understand what the underlying methodology of a rich Internet application really means.

Cross-browser Support

Too many times, in my work place as well as in online forums, I've encountered a common cry among many .NET developers: "Why doesn't my site work on Firefox and Safari?" Some even go so far as to make a blanket proclamation that they will support Internet Explorer only. That can be a scary proposition when you really think about it. Every year, the market share for Firefox grows exponentially. As of this writing, it accounts for about ten percent of total browser usage. That may not sound like a very large percentage, but if you step back from the equation, you realize that it's ten percent of the web population. That's **A LOT** of people. Why isolate those users right from the start?

Well, it does require extra effort on the developer's part to implement cross-browser support. You will encounter a few browser inconsistencies during various exercises throughout the book, but ultimately it will take trial and error and a whole lot of time with Google finding others that have resolved similar issues. Some have suggested that Mozilla-based browsers and Microsoft's Internet Explorer seem to be migrating towards common ground. That is certainly good news, but potentially a long time out.

Client-side Logic Handling

One of the benefits of Ajax technology is that it allows us to move some of the processing logic out to the client's computer, giving that computer the opportunity to help carry the load. Less strain on the server side of things can dramatically improve the scalability of your site. However, it is possible to overdo things. Bloated JavaScript is doing your users a grave injustice and will eventually lead to slower load times. Slower load times lead to angry users. Angry users will go somewhere else.

Application Installation

It is my personal opinion that a consistent rich Internet application will take advantage of preexisting software, i.e., the browser. Whether Internet Explorer or Firefox or any other web browser, your application should be generic enough to run on a majority of them. If I have to install a desktop application to access data, then it obviously cannot be classified as an RIA. For example, take a look at Figure 5-1, which shows Google Earth, an awesome mapping application.

This application (http://earth.google.com) is incredibly addictive, and it'll have you surfing the globe for hours. However, despite the fact that it is tied to the web for streaming content, it is not a rich Internet application, primarily because it is a Windows application and up until January of 2006 was not compatible with the Mac OS. If I have to install the core component (as shown in Figure 5-2), the application cannot be considered a dynamic web application.

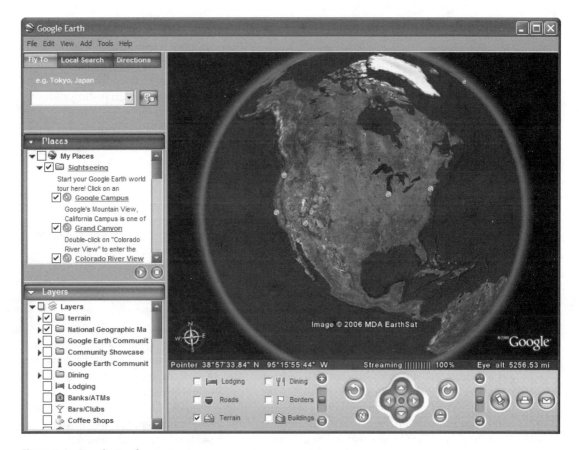

Figure 5-1. *Google Earth*

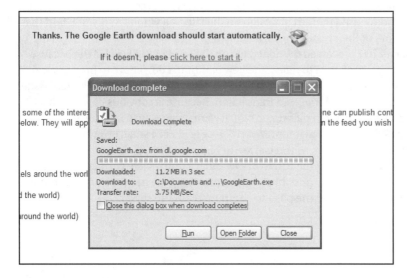

Figure 5-2. *Installing Google Earth*

Browser Transition Logic

One of the issues that you will eventually run into when working with Ajax technology is that it is quite easy to break the Back button on the browser. JavaScript and the Back button do not play nicely together. Some developers try to provide an easy path back to previous pages on their own site, but it is something that you'll want to monitor with testing and quality assurance verification.

So far we've discussed, briefly, what a rich Internet application should not be and what it could be. But I'd like to jump up on my little soapbox here for a moment and discuss some aspects of dynamic Internet applications and what they *should* be.

RIA Recommendations

Before you overrun your site with Ajax, we should discuss some tips and mistakes that you might want to bear in mind as you are designing pages. This is not meant to be a patterns-and-practices conversation, but rather an examination of some common concepts that seem to pop up across the web.

Focused Interaction

You should use Ajax controls where it makes sense to. I've come across a few sites where the developers absolutely Ajaxed the thing to death. Just because you can do something does not always mean that you should. When you choose to implement dynamic content on the site, it is imperative that the interactive portion of the site is obvious and easy to use. How many times have you been to a site and the first thought in your mind is, "Ummm . . . what do I do here?" Nothing will turn an anonymous user away from a site faster than confusion.

When you use an Ajax control that is primarily responsible for the direct modification of other content on the same page, you'll want to locate the two entities in close proximity to each other. This assures the viewer of immediate feedback to the interactive process by providing an easily found result. For instance, Flickr (http://www.flickr.com) tends to maintain a very stripped down and focused pattern of design on the site as a whole. And you'll find that the controls are neighbors of their result panes, as shown in Figure 5-3.

I know that the server has processed my added tag on the server after I click ADD because the tag list directly above it will change to reflect the new addition. I don't have to hunt around on the page to see if the action was accepted. I am a big fan of giving the user some kind of visual cue as to what is going on during the triggered transaction. Because an obvious page postback will not be available for the web user to pick up on, you'll want some way to indicate that something is going on. For instance, on Gmail (http://gmail.google.com), a small box will appear in the top-right corner to indicate activity, as you can see in Figure 5-4.

With this particular action I don't have to worry whether I didn't click correctly or at all. I don't have to worry that the server is possibly down or that the page has entered an infinite loop because I've inadvertently asked the page to compute pi on the server.

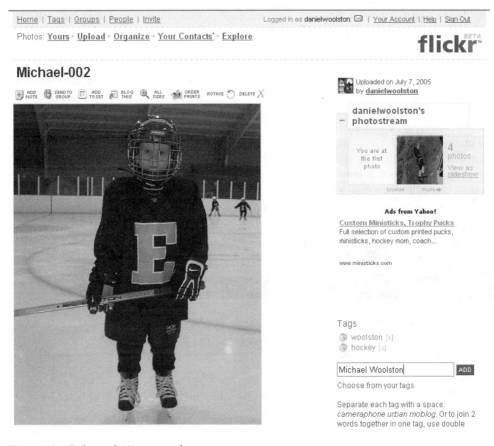

Figure 5-3. *Flickr and Ajax controls*

Figure 5-4. *Gmail feedback*

Page Disruptions

One of my biggest pet peeves (and I have many) when visiting a dynamic web site is when current page content is shifted around to accommodate timed events or data that is returned from an asynchronous call. If I'm enjoying the site and new content forces the material I'm already reading elsewhere, that makes me want to never visit the site again. For example, there is a popular sports-related site (they happen to have a television network as well) that typically has a **HUGE** banner at the top that will display for a moment and then collapse to a fourth of its original size. When it collapses, however, it shifts the rest of the page content back up an inch or two. I find that to be very disruptive to the user experience. If I'm clicking Load Image or something similar, I expect that the page will need to render its content again, and I can live with that. Timers or asynchronous events that move things around are increasingly bothersome.

For pages where content shift is absolutely necessary, it would be appropriate to differentiate the newer content from the old. An interesting online collaboration site accomplishes just such methodology with its dynamic content. Basecamp (http://www.basecamphq.com) allows companies or individuals the opportunity to manage various aspects of their projects online. One of the many tools that they implement is project messaging. If a new message is sent to the currently viewed project, they implement what is increasingly referred to as *Yellow Fade Technique* (YFT) to indicate content modification on the site, as shown in Figure 5-5.

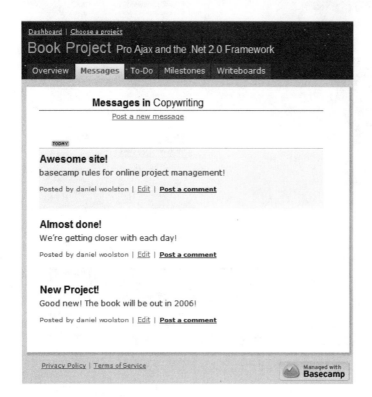

Figure 5-5. *Basecamp's Yellow Fade Technique*

The new content's background begins life as a bright yellow and will quickly fade to the current page background color. It's a fast, but eye-capturing, technique that notifies the user in a polite way that something new has hit the page.

Compelling Navigation

An engaging application should entice users to manipulate links, surf the site, and possibly buy the products. Getting the user to move from the home page and deeper into the website is often half the battle of good site design. Simply having a hyperlink or navigational tab is rather generic and unexciting. Wouldn't it be great if you could motivate users to click farther by giving them a taste of what is on the other side of the click? One essential tool to accomplishing that is a JavaScript hover (tooltip). Figure 5-6 (http://www.zondervan.com) illustrates how a tooltip can be so much more than just a single-line pop-up.

Figure 5-6. *Zondervan's hover message*

Notice that the hover is not a submenu but rather a detailed description of what lies beyond. The user will be more informed and therefore the overall satisfaction level will climb.

If at all possible, you should seek to avoid minor page transfers when the functionality that you want is somewhat trivial. For example, let's say you have a Create User Account page with a textbox asking for the alias that a user wishes to register. On many sites, the user will enter an insane amount of registration data and click Submit, only to be met rudely by the obnoxious "Username already taken. Click Back to try again." This particular process of try/submit/fail/retry can be easily remedied. Digg (http://www.digg.com) has a registration page that uses Ajax to query the database for a preexisting username, saving users the headache of annoying page bounces (see Figure 5-7).

After entering the requested username, the member-to-be clicks the check for availability button, and the page calls back to the server to check for the existence of the name. Following verification, the current page is updated with the acceptance/denial message without the need for a postback.

More sites are beginning to adopt this methodology, and I wholeheartedly encourage it. Ultimately it cuts down on server bandwidth, as users will not be submitting entire page loads to the server only to find out, for the thirteenth time, that their desired username has been taken.

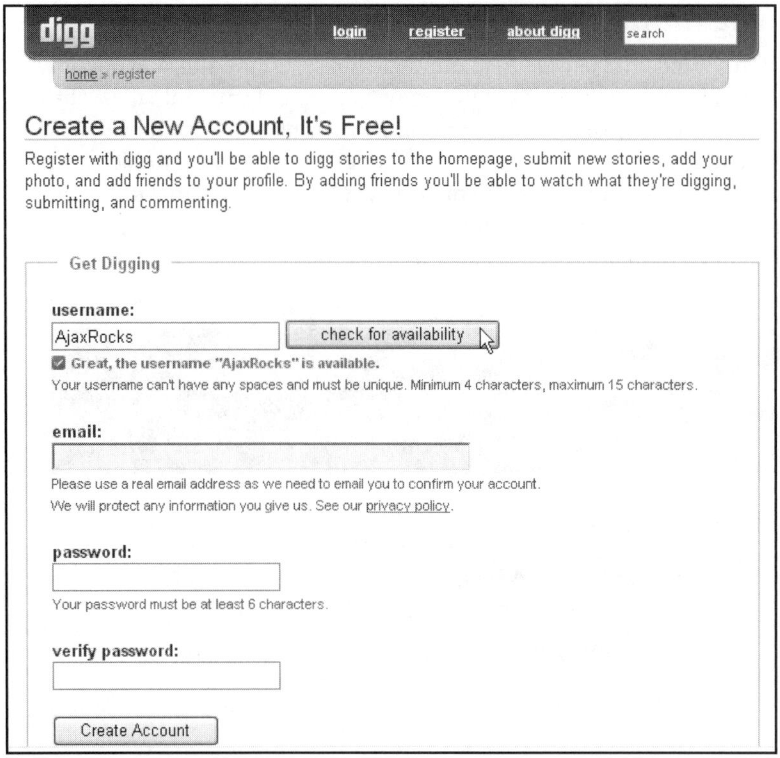

Figure 5-7. *Digg's seamless registration*

URL Linking

In the Ajax world of search and display, it is quite easy to bring content up to the browser dynamically. If you were to visit a community site where you've sought out and found a particular blog post that was displayed with Ajax technology, the URL for the parent page would not reflect the dynamic content included within.

The lack of proper method of URL referral becomes a bit frustrating if you find something online that you would like to refer to a friend or perhaps even bookmark for later. However, if you were to copy and paste the browser's URL, only the parent search page URL would be identifiable. This would leave you with the daunting task of describing to your friend the procedure they will have to endure if they want to see the same content. Not entirely a user-friendly process.

Kayak (http://www.kayak.com), for example, has an awesome Ajax-driven flight-scheduling application that allows you to search for and find competitive airfares with very little page transfer (see Figure 5-8). After selecting your desired flight plan, you may choose to book the flights with the appropriate airlines themselves. While this concept is certainly not new, Kayak's method of user interaction outclasses that of many of their competitors. After spending some time with the application, you'll immediately notice that a lot of dynamic content has been built into the web interface. Kayak makes heavy use of Ajax, and it shows.

Figure 5-8. *Kayak's "Google Suggest"-ish search box*

After selecting various options for travel, the site renders your possible flights for review, as you can see in Figure 5-9.

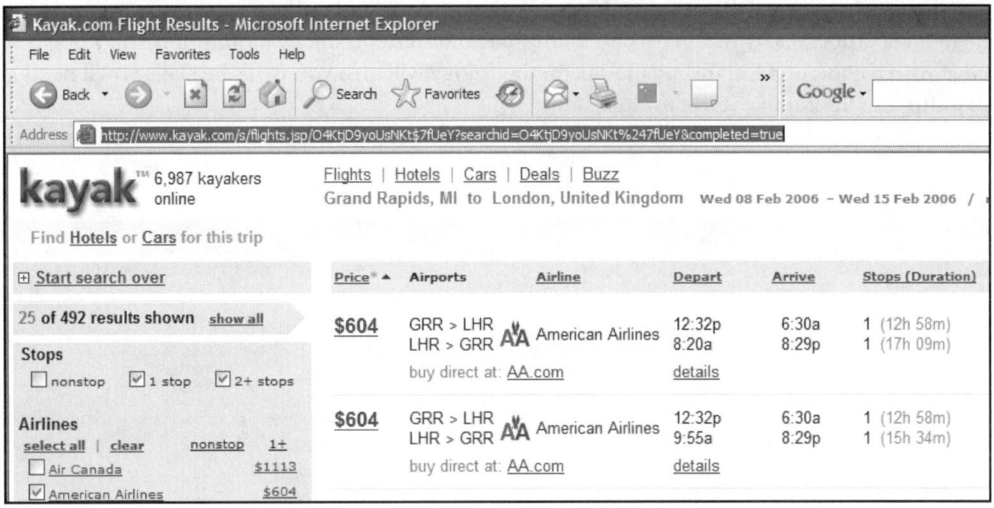

Figure 5-9. *Kayak search results*

OK, so now I have a selection of fares to consider. But what if I'm flying with my friend and I'd like to get their opinion of the rates? If I copy and paste the URL from the browser's address bar and send it to them, they'll attempt to access the site and receive an error, as shown in Figure 5-10.

Figure 5-10. *Nonworking URL for content referral*

It is certainly not an easy thing for developers to overcome. And, unfortunately, in many given situations, it will be a permanent drawback to implementing Ajax for large volumes of searchable content.

Summary

I bring these suggestions and drawbacks to the table so that you'll have a better understanding of what defines a rich Internet application and how Ajax can fit into dynamic web content as a whole. With more sites pushing the boundaries farther, it's exciting to see where the technology is leading. And it also helps us, as developers, to get a feel for what we assess to be a user-friendly experience by comparing the various designs that others host. One of the benefits of the web is that it allows us to learn from others' mistakes and build upon their successes.

The next chapter will continue down the dynamic content path as we discuss the various page-level processes by which we can manipulate content on the fly. Combining this knowledge with a good understanding of Ajax methodology will arm you with the skills you'll need to jump into interactive web development.

CHAPTER 6

■ ■ ■

CSS and the DOM

As you'll recall, we discussed how Ajax is not a singular technology, but rather a conglomeration of many. A growing number of individuals assume that by downloading a certain Ajax library and implementing it, they have encapsulated the concept of Ajax in its entirety. The name Ajax (Asynchronous JavaScript And XML) certainly indicates this to be true. One particular necessity of dynamic web development is the use of Cascading Style Sheets (CSS) and manipulation of the Document Object Model (DOM). However, CADAJAX (CSS And DOM Asynchronous JavaScript And XML) doesn't sound quite as elegant. Nonetheless, it is as vitally important as the other technologies, and you'll spend a considerable amount of time becoming acquainted with this toolset. A solid understanding of style sheets, the DOM, and how they fit into dynamic web development will only serve to further enhance your page content.

CSS

Cascading Style Sheets is a huge subject with a multitude of books documenting its contributions to the World Wide Web. While I won't dispute the fact that it is indeed an incredible technology for the realm of HTML markup, I want to constrain the context of our discussion to what is applicable to Ajax development. We'll take a summary examination of style sheets and concentrate on tasks that you'll find more useful when building dynamic web pages.

But before we get to that point, I must address the introductory question, "What is CSS?"

CSS was born as a recommendation by the World Wide Web Consortium (W3C) in response to issues raised by developers that HTML had reached the limits of its capabilities. Presentational markup had become a priority over the typical hypertext markup, which by 1996 had become limiting and sluggish. Thus CSS was born and quickly adopted by designers and programmers alike.

Understanding what CSS provides for you means that you need to know how things work without it, and then I'll throw a little style into the mix so that you can appreciate why you would use CSS at all.

HTML in its original form was meant for one thing: to mark up text displayed within the browser window. Much like a word processor, text had to be arranged and formatted in a particular fashion that would reproduce the look and feel of a printed paper document: paragraphs would be indented; headings would be larger and bolded; and lists would be bulleted. Therefore, typical document display in HTML would appear as follows:

```
<html xmlns="http://www.w3.org/1999/xhtml" >
<head>
    <title>Old School HTML</title>
</head>
<body>
    <form id="form1">
    <h1>Heading 1</h1>
    <p>HTML in its original form was meant for one thing:
     to "markup" text displayed within the browser window.
        Much like a word processor, text had to be arranged
          and formatted in a particular fashion that would
           reproduce the look and feel of a hard printed paper
           document.  Paragraphs would be indented.  Headings
             would be larger and bolded.  Lists would be bulleted.</p>
    <ul>
        <li>Item 1</li>
        <li>Item 2</li>
        <li>Item 3</li>
    </ul>
    </form>
</body>
</html>
```

When the preceding page is displayed in Internet Explorer, you'll have the rendered results shown in Figure 6-1.

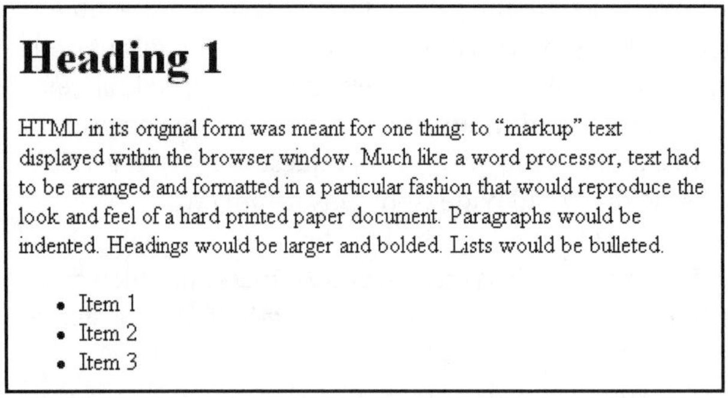

Figure 6-1. *Typical HTML rendering*

The main issue at stake here, however, is that not all browsers will display the same tags in the same way. And there is little that the developer can do within the bounds of HTML's ability to display the data. Sure, the <h1> tag is nice and all, but wouldn't it be great if we could make changes on a global scale that require that our <h1> tags be not only big and bolded, but also formatted in italics and colored gray? That's where the magic of style comes in. And you should note here that CSS is **NOT** HTML. It has a unique syntax, but don't let that fool you. It's just as easy to learn as HTML is.

Cascading Style Sheets, in general, define how HTML should be displayed. However, there are things that you can do in styles that cannot be accomplished in hypertext markup: display hyperlinks with no underline, create scrollable content regions, implement custom graphics for your list items, and so much more.

Style Elements

So what exactly is a *style*? It is coding that you apply to HTML, either inline within the HTML tags or externally (as we'll discuss momentarily). If we want to accomplish the previous task of modifying our <h1> tag to reflect italics as well as a grayed color, we can use the style attribute:

```
<html xmlns="http://www.w3.org/1999/xhtml" >
<head>
    <title>CSS Comparison</title>
</head>
<body>
    <form id="form1">
    <h1>Heading 1 - No Formatting</h1>
    <h1 style="font-style: italic; color: Gray;">Heading 1 - With Style</h1>
    </form>
</body>
</html>
```

When this is run in a browser, you'll find that the <h1> tag has been modified to reflect the desired changes, as shown in Figure 6-2.

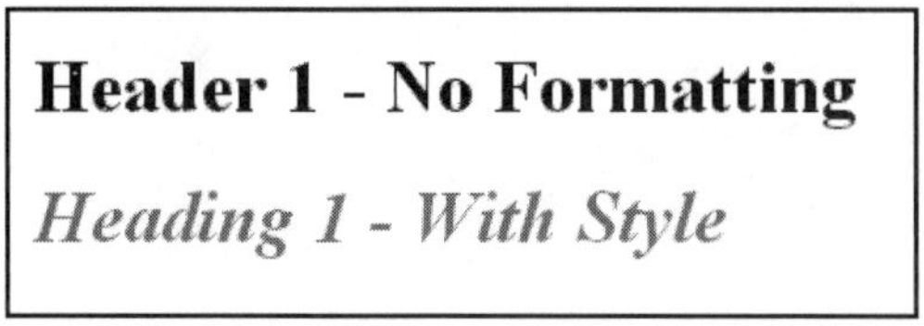

Figure 6-2. *CSS versus HTML*

Styles are, at their core, simply elements in much the same way that HTML tags are. However, HTML tags describe their content, whereas style elements describe their associative HTML tags. For instance, a car's color describes the car. Using the previous description, the car is the HTML tag, and the color is the style element. In our previous example, the inline style was applicable to the <h1> tag that it was nested within; therefore it was responsible for modifying that particular tag only. This is referred to as an *inline style*.

Inline Style

It is quite possible that you'll want to add CSS markup to a few individual HTML tags, as shown previously. Inline coding will have a common syntax for most of the hypertext tags that you'll add them to:

```
<htmlTag style="property: value;"></htmlTag>
```

Our sample web form did in fact adhere to that formatting:

```
<h1 style="font-style: italic; color: Gray;">Heading 1 - With Style</h1>
```

Examining the syntax statement, you'll find that `htmlTag` refers to the appropriate HTML tag that we are currently working with. Whether it is an `<a>`, `<p>`, or one of the many others, the syntax for inline coding will be the same.

As you'll see in a moment, maintaining this methodology can be tedious and wasteful. Inline styles, when used in repetition, tend to duplicate code, and ultimately that leads to an increase in application complexity and file size. It's generally recommended that styles be isolated in either an external file, which I'll cover in the "Site-wide Style Access" section, or an internal scripting block, which you'll find to be quite similar to a JavaScript code block.

Script Blocks

Page-level script blocks, as I've mentioned, are similar to JavaScript code blocks:

```
<html xmlns="http://www.w3.org/1999/xhtml" >
<head>
    <title>CSS Comparison</title>
    <style type="text/css">
        // Add some style here
    </style>
    <script type="text/javascript" language="javascript">
        // Add some JavaScript here
    </script>
</head>
<body>
    <form id="form1">
    <h1>Header 1 - No Formatting</h1>
    <h1 style="font-style: italic; color: Gray;">Heading 1 - With Style</h1>
    </form>
</body>
</html>
```

Once you're in the habit of putting your CSS into page-level blocks or externally linked files, you'll find it incrementally harder to go back to inline coding.

However, before we jump into adding some real content to our `<style>` blocks, you should understand a few key CSS concepts, which I'll cover next.

CSS Selectors

A *selector* does exactly what its name implies: it selects. What does it select? I'm glad you asked. If we have some style coding that reads

```
p
{
    color:gray;
    font-style: italic;
}
```

we're asking that the selector p find and apply the enclosed style against the selected p HTML elements. For any given selector, we have a few "rules" that we might take into consideration when manipulating HTML elements. We'll call those the *CSS rules*.

CSS Rules

Essentially, the CSS rules dictate the various ways in which HTML tags can be modified. They also dictate how CSS syntax varies depending on which tags you wish to apply the styles to. Let's take a quick look at these CSS rules and how they affect HTML markup.

HTML Tag Type Rule

This kind of rule applies the CSS properties to only the HTML tag indicated by the selector. For example:

```
<html xmlns="http://www.w3.org/1999/xhtml" >
<head>
    <title>CSS Comparison</title>
    <style type="text/css">
        h1
        {
            text-align: center;
        }

        p
        {
            color:gray;
            font-style: italic;
        }
    </style>
</head>
<body>
    <form id="form1">
    <h1>My Heading</h1>
    <p>This is my paragraph text.  It should display in Gray and Italics.</p>
    </form>
</body>
</html>
```

This would modify all `<p>` and `<h1>` tags that are listed on the page, if the rule is placed within the `<head>` tag of the document as shown in the preceding example. You'll find the results of viewing this page to be as shown in Figure 6-3.

Figure 6-3. *HTML tag type rule*

You could also apply the same set of styles to multiple HTML tags:

```
<style type="text/css">
    h1, p
    {
        text-align: center;
    }

    p
    {
        color:gray;
        font-style: italic;
    }
</style>
```

By appending the p tag to the h1 with a delimiting comma, we apply the bracketed style, in this case centered text, to both <p> tags and <h1> tags. We also apply the italic/gray style to <p> tags only with the other rule, with the results shown in Figure 6-4.

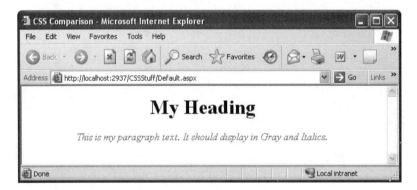

Figure 6-4. *Multiple HTML tags per style*

HTML ID Type Rule

This kind of rule applies the style to only a single HTML tag, designated by its id attribute:

```
<style type="text/css">
    #myParagraph
    {
        color:Gray;
        text-align: right;
    }
</style>
```

So, the preceding example modifies

```
<p id="myParagraph">This is my text</p>
```

Note that this code will only alter <p> tags with an id of myParagraph. If we were to include multiple <p> tags, of which only one has an id of myParagraph, we could verify that it changed the correct paragraph:

```
<html xmlns="http://www.w3.org/1999/xhtml" >
<head>
    <title>CSS Comparison</title>
    <style type="text/css">
        #myParagraph
        {
            color:gray;
            font-style: italic;
        }

    </style>
</head>
<body>
    <form id="form1">
    <h1>My Heading</h1>
    <p id="myParagraph">This is my paragraph text.
     It should display in Gray and Italics.</p>
    <p>This is normal paragraph text.  No formatting is expected here.</p>
    </form>
</body>
</html>
```

Despite the fact that we have two <p> tags, we have asked that only the <p> tag with an id of myParagraph be modified, and our results are predictable, as you can see in Figure 6-5.

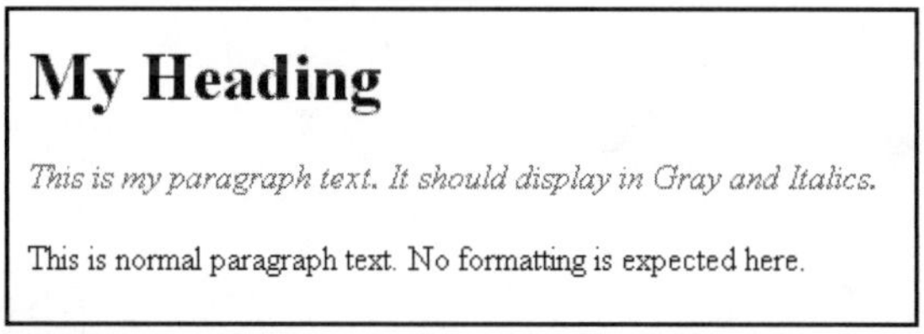

Figure 6-5. *HTML ID type rule*

CSS Class Type Rule

The ID type and HTML tag type rules are easy to implement. But what if we want to make changes to multiple elements without having to designate their HTML type first? We can easily accomplish this with the CSS class type rule. CSS classes allow you to set aside an easily accessible style rule that is not restricted by ID or HTML tag type:

```
<style type="text/css">
    .Gray
    {
        color:Gray;
    }
</style>
```

This modifies the following:

```
<p class="Gray">This is my text</p>
```

We create the style class by declaring it first with a period and then the class name as shown previously. We simply assign the class name to any tag that we wish to pick up the enclosed styling.

One of the more exciting aspects of style classes is that we can assign them on the fly. And it really becomes interesting if we tie the change into an event raised by the tag. For instance, we'll use the common onmouseover and onmouseout events that most HTML tags are capable of raising, and assign some dynamic styling in response to the actions taken:

```
<html xmlns="http://www.w3.org/1999/xhtml" >
<head>
    <title>CSS Comparison</title>
    <style type="text/css">
        .Gray
        {
            color:gray;
            font-weight: normal;
        }

        .Hover
        {
            color: black;
            font-weight: bold;
        }

    </style>
</head>
<body>
    <form id="form1">
    <h1>My Heading</h1>
    <p>This is normal paragraph text.  No formatting is expected here.</p>
    <p onmouseover="this.className='Hover';"
       onmouseout="this.className='Gray';">This is "special text"</p>
    </form>
</body>
</html>
```

We capture the paragraph's onmouseover and onmouseout events, and as you can see, we modify the class name for the HTML tag, which in turn modifies the text contained within the

<p> tags (see Figure 6-6). As you run the application and mouse over the special text, notice that it will turn black and bolded, returning to its normal state as you move off the text. It's a very powerful CSS technique that I'm sure you'll find much use for.

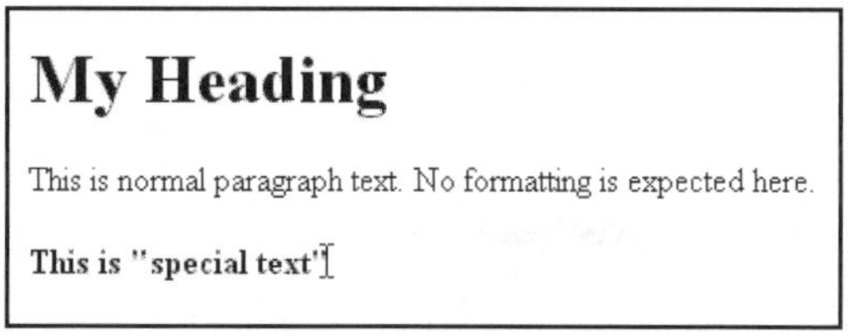

Figure 6-6. *Applying style with class*

CSS Comments

One of my pet peeves is uncommented code. It takes so little time to describe your code and can save considerable amounts of time on any subsequent development. Style sheets are a great place to throw some descriptive text into the mix. It's quite possible that some of your selectors may not be as self-describing as you'd like. Adding comments is a simple as

```
#divResults
{
    /* This is
     a comment block! */

    background-color:gainsboro;

    /* This is a single comment line */
}
```

Site-wide Style Access

Now that you've had a chance to see the CSS style block in action, we should examine what many refer to as *CSS hierarchy*. Simply put, where you put your style blocks will ordain what content has access to their attributes. For example, you now know that inline style attributes will modify only those HTML elements within which they reside. And we've also discussed how placing styles in the head of the document will affect the designated tags for that page. But wouldn't it be great if we could declare a style block that we could access from all of our site's pages?

Well here again, much like JavaScript, we can offload our CSS styles into an external file and simply add a reference to it:

```
<link href="myStyles.css" rel="stylesheet" type="text/css"/>
```

The link will seek out myStyles.css, and at runtime it will include the appropriate style sheet.

In Visual Studio 2005, we simply right-click the solution name, Add New Item, choose Style Sheet, and then we have a clean slate for dropping our styles into (see Figure 6-7).

Figure 6-7. *Added style sheet*

We add the following code to `myStyles.css` and then save the file:

```
.myStyleClass
{
        color:Gray;
        font-style:italic;
}
```

We now have a site-wide style class that we can simply assign to any HTML tag on any page:

```
<html xmlns="http://www.w3.org/1999/xhtml" >
<head>
    <title>Linked CSS Demo Page</title>
    <link href="myStyles.css" type="text/css" rel="stylesheet" />
</head>
<body>
    <form id="form1">
    <div>
    <p>This is normal text on Default.aspx</p>
    <p class="myStyleClass">This is text with Style applied.</p>
    </div>
    </form>
</body>
</html>
```

We simply assign the class name to the tag as if a style block were present within the page. When you stop to think about it, this allows you to create site-wide design patterns and make sweeping changes from the convenience of one individual file. I can't encourage you enough to implement this methodology when using style sheets on your next or current project.

You may be asking yourself at this point, "I've noticed that Cascading Style Sheets has the word 'cascading' in it. What's up with that?" And you would be right to ask that. *Cascading* refers to the possibility that a multitude of style options could be available for one single HTML tag. For example, let's say that you have an external CSS style sheet with a `<p>` style:

```
/* myStyles.css */
        p
        {
            color: red;
        }
```

And now let's assume that you also have a `<style>` block in your `<head>` section of the page as well:

```
<style>
p
{
        color: blue;
}
</style>
```

And finally, in the actual `<p>` tag itself on the same page, you have

```
<p style="color: green">This is text with cascading style.</p>
```

When the page is run, what color will the text be? If you guessed green, then you would be correct. The style that is closest to the HTML tag will win the right to modify the tag. However, what if we added some extra styling to the external `myStyles.css` that did not involve color?

For example:

```
/* myStyles.css */
p
{
        color:Gray;
        font-style:italic;
}
```

Let's also maintain the same HTML as described previously:

```
<html xmlns="http://www.w3.org/1999/xhtml" >
<head>
    <title>Cascading Style Demo Page</title>
    <link href="myStyles.css" type="text/css" rel="stylesheet" />
    <style type="text/css">
    p
    {
        color: blue;
    }
    </style>
</head>
<body>
    <form id="form1">
    <div>
        <p style="color: green">This is text with cascading style.</p>
    </div>
    </form>
</body>
</html>
```

You'll notice that we don't have `font-style` properties anywhere on our web page. So what will happen when we run this page? Take a look at Figure 6-8 to find out.

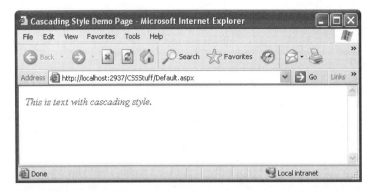

Figure 6-8. *Through the magic of black-and-white printing, the text appears gray, but it did in fact come out green.*

As expected, the font-style property cascaded down to the HTML tag because there were no other overriding properties as there were with the color change. Because nothing interrupted the flow of that style cascading down to the actual HTML, it modifies the text correctly.

But what if we don't want a particular style to be overridden by a cascading value? We can support that by including !important as an indicator to the page that this particular style should not be voted out by the styles further down the road:

```
/* myStyles.css */
p
{
        color:red !important;
        font-style:italic;
}
```

Despite the fact that my HTML tag appears as

```
<p style="color: green">This is text with cascading style.</p>
```

the browser will render the text in red, because !important has prioritized the style. Use this to enforce company or site restraints (for example, your boss wants all pages to have a background color of light blue), but use it with caution, as it could create hours of debugging headaches for developers who may not be aware of its existence.

Now that you have a pretty good idea of what CSS can do for you, we should take some time to see some real-world examples of styles in action. The possibilities are endless, and we could spend hundreds of pages with just this particular aspect of Ajax coding. But for now, I'll cover a few of the tasks that you may find yourself repeating in Ajax development.

CSS Element Alignment

One of the common misconceptions about style sheets is that they are beneficial for the look and feel of HTML objects only. Sure, I can use CSS to add cool color schemes and fancy font work, but that's not all that this technology is capable of. One of the more useful aspects of style sheets is that you can use them to dictate not only the format objects, but also where they should be placed on the page. Element alignment is equally important as the visual imagery. There is a growing trend among web designers to implement CSS locating rather than legacy tables, spans, etc.

Positioning

There are four basic position settings that we can apply to any given element to determine where it will appear on the page:

- static

- relative

- absolute

- fixed

Each setting has a direct impact on the placement of the tags associated with it, and the names are somewhat of an indication of how they'll render.

Static Positioning

By default, elements are positioned statically. *Static* simply means that elements will flow from one to another without interruption:

```
<%@ Page Language="C#" AutoEventWireup="true"
CodeFile="Default.aspx.cs" Inherits="Default" %>

<!DOCTYPE html PUBLIC "-//W3C//DTD XHTML 1.0 Transitional//EN"
"http://www.w3.org/TR/xhtml1/DTD/xhtml1-transitional.dtd">

<html xmlns="http://www.w3.org/1999/xhtml" >
<head>
    <title>CSS Positioning Demo Page</title>
    <style type="text/css">
    .stat
    {
        position: static;
    }
    </style>
</head>
<body>
    <form id="form1">
        <h2 class="stat">First Heading is 'Static'</h2>
        <h2 class="stat">Second Heading is 'Static'</h2>
    </form>
</body>
</html>
```

BLOCK VERSUS INLINE

It is pretty easy to confuse blocks and inlines if you've never worked with them, especially when comparing DIV tags with SPAN tags. Many developers tend to use them interchangeably, not realizing that they have a different wrap method. DIV tags are considered block-style elements, which means that any information after the DIV tag will be placed on the next line. DIV tags will also grow to occupy the entire line and will relocate other content if they have to. A SPAN tag, however, is considered an inline style element and will simply wrap other content around it. If you were to place a SPAN tag between two HTML buttons, they would nest up against the left and right sides of the SPAN tag. However, if you were to place a DIV tag between two buttons, you would end up with three lines, as the DIV tag desires its own line. They're greedy, but they're useful.

When you run this page, you'll find default placing of the elements, as shown in Figure 6-9.

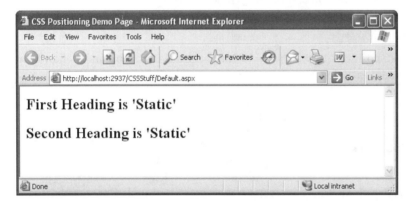

Figure 6-9. *Static positioning*

Because our <h2> elements are block-type elements, they wrap to the next available line.

Relative Positioning

When you apply a relative position to an element, you are almost always going to be supplying relative x and/or y coordinates as well. The position of the element will be relative to its original position on the page, as seen in Figure 6-10.

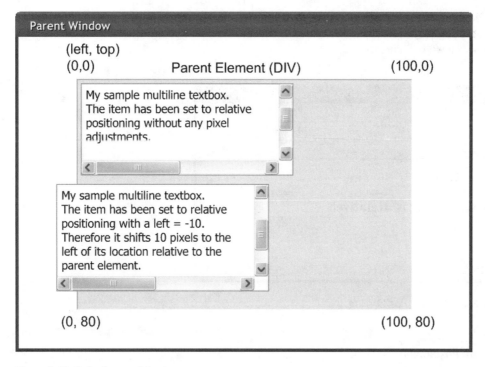

Figure 6-10. *Relative positioning*

If for some reason we want to shift a particular line a little to the left of where it would normally display, we simply implement relative positioning and assign a negative value to the left property:

```
<html xmlns="http://www.w3.org/1999/xhtml" >
<head>
    <title>CSS Positioning Demo Page</title>
    <style type="text/css">
    .rel
    {
        position: relative;
        left: -20px;
    }
    </style>
</head>
<body>
    <form id="form1">
        <h2>First Heading is Normal</h2>
        <h2 class="rel">Second Heading is 'Relative'</h2>
    </form>
</body>
</html>
```

You'll notice in the style block, we are asking to move the content 20 pixels to the left. When the page is displayed, you can see the effect that relative positioning has on the element, as shown in Figure 6-11.

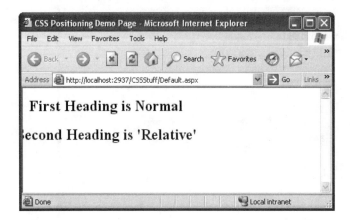

Figure 6-11. *Relative positioning*

Absolute Positioning

Absolute positioning allows you to detach an element from the rest of the page and basically move it around the browser window by assigning x,y coordinates in the style. The coordinates start at 0,0, which is the top left corner of the browser's available page display area (see Figure 6-12).

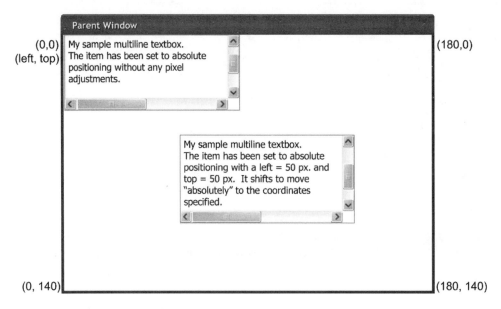

Figure 6-12. *Relative positioning*

By increasing the left value, we move the element to the right. By increasing the element's top value, we would be shifting the element further down the page:

```
<html xmlns="http://www.w3.org/1999/xhtml" >
<head>
    <title>CSS Positioning Demo Page</title>
    <style type="text/css">
    .abs
    {
        position:absolute;
        left:200px;
        top:150px
    }
    </style>
</head>
<body>
    <form id="form1">
        <h2>First Heading is Normal</h2>
        <h2 class="abs">Second Heading is 'Absolute'</h2>
    </form>
</body>
</html>
```

We should expect to see that the second line of text has been located at the x,y (top and left) coordinates that we have specified in our style, as shown in Figure 6-13.

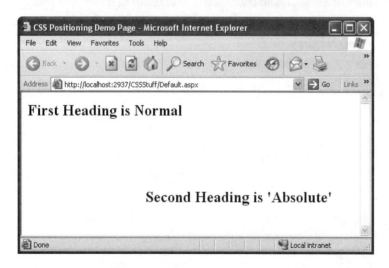

Figure 6-13. *Absolute positioning*

Absolute positioning is quite powerful and will be the positioning of choice for various dynamic tools that you'll use, such as hover tips, pop-up menus, and other content that you need to place at will on the user's page.

Fixed Positioning

I'm not going to spend any time discussing fixed positioning because, frankly, it is not supported by Internet Explorer. The summary description, however, is that it allows you to declare an x,y location, and scrolling will not affect the location of the element. Essentially, the element will float to maintain its assigned coordinates.

Element Visibility

One of the style sheet properties that you will find yourself using a lot is visibility. If you assign it a value of hidden, the element to which its rule applies is erased from the page, and any code will not have access to this element. Keep that in mind if you attempt to access this element from other code on the page. To show the content, you'll assign a value of visible:

```
.show
{
    visibility:visible;
}
.hide
{
    visibility:hidden;
}
```

One thing that you should note with the visibility property is that, while the HTML element is not visible to the user, space is still reserved on the page. You'll see an empty spot where the element used to be. Should you want the page to maintain its current layout, you would use the visibility property to prevent the imminent relocation of your controls. However, if you want the page to shift to occupy hidden content, use the display property instead:

```
<html xmlns="http://www.w3.org/1999/xhtml" >
<head>
    <title>CSS Display Demo Page</title>
    <style type="text/css">
    .hide
    {
        display:none;
    }
    </style>
</head>
<body>
    <form id="form1">
        Some Sample Text Before the button.
        <input id="Button1" type="button" value="Click to hide"
            onclick="this.className='hide';" />
        Text placed after the button.
    </form>
</body>
</html>
```

Here we dynamically change the class on the HTML button as a result of the onclick event. The class will, in turn, set the display property to none, subsequently turning off the button and shifting page content to fill the void, as shown in Figures 6-14 and 6-15.

Figure 6-14. *The display property before the click event*

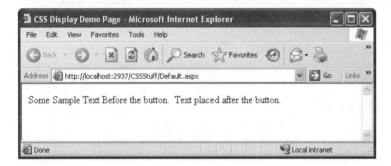

Figure 6-15. *The display property set to none*

There are a multitude of display values that can be assigned, but of current interest to us are the following:

- none: The element is not displayed.

- block: The element is displayed as block type. A line break is placed before and after the element.

- inline: The element is displayed as inline type. No line breaks are placed before or after.

- list-item: The element is displayed as a list item.

I encourage you to play around with the values, as you'll most definitely use all of them with Ajax development.

You've been given a cursory look at the basic skills that you will need if you are to implement CSS in your Ajax projects. It is a vital tool when dealing with dynamic web content, and you will need to have a good foundational understanding of style and how it modifies HTML content. However, it is imperative that we address what many call the sibling technology of Cascading Style Sheets: the DOM.

Document Object Model

In almost every online article that I have whipped out for research, I find CSS and the DOM paired together in the same sentence. One can hardly mention one without discussing the other. And for good reason: style sheets help us visually modify the content, and the DOM helps us to programmatically access that same content with JavaScript. The DOM becomes a bridge between the web page and our JavaScript coding. For Ajax development, this becomes an essential aspect of our approach. Before we can discuss what the DOM can do for your site, you should understand exactly what it is that you're dealing with.

How the DOM Came to Be

The Document Object Model as we know it today has, as you would expect, a tumultuous past. Like so much of web technology, it began life as two separate entities: Netscape DOM and Microsoft DOM. Netscape 2 provided us JavaScript access to the elements on the page. Microsoft would later roll out JavaScript support with version 3 of Internet Explorer. It didn't take long for the proprietary systems to become so drastically different that programmers found themselves having to browser-sniff and provide differing scripts to accommodate the battling browsers. Right around 1996, W3C released DOM Level 1 in an effort to level the playing field for content authors as they struggled to build cross-browser compatible pages. The spec provided generic access to page elements and was later adopted by Internet Explorer 5 and Netscape Navigator 6. There has been little change in the world of the DOM since then.

Definition of the DOM

Understanding the Document Object Model requires that you understand how an Internet web page is structured as referenced by the user's browser. The basic structure is tree-like, in that it has multiple branches that derive from root values. I'll refer to the branches of the tree as nodes to be consistent with most popular terminology. If you've ever worked with XML (Extensible Markup Language), you will find this an easy concept to grasp. The basic premise is that we have a root node that we'll build upon with other nodes that represent page elements. Let's take a quick look at a basic web page:

```
<%@ Page Language="C#" AutoEventWireup="true" CodeFile="Default.aspx.cs"
Inherits="Default" %>

<!DOCTYPE html PUBLIC "-//W3C//DTD XHTML 1.0 Transitional//EN"
 "http://www.w3.org/TR/xhtml1/DTD/xhtml1-transitional.dtd">

<html xmlns="http://www.w3.org/1999/xhtml" >
<head>
    <title>Document Object Model Demo Page</title>
</head>
```

```
<body>
    <form id="form1">
        <div id="divMain">
            <p id="pMyFirstParagraph">My Paragraph text.</p>
            <span id="spanMySpan" style="font-style:italic;
              font-weight:bold;">My Span text.</span>
        </div>
        <p id="pMySecondParagraph">More Paragraph text.</p>
    </form>
</body>
</html>
```

Each of the page elements, when thought of from a tree-view perception, will map out as shown in Figure 6-16.

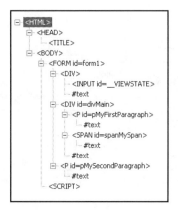

Figure 6-16. *Our page as a treeview*

As you can see, we have our base node HTML element and the consecutive nested elements follow.

Our treeview, from Figure 6-17, is a page-level representation of the current document. At the top (or root level) of the tree we have our Window object, within which all others must fall. Think of the Window object as an instantiated version of the browser and the document node as the page that you have loaded within the browser.

A node can have one to many child nodes, but only one parent node. We can access the nodes independent of their location in the tree by referring to their id attribute.

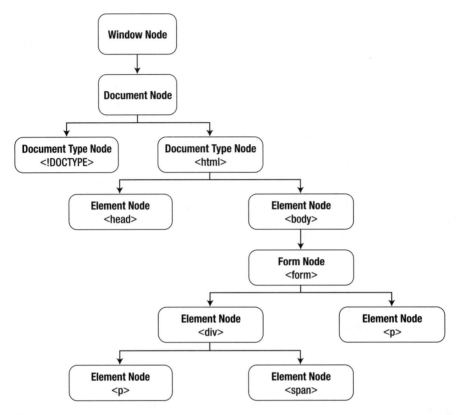

Figure 6-17. *The page translated as individual nodes*

Working with the DOM Node

You'll notice in the previous sample code that we have assigned unique id attributes to each HTML tag. It is this particular attribute that promotes the value in the Document Object Model, enabling page-level access to the tag as a whole. Assigning an ID is as simple as just plugging in a meaningful or company-standards-based name:

```
<span id="spanMySpan" style="font-style:italic; font-weight:bold;">
```

When the time comes for us to seek out and find this particular element with our JavaScript, we'll use the id attribute exclusively.

NAME VERSUS ID

You'll undoubtedly come across code where the name attribute is in use:

```
<span name="mySpan">My Span Text</span>
```

This attribute is being phased out, and you should concentrate your efforts on using the id attribute instead.

To isolate elements for JavaScript use, we'll make use of the document object's getElementById() method:

```
var thisSpan = document.getElementById("spanMySpan");
```

Once we have declared our containing variable and retrieved the element with the document's getElementById() method, we can manipulate the HTML element at will:

```
thisSpan.innerText = "Changed to something new!";
```

Let's drop this functionality into an actual web page and run it:

```
<%@ Page Language="C#" AutoEventWireup="true" CodeFile="Default.aspx.cs"
    Inherits="Default" %>

<!DOCTYPE html PUBLIC "-//W3C//DTD XHTML 1.0 Transitional//EN"
    "http://www.w3.org/TR/xhtml1/DTD/xhtml1-transitional.dtd">

<html xmlns="http://www.w3.org/1999/xhtml" >
<head>
    <title>Document Object Model Demo Page</title>
</head>

    <script type="text/javascript" language="javascript">
        function changeSpan()
        {
            var thisSpan = document.getElementById("spanMySpan");
            thisSpan.innerText = "Changed to something new!";
        }
    </script>

<body onload="changeSpan();">
    <form id="form1">
        <span id="spanMySpan">My Span text.</span>
    </form>
</body>
</html>
```

We've declared a JavaScript function that will be run after the body onload event has fired. Within that function, we will find and modify the <span> tag's inner content, as shown in Figure 6-18.

A majority of the work that you will do with the DOM and Ajax will almost always revolve around manipulation of page elements to reflect callback or updated dynamic data.

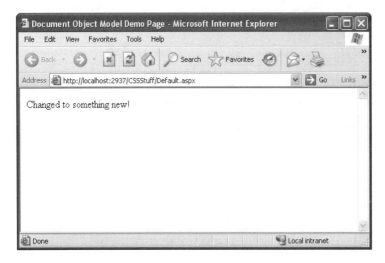

Figure 6-18. *The modified <span> tag*

Modifying Style Elements

You will likely want to modify the style of a page tag, and accomplishing that is just as easy as modifying the content value in the previous demo. We first obtain the element:

```
var thisSpan = document.getElementById("spanMySpan");
```

We can then modify the style of the object by accessing the `style` property as shown:

```
<script type="text/javascript" language="javascript">
    function changeSpan()
    {
        var thisSpan = document.getElementById("spanMySpan");
        thisSpan.style.position = 'absolute';
        thisSpan.style.top = '200px';
        thisSpan.style.left = '150px';
    }
</script>
```

Our results are predictable, as you can see in Figure 6-19.

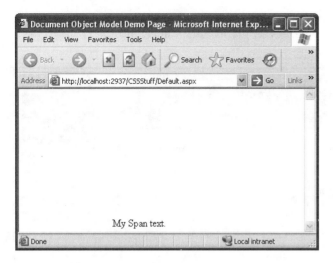

Figure 6-19. *Modified style data*

Debugging DOM issues

An indispensable tool that I have grown quite fond of lately is Microsoft's Developer Toolbar. It is a browser add-on that allows you to identify object information by clicking an object or by finding it in the treeview, as demonstrated in Figure 6-20.

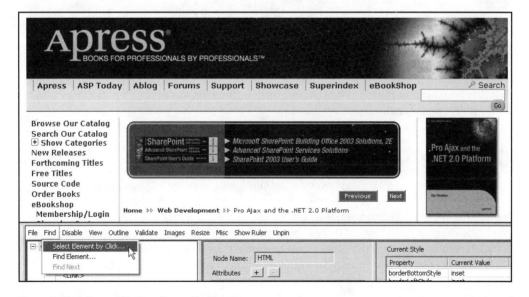

Figure 6-20. *Microsoft's Developer Toolbar*

If I click the book cover shown in Figure 6-20, I'll be given a breakdown of the element's location in the DOM as well as any applicable styling, as you see in Figure 6-21.

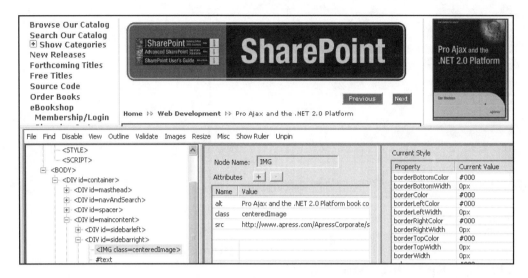

Figure 6-21. *Finding an element by click*

You can find the application on Microsoft's download site after searching for "Developer Toolbar": `http://www.microsoft.com/downloads`.

A version exists for the Mozilla/Firefox browser as well: `https://addons.mozilla.org/ extensions/moreinfo.php?id=60`.

It's free, and you'll find yourself saving a lot of time when you avoid having to view the source just to locate a misplaced tag.

Now that you've had an opportunity to work with CSS, DOM, JavaScript, and the XmlHttpRequest object, this would be an excellent time for you to see all of these technologies implemented in a sample application.

Using the Technology

In a few short chapters, I will be covering the cloning of Google's Suggest engine with a proprietary Ajax library, and subsequently we will be working with a variety of return data types. This application, however, is a generic low-grade version of the coming application, but it should give you a taste of things to come. We will be using CSS to assign visibility to a search results element; XmlHttpRequest to obtain those results; JSON as the data structure; JavaScript to call the appropriate functions; and, finally, DOM to display our results to the user.

In the sample application for this chapter, you should find a file structure that has two `.aspx` pages, `Default.aspx` and `dataFetch.aspx`. Our customer-facing web page will be the `Default.aspx`, so verify that it is indeed the startup page for our site by right-clicking the file and assigning it so. `dataFetch.aspx` is the process page that we will be calling asynchronously from `Default.aspx`. It will do nothing but gather the data, build the JSON string, and send it back to the callback function. Let's first take a look at what the application will do when run (see Figure 6-22).

Figure 6-22. *Our simple store finder application*

As we type within the textbox, we are asynchronously hitting the `dataFetch.aspx` page, getting search results that are like our current textbox value, and then populating a `<div>` tag's `innerHTML` content region with the results, as demonstrated in Figure 6-23.

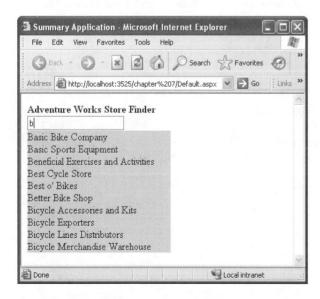

Figure 6-23. *The search results made it home.*

This simple application is a basic conglomeration of all of the technology that we have discussed so far. Let's take a look at the code on both the calling page and the destination page.

Default.aspx

As noted, this page is the front end that the user will interact with. If you open up both the `.aspx` view as well as the `.cs` coding view, you'll immediately notice that there is a huge void where you would imagine server-side code to exist:

```
using System;
using System.Data;
using System.Configuration;
using System.Web;
using System.Web.Security;
using System.Web.UI;
using System.Web.UI.WebControls;
using System.Web.UI.WebControls.WebParts;
using System.Web.UI.HtmlControls;

public partial class _Default : System.Web.UI.Page
{
    protected void Page_Load(object sender, EventArgs e)
    {

    }
}
```

The power of this application does not lie in the server-side coding. All of our work is being done with JavaScript in the client-side HTML view:

```
<%@ Page Language="C#" AutoEventWireup="true"
CodeFile="Default.aspx.cs" Inherits="_Default" %>

<!DOCTYPE html PUBLIC "-//W3C//DTD XHTML 1.0 Transitional//EN"
"http://www.w3.org/TR/xhtml1/DTD/xhtml1-transitional.dtd">

<html xmlns="http://www.w3.org/1999/xhtml" >
<script type="text/javascript" language="javascript">
 xmlhttp = false;
 var requestURL = "dataFetch.aspx?term=";

function getNames(currentTerm)
{

    if (currentTerm.length > 0)
    {
        // A proper term has been entered
        var url = requestURL + currentTerm;
```

```
        getHTTPRequestObject();

        if(xmlhttp)
        {
            xmlhttp.open("GET", url, true);
            xmlhttp.onreadystatechange = callback;
            xmlhttp.send(null);
        }
    }
    else
    {
        //No search term entered - empty the div
        var findDIV = document.getElementById("divResults")
        findDIV.className = 'hide';
    }
}

function callback(response)
{
        if(xmlhttp.readyState == 4)
        {
            if(xmlhttp.status ==200)
            {
                eval("var objResults = " + xmlhttp.responseText);

              var displaytext = "";

              for (var i=0; i < objResults.Results.shops.length; i++)
              {
                displaytext += objResults.Results.shops[i].Name + "<br>";
              }
              if(displaytext.length > 0)
              {
                    var findDIV = document.getElementById("divResults");
                    findDIV.className = 'show';
                    findDIV.innerHTML = displaytext;
              }

            }
        }
}
```

```
function getHTTPRequestObject()
{
    try
    {
        // Try legacy object first
        xmlhttp = new ActiveXObject("Msxml2.XMLHTTP");
    }
    catch(e)
    {
        try
        {
            // Try IE implementation now
            xmlhttp = new ActiveXObject("Microsoft.XMLHTTP");
        }
        catch(E)
        {
            xmlhttp = false;
        }
    }
    if(!xmlhttp && typeof XMLHttpRequest!= 'undefined')
    {
        // We must be using a Mozilla-based browser
        // so create a native request object now
        xmlhttp = new XMLHttpRequest();
    }
}
</script>


<head runat="server">
    <title>Summary Application</title>
    <style type="text/css">
    .hide
    {
        display:none;
    }
    .show
    {
        display:block;
        width:230px;
    }
    #divResults
    {
        background-color:gainsboro;
    }
    </style>
</head>
```

```
<body>
    <form id="form1" runat="server">
    <div>
        <strong>Adventure Works Store Finder</strong><br />
        <input type="text" id="txtName" autocomplete="off"
         onkeyup="getNames(this.value);" />
    </div>
    <div id="divResults"></div>
    </form>
</body>
</html>
```

Quite a bit of code for such a small application, but it does exactly what we're trying to accomplish. One of the benefits of Ajax development is that it allows us the opportunity to move work off of the servers and out to the client.

The code is pretty unassuming. We have a function that generates our XmlHttpRequest object for passing around on the form. We have our callback functions declared where we'll be iterating through the returned data and displaying the results to the user.

The heart of the code is the JSON disassembler, where we simply call the JavaScript eval() function and parse the object properties off into the <div> tag:

```
eval("var objResults = " + xmlhttp.responseText);

var displaytext = "";

for (var i=0; i < objResults.Results.shops.length; i++)
{
    displaytext += objResults.Results.shops[i].Name + "<br>";
}
if(displaytext.length > 0)
{
        var findDIV = document.getElementById("divResults");
        findDIV.className = 'show';
        findDIV.innerHTML = displaytext;
}
```

dataFetch.aspx.cs

Of course, we have to retrieve the data from somewhere, so let's take a look at the page that was called from our XmlHttpRequest method:

```
using System;
using System.Data;
using System.Configuration;
using System.Collections;
using System.Web;
using System.Web.Security;
using System.Web.UI;
```

```csharp
using System.Web.UI.WebControls;
using System.Web.UI.WebControls.WebParts;
using System.Web.UI.HtmlControls;
using System.Data.SqlClient;
using System.Text;
public partial class dataFetch : System.Web.UI.Page
{
    protected void Page_Load(object sender, EventArgs e)
    {
        string searchterm = Request.QueryString["term"];

        // You may need to modify this connection string to suit your environment
        SqlConnection conn = new SqlConnection("Data Source=(local);Initial
 Catalog=AdventureWorks;Integrated Security=SSPI");
        DataTable dtReturn = new DataTable();

        conn.Open();
        SqlCommand cmd = new SqlCommand
         ("Select Top 10 Name from Sales.Store where Name like
            @searchterm Order By Name", conn);
        SqlParameter param = new SqlParameter();
        param.ParameterName = "@searchterm";
        searchterm.Trim().Replace("'", "''");
        searchterm += "%";
        param.Value = searchterm;
        cmd.Parameters.Add(param);

        SqlDataAdapter adpt = new SqlDataAdapter(cmd);
        adpt.Fill(dtReturn);

        conn.Close();
        StringBuilder sb = new StringBuilder();
        sb.Append("{\"Results\": { \"shops\": [");

        for (int i = 0; i < dtReturn.Rows.Count; i++)
        {
            sb.Append("{\"Name\":\"" + (string)dtReturn.Rows[i]["Name"] +
"\"}");
            if (i <= (dtReturn.Rows.Count - 2))
            {
                sb.Append(",");
            }
        }
```

```
    sb.Append("]}}");

    Response.Write(sb.ToString());

  }
}
```

This particular page does nothing aside from generate a string that will be written out as response data. The string, however, is JSON-formatted text, assembled from the database query results. We could have easily built an XML file and returned that instead of JSON, but I really feel that JSON is appropriate for this sample. It's quick and has a smaller footprint than XML as well. If I'm only interested in passing back generic data for manipulation with JavaScript, JSON is always a good choice.

Also notice that on the client side of things, we have stripped all HTML coding from the .aspx file:

```
<%@ Page Language="C#" AutoEventWireup="true"
CodeFile="dataFetch.aspx.cs" Inherits="dataFetch" %>
```

While this is a rather simple application, it does illustrate all of the technology that we have studied up to this point. As we move forward, we'll be implementing an actual Ajax library that will encapsulate a majority of the code that we've prepared here. This will save us a boatload of time and frustration by giving us an out-of-the-box solution.

Summary

In this chapter, we've discussed Cascading Style Sheets and, as you've seen in the demo application, they have a very practical meaning in the world of software development. They're so much more than just visual management, and they can ultimately change the way that you work with web design as a whole. We've also taken a cursory look at the DOM and how we can isolate, manipulate, and render page-level elements from JavaScript. In the coming chapters, you will see how these learned skills will become indispensable to Ajax development.

CHAPTER 7

■ ■ ■

Ajax Frameworks

In the last few chapters, you have had the opportunity to work with a majority of the facets of Ajax development. As you worked through some of the sample code, you may have started to notice that there tended to be some redundancy to some of the code that you're pounding out. Wouldn't it be great if we could wrap the tedious and repetitious JavaScript and server-side code into a redistributable library? Yes, in fact, that would be awesome! Furthermore, it has already been done by a multitude of outstanding developers who have made the aforementioned libraries available to you. Most are free and open sourced to the world.

So you really understand Ajax as an entity rather than how it applies only to the world of .NET development, we should take a look at what other languages are doing with dynamic web programming. Sure, we'll take a look at the .NET stuff too, but we'll be spending a great deal of time with that in the coming chapters. For now, I want to make sure that you understand that there is a whole world of Ajax frameworks, libraries, and code snippets out there just waiting. And every day the community grows incrementally larger. So we should take a look at some non-.NET software packages in addition to the .NET distributions.

So really, what else is out there? The short answer: a great deal. There is literally a multitude of Ajax-driven libraries/frameworks and third-party packages out on the web just waiting for someone to give them a chance. Ultimately, they all accomplish the same thing as we've done so far: the browser fetches the data, and there is no postback.

I know it's a short description of a very large topic, and you might be thinking at this exact moment that Ajax is so much more than just those ten words. And you would be right. But I generalize because I want to point out the fact that, while most of the Ajax-enabled libraries and frameworks out there are really cool, they all serve the same purpose: dynamic retrieval and manipulation of data.

I would like to use this chapter as an opportunity for us to have a quick glance at some of the more popular products on the market.

Non-.NET and Cross-Platform

It is exciting to see Microsoft building new tools into their Visual Studio environment that facilitate a better and more interesting coding platform, but I'm intelligent enough to recognize that not every project out there will be a .NET endeavor. If, like me, you're employed in the world of consulting, you may not have the luxury of choosing the next coding platform. Therefore, I would be less of a friend to you if I didn't introduce you to some of the other products available in the Ajax world.

Ruby on Rails

Almost always, when I listen to a podcast, read an online article, or browse through white papers that deal with Ajax, Ruby on Rails seems to raise its hand and yell, "Pick me!"

Ruby on Rails, also known as Rails, is the product of David Heinemeier Hansson's framework development for the proprietary Basecamp (http://www.basecamphq.com). The product is coded in Ruby (http://www.ruby-lang.org), which is an open source development language that is quite similar to Perl and Python. Ruby, as a language, was released to the world in 1995 by Yukihiro Matsumoto. One of the coolest aspects of Ruby is that everything is an object. Functions are methods of objects and behave as such. Sound familiar?

There are a few variations of Rails available, each with a differing package of components. The Windows-enabled install package that I've worked with is available at http://instantrails.rubyforge.org and includes the Ruby language, Rails Framework, Apache server, and MySQL database platform. It has an easy-to-use installer that will install and configure all of these products without modifying the system environment. That's a good thing, in that you feel a little safer about installing it knowing full well that it won't trash your computer. The Instant Rails interface application is pretty simple to operate and has a fairly low footprint of resources, as you can see in Figure 7-1.

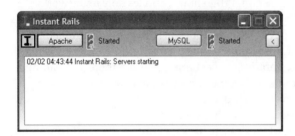

Figure 7-1. *The Instant Rails interface*

From this application, you can start the MySQL database, the Apache server, and the individual Rails applications. Starting a new Rails application is as simple as starting a console window, wherein you'll execute the appropriate command to generate a new application. All of this can be accomplished through the Instant Rails Applications console, shown in Figure 7-2.

The package also has a pair of starter applications to get you started. These will give you a good starting point as you attempt to do things the Rails way. The syntax will take a bit to get used to, but after building a few pages you'll get the hang of it.

As of this writing, there is a lack of serious visual IDEs available for the framework on the Windows platform. One of the applications that I have tried briefly is RadRails (http://www.radrails.org), which is shown in Figure 7-3. It is an open source product, as you would expect.

Figure 7-2. *The Instant Rails Application console*

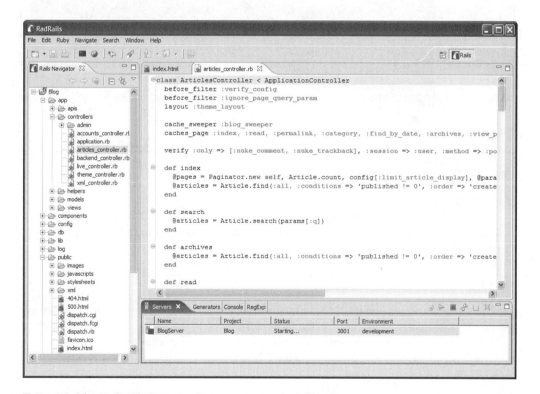

Figure 7-3. *The RadRails IDE*

Dojo Toolkit

The Dojo Toolkit (http://www.dojotoolkit.org) is a JavaScript library that encapsulates all of the functionality needed for dynamic web pages. The product is open source, and Ajax abilities are present by default. The sample applications that accompany the download are adequate to get you moving, but the documentation needs some help. As of the time of this writing, I was able to get their Mail application, shown in Figure 7-4, running in IE 6, but not IE 7. I'm sure they're on top of it and a newer, compatible version will come along shortly.

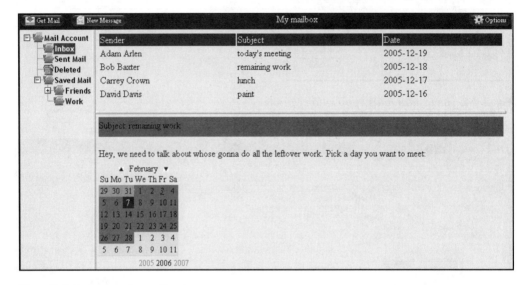

Figure 7-4. *Dojo sample application*

The power of the library resides in the widgets that they make available. They're fairly straightforward and require very little coding. The library is worth taking a look at, if only for curiosity's sake.

SAJAX

Another open-source option is SAJAX (http://www.modernmethod.com/sajax). Here again, it is primarily a third-party script that you'll reference from one of the many server-side platform stubs that they provide. Unfortunately, when I attempted to sample the ASP code block, I received instead the message shown in Figure 7-5.

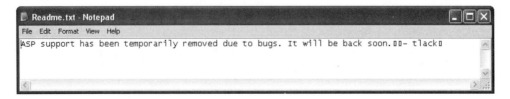

Figure 7-5. *ASP compatibility missing*

I was, however, able to access the Perl script, and it was pretty self explanatory. The supported platforms at the time of this writing are as follows:

- ASP (someday, I guess)

- ColdFusion

- Io

- Lua

- Perl

- PHP

- Python

- Ruby

The library seems to be well supported with forums, FAQs, and continuous updates.

xajax

xajax (`http://www.xajaxproject.org`) is a PHP library that is object oriented and customizable as well. It provides a JavaScript pump to client-side PHP coding. If you're looking to do dynamic PHP content, then in all likelihood this is the library for you.

They have an excellent wiki available for getting started with the product as well: `http://wiki.xajaxproject.org/Tutorials:Learn_xajax_in_10_Minutes`.

The site is updated on a fairly regular basis, and library updates seem to be on the move. I expect to see more of this product in the future.

DWR: Direct Web Remoting

DWR is a Java library that is open to the public at `http://getahead.ltd.uk/dwr/`. It mirrors Ajax for .NET in many ways syntactically. For example, both have calling and callback functions for interaction with server-side code. The illustrations that are provided have a resounding similarity to much of the coding that we'll do in this book.

If you're working with Java, you'll want to have a run at this. There is some initial setup, but the documentation out there makes it an easy task.

WebORB

Midnight Coders has built an Ajax presentation framework, called WebORB, that they currently retail at `http://www.themidnightcoders.com`. It's a pretty large application with a multitude of functionality. The package supports the .NET languages and Java. Here again, coding is similar to what we do here in the book.

The site has tons of coding help, decent support, and some really cool sample apps, as you can see in Figure 7-6.

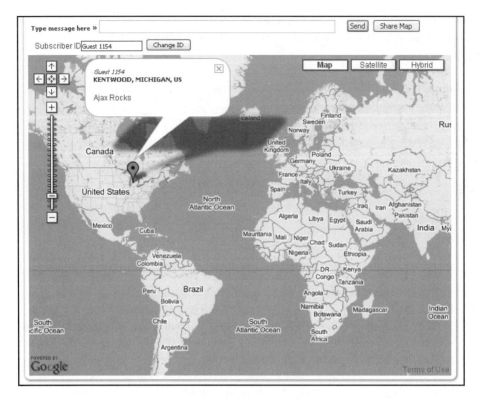

Figure 7-6. *WebORB Chat application*

Midnight Coders provides two versions of the library that I've found: standard and professional. Standard seems to be free "for most commercial applications," and professional has a few more options. You'll want to contact them for details and clarification on licensing.

.NET Frameworks and Libraries

One of the things that you'll hear me mention a few times in this book is that you should always keep in mind that the modern implementation of Ajax is a relatively new technology. I'll freely admit that DHTML and remoting have been around for years, but Ajax in its current manifestation is still quite young. And because of the relative youthfulness of the products available, you will find that most authors of the products in this section are not quite ready to roll their code out of beta just yet. They are most certainly works in progress and will continue to be so for some time.

Fortunately, the level of excitement is relatively high in the community, so we'll see constant updates and new products pop up on the radar. Ajax and the .NET Framework have been the subject of much interest by a large community of developers. With ASP.NET 2.0 beginning to wind up in the market place, people are excited to see where they will be able to take the next release of the technology.

Let's take a look at some of the more prominent Ajax for .NET implementations out on the web as we prepare to dissect and build in Chapter 8.

Michael Schwarz's Ajax.NET

In my current work project, I am using Michael's library exclusively. Having named the product Ajax.NET has seemingly enabled him to coin the term as well. I'd entertained some ideas of naming this book *Ajax.NET and the .NET Framework*, but as you can imagine, that could create some confusion for those of you who are familiar with Mr. Schwarz's work. But it is a sacrifice that I'm fully willing to make because his product deserves the exclusive nomenclature. You can find a fairly active blog and links to the content at `http://weblogs.asp.net/mschwarz/`.

There are a few things worth mentioning when considering his product:

- Open sourced DLL and source code.

- The licensing for the product is somewhat confusing and open for interpretation.

- Depends on HTTPHandler for DLL routing. If you're operating within an application framework, this could create some issues.

The sample code that he has provided will give you an excellent start towards implementing the library into your own projects. Implementing the code is similar to what we've already seen. Having the Ajax.NET DLL added to the project is not enough. You must also add the appropriate handler and configuration settings to your `web.config` file as well:

```
<configSections>
  <sectionGroup name="ajaxNet">
    <section name="ajaxSettings"
             type="AjaxPro.AjaxSettingsSectionHandler, AjaxPro"/>
  </sectionGroup>
</configSections>

<ajaxNet>
  <ajaxSettings>
    <urlNamespaceMappings>
    </urlNamespaceMappings>
    <jsonConverters>
      <add type="AJAXDemo.Examples.Classes.PersonConverter, AJAXDemo"/>
    </jsonConverters>
  </ajaxSettings>
</ajaxNet>

<httpHandlers>
  <add verb="POST,GET" path="ajaxpro/*.ashx"
       type="AjaxPro.AjaxHandlerFactory, AjaxPro"/>
</httpHandlers>
```

We first register the server-side page with the Ajax library (you will see this again later) by adding the following to the page load event:

```
protected void Page_Load(object sender, EventArgs e)
{
  AjaxPro.Utility.RegisterTypeForAjax(typeof(_Default));
}
```

Having accomplished that, we must identify Ajax-aware functions by prefixing the function name with an attribute as shown:

```
[AjaxPro.AjaxMethod]
public DateTime GetServerTime()
{
  return DateTime.Now;
}
```

We can now call the code dynamically from the client side. The calling function is simple:

```
function getServerTime()
{
  MyDemo._Default.GetServerTime(getServerTime_callback);
}
```

As is the callback function:

```
function getServerTime_callback(res)
{
  alert(res.value);
}
```

The library has the ability to pass many data types back to the JavaScript layer, including

- DataSets

- DataTables

- DataViews

- Arrays

- Collections

I think you'll be pleased with Michael's work. He has started and supports a Google group (http://groups.google.com/group/ajaxpro/) for the library, and his blog has a continuous flow of new and interesting Ajax.NET-related discussions. Definitely worth checking out.

Jason Diamond's Anthem

You will become quite familiar with this library by the time that you have finished this book. I chose to use his library for the sample applications that we'll work with. I decided on his work not because it is better, cheaper, or better supported, but rather because it is lightweight and easily explained. Like Michael Schwarz's Ajax.NET library, Jason has made the source code available for all to see. His current version, titled Anthem, is available at http://anthem-dot-net. sourceforge.net.

He also keeps a running blog at http://jason.diamond.name/weblog/.

Some key points concerning his library:

- Library has 1.1 and 2.0 tested compatibility.

- The documentation is a little weak, which he freely admits, but makes up for it with excellent code samples in both Visual Studio 2003 and Visual Studio 2005.

- You will only need to implement one class file for core functionality.

- No HTTPHandler needed.

Setting up the server side of things is similar to Michael Schwarz's process (sans the handler, of course). First we register the page:

```
private void Page_Load()
{
  Anthem.Manager.Register(this);
}
```

We then prefix the appropriate server-side function with an attribute:

```
[Anthem.Method]
public int Add(int a, int b)
{
  return a + b;
}
```

In the client-side calling function, we invoke the server-side function through Anthem (with the Anthem_InvokePageMethod()):

```
function DoAdd()
{
  Anthem_InvokePageMethod('Add', [document.getElementById('a').value, ➥
document.getElementById('b').value], ReturnTrip);
}
```

We specify the name of the client-side callback function in the calling function:

```
function ReturnTrip(result){alert(result.value);}
```

We'll work more with this library in the following chapters, so if something is raising some alarms, fear not. You will become intimately familiar with the full process of this library.

ComfortASP.NET

The ComfortASP.NET library (http://www.comfortasp.de) is open source and was released in August 2005, and gains popularity with every passing day. It is a powerful tool with a ton of configurable options to boot. The author, Daniel Zeiss, has a pretty detailed set of getting started instructions, complete with screenshots. Of particular interest to me was the Comfort-ASP.NET manager control, which has a pretty good design-time properties window, as you can see in Figure 7-7.

As is the case with Schwarz's library, this package also requires the use of HTTPHandlers and other various configuration settings within web.config.

You may be required to register with the site in order to download the latest version.

My exposure to this library has been minimal, so I encourage you to check it out for yourself to see if it's the right fit for your next project.

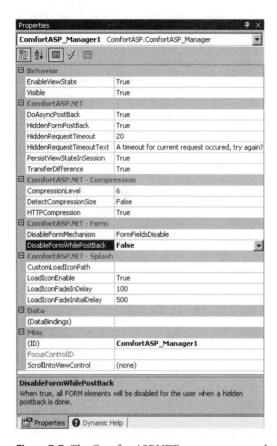

Figure 7-7. *The ComfortASP.NET manager control*

MagicAjax.NET

The real magic of MagicAjax.NET is that it is more of a control than an actual interactive library. The library provides you with an ajaxpanel control that you basically use as a wrapper for your dynamic controls. You handle the control events as you would handle classic ASP.NET event triggers. The only setup really necessary is a few lines of code in `web.config`, and you can then just drop the wrapper into the HTML. The download also comes with an excellent Visual Studio 2005 application that will help educate you on the intricacies of MagicAjax.NET's pioneer product.

The library has a pretty decent list of features:

- JavaScript not necessary for Ajax calls.

- Replaces ASP.NET postbacks with Ajax postbacks for controls inside of their panel.

- Page ViewState is accessible by both postback processes.

- Customizable JavaScript can be sent to the client via various helper methods.

You can check it out for yourself at `http://www.magicajax.net`.

Microsoft's Atlas

Of course, no discussion of ASP.NET-compatible Ajax libraries would be complete without mentioning Microsoft's Atlas. Billed as Microsoft's Ajax, the freshman software product is poised to bring legacy ASP.NET developers into the world of dynamic development by providing a seamless integration with their Visual Studio 2005 environment. A few controls, as well as the beta application, have been released to the public and are freely available for download: `http://atlas.asp.net`.

I'll be covering this product in detail, in Chapter 20, but for now let's just get a feel for what the basic feature set of the product will be:

- Object-oriented API development.

- Asynchronous calls to web services.

- Tight integration with Visual Studio 2005.

- Cross-platform. Yes, it's true, a Microsoft product that seeks to be cross-platform.

Program syntax is, yet again, similar to what we've grown accustomed to. Most of the sample applications that I've worked with, however, deal with asynchronous calls to web services, rather than server-side code. The setup is pretty much the same. You have external JavaScript that is brought into the `.aspx` page as well as the identification of the web service resource:

```
<atlas:ScriptManager runat="server" ID="scriptManager">
  <services>
    <atlas:servicereference path="HelloWorldService.asmx"
                            type="text/javascript" />
  </services>
</atlas:ScriptManager>
```

Calling the web service's web method is nearly identical to server-side calling functions in other libraries:

```
function DoSearch()
{
  var SrchElem = document.getElementById("SearchKey");
  Samples.AspNet.HelloWorldService.HelloWorld(SrchElem.value, OnRequestComplete);
}
```

Here's the callback function:

```
function OnRequestComplete(result)
{
  var RsltElem = document.getElementById("Results");
  RsltElem.innerHTML = result;
}
```

The syntax is slightly different, but the pattern remains the same. I don't want to get into too much detail and spoil the end of the book for you. We will visit this library again, and you will see it in action for yourself.

Summary

There are a **LOT** of Ajax frameworks/libraries out on the web, all jockeying for popularity and use. They all are worthy of trial and investigation, and your experience with them will be limited by only time and resources. I'm always on the prowl for the latest and greatest web technology, and these days, with all of the Ajax updates and new releases, I hardly have time for anything else. It is truly an exciting time to be in web development.

In the next chapter, we'll begin to translate what we've seen about all of the various dynamic technologies that make up Ajax into an investigative dissection of what goes into the construction of a basic Ajax library. Understanding the Ajax class library processes will force us to spend less time guessing about the functionality and more time embracing it.

PART 3

■ ■ ■

Concept to Code

In the previous seven chapters, we have concentrated primarily on the theories and concepts behind Ajax development. And while conceptual guidelines are useful, they can become meaningless if they're not expressed with source code. Automotive engineering would be pointless if the designs are never transitioned to the factory floor. As such, our Ajax ideas need to transition toward fully functioning, reusable Ajax applications.

■■■

Understanding the Library

If you're like me, you love third-party controls. Nothing saves more time than being able to simply drag and drop something onto a page and have it just work. For my personal web page, I use DotNetNuke (http://www.dotnetnuke.com) as the site portal, and I also have a few third-party DNN modules that I've purchased to use on the site. Sure, I probably could have written them. And given DNN's awesome documentation and ease of use, I'm quite sure that the actual writing of the product would have gone very smoothly. However, there is one sacrifice that I'm finding harder to make: time. So if an out-of-the-box solution comes along that can save me time and debugging headaches, I am 100 percent in favor of it.

This also explains my recent fascination with the various Ajax libraries that are popping up all over the web. We could all take the time to write the necessary JavaScript and C# class files so that we'll have a redistributable dynamic class library for ourselves, but honestly, who has time for that? If developers such as Michael Schwarz and Jason Diamond are willing to do the dirty work, then why not embrace the work that they have done and concentrate on the more interesting aspects of the site: design, structure, and usability? The less time that I have to spend worrying about the intricacies of the plumbing, the better. However, that does not mean that I'm unwilling to understand what is going on behind the scenes.

Implementing an Ajax library should be a process accompanied by a decent level of comprehension of the functionality that it provides. For this chapter, we'll create a small application that uses an Ajax library, and we'll also take a closer look at the code that is fired off within the library itself. Understanding this process may lead you to expand the existing product or perhaps build your own from scratch.

The Library

As I've mentioned before, tons of libraries are available for you out on the web, either free or at a minimal price. One in particular that I've grown quite fond of is Jason Diamond's Anthem library. His library has a few benefits for the purpose of implementation and dissection in our sample application:

- *Open source*: Jason has donated the code to the public.

- *One file*: Anthem.dll is all we'll need.

- *Easily illustrated*: The code is laid out in an easy-to-read manner.

- *Extendable*: You can modify it and call it your own.

There are two downloads that you'll want to grab: the Anthem files from Jason's site at `http://anthem-dot-net.sourceforge.net` as well as the sample application for this chapter.

Before we dive into the sample app, we need to first compile the Anthem library into a working DLL.

Installing the Library

Once you've downloaded the project files, you'll need to extract them to a working directory, as shown in Figure 8-1.

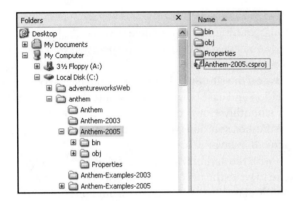

Figure 8-1. *Our Anthem file locations*

We'll cover the various files that make up the DLL in a moment, but for now, let's compile our DLL so that we can jump into a simple Ajax application:

1. In Visual Studio, open the `Anthem-2005.csproj` file found in the `Anthem-2005` folder.

2. Switch your Build configuration from Debug to Release.

3. Right-click the project name and choose Build.

4. Your DLL should now be accessible from the `/bin/Release` folder, as shown in Figure 8-2.

We now have a working `Anthem.dll` that we can access from our web applications.

Figure 8-2. *Anthem project files*

The Application

So what exactly does this website accomplish? Well, take a look at the finished product, shown in Figure 8-3.

Figure 8-3. *Simple Ajax application*

We have a relatively simple application with a textbox and a button. The user enters their name and clicks the button, subsequently returning a personalized greeting. The personalized greeting, however, is built on the server side rather than with JavaScript. A generalized sequence of events for this application can be described as follows:

1. We first make our web page Ajax aware.

2. The onclick event of the button is routed to a JavaScript function.

3. The JavaScript function calls an established Anthem method on the server side.

4. The client-side code creates a return string comprising "Hello" and the name, and returns that string back to the client.

5. A JavaScript function handles the returned data.

6. An alert box is popped up with the compiled greeting.

This is a pretty basic description of the overall process happening in our simple application. But as you've already discovered, with Ajax, there is so much more to understand.

Our site file structure has the basic necessities, as shown in Figure 8-4.

Figure 8-4. *Sample application file structure*

As you can see, we have a Bin folder added to the site. We have within that folder our referenced Anthem.dll file. It is that class library that encapsulates all of our Ajax functionality. We'll take a look at that in a moment; for now let's take a look at the ASP.NET page.

Our HTML is pretty generic:

```
<%@ Page Language="C#" AutoEventWireup="true"
 CodeFile="Default.aspx.cs" Inherits="_Default" %>

<!DOCTYPE html PUBLIC "-//W3C//DTD XHTML 1.0 Transitional//EN"
 "http://www.w3.org/TR/xhtml1/DTD/xhtml1-transitional.dtd">

<html xmlns="http://www.w3.org/1999/xhtml" >
<head runat="server">
    <title>Chapter 8 Sample Application</title>
</head>
<body>
<script type="text/javascript" language="javascript">
function CallAjaxFunction()
{
    var findName = document.getElementById("txtName");
```

```
    Anthem_InvokePageMethod('SayHello',[findName.value] , AjaxFunctionCallback);
}

function AjaxFunctionCallback(response)
{
    alert(response.value);
}
</script>
    <form id="frmMain" runat="server">
    <div>
        Enter your name:
        <asp:TextBox ID="txtName" runat="server" ></asp:TextBox>
        <input id="btnGo" type="button"
         onclick="CallAjaxFunction();" value="Say Hello" />
    </div>
    </form>
</body>
</html>
```

Let's also take a look at the server-side code before we begin describing processes:

```
using System;
using System.Data;
using System.Configuration;
using System.Web;
using System.Web.Security;
using System.Web.UI;
using System.Web.UI.WebControls;
using System.Web.UI.WebControls.WebParts;
using System.Web.UI.HtmlControls;

public partial class _Default : System.Web.UI.Page
{
    protected void Page_Load(object sender, EventArgs e)
    {
        // We must first register our page with the library
        Anthem.Manager.Register(this);
    }

    // We must preface our Ajax aware methods with [Ajax.Method()]
    [Anthem.Method]
    public string SayHello(string name)
    {
        // Create and return a new string
        return "Hello " + name + "!";
    }
}
```

As I mentioned before, in our generalized sequence of events, we must first register this page with the Anthem library. Our Page_Load event takes care of that for us:

```
protected void Page_Load(object sender, EventArgs e)
{
    // We must first register our page with the library
    Anthem.Manager.Register(this);
}
```

Having done this, we now need to declare any server-side methods as Ajax aware:

```
[Anthem.Method]
public string SayHello(string name)
{
    // Create and return a new string
    return "Hello " + name + "!";
}
```

By adding the [Anthem.Method] attribute to our function, we are informing the library that we'd like this function to be made available to the asynchronous process.

On the client side of things, we can call our method via Anthem_InvokePageMethod:

```
Anthem_InvokePageMethod('SayHello',[findName.value] , AjaxFunctionCallback);
```

Notice that the SayHello function name is the first parameter of the Anthem function. We supply any parameters (as an array) that SayHello requires as the second parameter. Finally, the client-side callback function is provided as the third parameter.

As you'll recall from our XmlHttpRequest example in Chapter 3, we receive a callback from our asynchronous work. And within that callback we manipulate the response value:

```
function AjaxFunctionCallback(response)
{
    alert(response.value);
}
```

So we can see that the current process is very similar to our previous demo with the Xml-HttpRequest object. What differentiates this example from the previous one is that we have encapsulated most of our XmlHttpRequest processes within Anthem.dll.

There are three core things that the library accomplishes for us:

- Generates and maintains our XmlHttpRequest object

- Calls our server-side code with the appropriate parameters

- Parses and returns various data types

Of course, as you read through the Anthem code, you'll notice that there are a multitude of capabilities represented within the library. To describe the entire library would undoubtedly take up an entire book. What I will do, to keep it down to a chapter, is show you the major class properties and methods of the library.

Examining the Anthem Library

As I'm sure you have discovered, one of the best ways to understand a new project is to walk the code in debug mode. I'll step through and describe most of the activity taking place within the Anthem Manager class.

Before we do that, we'll need to add the Anthem 2005 project to this solution.

Under File, select Open and then Project/Solution.

Find the Anthem-2005.csproj file in the Anthem-2005 directory. Remember to toggle the Add to Solution button prior to adding the project.

Once you've added the Anthem project, you'll have access to the code, while you debug the web application.

First we set a breakpoint on our page register statement, as shown in Figure 8-5.

```
public partial class _Default : System.Web.UI.Page
{
    protected void Page_Load(object sender, EventArgs e)
    {
        // we must first register our page with the library
        Anthem.Manager.Register(this);
    }

    // We must preface our Ajax aware methods with [Anthem.Method]
    [Anthem.Method]
    public string SayHello(string name)
    {
        // create and return a new string
        return "Hello " + name + "!";
    }
}
```

Figure 8-5. *Setting the first breakpoint*

When we run the application, we find that the Register method is the entry point to our library, which ultimately leads to the actual class registration method within Anthem.Manager.cs found in the Anthem project:

```
public static void Register(Page page)
{
    Register(page, page);
}

public static void Register(Control control)
{
    Register(control.Page, control);
}

private static void Register(
    Page page,
    Control control)
```

```
    {
        AddManager(page);
        Manager manager = GetManager();
        if (!object.ReferenceEquals(page, control))
        {
            manager.AddTarget(control);
        }
    }
```

We will supply the web page as a parameter to the Register function.

Our register method is going to accomplish one basic task. It will instantiate our Anthem Manager class as a control and add it to the page's collection of controls, as we can see if we step into the AddManager function:

```
    private static void AddManager(Page page)
    {
        if (!HttpContext.Current.Items.Contains("Anthem.Manager"))
        {
            Manager manager = new Manager();
            page.PreRender += new EventHandler(manager.OnPreRender);
            page.Error += new EventHandler(manager.OnError);
            manager._targets["Anthem.Manager"] = manager;
            HttpContext.Current.Items["Anthem.Manager"] = manager;
            manager.RegisterPageScript(page);
        }
    }
```

The AddManager first checks to see whether it has already added the appropriate class to the list of page controls; if not, it will add it for later use.

The PreRender function is then added as an EventHandler to the Anthem Manager. It essentially points the execution path toward the proper function calls. If you've called a server-side function, this code will point the compiler toward the proper page-level method:

```
    private void OnPreRender(object source, EventArgs e)
    {
        HttpContext context = HttpContext.Current;
        HttpRequest req = context.Request;
        HttpResponse resp = context.Response;

        if (!CheckIfRedirectedToLoginPage() && IsCallBack)
        {
            object targetObject = null;
            string methodName = null;
            if (req.Form["Anthem_PageMethod"] != null)
            {
                targetObject = source as Page;
                methodName = req.Form["Anthem_PageMethod"];
            }
```

```csharp
else if (req.Form["Anthem_MasterPageMethod"] != null)
{
    Page page = source as Page;
    if (page != null)
    {
        targetObject = page.Master;
        methodName = req.Form["Anthem_MasterPageMethod"];
    }
}

else if (req.Form["Anthem_ControlID"] != null &&
        req.Form["Anthem_ControlMethod"] != null)
{
    targetObject = _targets[req.Form["Anthem_ControlID"]];
    methodName = req.Form["Anthem_ControlMethod"];
}

object val = null;
string error = null;
if (targetObject == null)
{
    error = "CONTROLNOTFOUND";
}
else
{
    if (methodName != null && methodName.Length > 0)
    {
        MethodInfo methodInfo = FindTargetMethod(targetObject,
         methodName);
        if (methodInfo == null)
        {
            error = "METHODNOTFOUND";
        }
        else
        {
            try
            {
                object[] parameters =
                 ConvertParameters(methodInfo, req);
                val = InvokeMethod(targetObject,
                 methodInfo, parameters);
            }
            catch (Exception ex)
            {
                error = ex.Message;
            }
        }
    }
}
```

```
            context.Trace.IsEnabled = false;
            ConfigureResponse(resp);
            resp.Filter = new CallBackFilter(this, resp.Filter);
            _value = val;
            _error = error;
            _updatePage = req.Form["Anthem_UpdatePage"] == "true";
        }
    }

    object _value;
    string _error;
    bool _updatePage;
```

The instantiated manager is then added to the page items:

```
HttpContext.Current.Items["Anthem.Manager"] = manager;
```

It's important that we should also observe the manager.RegisterPageScript(page) called as the final step in our AddManager routine. It will add some dynamically generated JavaScript:

```
private void RegisterPageScript(Page page)
{
    HttpContext context = HttpContext.Current;
    string url = GetCallBackURL(context);
    string formID = GetFormID(page);

    string pageScript = @"<script type=""text/javascript"">
    var Anthem_DefaultURL = """ + url + @""";
    var Anthem_FormID = """ + formID + @""";
    </script>";
    page.ClientScript.RegisterClientScriptBlock
    (typeof(Manager), "pageScript", pageScript);
    page.ClientScript.RegisterClientScriptResource
    (typeof(Anthem.Manager), "Anthem.Anthem.js");
}
```

I've italicized the dynamic JavaScript code so as to set it apart from the C# code.

We add this code dynamically because we need to declare a few JavaScript variables with information that is available at runtime only:

```
var Anthem_DefaultURL = "Default.aspx?Anthem_Callback=True";
var Anthem_FormID = "frmMain";
```

The library will use these variables later to correctly route dynamic calls.

This would be a good time to take notice of a few things about the current page that is being built. You'll notice that we're adding an external JavaScript file to the page:

```
page.ClientScript.RegisterClientScriptResource
  (typeof(Anthem.Manager), "Anthem.Anthem.js");
```

Anthem.js

If we open up the `Anthem.js` file, we find a rather sizable file that encapsulates all of our client-side functionality:

```
function Anthem_AddEvent(obj, evType, fn, useCapture) {
    if (obj.addEventListener) {
        obj.addEventListener(evType, fn, useCapture);
        return true;
    } else if (obj.attachEvent) {
        var r = obj.attachEvent("on" + evType, fn);
        return r;
    } else {
        alert("Anthem_AddEvent could not add event!");
    }
}

function Anthem_GetXMLHttpRequest() {
    if (window.XMLHttpRequest) {
        return new XMLHttpRequest();
    } else {
        if (window.Anthem_XMLHttpRequestProgID) {
            return new
            ActiveXObject
            (window.Anthem_XMLHttpRequestProgID);
        } else {
            var progIDs = ["Msxml2.XMLHTTP.5.0",
            "Msxml2.XMLHTTP.4.0",
            "MSXML2.XMLHTTP.3.0",
            "MSXML2.XMLHTTP",
            "Microsoft.XMLHTTP"];
            for (var i = 0; i < progIDs.length; ++i)
            {
             var progID = progIDs[i];
             try {
                 var x = new ActiveXObject(progID);
                 window.Anthem_XMLHttpRequestProgID = progID;
                     return x;
             } catch (e) {
             }
            }
        }
    }
    return null;
}
```

```
function Anthem_CallBack(url, target, id, method, args, clientCallBack,
clientCallBackArg, includeControlValuesWithCallBack,
updatePageAfterCallBack) {
      if (window.Anthem_PreCallBack) {
            var preCallBackResult = Anthem_PreCallBack();
            if (!(typeof preCallBackResult == "undefined" || preCallBackResult)) {
                  if (window.Anthem_CallBackCancelled) {
                        Anthem_CallBackCancelled();
                  }
                  return null;
            }
      }
      var x = Anthem_GetXMLHttpRequest();
      var result = null;
      if (!x) {
            result = { "value":null, "error":"NOXMLHTTP" };
            Anthem_DebugError(result.error);
            if (clientCallBack) {
                  clientCallBack(result, clientCallBackArg);
            }
            return result;
      }
      x.open("POST", url ? url : Anthem_DefaultURL, clientCallBack ? true : false);
      x.setRequestHeader("Content-Type", "application/x-www-form-urlencoded;
        charset=utf-8");
      if (clientCallBack) {
            x.onreadystatechange = function() {
                  if (x.readyState != 4) {
                        return;
                  }
                  Anthem_DebugResponseText(x.responseText);
                  result = Anthem_GetResult(x);
                  if (result.error) {
                        Anthem_DebugError(result.error);
                  }
                  if (updatePageAfterCallBack) {
                        Anthem_UpdatePage(result);
                  }
                  Anthem_EvalClientSideScript(result);
                  clientCallBack(result, clientCallBackArg);

                  //x.onreadystatechange = function() {};
                  x = null;
```

```
                  if (window.Anthem_PostCallBack) {
                        Anthem_PostCallBack();
                  }
            }
      }
var encodedData = "";
if (target == "Page") {
      encodedData += "&Anthem_PageMethod=" + method;
} else if (target == "MasterPage") {
      encodedData += "&Anthem_MasterPageMethod=" + method;
} else if (target == "Control") {
      encodedData += "&Anthem_ControlID=" + id.split(":").join("_");
      encodedData += "&Anthem_ControlMethod=" + method;
}
  if (args) {
        for (var argsIndex = 0; argsIndex < args.length; ++argsIndex) {
              if (args[argsIndex] instanceof Array) {
                    for (var i = 0; i < args[argsIndex].length; ++i) {
                          encodedData += "&Anthem_CallBackArgument" +
                          argsIndex + "=" +
                          encodeURIComponent(args[argsIndex][i]);
                    }
              } else {
                    encodedData += "&Anthem_CallBackArgument" +
                    argsIndex + "=" + encodeURIComponent(args[argsIndex]);
              }
        }
  }
  if (updatePageAfterCallBack) {
        encodedData += "&Anthem_UpdatePage=true";
  }
  if (includeControlValuesWithCallBack) {
        var form = document.getElementById(Anthem_FormID);
        if (form != null) {
              for (var elementIndex = 0; elementIndex < form.length;
                    ++elementIndex) {
                    var element = form.elements[elementIndex];
                    if (element.name) {
                          var elementValue = null;
                          if (element.nodeName == "INPUT") {
                                var inputType =
                                element.getAttribute("TYPE").toUpperCase();
```

```
                    if (inputType == "TEXT" ||
                        inputType == "PASSWORD" ||
                        inputType == "HIDDEN") {
                            elementValue = element.value;
                    } else if (inputType == "CHECKBOX" ||
                            inputType == "RADIO") {
                        if (element.checked) {
                            elementValue = element.value;
                        }
                    }
                } else if (element.nodeName == "SELECT") {
                    if (element.multiple) {
                        elementValue = [];
                        for (var i = 0; i < element.length; ++i) {
                            if (element.options[i].selected) {
                            elementValue.push
                            (element.options[i].value);
                            }
                        }
                    } else {
                        elementValue = element.value;
                        if (elementValue == "") {
                            elementValue = null;
                        }
                    }
                } else if (element.nodeName == "TEXTAREA") {
                    elementValue = element.value;
                }
                if (elementValue instanceof Array) {
                    for (var i = 0; i < elementValue.length; ++i) {
                            encodedData +=
                            "&" + element.name +
                            "=" +
                            encodeURIComponent(elementValue[i]);
                    }
                } else if (elementValue != null) {
                        encodedData +=
                        "&" + element.name +
                        "=" + encodeURIComponent(elementValue);
                }
            }
        }
    }
    // ASP.NET 1.1 won't fire any events if neither of the following
    // two parameters are in the request, so make sure they're
    // always in the request.
```

```
            if (typeof form.__VIEWSTATE == "undefined") {
                encodedData += "&__VIEWSTATE=";
            }
            if (typeof form.__EVENTTARGET == "undefined") {
                encodedData += "&__EVENTTARGET=";
            }
        }
    }
    Anthem_DebugRequestText(encodedData.split("&").join("\n&"));
    x.send(encodedData);
    if (!clientCallBack) {
        Anthem_DebugResponseText(x.responseText);
        result = Anthem_GetResult(x);
        if (result.error) {
            Anthem_DebugError(result.error);
        }
        if (updatePageAfterCallBack) {
            Anthem_UpdatePage(result);
        }
        Anthem_EvalClientSideScript(result);
    }
    return result;
}

function Anthem_GetResult(x) {
    var result = { "value": null, "error": "BADRESPONSE"};
    try {
        result = eval("(" + x.responseText + ")");
    } catch (e) {
        if (x.responseText.length == 0) {
            alert("response text had 0 length!");
        } else {
            alert("error evaluating response text:\n" + x.responseText);
        }
    }
    return result;
}

function Anthem_SetHiddenInputValue(form, name, value) {
    if (form[name]) {
        form[name].value = value;
    } else {
        var input = document.createElement("input");
        input.setAttribute("name", name);
        input.setAttribute("type", "hidden");
```

```
                input.setAttribute("value", value);
                form.appendChild(input);
                form[name] = input;
        }
}


function Anthem_FireEvent(eventTarget, eventArgument, clientCallBack,
 clientCallBackArg, includeControlValuesWithCallBack,
 updatePageAfterCallBack) {
        var form = document.getElementById(Anthem_FormID);
        Anthem_SetHiddenInputValue(form, "__EVENTTARGET", eventTarget);
        Anthem_SetHiddenInputValue(form, "__EVENTARGUMENT", eventArgument);
        Anthem_CallBack(null, null, null, null, null, clientCallBack,
         clientCallBackArg, includeControlValuesWithCallBack,
         updatePageAfterCallBack);
        form.__EVENTTARGET.value = "";
        form.__EVENTARGUMENT.value = "";
}


function Anthem_UpdatePage(result) {
        var form = document.getElementById(Anthem_FormID);
        if (result.viewState) {
            Anthem_SetHiddenInputValue(form, "__VIEWSTATE", result.viewState);
        }
        if (result.viewStateEncrypted) {
            Anthem_SetHiddenInputValue(form, "__VIEWSTATEENCRYPTED",
             result.viewStateEncrypted);
        }
        if (result.eventValidation) {
            Anthem_SetHiddenInputValue(form, "__EVENTVALIDATION",
             result.eventValidation);
        }
        if (result.controls) {
            for (var controlID in result.controls) {
                var containerID = "__" + controlID.split("$").join("_") + "__";
                var control = document.getElementById(containerID);
                if (control) {
                    control.innerHTML = result.controls[controlID];
                    if (result.controls[controlID] == "") {
                        control.style.display = "none";
                    } else {
                        control.style.display = "";
                    }
                }
            }
        }
}
```

```
function Anthem_EvalClientSideScript(result) {
    if (result.script) {
        for (var i = 0; i < result.script.length; ++i) {
            try {
                eval(result.script[i]);
            } catch (e) {
                alert("Error evaluating client-side script!\n\nScript: "
                + result.script[i] + "\n\nException: " + e);
            }
        }
    }
}

function Anthem_DebugRequestText(text) {
}

function Anthem_DebugResponseText(text) {
}

function Anthem_DebugError(text) {
}

function Anthem_InvokePageMethod(methodName, args, callBack, context) {
    return Anthem_CallBack(null, "Page", null, methodName, args,
      callBack, context, true, true);
}

function Anthem_InvokeMasterPageMethod(methodName, args, callBack, context) {
    return Anthem_CallBack(null, "MasterPage", null, methodName, args,
      callBack, context, true, true);
}

function Anthem_InvokeControlMethod(id, methodName, args, callBack, context) {
    return Anthem_CallBack(null, "Control", id, methodName, args,
      callBack, context, true, true);
}

function AnthemButton_Click(
    button,
    id,
    causesValidation,
    textDuringCallBack,
    enabledDuringCallBack,
    preCallBackFunction,
    postCallBackFunction,
    callBackCancelledFunction,
    includeControlValuesWithCallBack,
    updatePageAfterCallBack
) {
```

```
        var preCallBackResult = true;
        if (preCallBackFunction) {
            preCallBackResult = preCallBackFunction(button);
        }
        if (typeof preCallBackResult == "undefined" || preCallBackResult) {
            var valid = true;
            if (causesValidation && typeof Page_ClientValidate == "function") {
                valid = Page_ClientValidate();
            }
            if (valid) {
                var text = button.value;
                if (textDuringCallBack) {
                    button.value = textDuringCallBack;
                }
                var enabled = !button.disabled;
                button.disabled = !enabledDuringCallBack;
                Anthem_FireEvent(
                    id,
                    "",
                    function(result) {
                        if (postCallBackFunction) {
                            postCallBackFunction(button);
                        }
                        button.disabled = !enabled;
                        button.value = text;
                    },
                    null,
                    includeControlValuesWithCallBack,
                    updatePageAfterCallBack
                );
            }
        } else if (callBackCancelledFunction) {
            callBackCancelledFunction(button);
        }
    }

    function AnthemLinkButton_Click(
        button,
        id,
        causesValidation,
        textDuringCallBack,
        enabledDuringCallBack,
        preCallBackFunction,
        postCallBackFunction,
        callBackCancelledFunction,
        includeControlValuesWithCallBack,
        updatePageAfterCallBack
    ) {
```

```
        var preCallBackResult = true;
        if (preCallBackFunction) {
            preCallBackResult = preCallBackFunction(button);
        }
        if (typeof preCallBackResult == "undefined" || preCallBackResult) {
            var valid = true;
            if (causesValidation && typeof Page_ClientValidate == "function") {
                valid = Page_ClientValidate();
            }
            if (valid) {
                var text = button.innerHTML;
                if (textDuringCallBack) {
                    button.innerHTML = textDuringCallBack;
                }
                var enabled = !button.disabled;
                button.disabled = !enabledDuringCallBack;
                Anthem_FireEvent(
                    id,
                    "",
                    function(result) {
                        if (postCallBackFunction) {
                            postCallBackFunction(button);
                        }
                        button.disabled = !enabled;
                        button.innerHTML = text;
                    },
                    null,
                    includeControlValuesWithCallBack,
                    updatePageAfterCallBack
                );
            }
        } else if (callBackCancelledFunction) {
            callBackCancelledFunction(button);
        }
}

function AnthemImageButton_Click(
    button,
    id,
    causesValidation,
    imageUrlDuringCallBack,
    enabledDuringCallBack,
    preCallBackFunction,
    postCallBackFunction,
    callBackCancelledFunction,
    includeControlValuesWithCallBack,
    updatePageAfterCallBack
) {
```

```
        var preCallBackResult = true;
    if (preCallBackFunction) {
        preCallBackResult = preCallBackFunction(button);
    }
    if (typeof preCallBackResult == "undefined" || preCallBackResult) {
        var valid = true;
        if (causesValidation && typeof Page_ClientValidate == "function") {
            valid = Page_ClientValidate();
        }
        if (valid) {
            var imageUrl = button.src;
            if (imageUrlDuringCallBack) {
                button.src = imageUrlDuringCallBack;
            }
            var enabled = !button.disabled;
            button.disabled = !enabledDuringCallBack;
            Anthem_FireEvent(
                id,
                "",
                function(result) {
                    if (postCallBackFunction) {
                        postCallBackFunction(button);
                    }
                    button.disabled = !enabled;
                    button.src = imageUrl;
                },
                null,
                includeControlValuesWithCallBack,
                updatePageAfterCallBack
            );
        }
    } else if (callBackCancelledFunction) {
        callBackCancelledFunction(button);
    }
}

function AnthemTextBox_TextChanged(textBox, id,
 includeControlValuesWithCallBack, updatePageAfterCallBack) {
    Anthem_FireEvent(id, "", function(result) {}, null,
      includeControlValuesWithCallBack, updatePageAfterCallBack);
}

function AnthemRadioButtonList_OnClick(e) {
    var target = e.target || e.srcElement;
    var eventTarget = target.id.split("_").join("$");
    Anthem_FireEvent(eventTarget, "", function() {}, null, true, true);
}
```

Some of the preceding code should be quite familiar, as it is similar to the previous Xml-HttpRequest work that was discussed in Chapter 3. The basic knowledge that we need to take from this JavaScript is that our request and response processes are handled for us here.

The addition of the external JavaScript file is the last in line of execution, so if we simply continue the debugging process by pressing F5, we'll soon be met by the waiting web application, as you see in Figure 8-6.

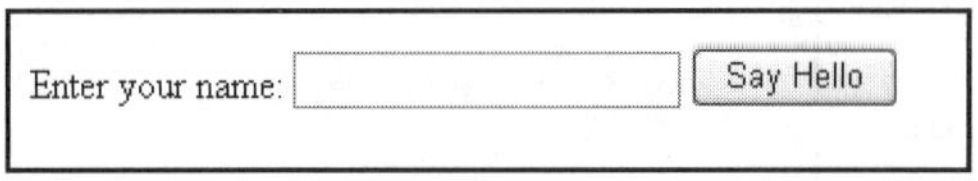

Figure 8-6. *The waiting application*

For the purposes of this demonstration, enter some data into the text field and click the Say Hello button. You should now be dropped back into the Page_Load event:

```
protected void Page_Load(object sender, EventArgs e)
{
    // We must first register our page with the library
    Anthem.Manager.Register(this);
}
```

However, on this pass through, you'll notice some very interesting details about the page process. As before, we are sent into the Register function where we will rebuild the manager class with the updated page controls (i.e., we've modified the textbox value now).

As you step through into the AddManager function, notice by watching the Locals window that a few of the properties have been modified, most notably the IsCallBack now reflects the current calling state, as shown in Figure 8-7.

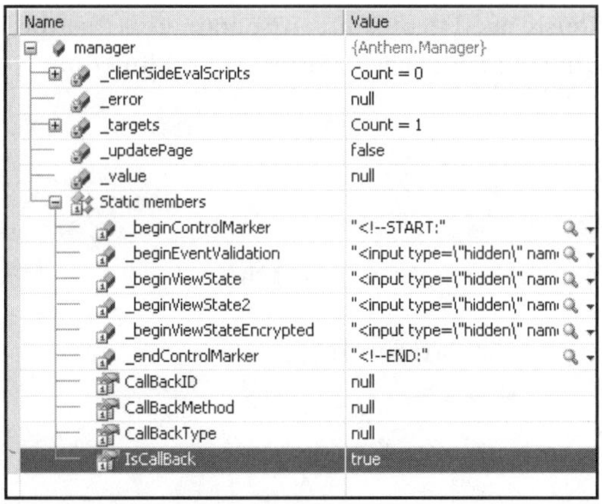

Figure 8-7. *The callback process examined*

We'll eventually step into the PreRender function, where our server-side method will be executed (as previously discussed). The current page and method data is made available, as shown in Figure 8-8.

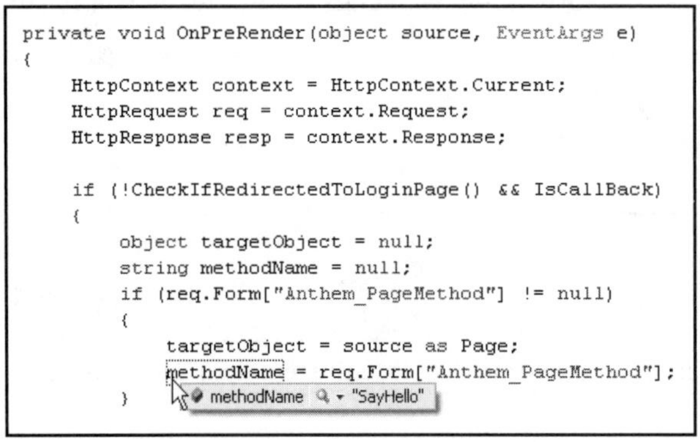

```
private void OnPreRender(object source, EventArgs e)
{
    HttpContext context = HttpContext.Current;
    HttpRequest req = context.Request;
    HttpResponse resp = context.Response;

    if (!CheckIfRedirectedToLoginPage() && IsCallBack)
    {
        object targetObject = null;
        string methodName = null;
        if (req.Form["Anthem_PageMethod"] != null)
        {
            targetObject = source as Page;
            methodName = req.Form["Anthem_PageMethod"];
        }  methodName  Q ▾ "SayHello"
```

Figure 8-8. *PreRender process*

We can quickly identify the SayHello function name as the methodName, and we know we'll be looking to execute that asynchronously with the InvokeMethod() call, found later in the PreRender function:

```
try
{
    object[] parameters = ConvertParameters(methodInfo, req);
    val = InvokeMethod(targetObject, methodInfo, parameters);
}
```

Prior to executing the target code, we obviously need to pull out any parameters that the server-side function may be in need of. We do that with our ConvertParameters() function:

```
static object[] ConvertParameters(
    MethodInfo methodInfo,
    HttpRequest req)
{
 object[] parameters = new object[methodInfo.GetParameters().Length];
 int i = 0;
 foreach (ParameterInfo paramInfo in methodInfo.GetParameters())
  {
   object param = null;
   string paramValue = req.Form["Anthem_CallBackArgument" + i];
   if (paramValue != null)
   {
     if (paramInfo.ParameterType.IsArray)
```

```
    {
      Type type = paramInfo.ParameterType.GetElementType();
      string[] values = req.Form.GetValues("Anthem_CallBackArgument" + i);
      Array array = Array.CreateInstance(type, values.Length);

      for (int index = 0; index < values.Length; index++)
      {
        array.SetValue(Convert.ChangeType(values[index], type), index);
      }
      param = array;
    }
    else
    {
      param = Convert.ChangeType(paramValue, paramInfo.ParameterType);
    }
  }
  parameters[i] = param;
  ++i;
  }
return parameters;
}
```

Now that we have the proper parameters needed for execution of the actual Anthem method, we can now call the Invoke method, which will finish the asynchronous process by running the server-side function and subsequently handing off to the client-side callback function:

```
static object InvokeMethod(
    object target,
    MethodInfo methodInfo,
    object[] parameters)
{
    object val = null;
    try
    {
        val = methodInfo.Invoke(target, parameters);
    }
    catch (TargetInvocationException ex)
    {
        // TargetInvocationExceptions should have the actual
        // exception the method threw in its InnerException
        // property.
        if (ex.InnerException != null)
        {
            throw ex.InnerException;
        }
        else
```

```
        {
            throw ex;
        }
    }
    return val;
}
```

After we execute val = methodInfo.Invoke(target, parameters);, the application will finish
up the async process, and we'll be met by our infamous alert box, as shown in Figure 8-3.

But didn't we discuss earlier that Jason Diamond's library could pass and manipulate
.NET data types (DataSets, DataTables, etc.) from within the library? Yes, we did. How fortu-
nate that you should remember that. As we stepped through our sample code, one particular
event that we didn't stop on was the overridden close method:

```
 public override void Close()
{
    base.Close();
    _manager.WriteResult(_next, _buffer);
    _next.Close();
}
```

We are interested in the WriteResult call that is being made with our callback function's
return value (you remember, the string from SayHello). It is within WriteResult that we find
our return type parsing, and if you think about it, this is where you can really start to extend
the library by adding your own parsing methods. Jason was kind enough to include a majority
of the types that most .NET developers will use on a regular basis. We can find those within the
correlated methods connected to WriteResult:

```
public static void WriteResult(
    HttpResponse resp,
    object val,
    string error)
{
    StringBuilder sb = new StringBuilder();
    try
    {
        WriteValueAndError(sb, val, error, null, null, null, null);
    }
    catch (Exception ex)
    {
        // If an exception was thrown while formatting the
        // result value, we need to discard whatever was
        // written and start over with nothing but the error
        // message.
        sb.Length = 0;
        WriteValueAndError(sb, null, ex.Message, null, null, null, null);
    }
    resp.Write(sb.ToString());
}
```

```csharp
static void WriteValueAndError(
    StringBuilder sb,
    object val,
    string error,
    string viewState,
    string viewStateEncrypted,
    string eventValidation,
    Hashtable controls)
{
    sb.Append("{\"value\":");
    WriteValue(sb, val);
    sb.Append(",\"error\":");
    WriteValue(sb, error);
    if (viewState != null)
    {
        sb.Append(",\"viewState\":");
        WriteValue(sb, viewState);
    }
    if (viewStateEncrypted != null)
    {
        sb.Append(",\"viewStateEncrypted\":");
        WriteValue(sb, viewStateEncrypted);
    }
    if (eventValidation != null)
    {
        sb.Append(",\"eventValidation\":");
        WriteValue(sb, eventValidation);
    }
    if (controls != null && controls.Count > 0)
    {
        sb.Append(",\"controls\":{");
        foreach (DictionaryEntry control in controls)
        {
            sb.Append("\"" + control.Key + "\":");
            WriteValue(sb, control.Value);
            sb.Append(",");
        }
        --sb.Length;
        sb.Append("}");
    }
    if (GetManager()._clientSideEvalScripts.Count > 0)
    {
        sb.Append(",\"script\":[");
        foreach (string script in GetManager()._clientSideEvalScripts)
```

```
        {
            WriteValue(sb, script);
            sb.Append(",");
        }
        --sb.Length;
        sb.Append("]");
    }
    sb.Append("}");
}

public static void WriteValue(StringBuilder sb, object val)
{
    if (val == null || val == System.DBNull.Value)
    {
        sb.Append("null");
    }
    else if (val is string || val is Guid)
    {
        WriteString(sb, val.ToString());
    }
    else if (val is bool)
    {
        sb.Append(val.ToString().ToLower());
    }
    else if (val is double ||
        val is float ||
        val is long ||
        val is int ||
        val is short ||
        val is byte ||
        val is decimal)
    {
        sb.Append(val);
    }
    else if (val.GetType().IsEnum)
    {
        sb.Append((int)val);
    }
    else if (val is DateTime)
    {
        sb.Append("new Date(\"");
        sb.Append(((DateTime)val).ToString("MMMM, d yyyy HH:mm:ss", new
                CultureInfo("en-US", false).DateTimeFormat));
        sb.Append("\")");
    }
    else if (val is DataSet)
```

```
    {
        WriteDataSet(sb, val as DataSet);
    }
    else if (val is DataTable)
    {
        WriteDataTable(sb, val as DataTable);
    }
    else if (val is DataRow)
    {
        WriteDataRow(sb, val as DataRow);
    }
    else if (val is IEnumerable)
    {
        WriteEnumerable(sb, val as IEnumerable);
    }
    else
    {
        WriteObject(sb, val);
    }
}

static void WriteString(StringBuilder sb, string s)
{
    sb.Append("\"");
    foreach (char c in s)
    {
        switch (c)
        {
            case '\"':
                sb.Append("\\\"");
                break;
            case '\\':
                sb.Append("\\\\");
                break;
            case '\b':
                sb.Append("\\b");
                break;
            case '\f':
                sb.Append("\\f");
                break;
            case '\n':
                sb.Append("\\n");
                break;
            case '\r':
                sb.Append("\\r");
                break;
```

```
            case '\t':
                sb.Append("\\t");
                break;
        default:
                int i = (int)c;
                if (i < 32 || i > 127)
                {
                    sb.AppendFormat("\\u{0:X04}", i);
                }
                else
                {
                    sb.Append(c);
                }
                break;
        }
    }
    sb.Append("\"");
}

static void WriteDataSet(StringBuilder sb, DataSet ds)
{
    sb.Append("{\"Tables\":{");
    foreach (DataTable table in ds.Tables)
    {
        sb.AppendFormat("\"{0}\":", table.TableName);
        WriteDataTable(sb, table);
        sb.Append(",");
    }
    // Remove the trailing comma.
    if (ds.Tables.Count > 0)
    {
        --sb.Length;
    }
    sb.Append("}}");
}

static void WriteDataTable(StringBuilder sb, DataTable table)
{
    sb.Append("{\"Rows\":[");
    foreach (DataRow row in table.Rows)
    {
        WriteDataRow(sb, row);
        sb.Append(",");
    }
    // Remove the trailing comma.
    if (table.Rows.Count > 0)
```

```
    {
        --sb.Length;
    }
    sb.Append("]}");
}

static void WriteDataRow(StringBuilder sb, DataRow row)
{
    sb.Append("{");
    foreach (DataColumn column in row.Table.Columns)
    {
        sb.AppendFormat("\"{0}\":", column.ColumnName);
        WriteValue(sb, row[column]);
        sb.Append(",");
    }
    // Remove the trailing comma.
    if (row.Table.Columns.Count > 0)
    {
        --sb.Length;
    }
    sb.Append("}");
}

static void WriteEnumerable(StringBuilder sb, IEnumerable e)
{
    bool hasItems = false;
    sb.Append("[");
    foreach (object val in e)
    {
        WriteValue(sb, val);
        sb.Append(",");
        hasItems = true;
    }
    // Remove the trailing comma.
    if (hasItems)
    {
        --sb.Length;
    }
    sb.Append("]");
}

static void WriteObject(StringBuilder sb, object o)
```

```csharp
{
    MemberInfo[] members = o.GetType().GetMembers(BindingFlags.Instance |
     BindingFlags.Public);
    sb.Append("{");
    bool hasMembers = false;
    foreach (MemberInfo member in members)
    {
        bool hasValue = false;
        object val = null;
        if ((member.MemberType & MemberTypes.Field) == MemberTypes.Field)
        {
            FieldInfo field = (FieldInfo)member;
            val = field.GetValue(o);
            hasValue = true;
        }
        else if ((member.MemberType & MemberTypes.Property) ==
                MemberTypes.Property)
        {
            PropertyInfo property = (PropertyInfo)member;
            if (property.CanRead && property.GetIndexParameters().Length == 0)
            {
                val = property.GetValue(o, null);
                hasValue = true;
            }
        }
        if (hasValue)
        {
            sb.Append("\"");
            sb.Append(member.Name);
            sb.Append("\":");
            WriteValue(sb, val);
            sb.Append(",");
            hasMembers = true;
        }
    }
    if (hasMembers)
    {
        --sb.Length;
    }
    sb.Append("}");
}
```

You should also notice that the StringBuilder is assembling JSON text as the default transfer text back to the client side.

For example, in a coming chapter, we'll be building a DataTable and passing it back to the client side for interpretation. We call the DataTable parser from earlier:

```
static void WriteDataTable(StringBuilder sb, DataTable table)
{
    sb.Append("{\"Rows\":[");
    foreach (DataRow row in table.Rows)
    {
        WriteDataRow(sb, row);
        sb.Append(",");
    }
    // Remove the trailing comma.
    if (table.Rows.Count > 0)
    {
        --sb.Length;
    }
    sb.Append("]}");
}
```

Ultimately, a JSON object is created for us that is a representation of a DataTable:

```
{"value":{"Rows":[{"Name":"Basic Bike Company"},
{"Name":"Basic Sports Equipment"},
{"Name":"Beneficial Exercises and Activities"},
{"Name":"Best Cycle Store"},{"Name":"Best o' Bikes"},
{"Name":"Better Bike Shop"},{"Name":"Bicycle Accessories and Kits"},
{"Name":"Bicycle Exporters"},{"Name":"Bicycle Lines Distributors"},
{"Name":"Bicycle Merchandise Warehouse"}]},"error":null}
```

Converting a DataSet continues the same pattern:

```
static void WriteDataSet(StringBuilder sb, DataSet ds)
{
    sb.Append("{\"Tables\":{");
    foreach (DataTable table in ds.Tables)
    {
        sb.AppendFormat("\"{0}\":", table.TableName);
        WriteDataTable(sb, table);
        sb.Append(",");
    }
    // Remove the trailing comma.
    if (ds.Tables.Count > 0)
    {
        --sb.Length;
    }
    sb.Append("}}");
}
```

The preceding code will render the JSON object as

```
{"value":{"Tables":{"stores":{"Rows":
[{"Name":"Basic Bike Company"},
{"Name":"Basic Sports Equipment"},
{"Name":"Beneficial Exercises and Activities"},
{"Name":"Best Cycle Store"},
{"Name":"Best o' Bikes"},
{"Name":"Better Bike Shop"},
{"Name":"Bicycle Accessories and Kits"},
{"Name":"Bicycle Exporters"},
{"Name":"Bicycle Lines Distributors"},
{"Name":"Bicycle Merchandise Warehouse"}]}}},
"error":null}
```

The Anthem library provides these data conversions "out of the box" and, more importantly, they can be modified to fit whatever role Ajax may be taking in your current application.

Summary

In this chapter, we've discussed one of the many Ajax libraries available to .NET developers. I encourage you to experiment with the product, optimizing and extending it to meet your project demands. Also, be sure to keep up with Jason Diamond's blog, as I'm sure that he will continue to update the library as new functionality comes to light.

In the coming chapters, we'll really start pushing the Ajax library as we build sample applications that mimic some of the more popular Ajax web controls that have caught the public eye recently. We've covered a majority of the core knowledge that we'll now need to build truly dynamic web content.

■ ■ ■

CHAPTER 9

Ajax and Web Services

A few years back, web services were all the rage. Microsoft, Sun, and others were touting the technology as the next big thing for online communication. And honestly, I was somewhat intimidated by them. I thought for sure that the acronyms alone would kill me. Tech terms were flying about like crazy: SOAP, XML, REST, WSDL, and DISCO. I also thought anything with that many acronyms must be terribly demanding and difficult to learn. But I knew that if Microsoft was pushing it, I would eventually be forced to jump into the web services water. I was pleasantly surprised and relieved to find that not only was the technology not that difficult, but also Visual Studio encapsulated most of the interface into an easy-to-use project template.

I love it when I can gradually adapt to a new technology, and web services are no different. Either you can choose to be a SOAP-wielding, WSDL-creating, web services guru or you can opt for the quick-and-easy ASP.NET web services project. For the purposes of this book, we'll take the latter approach. This technology can be as hard as you want it to be, but we have enough to worry about with Ajax, so we'll not carry any more load than necessary. I do encourage you to check out Apress' site (http://www.apress.com) for more material on ASP.NET web services.

So What Is a Web Service?

Obviously, you'll want to read this first section if you have had little or no exposure to creating or consuming an ASP.NET 2.0 web service. Otherwise, feel free to skim ahead to the good stuff.

An Internet web service is nothing more than a method of exchanging data on the web. The really cool part is that the service providers are platform independent. Let's say that Joe Johnson of Johnson's Auto Parts wants to have an online part lookup web service for his online retail portal. Joe only knows Java, and he knows it well enough to set up a web service.

Along comes his online buddy, Bob, who would like to help Joe out by setting up an access point on his auto collectors site for users to find rare and discontinued parts. Bob, however, only knows ASP.NET and not Java. Can Bob's auto site still retrieve data from Joe's parts portal? Yes it can, because the beauty of web services is that they communicate in plain XML text. Commonly known as SOAP (Simple Object Access Protocol) envelopes, these textual messages are responsible for transferring the request and response text in an ambiguous fashion.

SOAP

SOAP is structured data and is therefore similar to some of the data that we've already worked with. We'll not dive too deeply into SOAP other than to take a look at the format and usage of the data.

As we discussed earlier, SOAP is an XML dialect. This package is also known as the SOAP envelope. As you would expect, the envelope is responsible for containing data that will be shipped across the web. Inside of an individual envelope, you'll find the header and body sections as is typical with most HTTP activity. Typically, you'll send SOAP envelopes to and from their destination with HTTP POST, so you'll have HTTP instructions in the message as well. With that in mind, understand that the POST request is not entirely XML; however, the contained SOAP package is.

Let's revisit our example from earlier. Johnson's Auto Parts has an online web service. The web service provides many methods from which we can access various part quantities, pricing, and stock levels. In particular, Bob is interested in the GetQuantity method, as he already has a part number and just wants to see whether Joe has the thing lying around. Bob will need to submit a SOAP message to the web service asking for the quantity. His request is similar to the following:

```
POST /Service HTTP/1.1
Host: http://joejohnsonspartshopservice.com
Content-Type: text/xml; charset=utf-8
Content-Length: length
SOAPAction: "http://joejohnsonspartshopservice.com/GetQuantity"

<?xml version="1.0" encoding="utf-8"?>
<soap:Envelope xmlns:xsi="http://www.w3.org/2001/XMLSchema-instance"
 xmlns:xsd="http://www.w3.org/2001/XMLSchema"
 xmlns:soap="http://schemas.xmlsoap.org/soap/envelope/">
  <soap:Body>
    <GetQuantity xmlns="http://joejohnsonspartshopservice.com/">
      <PartNumber>ford0019901</PartNumber>
    </GetQuantity>
  </soap:Body>
</soap:Envelope>
```

Joe's Java-based web service accepts the message, looks up the data, and then returns the following SOAP response:

```
HTTP/1.1 200 OK
Content-Type: text/xml; charset=utf-8
Content-Length: length

<?xml version="1.0" encoding="utf-8"?>
<soap:Envelope xmlns:xsi="http://www.w3.org/2001/XMLSchema-instance"
 xmlns:xsd="http://www.w3.org/2001/XMLSchema"
 xmlns:soap="http://schemas.xmlsoap.org/soap/envelope/">
  <soap:Body>
    <GetQuantityResponse xmlns="http://joejohnsonspartshopservice.com/">
      <GetQuantityResult>5</GetQuantityResult>
    </GetQuantityResponse>
  </soap:Body>
</soap:Envelope>
```

Obviously, this is not from a real web service, as you can tell from the namespace defaults and lack of real data. But it illustrates that SOAP has the HTTP functionality of request and response. Notice the status of 200 from the response, indicating the call was successful. Also notice that Joe's web service takes the original message and concatenates `Response` and `Result` to the respective calls from Bob's message submission.

There are a ton of things that you can do with SOAP messaging that are **WAY** beyond the context of this book. Fortunately for us, we really don't have to do anything with SOAP, so long as we stay within the confines of Visual Studio. It will generate all of these envelopes for us via the web service proxy, allowing us to concentrate on building and consuming web services.

Affecting Ajax

So what does this mean for Ajax? Well two things. As you'll see with the coming demonstration, we are still able to access web service calls from within an asynchronous process in much the same way we are able to call a database. Also, as we migrate or just plain move to Microsoft's Atlas, we'll be able to call the web service directly from the client-side code.

Realistically, we could call a web service with XmlHttpRequest, parse the SOAP message, and make use of the data, but I'd like to concentrate on making use of the Ajax libraries that we have available to use now. As I've said before, keep abreast of the various libraries available; I'm sure that the functionality will be there eventually. But for now, we'll do things the n-tier way and keep our service calls on the server side.

Creating the Web Service

This would be a good time to go ahead and create a web service that we'll publish and make available to our Ajax-enabled applications.

Start Visual Studio 2005 and then select File ➤ New ➤ Web Site.

When you're presented with the project type selection, click ASP.NET Web Service. Before clicking OK, we need to make a few other changes to this particular window. Because we are building a web service, we should make this available to IIS. In the Location drop-down, select HTTP. You'll also notice that you're presented with new options now, as shown in Figure 9-1.

Click Browse. A new window will appear. We'll create a virtual directory to hold our web service and give it a permanent location on the computer.

Select IIS on the left and then select Create New Web Application as shown in Figure 9-2.

Name the application wsAdventureWorks and click OK.

When you return to the New Web Site window, you can now choose OK and let Visual Studio build the project (finally).

Your solution should look very similar to that of Figure 9-3.

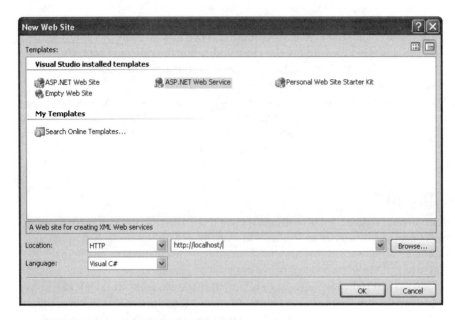

Figure 9-1. *Creating the HTTP Web Service*

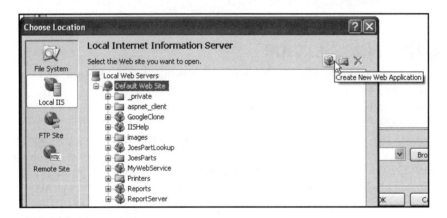

Figure 9-2. *Creating an IIS application*

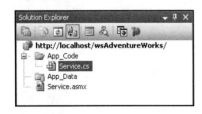

Figure 9-3. *wsAdventureWorks solution files*

We're finally ready to write some code. Let's first take care of some housekeeping in our
.cs file. We have some default namespaces that we should modify. You don't have to use a real
website, as they are really just for distinctive data separation. By implementing a proper naming schema for your namespaces, you'll avoid collisions with other published web services.

```
using System;
using System.Web;
using System.Web.Services;
using System.Web.Services.Protocols;

[WebService(Namespace = "http://adventureworksSystem.com/")]
[WebServiceBinding(ConformsTo = WsiProfiles.BasicProfile1_1)]
public class Service : System.Web.Services.WebService
{
    public Service () {
        // Uncomment the following line if using designed components
        //InitializeComponent();
    }

    [WebMethod]
    public string HelloWorld() {
        return "Hello World";
    }

}
```

We will leave the HelloWorld method in there for now. We'll modify that in a moment.

Save your project so that you won't have to do this all over again if something happens
to your PC.

So now we have this generic web service ready for some functionality. But what do we
want it to do? Let's model our web service after our earlier data lookup and provide a simple
parameter/lookup database query. Our AdventureWorks database has a Production.Product
table with a multitude of products. Let's build a web service that returns a DataSet of products
that have a list price that is equal to, or less than, a dollar value that we will supply as a parameter. We'll be implementing a single WebMethod to return a list of products based on the current
price limitation. Modify Service.cs as follows:

```
using System;
using System.Web;
using System.Web.Services;
using System.Web.Services.Protocols;
using System.Data;
using System.Data.SqlClient;
```

```
[WebService(Namespace = "http://adventureworksSystem.com/")]
[WebServiceBinding(ConformsTo = WsiProfiles.BasicProfile1_1)]
public class Service : System.Web.Services.WebService
{
    public Service()
    {
        // Uncomment the following line if using designed components
        //InitializeComponent();
    }


    [WebMethod]
    public DataSet GetProducts(decimal MaxAmount)
    {
        SqlConnection conn = new SqlConnection("Data Source=(local); ➥
Initial Catalog=AdventureWorks;Integrated Security=SSPI");
        DataSet dsReturn = new DataSet();

        conn.Open();
        // Go get the products where the price is less than
        //  or equal to the parameter
        SqlCommand cmd = new SqlCommand("Select ProductID, Name,
         ListPrice from Production.Product
         where ListPrice <= @maxamount and ListPrice <> 0", conn);
        SqlParameter param = new SqlParameter();
        param.ParameterName = "@maxamount";
        param.Value = MaxAmount;
        cmd.Parameters.Add(param););

        SqlDataAdapter adpt = new SqlDataAdapter(cmd);

        adpt.Fill(dsReturn, "Products");

        conn.Close();
        return dsReturn;
    }
}
```

Before we build and try out the web service, you'll want to verify that the ASPNET user account has rights to the AdventureWorks database, if you're going to use SSPI security.

Add the preceding code to your .cs file and save your work.

Now let's take a look at the process of invoking our web service. One of the coolest features of Visual Studio is that it provides functionality to demo your web service before you turn it loose to the world. It's a pretty straightforward process, and you'll find that the interface is easy to use.

Start your project in Visual Studio. After a moment, Internet Explorer will present you with the screen shown in Figure 9-4.

Figure 9-4. *Sampling the service*

Our interface is presenting for our review the available web methods for the called service. In our case, we have only one: GetProducts. We made that particular function available in the code by prefixing the function name with the WebMethod attribute:

```
[WebMethod]
public DataSet GetProducts(decimal MaxAmount)
{...}
```

To demo this function, we simply click the hyperlink and wait while we are given the interactive portion of the service, as shown in Figure 9-5.

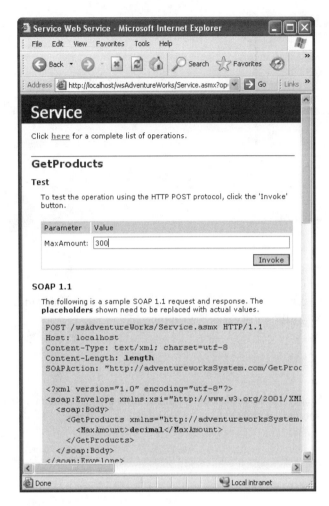

Figure 9-5. *Adding parameters*

We supply the parameters for our call and click the Invoke button. The results are delivered to us via XML, as shown in Figure 9-6.

As you can see from scrolling through the results, we have a ton of information returned. We could refine our SQL string to pare the results down to a few fields, but we'll leave that for another day. For now, go ahead and stop debugging the application and close Visual Studio 2005.

Figure 9-6. *Web service results*

Building the Ajax Application

Now that we have a running web service out on IIS, let's continue with web services implementation by building a simple client that will make a call to the service and return the results.

Start Visual Studio 2005 and create a new ASP.NET website as we've done before. Don't forget to set your Location back to File System, as shown in Figure 9-7.

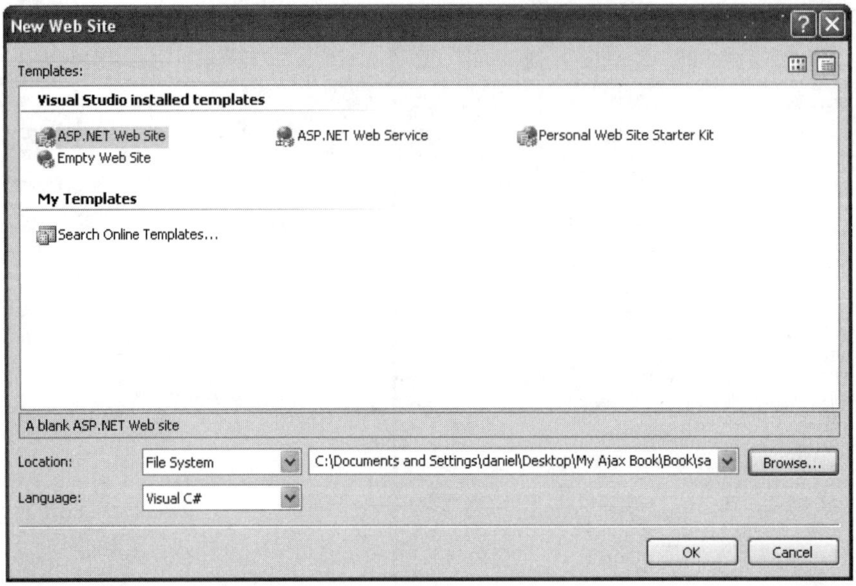

Figure 9-7. *Creating a new website*

After Visual Studio prepares our project files, we'll need to add a web reference so that we'll have access to the web service via our code. Right-click the project name and choose Add Web Reference, as shown in Figure 9-8.

Figure 9-8. *Adding a web reference*

You'll be asked to browse for web services. You'll want to click the Web Services on the Local Machine link. The application will spend a moment searching your box for running web services. After a moment, it will present you with any running services that you may have on IIS.

You should be able to see your service listed with the accompanying wsAdventureWorks information. Click the Service link. You'll visit a familiar page listing the available methods as you've seen before when sampling the web service. We need to change the web reference name as it appears in Figure 9-9.

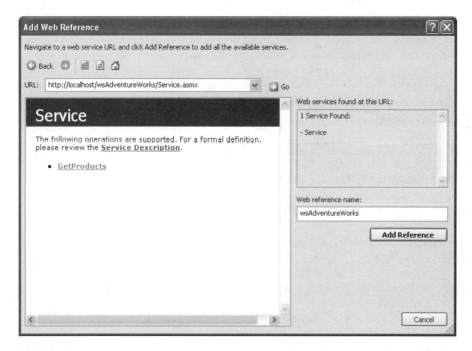

Figure 9-9. *Adding our reference*

After changing the name, click the Add Reference button. Our web service will now be added to the list of references for our project. You'll also notice that Visual Studio adds a few things for good measure: Service.disco, Service.discomap, and Service.wsdl.

Service.disco and Service.discomap help outside resources locate the web service. Service.wsdl describes what the web service is capable of.

Let's start working with our new web service via code by first building the user interface, as shown in Figure 9-10.

Figure 9-10. *The client interface*

We only need the text, textbox, and button for this particular example. Modify your Default.aspx code to reflect the following:

```
<%@ Page Language="C#" AutoEventWireup="true"
 CodeFile="Default.aspx.cs" Inherits="_Default" %>

<!DOCTYPE html PUBLIC "-//W3C//DTD XHTML 1.0 Transitional//EN"
 "http://www.w3.org/TR/xhtml1/DTD/xhtml1-transitional.dtd">
```

```html
<html xmlns="http://www.w3.org/1999/xhtml" >
  <head runat="server">
    <title>Web Service Test</title>
  </head>
  <body>
    <script type="text/javascript" language="javascript">
    function GetProductsList()
    {
        var maxamount = document.getElementById("txtPrice").value;

        Anthem_InvokePageMethod('GetProducts', [maxamount], ProductsCallback);
    }
    function ProductsCallback(response)
    {
        var findDiv = document.getElementById("divResults");
        findDiv.innerHTML = response.value;
    }
    </script>

    <form id="frmWebServiceTest" runat="server">
      <div>
        Enter Max Price: 
        <asp:TextBox ID="txtPrice" runat="server"
                     autocomplete="off"></asp:TextBox> 
        <button id="btnGo" onclick="GetProductsList();">
          Go!</button>
        <br />
        <div id="divResults"></div>
      </div>
    </form>
  </body>
</html>
```

Most, if not all, of this code should be very familiar from the preceding chapter's demo application. We have a pair of calling and callback JavaScript functions that hit the server side as a result of the button's onclick event. The text is generated and returned via the response object and will be sent out to the div tag's innerHTML.

Let's take a look at how we're communicating with the web service on the server side:

```csharp
using System;
using System.Data;
using System.Configuration;
using System.Web;
using System.Web.Security;
using System.Web.UI;
using System.Web.UI.WebControls;
using System.Web.UI.WebControls.WebParts;
using System.Web.UI.HtmlControls;
using System.Text;
```

```
public partial class _Default : System.Web.UI.Page
{
    protected void Page_Load(object sender, EventArgs e)
    {
        // Dont forget to register your pages!
        Anthem.Manager.Register(this);
    }


     [Anthem.Method]
    public string GetProducts(string maxPrice)
    {
        decimal maxAmount = Decimal.Parse(maxPrice);

        DataSet newData = new DataSet();

        // Create a new instance of the web service
        wsAdventureWorks.Service myWebService = new wsAdventureWorks.Service();

        // Now assign the output of the web service to our DataSet
        newData = myWebService.GetProducts(maxAmount);


        StringBuilder sb = new StringBuilder();

        // Iterate thru the table rows, building an HTML table as we go
        if (newData.Tables["Products"].Rows.Count > 0)
        {
            sb.Append("<table>");
            sb.Append("<tr><td>Product ID</td><td>Product Name</td>
             <td>List Price</td></tr>");

            foreach(DataRow dr in newData.Tables["Products"].Rows)
            {
                sb.Append("<tr>");
                sb.Append("<td>");
                sb.Append(dr["ProductID"]);
                sb.Append("</td>");
                sb.Append("<td>");
                sb.Append(dr["Name"]);
                sb.Append("</td>");
                sb.Append("<td align='right'>");
                sb.Append(String.Format("{0:c}", dr["ListPrice"]));
                sb.Append("</td>");
                sb.Append("</tr>");
            }
            sb.Append("</table>");
        }
```

```
        // We'll return the HTML table to the client side for
        // assignment to the innerHTML property
        return sb.ToString();
    }
}
```

We have only one Ajax method in this sample application, and its primary responsibility is to invoke the web service method and manipulate the results.

We must first instantiate the web service:

```
wsAdventureWorks.Service myWebService = new wsAdventureWorks.Service();
```

And then we invoke the GetProducts method:

```
newData = myWebService.GetProducts(maxAmount);
```

Once the data is returned, we simply parse through it, building an HTML table as we go. That table is then returned back to the callback function on the client where it is assigned to the divResults innerHTML property:

```
function ProductsCallback(response)
{
    var findDiv = document.getElementById("divResults");
    findDiv.innerHTML = response.value;
}
```

Once we run the application, we're asked to input an amount. Let's enter 125 and click the Go! button. Our results are fetched from the web service asynchronously and displayed as expected (see Figure 9-11).

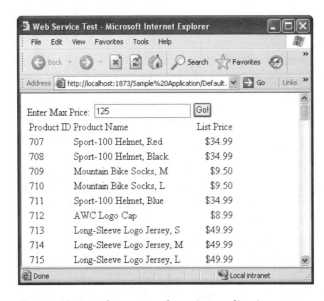

Figure 9-11. *Asynchronous web service application*

So there you have it. We have built an Ajax application that can access web services asynchronously. There really is little difference between this and a database application implementing the same Ajax library. We simply point our Ajax method content toward an Internet web service rather than a data store.

Accessing with XmlHttpRequest

OK, at this point you may be asking the question, "But what if I **really** want to access a web service from the client side?" As I've said before, aside from Atlas, most modern Ajax libraries do not have an implementation available for client-side access. It is possible, however, to use the XmlHttpRequest object to communicate with those pesky web services. As the developers, we will have to write the code to parse the inbound and outbound XML, as we'll be stepping outside of the Ajax library comfort zone. But this can be done, and I would do you a great disservice if I didn't at least show you how.

Using the same WebSite project from the previous example (the one we just finished), right-click the project name and select Add New Item. We'll be adding a new Web Form, naming it xhrAccess.aspx as shown in Figure 9-12.

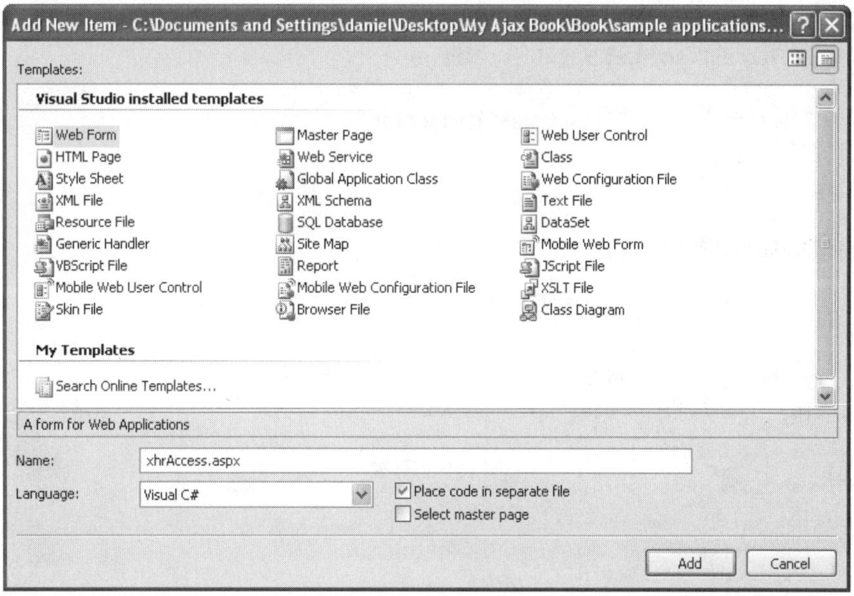

Figure 9-12. *Adding the new form*

Because we'll be doing everything with JavaScript, we don't need to concern ourselves with registration of Ajax library components. We'll not be making any use of the library at all, in fact.

We will, however, be drawing on previous chapter code, and you may find it easier to just copy and paste from those appropriate chapter examples rather than typing it from the book.

To communicate with a web service with only the XmlHttpRequest object, our application will need to accomplish a few things:

- Instantiate a cross-browser XmlHttpRequest object.

- Create a SOAP envelope for transmission.

- Parse the XML-SOAP results on the client side.

- Display the parsed XML on the client.

Let's take a look at the complete .aspx code and then I'll describe the individual sections in detail:

```
<%@ Page Language="C#" AutoEventWireup="true"
 CodeFile="xhrAccess.aspx.cs" Inherits="xhrAccess" %>

<!DOCTYPE html PUBLIC "-//W3C//DTD XHTML 1.0 Transitional//EN"
 "http://www.w3.org/TR/xhtml1/DTD/xhtml1-transitional.dtd">

<html xmlns="http://www.w3.org/1999/xhtml" >
  <head runat="server">
    <title>XmlHttpRequest and Web Services</title>
  </head>
  <script type="text/javascript" language="javascript">
  var xmlhttp = false;
  var objXmlDoc;

  function getHTTPRequestObject()
  {
      try
      {
          // Try legacy object first
          xmlhttp = new ActiveXObject("Msxml2.XMLHTTP");
      }
      catch(e)
      {
          try
          {
              // Try IE implementation now
              xmlhttp = new ActiveXObject("Microsoft.XMLHTTP");
          }
          catch(E)
          {
              xmlhttp = false;
          }
      }
```

```
    if(!xmlhttp && typeof XMLHttpRequest!= 'undefined')
    {
        // We must be using a Mozilla-based browser
        // so create a native request object now
        xmlhttp = new XMLHttpRequest();
    }
}

function GetProductsList()
{
    // Instantiate XmlHttpRequest object
    getHTTPRequestObject();

    // First get the textbox value.
    var maxamount = document.getElementById("txtPrice").value;

    var serviceUrl = "http://localhost/wsAdventureWorks/Service.asmx";
    var serviceNamespace = "http://adventureworksSystem.com/Products"

    // Build the SOAP envelope now
    var strEnvelope = "<soap:Envelope xmlns:xsi=\"http://www.w3.org/2001/
    XMLSchema-instance\"" +
     " xmlns:xsd=\"http://www.w3.org/2001/XMLSchema\" " +
     " xmlns:soap=\"http://schemas.xmlsoap.org/soap/envelope/\">\n" +
     "  <soap:Body>\n" +
     "    <GetProducts xmlns=\"http://adventureworksSystem.com/Products\" >\n" +
     "        <MaxAmount>" + maxamount + "</MaxAmount>\n" +
     "    </GetProducts>" + "  </soap:Body>" + "</soap:Envelope>";

    var serviceAction = serviceNamespace + "/GetProducts";

    xmlhttp.open("POST", serviceUrl, true);

    // Assign the callback function
    xmlhttp.onreadystatechange = processResults;
    xmlhttp.setRequestHeader("Content-Type", "text/xml");
    xmlhttp.setRequestHeader("SOAPAction", serviceAction);
    xmlhttp.send(strEnvelope);

}
```

```
function processResults()
{
    if (xmlhttp.readyState == 4)
    {
        if (xmlhttp.status == 200)
        {
            // Create the XML object
            objXmlDoc = new ActiveXObject("Msxml2.DOMDocument");

            var serviceResponse = xmlhttp.responseText;

            objXmlDoc.loadXML(serviceResponse);

            if (objXmlDoc.parseError.errorCode != 0)
            {
                var xmlErr = objXmlDoc.parseError;
                alert("oops: " + xmlErr.reason);
            }
            else
            {
                ParseDataSet();
            }
        }
        else
        {
            alert(xmlhttp.statusText);
        }
    }
}

function ParseDataSet()
{
    objNodeList = objXmlDoc.getElementsByTagName("Products");

    var stringout = "";
    if(objNodeList.length > 0)
    {
        stringout = "<table>" +
        "<tr><td>Product ID</td><td>Name</td><td>List Price</td></tr>";
```

```
        }
    for (var i = 0; i < objNodeList.length; i++)
    {
        var dataNodeList;
        var ProductIDNode;
        var ProductNameNode;

        dataNodeList = objNodeList[i];

        ProductIDNode = getParsedElement(dataNodeList, "ProductID");
        ProductNameNode = getParsedElement(dataNodeList, "Name");
        PriceNode = getParsedElement(dataNodeList, "ListPrice");

        stringout = stringout + "<tr><td>" + ProductIDNode + "</td><td>" +
         ProductNameNode + "</td><td align='right'>" + PriceNode + "</td></tr>";

    }
    if(objNodeList.length > 0)
    {
        stringout = stringout + "</table>";
    }
    document.getElementById("divResults").innerHTML = stringout;
}

function getParsedElement(source, child)
{
    var childNode = source.getElementsByTagName(child);
    return childNode[0].firstChild.nodeValue;
}
</script>

<body>
  <form id="frmXHRWS" runat="server">
    <div>
      Enter Max Price: 
      <asp:TextBox ID="txtPrice" runat="server"></asp:TextBox>
      <button id="btnGo" onclick="GetProductsList();" type="button">
        Go!</button>
      <br />
      <div id="divResults"></div>
    </div>
  </form>
</body>
</html>
```

The preceding HTML has set up our user interface in the same fashion as the previous demo (see Figure 9-13).

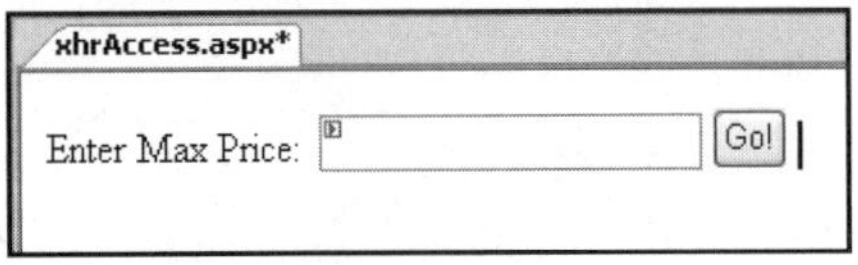

Figure 9-13. *User interface*

The onclick event of our button kick starts the GetProductsList() function and ultimately leads to the creation of the XmlHttpRequest object. We need a function that will create the object with inclusive cross-browser support:

```
function getHTTPRequestObject()
{
    try
    {
        // Try legacy object first
        xmlhttp = new ActiveXObject("Msxml2.XMLHTTP");
    }
    catch(e)
    {
        try
        {
            // Try IE implementation now
            xmlhttp = new ActiveXObject("Microsoft.XMLHTTP");
        }
        catch(E)
        {
            xmlhttp = false;
        }
    }
    if(!xmlhttp && typeof XMLHttpRequest!= 'undefined')
    {
        // We must be using a Mozilla-based browser
        // so create a native request object now
        xmlhttp = new XMLHttpRequest();
    }
}
```

This particular routine should be familiar to you, as you've seen it before in Chapter 3. We simply instantiate an XmlHttpRequest object dependent on the client's browser and assign it to a page-level variable. Once we've accomplished this, we'll have full access to all of the functionality that we'll need to asynchronously call the web service.

We will need a placeholder for the web service location and namespace, as we will be assigning them to our delivered message as well:

```
var serviceUrl = "http://localhost/wsAdventureWorks/Service.asmx";
var serviceNamespace = "http://adventureworksSystem.com/Products"
```

Because we are calling a web service, we'll need to create a SOAP envelope manually. This is not as difficult as it seems. When we ran the web service after creating it in Visual Studio, the test harness actually gave us some pointers on how we could possibly build the SOAP POST for ourselves, as shown in Figure 9-14.

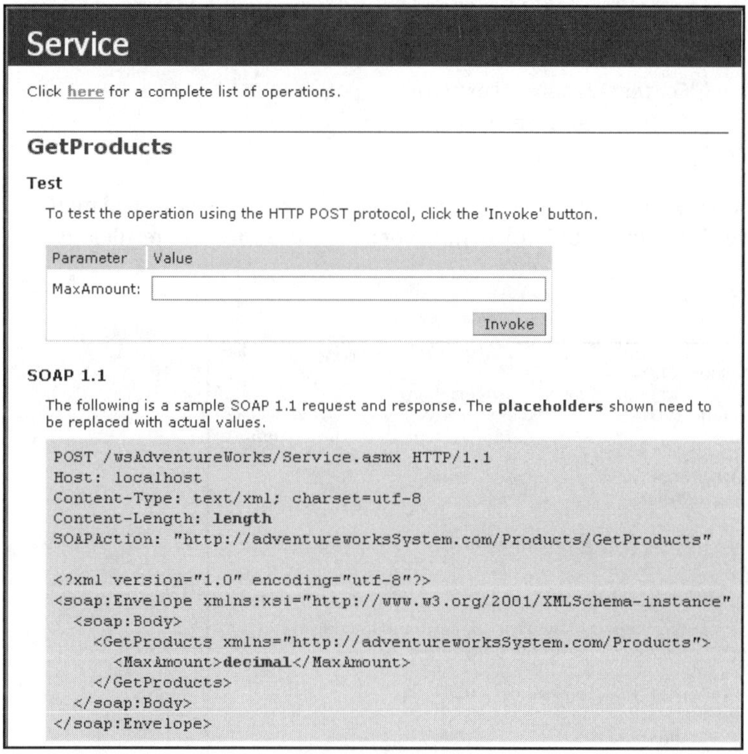

Figure 9-14. *Test harness for the web service*

As you can see, the XML structure for the SOAP message is laid out for us. We will fashion our own envelope based on this information.

We build the SOAP envelope as shown:

```
// Build the SOAP envelope now
var strEnvelope = "<soap:Envelope xmlns:xsi=\"http://www.w3.org/2001/
  XMLSchema-instance\"" +
  " xmlns:xsd=\"http://www.w3.org/2001/XMLSchema\" " +
  " xmlns:soap=\"http://schemas.xmlsoap.org/soap/envelope/\">\n" +
  " <soap:Body>\n" +
  "   <GetProducts xmlns=\"http://adventureworksSystem.com/Products\" >\n" +
  "     <MaxAmount>" + maxamount + "</MaxAmount>\n" +
  "   </GetProducts>" + "   </soap:Body>" + "</soap:Envelope>";
```

As you can see, we're dynamically assigning the MaxAmount parameter value to the body of the SOAP envelope, based on the value found in the text field:

```
var maxamount = document.getElementById("txtPrice").value;
```

We need to tell the XmlHttpRequest object which function we would like to have handle the return data once the objects request status has completed:

```
xmlhttp.onreadystatechange = processResults;
```

We'll take a look at the processResults() function in a moment, but first we must assign the various POST attributes and send the asynchronous call on its way:

```
xmlhttp.setRequestHeader("Content-Type", "text/xml");
xmlhttp.setRequestHeader("SOAPAction", serviceAction);
xmlhttp.send(strEnvelope);
```

The SOAP package will work its way out to the web service, invoke the appropriate method, and return with a serialized DataSet of our information. For a MaxAmount of 4, our result is as shown in Figure 9-15.

```xml
<?xml version="1.0" encoding="utf-8" ?>
- <DataSet xmlns="http://adventureworksSystem.com/Products">
  - <xs:schema id="NewDataSet" xmlns=""
      xmlns:xs="http://www.w3.org/2001/XMLSchema" xmlns:msdata="urn:schemas-
      microsoft-com:xml-msdata">
    - <xs:element name="NewDataSet" msdata:IsDataSet="true"
        msdata:UseCurrentLocale="true">
      - <xs:complexType>
        + <xs:choice minOccurs="0" maxOccurs="unbounded">
        </xs:complexType>
      </xs:element>
    </xs:schema>
  - <diffgr:diffgram xmlns:msdata="urn:schemas-microsoft-com:xml-msdata"
      xmlns:diffgr="urn:schemas-microsoft-com:xml-diffgram-v1">
    - <NewDataSet xmlns="">
      - <Products diffgr:id="Products1" msdata:rowOrder="0">
          <ProductID>873</ProductID>
          <Name>Patch Kit/8 Patches</Name>
          <ListPrice>2.2900</ListPrice>
        </Products>
      - <Products diffgr:id="Products2" msdata:rowOrder="1">
          <ProductID>922</ProductID>
          <Name>Road Tire Tube</Name>
          <ListPrice>3.9900</ListPrice>
        </Products>
      </NewDataSet>
    </diffgr:diffgram>
  </DataSet>
```

Figure 9-15. *The full XML results*

We'll receive this information back on the client side, within the callback function:

```
function processResults()
{
    if (xmlhttp.readyState == 4)
    {
        if (xmlhttp.status == 200)
        {
            // Create the XML object
            objXmlDoc = new ActiveXObject("Msxml2.DOMDocument");

            var serviceResponse = xmlhttp.responseText;

            objXmlDoc.loadXML(serviceResponse);

            if (objXmlDoc.parseError.errorCode != 0)
            {
                var xmlErr = objXmlDoc.parseError;
                alert("oops: " + xmlErr.reason);
            }
            else
            {
                ParseDataSet();
            }
        }
        else
        {
            alert(xmlhttp.statusText);
        }
    }
}
```

The DataSet has now made its way to the client side, but in its serialized state there isn't much that we can do with it on the browser. We'll need to parse the data by calling the ParseDataSet() function. Within that function, we'll iterate through the XML nodes, building an HTML table for assignment to the div's innerHTML property:

```
function ParseDataSet()
{
    objNodeList = objXmlDoc.getElementsByTagName("Products");

    var stringout = "";
    if(objNodeList.length > 0)
    {
        stringout = "<table>" +
        "<tr><td>Product ID</td><td>Name</td><td>List Price</td></tr>";

    }
    for (var i = 0; i < objNodeList.length; i++)
    {
        var dataNodeList;
        var ProductIDNode;
        var ProductNameNode;
```

```
        dataNodeList = objNodeList[i];

        ProductIDNode = getParsedElement(dataNodeList, "ProductID");
        ProductNameNode = getParsedElement(dataNodeList, "Name");
        PriceNode = getParsedElement(dataNodeList, "ListPrice");

        stringout = stringout + "<tr><td>" + ProductIDNode + "</td><td>" +
         ProductNameNode + "</td><td align='right'>" + PriceNode + "</td></tr>";
    }
    if(objNodeList.length > 0)
    {
        stringout = stringout + "</table>";
    }
    document.getElementById("divResults").innerHTML = stringout;
}

function getParsedElement(source, child)
{
    var childNode = source.getElementsByTagName(child);
    return childNode[0].firstChild.nodeValue;
}
```

All of the Ajax functionality is handled on the client side. The server side coding is void of any content:

```
using System;
using System.Data;
using System.Configuration;
using System.Collections;
using System.Web;
using System.Web.Security;
using System.Web.UI;
using System.Web.UI.WebControls;
using System.Web.UI.WebControls.WebParts;
using System.Web.UI.HtmlControls;

public partial class xhrAccess : System.Web.UI.Page
{
    protected void Page_Load(object sender, EventArgs e)
    {
        // Nothing here but an empty shell
    }
}
```

After running the application, we discover that the output is nearly identical to that of the ASP.NET server-side application that we wrote earlier, as you see in Figure 9-16.

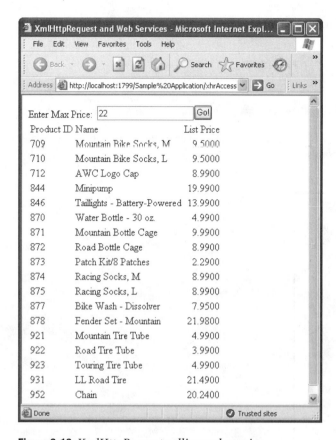

Figure 9-16. *XmlHttpRequest calling web service*

Well, it almost looks the same. Our List Price column is not formatted for currency standards as it was with the .NET version. Before we were able to do a String.Format function call, but we are working in JavaScript now and must make use of a custom function to accomplish that formatting:

```
function formatCurrency(amount)
{
    var i = parseFloat(amount);
    if(isNaN(i)) { i = 0.00; }
    var minus = '';
    if(i < 0) { minus = '-'; }
    i = Math.abs(i);
    i = parseInt((i + .005) * 100);
    i = i / 100;
    s = new String(i);
    if(s.indexOf('.') < 0) { s += '.00'; }
    if(s.indexOf('.') == (s.length - 2)) { s += '0'; }
    s = minus + s;
    return s;
}
```

Simply modify the table row builder so that the List Price column is run through the formatter:

```
stringout = stringout + "<tr><td>" + ProductIDNode +
  "</td><td>" + ProductNameNode +
  "</td><td align='right'>" +
  formatCurrency(PriceNode) + "</td></tr>";
```

And now our results are in line with the previous .NET server-side application from earlier in the chapter, as Figure 9-17 illustrates.

Enter Max Price: 33		Go!
Product ID	Name	List Price
709	Mountain Bike Socks, M	9.50
710	Mountain Bike Socks, L	9.50
712	AWC Logo Cap	8.99
843	Cable Lock	25.00
844	Minipump	19.99
845	Mountain Pump	24.99
846	Taillights - Battery-Powered	13.99
858	Half-Finger Gloves, S	24.49
859	Half-Finger Gloves, M	24.49
860	Half-Finger Gloves, L	24.49
870	Water Bottle - 30 oz.	4.99
871	Mountain Bottle Cage	9.99
872	Road Bottle Cage	8.99
873	Patch Kit/8 Patches	2.29
874	Racing Socks, M	8.99
875	Racing Socks, L	8.99
877	Bike Wash - Dissolver	7.95
878	Fender Set - Mountain	21.98

Figure 9-17. *Formatted List Price column*

Summary

So we have successfully accessed a web service with only an XmlHttpRequest object and nothing more. Having witnessed the various parsing and intricacies of the SOAP envelope, perhaps you can see why I had claimed earlier that it is far easier to access web services from server-side code than from manually constructed client-side functions. Implementing an Ajax method, with web service functionality, is unbelievably easier and faster to roll out.

In the following chapters, we will continue to work with the Ajax library, building even more sample applications from which we can continue to derive various tidbits of information that we'll carry on to other Ajax projects.

CHAPTER 10

■ ■ ■

Tagging with Ajax

It seems that just about everybody these days has a Flickr (http://www.flickr.com) account for hosting and distributing pictures.

While the idea of free image hosting has been around for quite some time, where Flickr differs is in its usage of tagging. Essentially, tagging is nothing more than associating some text with a particular object. Let's say you've just uploaded pictures of your one-year-old child with a face full of their very first chocolate birthday cake. Another registered user can browse your images and add a tag to the cheesy-grinned birthday boy that might read "Cute" or perhaps "Messy." That particular text becomes a "bookmarked" tag within the Flickr system. Now imagine that there are 3,000 other images out there that have been tagged with the text "Messy." Browsing to the tag lists generated by the site (as shown in Figure 10-1) and clicking the aforementioned link would bring up thumbnails of 3,000 various images.

All time most popular tags

Figure 10-1. *Flickr's tag cloud*

What the site has done is put the power and responsibility of content classification into the hands of the very users themselves! That's an awesome concept for community building!

Of particular interest to us, in the context of this chapter, is the actual tagging portion of Flickr's site, whereby users enter their tags and the Ajax code asynchronously delivers and updates the users' text. We'll build a sample application to replicate that behavior, and you'll be able to see firsthand the introductory steps needed for asynchronous interaction between your server-side code layer and your client-side interface.

Obviously we're going to need a few things before we get started. In the sample code for Chapter 10, you'll find not only the Visual Studio WebSite files, but also a SQL script for creating the database and table needed for this example. Before running the script against the database, we need to create a database as the destination. In Enterprise Manager, create a new database on the server, naming it AjaxTaggingSample. Now open Query Analyzer and execute the script to create and populate the tagging database:

```
USE [AjaxTaggingSample]
GO
SET ANSI_NULLS ON
GO
SET QUOTED_IDENTIFIER ON
GO
SET ANSI_PADDING ON
GO
CREATE TABLE [dbo].[ImageTags](
        [id] [int] IDENTITY(1,1) NOT NULL,
        [ImageID] [int] NULL,
        [TagName] [varchar](50) COLLATE SQL_Latin1_General_CP1_CI_AS NULL
) ON [PRIMARY]

GO

USE [AjaxTaggingSample]
GO

Insert into ImageTags (ImageID, TagName)
select 1, 'Kids'
union all
select 2, 'Hockey'
union all
select 3, 'Gotcha!'
```

```
union all
select 3, 'Cheesy'
union all
select 4, 'Prowler'

GO


SET ANSI_PADDING OFF
```

After a successful execution, you should be able to browse the table and find a few tags waiting for the application's use.

If you're not using Microsoft SQL Server or SQL Server Express, don't worry. Just create a database and table structure in your preferred database platform as demonstrated in the following steps and verify your connection string information in the sample code.

Creating the Database

Your database should be named AjaxTaggingSample to avoid naming conflicts with the sample code. Create a table with the structure and columns as shown in Figure 10-2.

Table - dbo.ImageTags		
Column Name	Data Type	Allow Nulls
id	int	☐
ImageID	int	☑
TagName	varchar(50)	☑
		☐

Figure 10-2. *ImageTags table*

If you're not going to execute the SQL script included with the chapter download (available from the Apress Source Code web page at http://www.apress.com/book/download.html), you'll want to populate the table now with some preexisting data for the images we'll display later.

___

■Note The column id is an identity column, typical with most lookup tables. It should auto-increment with each row entered.

___

Use Figure 10-3 as a guide for entering sample data into the ImageTags table.

After you've finished creating the database and entering the sample information, you'll be ready for the Ajax tagging sample!

Table - dbo.ImageTags		
id	ImageID	TagName
1	1	Kids
2	2	Hockey
3	3	Gotcha!
4	3	Cheesy
5	4	Prowler
NULL	*NULL*	*NULL*

Figure 10-3. *Sample tags*

The Tagging Application

Now let's take a look at the Visual Studio project that you've hopefully downloaded from the Apress Source Code web page. You should find within the WebSite a variety of components, as shown in Figure 10-4.

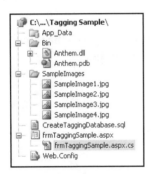

Figure 10-4. *Tagging application structure*

Our `Anthem.dll` encapsulates the functionality of the XMLHttpRequest object; without it our application will sit lifeless and dull. Throughout the chapter, when I refer to the "Ajax class," I'm referring to our `Anthem.dll` and its functionality.

So we have the application downloaded, open, and ready to go. We have our database set up and ready for action, so let's not disappoint it! Fire up the sample program and let's see what the end result should be, which should look like what appears in Figure 10-5, and then come back to the chapter and dissect the project.

When the web page loads, you'll be greeted by four awesome pictures that I've included within the `SampleImages` folder. As you move the mouse across each image, you'll notice that it becomes "clickable." Clicking an image will then begin the amazing asynchronous process of going out to the database, retrieving the tags, and returning to populate your page with the appropriate information. Did you notice something incredible? No postback! Everything happened behind the scenes via our Ajax class and its ability to submit and accept the XML request. The application also allows us to enter and delete our own tags, rounding off a complete user tagging experience.

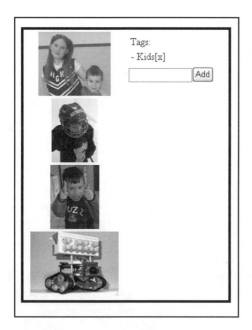

Figure 10-5. *Sample application in action*

First you should examine the client-side HTML, so that you'll understand how the client's actions kicked off the first round of events.

HTML Code

Take a moment to read through the HTML code:

```
<%@ Page Language="C#" AutoEventWireup="true"
 CodeFile="frmTaggingSample.aspx.cs"
Inherits="frmTaggingSample" %>

<!DOCTYPE html PUBLIC "-//W3C//DTD XHTML 1.0 Transitional//EN"
"http://www.w3.org/TR/xhtml1/DTD/xhtml1-transitional.dtd">

<html xmlns="http://www.w3.org/1999/xhtml" >
      <head>
            <title>Sample Tagging Application</title>
        <script language="javascript" type="text/javascript">
        // Let's establish a placeholder variable for storing the user's
        // selected image ID here
        var currentImage = null;
```

```
function LoadTags(imageID)
{
// We'll call our Ajax method within the CSharp file from here
// and redirect the resulting data to the Callback function.
    Anthem_InvokePageMethod('LoadImageTags',[imageID] , LoadTagsCallBack);
    currentImage = imageID
}

function LoadTagsCallBack(result)
{
// Our tags have been loaded and the result.value
// will contain the HTML table that we build on the
// code side. We'll find the DIV tag in the document
// and then "bind" the new HTML to the innerHTML
// property.
    var thisElement = document.getElementById('divTags');
    thisElement.innerHTML = result.value;
}

function AddTag()
{
// We'll store the current image ID in the hidden control
// so that we can demonstrate Page access later. We'll
// also use that value for our Insert statement as well.
    var findthis = document.getElementById('hidImageID');
    findthis.value = currentImage;

// We'll add a tag to the images database collection of tags.
// To do that we'll make use of the hidden control's viewstate to
// store the ID of the last image selected. This will give you a
// chance to see Ajax's ability to access the Page state.
    var thisElement = document.getElementById('txtTagName');
    Anthem_InvokePageMethod('AddTag',[thisElement.value] ,
    AddTagCallBack);
}


function AddTagCallBack(result)
{
// After the tag has been entered we'll come back here for display.
    LoadTags(currentImage);

// Let's remove the user's entry from the textbox now that the
// tag has been entered and posted.
    var findTextBox = document.getElementById('txtTagName');
    findTextBox.value = '';

}
```

```
function DeleteTag(imageID, tagName)
      {
      // We'll allow the user the ability to delete a tag from a particular image.
      // Again we'll need to use the image ID stored in the hidden control as a
      // reference for which image to delete against the tagging database.

            var findthis = document.getElementById('hidImageID');
            findthis.value = imageID;

      // Now the call is made to the code-side method for deletion.
      // We provide the tag name as the first parameter and the Java-side callback
      // function for the return trip.
            Anthem_InvokePageMethod('DeleteTag',[tagName] , DeleteTagCallBack);

      }

      function DeleteTagCallBack(result)
      {
      // After deleting the tag, we'll redisplay the list again.
            LoadTags(currentImage);
      }

      </script>
</head>
      <body>
            <form id="Form1" method="post" runat="server">
            <table style="BORDER-RIGHT: black solid;
             BORDER-TOP: black solid;
             BORDER-LEFT: black solid;
             WIDTH: 336px;
             BORDER-BOTTOM: black solid;
             HEIGHT: 414px">
            <tr>
            <td valign="top" align="center">

                  <div id="divImage1"
                   onmouseover="this.style.cursor='hand';"
                   onclick="LoadTags(1);" runat="server">
                  <img src="SampleImages\SampleImage1.JPG"
                    alt="SampleImage1" />
                  </div>

                  <div id="divImage2"
                   onmouseover="this.style.cursor='hand';"
                   onclick="LoadTags(2);" runat="server">
                  <img src="SampleImages\SampleImage2.JPG"
                   alt="SampleImage2" />
                  </div>
```

```
                        <div id="divImage3"
                         onmouseover="this.style.cursor='hand';"
                         onclick="LoadTags(3);" runat="server">
                        <img src="SampleImages\SampleImage3.JPG"
                         alt="SampleImage3" />
                        </div>

                        <div id="divImage4"
                         onmouseover="this.style.cursor='hand';"
                         onclick="LoadTags(4);" runat="server">
                        <img src="SampleImages\SampleImage4.JPG"
                         alt="SampleImage4" />
                        </div>

                </td>
                <td valign="top">
                    <table>
                        <tr>
                            <td valign="top">
                                        <div id="divTags"></div>
                            </td>
                        </tr>
                        <tr valign="bottom">
                            <td align="right"><asp:textbox id="txtTagName"
                                runat="server"
                    Width="96px"></asp:textbox><input onclick="AddTag();"
                    type="button" value="Add" /></td>
                        </tr>
                    </table>
                </td>
        </tr>
        </table>
<input id="hidImageID" type="hidden" name="hidImageID" runat="server" />
            </form>
        </body>
</html>
```

The fun really begins with the image click event that is found in the embedded JavaScript for the onclick event of the div tag that you've wrapped around the image:

```
<div id="divImage1" onmouseover="this.style.cursor='hand';"
onclick="LoadTags(1);" runat="server">
<IMG src="SampleImages\SampleImage1.JPG"></div>
```

The onclick event associated with SampleImage1, as just shown, will call the JavaScript function LoadTags(). Notice that we have added the picture's ImageID as a static parameter for the call. That's fine for the purpose of this exercise, but later you'll see how to add dynamic information to this embedded script.

We're still in the context of the client-side coding, as we haven't dropped into the Ajax methods just yet. Our click event has taken us to the first step in sending our request out:

```
function LoadTags(imageID)
{
// We'll call our Ajax method within the CSharp file from here
// and redirect the resulting data to the Callback function.
        InvokePageMethod('LoadImageTags',[imageID] , LoadTagsCallBack);
        currentImage - imageID
}
```

The function accepts our imageID (which we provided statically) and in turn looks to call some function named InvokePageMethod. Within the InvokePageMethod function, we place a call to the server-side function LoadImageTags, supplying it with the necessary data.

Notice that three parameters are included within this particular function call. The first, as I mentioned before, is the name of the server-side function. The second is an obvious usage of the image ID that we'll need for our database efforts. The third parameter is an interesting manifestation, however. LoadTagsCallBack is our client-side receiving call that any server-side results should seek out when they're on the return trip home. Essentially this is our return address for the LoadTags message that is sent out to the server. We'll also drop the current image ID into a page-level variable for later use.

C# Code

Let's take a look at the C# function that LoadTags() is attempting to communicate with:

```
[Anthem.Method]
public string LoadImageTags(int ImageID)
{

//      This is our Ajax-ready function for loading the tags
//      associated with the
//      selected picture.
//      We'll build an HTML table and return that as a
//      string to the Ajax Callback
//      function.

// Let's go grab our data here
string strHTMLOutput = null;

SqlConnection conn = new SqlConnection("Data Source=(local);
Initial Catalog=AjaxTaggingSample;Integrated Security=SSPI");
```

```
SqlDataReader rdr = null;
      try
      {
      // This is typical ADO.NET processing here to insert our new
      // tag into the database.
      conn.Open();
      SqlCommand cmd = new SqlCommand("SELECT * FROM ImageTags
       WHERE ImageID = @imageid", conn);
      SqlParameter param  = new SqlParameter();
      param.ParameterName = "@imageid";
      param.Value         = ImageID;
      cmd.Parameters.Add(param);
      rdr = cmd.ExecuteReader();

      // We'll build our HTML table here
      System.IO.StringWriter swResponse = new System.IO.StringWriter();
      System.Web.UI.HtmlTextWriter htwResponse = new
        System.Web.UI.HtmlTextWriter(swResponse);

      HtmlTable tblResult = new HtmlTable();
      HtmlTableRow rowResult = new HtmlTableRow();
      HtmlTableCell cellResult = new HtmlTableCell();
      //  We'll add a table title here
      rowResult = new HtmlTableRow();
      cellResult = new HtmlTableCell();
      cellResult.InnerText = "Tags:";
      rowResult.Cells.Add(cellResult);
      tblResult.Rows.Add(rowResult);

      //  For each row in the returned datareader, we'll build an HTML row
      //  and add it to the HTML table for rendering within the DIV tag.
      while (rdr.Read())
      {
            rowResult = new HtmlTableRow();
            cellResult = new HtmlTableCell();

      // The tag is added to the innerText of the cell
      StringBuilder strInnerHtml = new StringBuilder();
      strInnerHtml.Append("- " + rdr["TagName"].ToString());
      strInnerHtml.Append("<DIV id='btnDelete'
       style=\"CURSOR:hand; DISPLAY:inline;\"");
      strInnerHtml.Append("onclick=\"DeleteTag
       ('" + ImageID.ToString() + "', '");
      strInnerHtml.Append(rdr["TagName"].ToString() + "');\"
       align='left'>[x]</DIV>");

      cellResult.InnerHtml = strInnerHtml.ToString();
```

```
        rowResult.Cells.Add(cellResult);
        tblResult.Rows.Add(rowResult);
        }

        //  Dump the HTML table out to the StringWriter
        tblResult.RenderControl(htwResponse);
        strHTMLOutput = swResponse.ToString();
}
finally
{
        // Close the reader
        if (rdr != null)
{
        rdr.Close();
}
        if (conn != null)
{
                conn.Close();
        }
}

//  Now we'll store the image's ID in the hidden control for later usage:
                this.hidImageID.Value = ImageID.ToString();
                return strHTMLOutput;
}
```

Really, two things are happening in this function. First, we're accessing the database and retrieving the tags for the ImageID that was provided. Second, we're building an HTML table with the StringBuilder class to return to the client side. One of the first requirements for the Anthem.dll to function correctly is that you must prefix the function name with the Anthem.Method designator as shown:

```
[Anthem.Method]
public string LoadImageTags(int ImageID)
```

Without that preface, the function won't be available to JavaScript during the render phase, and essentially it will be nonexistent and unavailable to the client. But wait a minute! How does the page know that this function is an Ajax-ready component? If you look at the Page_Load method in the code behind, you'll notice that we've declared this particular page to be "ready and available" for Ajax efforts and therefore any inclusive functions (prefixed correctly) will be available for Ajax calls.

```
private void Page_Load(object sender, System.EventArgs e)
{
        // We need to register this page with the Ajax class, so that it is
        // Ajax aware.

        Anthem.Manager.Register(this);
```

```
    // That is all that is needed for the ready reception of Ajax calls.
    // Pretty cool? Yes it is!
}
```

The Anthem.Manager establishes that this page is now registered with the Ajax engine and any methods marked as [Anthem.Method] will be available for the JavaScript rendering process.

Let's shift back to our server-side code-behind file and continue our dissection of the LoadImageTags method. One noticeable question that you should be raising at the moment is why there is only one parameter in the function call.

```
[Anthem.Method]
public string LoadImageTags(int ImageID)
```

Shouldn't the callback function be included with the ImageID? No. During the Ajax interpretation of the call, the callback method isn't required for the server-side code, as we will be parsing that particular address when we build the appropriate JavaScript methods. (Actually "we" won't be building those methods. Our Ajax muscle will be pushing that code around for us.)

The ADO.NET actions are pretty typical for our particular usage of the tagging database. We simply take an ImageID in as a parameter and ask for all of the tags in return. That information is loaded in the DataReader and patiently waits for us to put it to work.

Our next task is to build a string representation of an HTML table to pass back to the client side. If you review the posted function on the previous pages, you'll find that the heart of the table lies within this particular StringBuilder activity:

```
StringBuilder strInnerHtml = new StringBuilder();
strInnerHtml.Append("- " + rdr["TagName"].ToString());
strInnerHtml.Append("<DIV id='btnDelete'
  style=\"CURSOR:hand; DISPLAY:inline;\"");
strInnerHtml.Append("onclick=\"DeleteTag
  ('" + ImageID.ToString() + "', '");
strInnerHtml.Append(rdr["TagName"].ToString() + "');\"
  align='left'>[x]</DIV>");

cellResult.InnerHtml = strInnerHtml.ToString();
```

If you recall, the application displayed the tags with the structure shown in Figure 10-6.

Tags:
- Prowler[x]
- Robotics[x]
- Hobby[x]

[   ] [Add]

Figure 10-6. *Tag structure*

Obviously we need to display the tag, so we simply dump that out as regular text. We don't really need to create any form of user interaction with said tag at the moment. In a real-world application (similar to Flickr's), you'd want to make the tag name a hyperlink that would perhaps lead to another form responsible for rendering all of the images that you've tagged with the chosen text. However, our current user is interested only in being able to delete the tag from the database by clicking the [x]. If you walk through the StringBuilder on a step-by-step basis, you'll see how we've systematically built a DIV tag that allows us that exact ability. The rendered script would look something like this:

```
Kids <DIV id='btnDelete' style="Cursor:hand;DISPLAY:inline;");
 onclick="DeleteTag('1', 'Kids');" align='left'>[x]</DIV>
```

As you can see, we've dynamically built the DIV tag with the information we're retrieving on a line-by-line basis from the DataReader. All of this is added to the StringBuilder that we're appending, and in the end we use the ToString() function to write it out to our return variable:

```
// Dump the HTML table out to the StringWriter
    tblResult.RenderControl(htwResponse);
    strHTMLOutput = swResponse.ToString();
    return strHTMLOutput;
```

Because this is an Ajax method, our return statement will actually return us to our call-back function now. Our HTML string is now on the return path home seeking out the function that we established as the callback:

```
function LoadTagsCallBack(result)
{
        // Our tags have been loaded and the result.value
        // will contain the HTML table that we build on the
        // code side. We'll find the DIV tag in the document
        // and then "bind" the new HTML to the innerHTML
        // property.

var thisElement = document.getElementById('divTags');
        thisElement.innerHTML = result.value;
}
```

Our LoadTagsCallBack() function accepts one generic "result," which in this case is our HTML string. In the document object, we'll seek out and find the divTags control and quickly assign the string to the innerHTML property. Our browser recognizes the change and "presto-chango," our data is displayed! We've made a round trip from the client to server, asynchronously and with very little effort. If you examine the sample code further, you'll find that the same model is used repeatedly for each of the function calls. The entire introductory process is the same:

1. We designate our page as an Ajax registered entity:

   ```
   Anthem.Manager.Register(this);
   ```

2. Our client-side events call the server-side functions, providing parameters and a call-back "address:"

   ```
   Anthem_InvokePageMethod('LoadImageTags',[imageID] , LoadTagsCallBack);
   ```

3. Our code-behind function accepts the call, processes the server-side activities, and then starts the journey back to the callback function:

```
[Anthem.Method]
public string LoadImageTags(int ImageID)
...
return strHTMLOutput;
```

4. The Ajax callback waits patiently for your return. When it "discovers" your data coming home, it subsequently pushes that data back out to your browser:

```
function LoadTagsCallBack(result)
    ...
var thisElement = document.getElementById('divTags');
thisElement.innerHTML = result.value;
```

I've included the .cs file for quick review, but I recommend that you download the chapter sample applications as well:

```
//frmTaggingSample.aspx.cs

using System;
using System.Collections;
using System.ComponentModel;
using System.Data;
using System.Data.SqlClient;
using System.Drawing;
using System.Text;
using System.Web;
using System.Web.SessionState;
using System.Web.UI;
using System.Web.UI.WebControls;
using System.Web.UI.HtmlControls;

public partial class frmTaggingSample : System.Web.UI.Page
{
    protected void Page_Load(object sender, EventArgs e)
    {
        // We need to register this page with the Ajax class, so that it is
        // Ajax aware.

        Anthem.Manager.Register(this);

        // That is all that is needed for the ready reception of Ajax
        // calls.
        // Pretty cool?  Yes it is!
    }
```

```
[Anthem.Method]
public string LoadImageTags(int ImageID)
{

//      This is our Ajax ready function for loading the tags
//   associated with the
//        selected picture.
//   We'll build an HTML table and return that as a string to the
//   Ajax callback
//   function.

//   Let's go grab our data here

string strHTMLOutput = null;
SqlConnection conn = new SqlConnection("Data Source=(local);
Initial Catalog=AjaxTaggingSample;Integrated Security=SSPI");

    SqlDataReader rdr = null;

    try
    {

conn.Open();
SqlCommand cmd = new SqlCommand("SELECT * FROM ImageTags WHERE
 ImageID = @imageid", conn);
        SqlParameter param  = new SqlParameter();
        param.ParameterName = "@imageid";
        param.Value         = ImageID;
        cmd.Parameters.Add(param);

        rdr = cmd.ExecuteReader();

        // We'll build our HTML table here
        System.IO.StringWriter swResponse = new System.IO.StringWriter();
        System.Web.UI.HtmlTextWriter htwResponse = new
         System.Web.UI.HtmlTextWriter(swResponse);

        HtmlTable tblResult = new HtmlTable();
        HtmlTableRow rowResult = new HtmlTableRow();
        HtmlTableCell cellResult = new HtmlTableCell();

        // We'll add a table title here
        rowResult = new HtmlTableRow();
        cellResult = new HtmlTableCell();
        cellResult.InnerText = "Tags:";
        rowResult.Cells.Add(cellResult);
        tblResult.Rows.Add(rowResult);
```

```
// For each row in the returned datareader, we'll build an HTML row
// and add it to the HTML table for rendering within the DIV tag.
while (rdr.Read())
{
        rowResult = new HtmlTableRow();
        cellResult = new HtmlTableCell();

        // The tag is added to the innerText of the cell
        StringBuilder strInnerHtml = new StringBuilder();
        strInnerHtml.Append("- " + rdr["TagName"].ToString());
        strInnerHtml.Append("<DIV id='btnDelete'
          style=\"CURSOR:hand;
          DISPLAY:inline;\"");
        strInnerHtml.Append("onclick=\"DeleteTag
         ('" + ImageID.ToString() + "','");

        strInnerHtml.Append(rdr["TagName"].ToString() +
         "');\" align='left'>[x]</DIV>");

        cellResult.InnerHtml = strInnerHtml.ToString();

        rowResult.Cells.Add(cellResult);
        tblResult.Rows.Add(rowResult);
}


        // Dump the HTML table out to the StringWriter
        tblResult.RenderControl(htwResponse);
        strHTMLOutput = swResponse.ToString();
}
finally
{
        // Close the reader
        if (rdr != null)
        {
        rdr.Close();
        }
                        if (conn != null)
                        {
                        conn.Close();
                        }
}

//      Now we'll store the image's ID in the hidden control for later usage:
this.hidImageID.Value = ImageID.ToString();

return strHTMLOutput;
}
```

```
[Anthem.Method]
public void AddTag(string TagName)
{
// We'll add our tag here

// The application retrieves the ImageID from the value
// of the hidden control. We have access to the page state!

int intImageID = Convert.ToInt32(this.hidImageID.Value);

//  Your DB connection string may be different based on the security settings
//  that you have established. On my machine I'm using integrated security
//  for access.
      SqlConnection conn = new SqlConnection
       ("Data Source=(local);Initial Catalog=AjaxTaggingSample;
        Integrated Security=SSPI");

      try
      {
      // This is typical ADO.NET processing here to insert our new tag into the
      // database.
      conn.Open();
      SqlCommand cmd = new SqlCommand("INSERT INTO ImageTags
       VALUES(@imageid, @tagname)", conn);
      cmd.Parameters.Add(new SqlParameter("@imageid", SqlDbType.Int));
      cmd.Parameters["@imageid"].Value = intImageID;
      cmd.Parameters.Add(new SqlParameter("@tagname", SqlDbType.VarChar, 50));
      cmd.Parameters["@tagname"].Value = TagName;

      cmd.ExecuteNonQuery();

      }
      catch (Exception e)
      {
            // We'll just do simple error handling here.
            Response.Write(e.Message);
      }
      finally
      {
            conn.Close();
      }

}
```

```
[Anthem.Method]
public void DeleteTag(string TagName)
{
        // We'll delete the selected tag from the database here.
        // The application retrieves the ImageID from the value
        // of the hidden control. We have access to the page state!
        int intImageID = Convert.ToInt32(this.hidImageID.Value);

        //  Your DB connection string may be different based on the security settings
        //  that you have established. On my machine I'm using integrated security
        //  for access.
        SqlConnection conn = new SqlConnection("Data Source=(local);
         Initial Catalog=AjaxTaggingSample;Integrated Security=SSPI");

        try
        {
        // This is typical ADO.NET processing here to insert our new tag into the
        // database.
        // Need help with database development?  http://www.apress.com has a huge
        // selection of .NET books to get you started!

        conn.Open();
        SqlCommand cmd = new SqlCommand("DELETE FROM ImageTags WHERE ImageID =
                @imageid and TagName = @tagname", conn);
        cmd.Parameters.Add(new SqlParameter("@imageid", SqlDbType.Int));
        cmd.Parameters["@imageid"].Value = intImageID;
        cmd.Parameters.Add(new SqlParameter("@tagname",SqlDbType.VarChar, 50));
        cmd.Parameters["@tagname"].Value = TagName;

        cmd.ExecuteNonQuery();

        }
        catch (Exception e)
        {
                // We'll just do simple error handling here.
                Response.Write(e.Message);
        }
        finally
        {
                conn.Close();
        }
}

}
```

Summary

In this chapter, we've built an introductory application capable of asynchronous server-side activities. Even with such a basic start, you should be able to see that so many things are now possible. Continue to examine the other events and methods in the code-behind file for this project, and don't be afraid to experiment with the various calls. If you're really energetic, try to create the code that will dynamically load images at runtime and associate it with your tags. Tagging is an exciting feature to add to any community-driven content site, and it's not an incredibly hard technology to build.

In the next chapter, we'll begin to look a little deeper into the Ajax library. We'll take a look at an application that will "clone" the Google Suggest search component.

CHAPTER 11

∎∎∎

Cloning Google Suggest

I'll be the first to admit that I'm addicted to technology. I'm captivated by anything shiny and new, especially if it plugs in and makes noise. My computer room has an ominous hum at night because of this addiction, and my house probably consumes more energy than some third-world countries. Fortunately, by having a career in IT, I can rationalize it all as "necessary for the job." That's what I tell my wife anyway.

When something comes along that is new, useful, and, more importantly, **FREE!**, I get pretty excited. At the tail end of 2005, Google Labs released the beta of Google Suggest. What's really amazing is that the product was developed by Kevin Gibbs and others as part-time work. The folks at Google are gracious enough to allow their developers to utilize 20 percent of their working week in pursuit of personal side projects. Google Suggest is one such endeavor to spring forth from that investment.

Introducing Google Suggest

Essentially the Google Suggest site accomplishes one thing. As you type a search term, the page hits the Google database and queries for results that match what you've typed so far, as shown in Figure 11-1. This is essentially the auto-complete functionality that we've all become accustomed to in desktop applications.

To really appreciate the application, you should visit the Google Suggest site yourself at `http://labs.google.com/suggest`. You'll soon find yourself addicted, too.

At this exact moment, you might be thinking, "The ability to auto-complete web controls has been around for a while now." And to that I would reply, "You're exactly correct!" I'm not saying that Google has invented or necessarily revolutionized this particular technology. However, I would offer my opinion that Google has been responsible for bringing a lot of people to the DHTML table who otherwise would have sought other methodologies. Remote scripting has been around for a while, there's no denying that. But the process had seemingly dwindled to the point where it was a tough implementation for developers to sell. When Google Suggest hit in December 2005, a number of IT managers and application customers looked at what the Google folks had produced and were, like me, immediately captivated.

Web   Images   Groups   News   Froogle   Local^New!   **more »**

		Advanced Search
micro**soft**		Preferences
microsoft	188,000,000 results	Language Tools
microsoft antispyware	2,410,000 results	
microsoft.com	1 result	
microsoft spyware	5,920,000 results	
As you type, Goo| microsoft word	14,800,000 results |sults. Learn more
microsoft office	17,100,000 results	
microsoft anti spyware	3,480,000 results	
microsoft updates	12,800,000 results	
microsoft clip art	2,200,000 results	
microsoft clipart	847,000 results	

Figure 11-1. *Google Suggest at work*

Implementing Google Suggest

So, as .NET developers, can we reproduce this as an Ajax.NET application? You bet we can!
First and foremost, you must understand that at its heart, Google Suggest is primarily a drop-
down List with auto-complete functionality. To reproduce the application in its current state
would require a huge amount of coding and narrative, so we'll take a few of the key features
and implement those instead.

Obviously, we don't have access to a few terabytes of web data to build queries against,
but what we do have is the AdventureWorks database. You may have to visit the Microsoft
Download Center (http://www.microsoft.com/downloads) if in fact you are missing the database. It's free and a relatively small download (23MB). We'll use the sales.store table as our
data source because it should give us a decent range of results to work with. Feel free to modify the connection strings and schema if you have access to a database with a larger quantity
of data (for example, employees, medical records, or retail products). For now, the sales.store
table has approximately 700 rows to work with, and that should suffice for our example.

The primary purpose of this chapter is to demonstrate how data can be passed back to
code executing on the client. You should find in the chapter's sample application a collection
of three web forms and their associated code-behind files:

- SearchPage.aspx and SearchPage.aspx.cs

- SearchPage_DataSets.aspx and SearchPage_DataSets.aspx.cs

- SearchPage_Objects.aspx and SearchPage_Objects.aspx.cs

SearchPage.aspx

The search page is our first stop in code review:

```
<%@ Page Language="C#" AutoEventWireup="true"
CodeFile="SearchPage.aspx.cs" Inherits="SearchPage" %>
```

```
<!DOCTYPE html PUBLIC "-//W3C//DTD XHTML 1.0 Transitional//EN"
"http://www.w3.org/TR/xhtml1/DTD/xhtml1-transitional.dtd">

<html xmlns="http://www.w3.org/1999/xhtml" >
  <head>
    <title>Google Clone Demo</title>
    <style type="text/css">
      .mouseOut{ background: #ccccff; color: #0000000; }
      .mouseOver{ background: #FFFAFA; color: #0000000; }
    </style>

    <script type="text/javascript">
    function ShowDiv(divid)
    {
        if (document.layers) document.layers[divid].visibility="show";
        else document.getElementById(divid).style.visibility="visible";
    }

    function HideDiv(divid)
    {
        if (document.layers) document.layers[divid].visibility="hide";
        else document.getElementById(divid).style.visibility="hidden";
    }

    function BodyLoad()
    {
        HideDiv("searchresults");
        // Set focus to the input box
        document.form1.keyword.focus();
    }

    function ClearResults()
    {
        // Remove existing rows in results table
        var resultsdiv = document.getElementById("searchresults");
        var counter = resultsdiv.childNodes.length;
        for (var i = counter -1; i >= 0; i--)
        {
            resultsdiv.removeChild(resultsdiv.childNodes[i]);
        }
    }

    function LoadResults(searchterm)
    {
        if (searchterm.length == 0)
        {
```

```
            // If the input box is empty, let's dump all the rows
            // from the results table
            ClearResults();
            HideDiv("searchresults");
            return;
        }

        // Fetch results from server side
        // This is our actual Ajax call
        Anthem_InvokePageMethod('RetrieveRows',[searchterm] , LoadResultsCallback);
    }

    function LoadResultsCallback(result)
    {
        // The XmlHttpRequest will return to this function.

        ShowDiv("searchresults");
        ClearResults();

        // Callback results from Ajax call.
        // We'll assign the inbound DataTable
        // to the items variable
        var items = result.value;

        var count = items.Rows.length;

        // We'll create a table object in the DOM
        var divResults = document.getElementById("searchresults");
        var tblTable = document.createElement("table");
        var tablebody = document.createElement("tbody");
        var tablerow, tablecell, tablenode;

        // Loop through each of the rows in the DataTable
        for (var i = 0; i < count; i++)
        {
            var currenttext = items.Rows[i].Name;

            // We'll create each table row and append it to the
            // table body
            tablerow = document.createElement("tr");
            tablecell = document.createElement("td");
            // Build the cell attributes and functions
            tablecell.onmouseover = function(){this.className='mouseOver';};
            tablecell.onmouseout = function(){this.className='mouseOut';};
            tablecell.setAttribute("border", "0");
            tablecell.onclick = function(){ReplaceInput(this);};
            tablenode = document.createTextNode(currenttext);
```

```
                tablecell.appendChild(tablenode);
                tablerow.appendChild(tablecell);
                tablebody.appendChild(tablerow);
            }

        // Add the table body to the table
        tblTable.appendChild(tablebody);
        // Add the table to the div tag
        divResults.appendChild(tblTable);
    }

    function ReplaceInput(tablecell)
    {
        // Swap Input box value with the value selected by
        // the user's mouse click
        var inputbox = document.getElementById("keyword");
        inputbox.value = tablecell.firstChild.nodeValue;
        ClearResults();
        HideDiv("searchresults");
    }

    </script>
</head>

<body onload="BodyLoad();">
    <form id="form1" method="post" runat="server">
        <p><strong style="FONT-SIZE: 24pt">AJAX.NET</strong><br />
            <strong>Google Suggest Demo:</strong></p>
        <input name="keyword" onkeyup="LoadResults(this.value)"
               style="WIDTH:500px" autocomplete="off" />
        <div align="left" class="box" id="searchresults"
             style="WIDTH:500px;BACKGROUND-COLOR:#ccccff">
        </div>
    </form>
</body>
</html>
```

SearchPage.aspx.cs

Now that we've seen the page, here's the code-behind file:

```
using System;
using System.Data;
using System.Configuration;
using System.Collections;
using System.Web;
using System.Web.Security;
using System.Web.UI;
```

```csharp
using System.Web.UI.WebControls;
using System.Web.UI.WebControls.WebParts;
using System.Web.UI.HtmlControls;
using System.Data.SqlClient;

public partial class SearchPage : System.Web.UI.Page
{
    protected void Page_Load(object sender, EventArgs e)
    {
        // We need to register this page with Ajax class, so that it is
        // Ajax.NET aware.
        Anthem.Manager.Register(this);
    }

    [Anthem.Method]
    public DataTable RetrieveRows(string searchterm)
    {
        SqlConnection conn = new SqlConnection("Data Source=(local); ➥
          Initial Catalog=AdventureWorks;Integrated Security=SSPI");
        DataTable dtReturn = new DataTable();

        conn.Open();
        // Go get the top 10 store names that are like user's search criteria
        SqlCommand cmd = new SqlCommand
        ("SELECT TOP 10 Name FROM Sales.Store WHERE Name
          LIKE @searchterm ORDER BY Name", conn);
        SqlParameter param = new SqlParameter();
        param.ParameterName = "@searchterm";
        searchterm.Trim().Replace("'", "''");
        searchterm += "%";
        param.Value = searchterm;
        cmd.Parameters.Add(param);

        SqlDataAdapter adpt = new SqlDataAdapter(cmd);
        adpt.Fill(dtReturn);
        conn.Close();

        // Send the DataTable back to the CallBack function
        return dtReturn;
    }
}
```

SearchPage_DataSets.aspx

Next, here's the page that uses DataSets:

```
<%@ Page Language="C#" AutoEventWireup="true"
CodeFile="SearchPage_DataSets.aspx.cs" Inherits="SearchPage_DataSets" %>
```

```html
<!DOCTYPE html PUBLIC "-//W3C//DTD XHTML 1.0 Transitional//EN"
"http://www.w3.org/TR/xhtml1/DTD/xhtml1-transitional.dtd">

<html xmlns="http://www.w3.org/1999/xhtml" >
  <head>
    <title>Google Clone Demo</title>
    <style type="text/css">
      .mouseOut{ background: #ccccff; color: #0000000; }
      .mouseOver{ background: #FFFAFA; color: #0000000; }
    </style>

    <script type="text/javascript">
    function ShowDiv(divid)
    {
        if (document.layers) document.layers[divid].visibility="show";
        else document.getElementById(divid).style.visibility="visible";
    }

    function HideDiv(divid)
    {
        if (document.layers) document.layers[divid].visibility="hide";
        else document.getElementById(divid).style.visibility="hidden";
    }

    function BodyLoad()
    {
        HideDiv("searchresults");
        // Set focus to the input box
        document.form1.keyword.focus();
    }

    function ClearResults()
    {
        // Remove existing rows in results table
        var resultsdiv = document.getElementById("searchresults");
        var counter = resultsdiv.childNodes.length;
        for (var i = counter -1; i >= 0; i--)
        {
            resultsdiv.removeChild(resultsdiv.childNodes[i]);
        }
    }

    function LoadResults(searchterm)
    {
        if (searchterm.length == 0)
        {
```

```
            // If the input box is empty, let's dump all the
            // rows from the results table
            ClearResults();
            HideDiv("searchresults");
            return;
        }

    // Fetch results from server side
    // This is our actual Ajax call
    Anthem_InvokePageMethod('RetrieveRows',[searchterm] , LoadResultsCallback);
}

function LoadResultsCallback(result)
{
    // The XmlHttpRequest will return to this function.

    ShowDiv("searchresults");
    ClearResults();

    // Callback results from Ajax call.
    // We'll assign the inbound DataTable
    // to the items variable
    var items = result.value;

    var count = items.Tables.stores.Rows.length;

    // We'll create a table object in the DOM
    var divResults = document.getElementById("searchresults");
    var tblTable = document.createElement("table");
    var tablebody = document.createElement("tbody");
    var tablerow, tablecell, tablenode;

    // Loop through each of the rows in the DataTable
    for (var i = 0; i < count; i++)
    {
        var currenttext = items.Tables.stores.Rows[i].Name;

        // We'll create each table row and append it to the
        // table body
        tablerow = document.createElement("tr");
        tablecell = document.createElement("td");
        // Build the cell attributes and functions
        tablecell.onmouseover = function() {this.className='mouseOver';};
        tablecell.onmouseout = function() {this.className='mouseOut';};
        tablecell.setAttribute("border", "0");
        tablecell.onclick = function(){ReplaceInput(this);};
```

```
            tablenode = document.createTextNode(currenttext);
            tablecell.appendChild(tablenode);
            tablerow.appendChild(tablecell);
            tablebody.appendChild(tablerow);
        }

        // Add the table body to the table
        tblTable.appendChild(tablebody);
        // Add the table to the div tag
        divResults.appendChild(tblTable);
    }

    function ReplaceInput(tablecell)
    {
        // Swap Input box value with the value selected by
        // the user's mouse click
        var inputbox = document.getElementById("keyword");
        inputbox.value = tablecell.firstChild.nodeValue;
        ClearResults();
        HideDiv("searchresults");
    }

    </script>
</head>

<body onload="BodyLoad();">
    <form id="form1" method="post" runat="server">
        <p><strong style="FONT-SIZE: 24pt">AJAX.NET</strong><br />
            <strong>Google Suggest Demo:</strong></p>
        <input name="keyword" onkeyup="LoadResults(this.value)"
                style="WIDTH:500px" autocomplete="off" />
        <div align="left" class="box" id="searchresults"
                style="WIDTH:500px;BACKGROUND-COLOR:#ccccff">
        </div>
    </form>
</body>
</html>
```

SearchPage_DataSets.aspx.cs

The following is the code-behind file that uses DataSets:

```
using System;
using System.Data;
using System.Configuration;
using System.Collections;
using System.Web;
```

```
using System.Web.Security;
using System.Web.UI;
using System.Web.UI.WebControls;
using System.Web.UI.WebControls.WebParts;
using System.Web.UI.HtmlControls;
using System.Data.SqlClient;

public partial class SearchPage_DataSets : System.Web.UI.Page
{
    protected void Page_Load(object sender, EventArgs e)
    {
        // We need to register this page with the Ajax class, so that it is
        // Ajax.NET aware.
        Anthem.Manager.Register(this);
    }

    [Anthem.Method]
    public DataSet RetrieveRows(string searchterm)
    {
        SqlConnection conn = new SqlConnection(
            "Data Source=(local);Initial Catalog=AdventureWorks; ➡
            Integrated Security=SSPI");
        DataTable dtReturn = new DataTable();

        conn.Open();
        // Go get the top 10 store names from AdventureWorks that
        // are like user's search criteria
        SqlCommand cmd = new SqlCommand("SELECT TOP 10 Name From Sales.Store
          WHERE Name LIKE @searchterm ORDER BY Name", conn);
        SqlParameter param = new SqlParameter();
        param.ParameterName = "@searchterm";
        searchterm.Trim().Replace("'", "''");
        searchterm += "%";
        param.Value = searchterm;
        cmd.Parameters.Add(param);
        SqlDataAdapter adpt = new SqlDataAdapter(cmd);
        DataSet dsCustomers = new DataSet();
        adpt.Fill(dsCustomers, "stores");

        conn.Close();

        // Send the DataTable back to the CallBack function
        return dsCustomers;
    }
}
```

SearchPage_Objects.aspx

Now, let's see the search page that uses objects:

```
<%@ Page Language="C#" AutoEventWireup="true"
 CodeFile="SearchPage_Objects.aspx.cs"
 Inherits="SearchPage_Objects" %>

<!DOCTYPE html PUBLIC "-//W3C//DTD XHTML 1.0 Transitional//EN"
"http://www.w3.org/TR/xhtml1/DTD/xhtml1-transitional.dtd">

<html xmlns="http://www.w3.org/1999/xhtml" >
  <head>
    <title>Google Clone Demo</title>
    <style type="text/css">
      .mouseOut{ background: #ccccff; color: #0000000; }
      .mouseOver{ background: #FFFAFA; color: #0000000; }
    </style>

    <script type="text/javascript">
    function ShowDiv(divid)
    {
        if (document.layers) document.layers[divid].visibility="show";
        else document.getElementById(divid).style.visibility="visible";
    }

    function HideDiv(divid)
    {
        if (document.layers) document.layers[divid].visibility="hide";
        else document.getElementById(divid).style.visibility="hidden";
    }

    function BodyLoad()
    {
        HideDiv("searchresults");
        // Set focus to the input box
        document.form1.keyword.focus();
    }

    function ClearResults()
    {
        // Remove existing rows in results table
        var resultsdiv = document.getElementById("searchresults");
        var counter = resultsdiv.childNodes.length;
        for (var i = counter -1; i >= 0; i--)
        {
            resultsdiv.removeChild(resultsdiv.childNodes[i]);
        }
    }
```

```
function LoadResults(searchterm)
{
    if (searchterm.length == 0)
    {
        // If the input box is empty, let's dump all the
        // rows from the results table
        ClearResults();
        HideDiv("searchresults");
        return;
    }

    // Fetch results from server side.
    // This is our actual Ajax call
    Anthem_InvokePageMethod('RetrieveRows',[searchterm] , LoadResultsCallback);
}

function LoadResultsCallback(result)
{
    // The XmlHttpRequest will return to this function.

    ShowDiv("searchresults");
    ClearResults();

    // Callback results from Ajax call.
    // We'll assign the inbound object collection
    // to the items variable
    var items = result.value;

    var count = items.length;

    // We'll create a table object in the DOM
    var divResults = document.getElementById("searchresults");
    var tblTable = document.createElement("table");
    var tablebody = document.createElement("tbody");
    var tablerow, tablecell, tablenode;

    // Loop through each of the rows in the DataTable
    for (var i = 0; i < count; i++)
    {
        var currenttext = items[i].Name;

        // We'll create each table row and append it to the
        // table body
        tablerow = document.createElement("tr");
        tablecell = document.createElement("td");
        // Build the cell attributes and functions
        tablecell.onmouseover = function() {this.className='mouseOver';};
```

```
            tablecell.onmouseout = function() {this.className='mouseOut';};
            tablecell.setAttribute("border", "0");
            tablecell.onclick = function(){ReplaceInput(this);};
            tablenode = document.createTextNode(currenttext);
            tablecell.appendChild(tablenode);
            tablerow.appendChild(tablecell);
            tablebody.appendChild(tablerow);
        }

        // Add the table body to the table
        tblTable.appendChild(tablebody);
        // Add the table to the div tag
        divResults.appendChild(tblTable);
    }

    function ReplaceInput(tablecell)
    {
        // Swap Input box value with the value selected by
        // the user's mouse click
        var inputbox = document.getElementById("keyword");
        inputbox.value = tablecell.firstChild.nodeValue;
        ClearResults();
        HideDiv("searchresults");
    }

    </script>
</head>

<body onload="BodyLoad();">
    <form id="form1" method="post" runat="server">
        <p><strong style="FONT-SIZE: 24pt">AJAX.NET</strong><br />
        <strong>Google Suggest Demo:</strong></p>
        <input name="keyword" onkeyup="LoadResults(this.value)"
                style="WIDTH:500px" autocomplete="off" />
        <div align="left" class="box" id="searchresults"
                style="WIDTH:500px;BACKGROUND-COLOR:#ccccff">
        </div>
    </form>
</body>
</html>
```

SearchPage_Objects.aspx.cs

Finally, here's the code-behind file for the last implementation:

```
using System;
using System.Data;
using System.Configuration;
```

```csharp
using System.Collections;
using System.Web;
using System.Web.Security;
using System.Web.UI;
using System.Web.UI.WebControls;
using System.Web.UI.WebControls.WebParts;
using System.Web.UI.HtmlControls;
using System.Data.SqlClient;

public partial class SearchPage_Objects : System.Web.UI.Page
{
    protected void Page_Load(object sender, EventArgs e)
    {
        // We need to register this page with Ajax class, so that it is
        // Ajax.NET aware.
        Anthem.Manager.Register(this);

    }


    [Anthem.Method]
    public StoreCollection RetrieveRows(string searchterm)
    {

        SqlConnection conn = new SqlConnection(
            "Data Source=(local);Initial Catalog=AdventureWorks; ➥
             Integrated Security=SSPI");
        DataTable dtReturn = new DataTable();

        conn.Open();
        // Go get the top 10 store names from AdventureWorks that are
        // like user's search criteria
        SqlCommand cmd = new SqlCommand("SELECT TOP 10 Name FROM Sales.Store
          WHERE Name LIKE @searchterm ORDER BY Name", conn);
        SqlParameter param = new SqlParameter();
        param.ParameterName = "@searchterm";
        searchterm.Trim().Replace("'", "''");
        searchterm += "%";
        param.Value = searchterm;
        cmd.Parameters.Add(param);
        SqlDataAdapter adpt = new SqlDataAdapter(cmd);
        adpt.Fill(dtReturn);

        conn.Close();

        StoreCollection strCollection = new StoreCollection();
```

```
    for (int i = 0; i < dtReturn.Rows.Count; i++)
    {
        Store stre = new Store();
        stre.Name = (string)dtReturn.Rows[i]["Name"];
        strCollection.Add(stre);
    }

    // Send the CustomerCollection back to the CallBack function
    return strCollection;
    }
}
```

Before we dive into the code, right-click SearchPage.aspx and set it as the default startup page. Once you've started the application, you should be met with a textbox like the one in Figure 11-2.

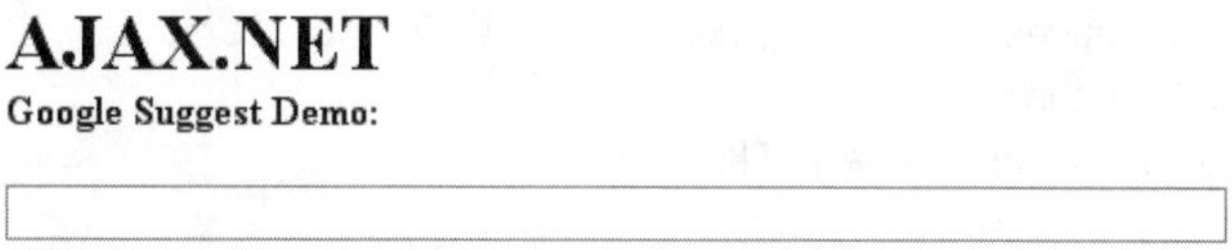

AJAX.NET
Google Suggest Demo:

Figure 11-2. *SearchPage.aspx*

As you begin typing in the textbox, a list of results will be displayed immediately below the textbox. Notice also that as you mouse over each of the search results, the selection will become highlighted. If you subsequently click the highlighted option, it will in turn become the chosen text inside of the textbox, as shown in Figure 11-3.

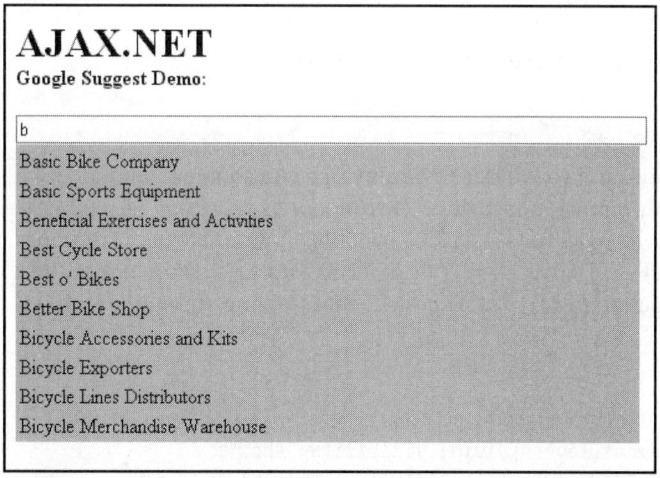

AJAX.NET
Google Suggest Demo:

b

Basic Bike Company
Basic Sports Equipment
Beneficial Exercises and Activities
Best Cycle Store
Best o' Bikes
Better Bike Shop
Bicycle Accessories and Kits
Bicycle Exporters
Bicycle Lines Distributors
Bicycle Merchandise Warehouse

Figure 11-3. *SearchPage.aspx in action*

If you start and run the other two web pages, you'll have similar results. However, the mechanism by which the data is delivered to the client-side function is quite different. The first example we'll look at is using a DataTable to pass the results to the client side.

Using a DataTable

If you open up `SearchPage.aspx.cs` and examine the `RetrieveRows` function, you'll notice that we're passing a DataTable back to the JavaScript call:

```
[Anthem.Method]
public DataTable RetrieveRows(string searchterm)
{
    SqlConnection conn = new SqlConnection("Data Source=(local); ➥
        Initial Catalog=AdventureWorks;Integrated Security=SSPI");
    DataTable dtReturn = new DataTable();

    conn.Open();
    // Go get the top 10 store names that are like user's search criteria
    SqlCommand cmd = new SqlCommand
      ("SELECT TOP 10 Name FROM Sales.Store WHERE Name
        LIKE @searchterm ORDER BY Name", conn);
    SqlParameter param = new SqlParameter();
    param.ParameterName = "@searchterm";
    searchterm.Trim().Replace("'", "''");
    searchterm += "%";
    param.Value = searchterm;
    cmd.Parameters.Add(param);

    SqlDataAdapter adpt = new SqlDataAdapter(cmd);
    adpt.Fill(dtReturn);
    conn.Close();

    // Send the DataTable back to the CallBack function
    return dtReturn;
}
```

This is typical ADO.NET code, and you're free to modify the data source to implement another database by changing the connection string. The function is expecting the client to supply the `searchterm` and will in turn deliver a DataTable with the appropriate query response. Now that we know what the back-end server-side code is serving up, let's take a look at the JavaScript functions that manipulate the `div` tag responsible for holding our popped-up search results:

```
function ShowDiv(divid)
{
    if (document.layers) document.layers[divid].visibility="show";
    else document.getElementById(divid).style.visibility="visible";
}
```

```
function HideDiv(divid)
{
    if (document.layers) document.layers[divid].visibility="hide";
    else document.getElementById(divid).style.visibility="hidden";
}

function BodyLoad()
{
    HideDiv("searchresults");
    // Set focus to the input box
    document.form1.keyword.focus();
}
```

We've placed our JavaScript in the HEAD block so that it will be available to page events that may be triggered through user interaction. You'll also notice that we're doing some typical manipulation of the div that pops up our search results (nested within the div as an HTML table). What if this is a return trip and we have existing rows? Won't we need to clear those out of the table? Excellent questions; let's take a look at the function that accomplishes this by identifying each of the div's child nodes and eliminating them.

```
function ClearResults()
{
    // Remove existing rows in results table
    var resultsdiv = document.getElementById("searchresults");
    var counter = resultsdiv.childNodes.length;
    for (var i = counter -1; i >= 0; i--)
    {
        resultsdiv.removeChild(resultsdiv.childNodes[i]);
    }
}
```

Our for loop iterates through each of the div's child nodes and promptly destroys them with the resultsdiv.removeChild() call.

So now we have an empty div waiting in the wings. The true power of the application is, of course, in the request and receipt of the search data. You'll notice in the HTML of the sample application that our input box has an onkeyup attribute established for us:

```
<input name="keyword" onkeyup="LoadResults(this.value)" style="WIDTH:500px" />
```

The onkeyup event is routing to the LoadResults function and carrying the text value that the user has supplied along with it.

Our user has entered a keystroke, and we're now in a position where we need to send that off to our waiting C# function on the server side for processing. That is accomplished in the LoadResults() call:

```
function LoadResults(searchterm)
{
    if (searchterm.length == 0)
    {
        // If the input box is empty, let's dump all
        // the rows from the results table
        ClearResults();
        HideDiv("searchresults");
        return;
    }


    // Fetch results from server side.
    // This is our actual Ajax call
    Anthem_InvokePageMethod('RetrieveRows',[searchterm] , LoadResultsCallback);

}
```

One immediate action that needs to take place is to recognize whether or not the input box does indeed have any text within it. It's quite possible that the user may have triggered the keyup event with the backspace key and in turn left us with an empty search string. If that is the situation here, the next step is to call ClearResults(), removing existing data and subsequently hiding the pop-up div box. If, however, our user has actually entered some data, we'll call the Anthem_InvokePageMethod() function, providing our server-side function name, search term, and callback address as the appropriate parameters, and wait for the data to come home.

A DataTable is generated on the server side (see previous RetrieveRows(string searchterm) database code) and returned to LoadResultsCallback():

```
function LoadResultsCallback(result)
{
    // The XmlHttpRequest will return to this function.

    ShowDiv("searchresults");
    ClearResults();

    // Callback results from Ajax call
    // We'll assign the inbound DataTable
    // to the items variable
    var items = result.value;

    var count = items.Rows.length;

    // We'll create a table object in the DOM
    var divResults = document.getElementById("searchresults");
    var tblTable = document.createElement("table");
    var tablebody = document.createElement("tbody");
    var tablerow, tablecell, tablenode;
```

```
    // Loop through each of the rows in the DataTable
    for (var i = 0; i < count; i++)
    {
        var currenttext = items.Rows[i].Name;

        // We'll create each table row and append it to the
        // table body
        tablerow = document.createElement("tr");
        tablecell = document.createElement("td");
        // Build the cell attributes and functions
        tablecell.onmouseover = function(){this.className='mouseOver';};
        tablecell.onmouseout = function(){this.className='mouseOut';};
        tablecell.setAttribute("border", "0");
        tablecell.onclick = function(){ReplaceInput(this);};
        tablenode = document.createTextNode(currenttext);
        tablecell.appendChild(tablenode);
        tablerow.appendChild(tablecell);
        tablebody.appendChild(tablerow);
    }

    // Add the table body to the table
    tblTable.appendChild(tablebody);
    // Add the table to the div tag
    divResults.appendChild(tblTable);
}
```

Something to note in the preceding code is how the DataTable is handled on the client side after delivery. The count of rows in the table is first obtained:

```
var count = items.Rows.length;
```

And the text in the Name field is extracted from that row during the iteration:

```
var currenttext = items.Rows[i].Name;
```

Notice that we're using the column name in proper context. That's an awesome maintenance tool for upkeep and modifications made later on. A majority of the remaining function script is pretty self-explanatory. We create table elements, populate them, and append them as necessary. We then append the table to the div tag, and the data is then displayed to the user.

But what if we're passing back a DataSet rather than a DataTable? Fortunately, our library is prepared for that as well.

Using a DataSet

You'll find in the chapter's sample application another form in the project aptly named SearchPage_DataSets.aspx. Right-click this form and run the solution. Notice anything different about the usability of this version of the clone? Probably not. However, if you take a look at the code, you'll find that there are a few minor variations. Our C# code is nearly the same aside from the DataAdapter's filling of the DataSet rather than the DataTable:

```
[Anthem.Method]
public DataSet RetrieveRows(string searchterm)
{
    SqlConnection conn = new SqlConnection(
        "Data Source=(local);Initial Catalog=AdventureWorks; ➥
          Integrated Security=SSPI");
    DataTable dtReturn = new DataTable();

    conn.Open();
    // Go get the top 10 store names from AdventureWorks that
    // are like user's search criteria
    SqlCommand cmd = new SqlCommand("SELECT TOP 10 Name FROM Sales.Store
      WHERE Name LIKE @searchterm ORDER BY Name", conn);
    SqlParameter param = new SqlParameter();
    param.ParameterName = "@searchterm";
    searchterm.Trim().Replace("'", "''");
    searchterm += "%";
    param.Value = searchterm;
    cmd.Parameters.Add(param);
    SqlDataAdapter adpt = new SqlDataAdapter(cmd);
    DataSet dsCustomers = new DataSet();
    adpt.Fill(dsCustomers, "stores");

    conn.Close();

    // Send the DataTable back to the CallBack function
    return dsCustomers;
}
}
```

Nothing truly exciting here, but note that we are returning a DataSet to the client side this time.

Back on the client side, the only change that will differentiate this form from the previous DataTable version is the callback function LoadResultsCallBack:

```
function LoadResultsCallback(result)
{
    // The XmlHttpRequest will return to this function.

    ShowDiv("searchresults");
    ClearResults();

    // Callback results from Ajax call.
    // We'll assign the inbound DataTable
    // to the items variable
    var items = result.value;
```

```
var count = items.Tables.stores.Rows.length;

// We'll create a table object in the DOM
var divResults = document.getElementById("searchresults");
var tblTable = document.createElement("table");
var tablebody = document.createElement("tbody");
var tablerow, tablecell, tablenode;

// Loop through each of the rows in the DataTable
for (var i = 0; i < count; i++)
{
    var currenttext = items.Tables.stores.Rows[i].Name;

    // We'll create each table row and append it to the
    // table body
    tablerow = document.createElement("tr");
    tablecell = document.createElement("td");
    // Build the cell attributes and functions
    tablecell.onmouseover = function(){this.className='mouseOver';};
    tablecell.onmouseout = function(){this.className='mouseOut';};
    tablecell.setAttribute("border", "0");
    tablecell.onclick = function(){ReplaceInput(this);};
    tablenode = document.createTextNode(currenttext);
    tablecell.appendChild(tablenode);
    tablerow.appendChild(tablecell);
    tablebody.appendChild(tablerow);
}

// Add the table body to the table
tblTable.appendChild(tablebody);
// Add the table to the div tag
divResults.appendChild(tblTable);
}
```

On the server side, the DataSet was filled and was named `stores`, as you can see from the following snippet:

```
adpt.Fill(dsCustomers, "stores");
```

Within our JavaScript code, we find something similar to the DataTable call, but we're now utilizing the DataSet's proper name as well as the column within the iterated row:

```
var currenttext = items.Tables.stores.Rows[i].Name;
```

In the end, we accomplish the same as before. We've retrieved SQL data and parsed it into the HTML table that is ultimately brought back to the browser.

Using a Custom Data Object

Moving on, the final form in our project (SearchPage_Objects.aspx) ups the intensity in our data manipulation plan a little more. It is here that we'll create a custom business object and a corresponding collection and make use of both. We could have easily incorporated "generics" rather than collections, but for simplicity and backwards compatibility (VS 2003), I've decided to opt for the collection.

Right-click the SearchPage_Objects.aspx page and set it as the default page. Run the application and notice that the functionality is consistent with previous examples. However, in this example we're creating a business object called store that is nothing more than a class with one property (Name):

```
using System;
using System.Data;
using System.Configuration;
using System.Web;
using System.Web.Security;
using System.Web.UI;
using System.Web.UI.WebControls;
using System.Web.UI.WebControls.WebParts;
using System.Web.UI.HtmlControls;

[Serializable]
public class Store
{
    public Store()
    {
        //
        // TODO: Add constructor logic here
        //
    }

    // We only need one property for the purposes of this demo.

    private string _storename = string.Empty;
    /// <summary>
    /// Stores Name
    /// </summary>
    public string Name
    {
        get{return _storename;}
        set{_storename = value;}
    }
}
```

The StoreCollection object was generated with a template-generation tool and contains nothing more than your typical collection-based methods (Add, Remove, and so on).

```
using System;
using System.Collections;
using System.Xml;

[Serializable]
public class StoreCollection : CollectionBase
{
    public StoreCollection()
    {
    }

    public StoreCollection(Store[] value)
    {
        this.AddRange(value);
    }

    public Store this[int index]
    {
        get { return ((Store)(this.List[index])); }
    }

    public int Add(Store value)
    {
        return this.List.Add(value);
    }

    public void AddRange(Store[] value)
    {
        for (int i = 0; (i < value.Length); i = (i + 1))
        {
            this.Add(value[i]);
        }
    }
}
```

```csharp
public void AddRange(StoreCollection value)
{
    for (int i = 0; (i < value.Count); i = (i + 1))
    {
        this.Add((Store)value.List[i]);
    }
}

public bool Contains(Store value)
{
    return this.List.Contains(value);
}

public void CopyTo(Store[] array, int index)
{
    this.List.CopyTo(array, index);
}

public int IndexOf(Store value)
{
    return this.List.IndexOf(value);
}

public void Insert(int index, Store value)
{
    List.Insert(index, value);
}

public void Remove(Store value)
{
    List.Remove(value);
}

public new StoreEnumerator GetEnumerator()
{
    return new StoreEnumerator(this);
}

public class StoreEnumerator : IEnumerator
{
    private IEnumerator _enumerator;
    private IEnumerable _temp;

    public StoreEnumerator(StoreCollection mappings)
    {
    _temp = ((IEnumerable)(mappings));
    _enumerator = _temp.GetEnumerator();
    }
```

```csharp
public Store Current
{
    get { return ((Store)(_enumerator.Current)); }
}

object IEnumerator.Current
{
    get { return _enumerator.Current; }
}

public bool MoveNext()
{
    return _enumerator.MoveNext();
}

bool IEnumerator.MoveNext()
{
    return _enumerator.MoveNext();
}

public void Reset()
{
    _enumerator.Reset();
}

void IEnumerator.Reset()
{
    _enumerator.Reset();
}
    }
}
```

Let's give some attention to how the business class is built and consequently sent back to the client. The RetrieveRows() function is similar to the others in its data obtainment. However, you'll notice that we're cycling through the DataTable's set of rows and building class properties (in this case, we're only building one) on the fly. After we package the Store object, we pack that into our collection and move on to the next DataTable row:

```csharp
[Anthem.Method]
public StoreCollection RetrieveRows(string searchterm)
{
    SqlConnection conn = new SqlConnection(
        "Data Source=(local);Initial Catalog=AdventureWorks; ➥
        Integrated Security=SSPI");
    DataTable dtReturn = new DataTable();
```

```
    conn.Open();
    // Go get the top 10 store names from AdventureWorks that are
    // like user's search criteria
    SqlCommand cmd = new SqlCommand("SELECT TOP 10 Name FROM Sales.Store
        WHERE Name LIKE @searchterm ORDER BY Name", conn);
    SqlParameter param = new SqlParameter();
    param.ParameterName = "@searchterm";
    searchterm.Trim().Replace("'", "''");
    searchterm += "%";
    param.Value = searchterm;
    cmd.Parameters.Add(param);
    SqlDataAdapter adpt = new SqlDataAdapter(cmd);
    adpt.Fill(dtReturn);

    conn.Close();

    StoreCollection strCollection = new StoreCollection();

    for (int i = 0; i < dtReturn.Rows.Count; i++)
    {
        Store stre = new Store();
        stre.Name = (string)dtReturn.Rows[i]["Name"];
        strCollection.Add(stre);
    }

    // Send the CustomerCollection back to the CallBack function
    return strCollection;
}
```

After building the collection, you'll notice that the return type of our Anthem method is a StoreCollection. What is really interesting to see is that our LoadResultsCallback() function makes use of the collection in much the same way as it would had we returned a typical JavaScript array:

```
function LoadResultsCallback(result)
{
    // The XmlHttpRequest will return to this function.

    ShowDiv("searchresults");
    ClearResults();

    // Callback results from Ajax call.
    // We'll assign the inbound object collection
    // to the items variable
    var items = result.value;
```

```
var count = items.length;

// We'll create a table object in the DOM
var divResults = document.getElementById("searchresults");
var tblTable = document.createElement("table");
var tablebody = document.createElement("tbody");
var tablerow, tablecell, tablenode;

// Loop through each of the rows in the DataTable
for (var i = 0; i < count; i++)
{
    var currenttext = items[i].Name;

    // We'll create each table row and append it to the
    // table body
    tablerow = document.createElement("tr");
    tablecell = document.createElement("td");
    // Build the cell attributes and functions
    tablecell.onmouseover = function(){this.className='mouseOver';};
    tablecell.onmouseout = function(){this.className='mouseOut';};
    tablecell.setAttribute("border", "0");
    tablecell.onclick = function(){ReplaceInput(this);};
    tablenode = document.createTextNode(currenttext);
    tablecell.appendChild(tablenode);
    tablerow.appendChild(tablecell);
    tablebody.appendChild(tablerow);
}

// Add the table body to the table
tblTable.appendChild(tablebody);
// Add the table to the div tag
divResults.appendChild(tblTable);
}
```

Here again, what differentiates this particular methodology is how we handle the data coming back from the C# code. We extract the Name by isolating the Store object by index and revealing the object's solitary property:

```
var currenttext = items[i].Name;
```

Keeping with the previous pattern, we build the HTML table in the same fashion and send that off to the browser.

So far, we've examined how we get the user's search term translated into data and the interesting channels of returning the queried results back to the client. Let's move on to some of the more functional aspects of the application.

Expanding the Application

Now that we can return context-sensitive data to the browser, we need to add more user-friendly features. To that end, when the user places their cursor over a return row, we want to highlight their current location, as Figure 11-4 demonstrates.

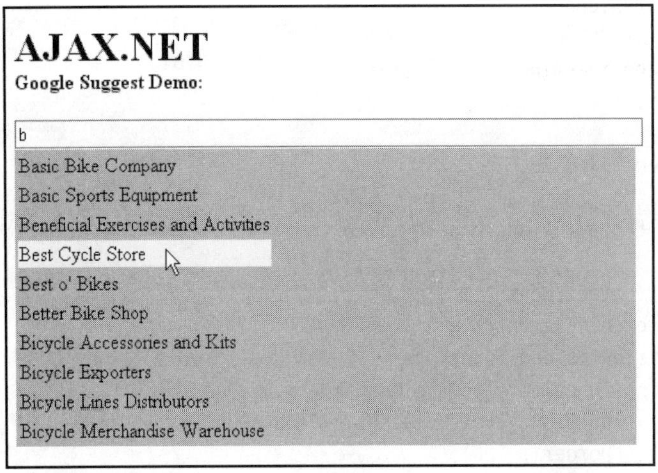

Figure 11-4. *SearchPage.aspx mouseover event*

To accomplish this, we'll assign a style class to the individual cells in each corresponding row:

```
tablecell.onmouseover = function(){this.className='mouseOver';};
tablecell.onmouseout = function(){this.className='mouseOut';};
```

Having established the appropriate class assignments, we now need to implement the style properties:

```
<style type="text/css">
  .mouseOut{ background: #ccccff; color: #0000000; }
  .mouseOver{ background: #FFFAFA; color: #0000000; }
</style>
```

We've now enabled mouseover and mouseout event handling that will render the results displayed in Figure 11-4.

Undoubtedly, in your own applications that will utilize this type of data display, you'll want to allow for click event functionality. In our sample application, we simply intercept the event and dump the chosen search result into the input box:

```
function ReplaceInput(tablecell)
{
    // Swap Input box value with the value selected by
    // the user's mouse click
    var inputbox = document.getElementById("keyword");
    inputbox.value = tablecell.firstChild.nodeValue;
    ClearResults();
    HideDiv("searchresults");
}
```

Figure 11-5 illustrates how this will appear.

AJAX.NET

Google Suggest Demo:

Best Cycle Store

Figure 11-5. *After the click event*

Having worked through a few variations of the Google Suggest clone, we can see that the ability to preempt user input is not only possible, but pretty darn cool too. While it is a rather simple application, we can build upon the foundation, adding further bells and whistles.

Possible Extensions

In a real-world implementation, you might redirect the user to another details page or perhaps initiate more server-side activity.

The real Google Suggest application has a ton of functionality, some of which we have touched on in this chapter. There are other features that you may or may not want to add into your own search page. For instance, Google fills in the rest of the input box with the remaining characters of the first search result (see Figure 11-6).

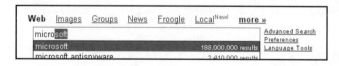

Figure 11-6. *Google auto-complete*

Google also caches your previous search result to prevent another server hit if the user presses their backspace key.

Both of these options are JavaScript-driven functions that will involve client-side manipulation of search results, and I encourage you to experiment with your own concept and design. We've built the primary structure of the Google Suggest application, and the rest is up to you!

Summary

Our Google Suggest clone example has not only reproduced the functionality of type-ahead, but you've also had the chance to work with a variety of data types and explore your ability to pass those types from server side to client side at will. You've learned some pretty important core Ajax concepts, and in the next chapter, we'll take an in-depth look at packaging Ajax capabilities into custom user controls and dive into the various caveats and limitations involved.

CHAPTER 12

■ ■ ■

User Controls and Ajax.NET

In the previous two chapters, we've taken a pretty good look at what Ajax can do for our dynamic web applications. And like most web applications, there exists a strong possibility that you'll want to reuse various Ajax components throughout your site. Web user controls have had a huge impact on developer productivity and web application design. In the past, we would have to cut and paste huge blocks of code into each individual page if we wanted to reproduce functionality across the site. For instance, without user controls, we would have to reproduce the Google Suggest clone code repeatedly for each desired placement of the type-ahead search box. This is simply not feasible for a structured environment, and thankfully we don't have to endure it. To this end, in this chapter we'll focus on web user controls and how we can embed Ajax functionality in those as well. There are certain caveats to implementation, and I'll point them out as we progress through the sample code.

I'm quite sure that by now you've plowed through Chapter 11 and have customized the Suggest box to facilitate various search functions within your own enterprise. And undoubtedly you have impressed your project manager with your fancy whiz-bang textbox. So much so that now there's much anticipation for how you'll be implementing that awesome functionality through the rest of your corporate web structure. After the applause and pay raises, you've taken a moment to realize that you've only just included the controls and coding on the search page and that accomplishing your new requirements will definitely require the use of a user control.

Before we transmogrify our Suggest clone into a user control, let's take a look at some of the minor idiosyncrasies you need to be aware of as we build some small applications that will push us towards the end goal of being able to simply drag and drop the clone onto any web page. In previous chapters, you downloaded and examined the project files, primarily to save time. Because this project application is so much smaller, I'll walk you through it step by step.

Setting Up Our Solution

Our first task is to set up our solution.

1. Start Visual Studio 2005 and select New ➤ WebSite.

2. When asked to name your site, enter **UserControlExample**.

3. Rename `Default.aspx` to `TestingForm.aspx`.

4. Right-click the website name and select Add New Item.

5. Select Web User Control and name it ucNameTest.ascx.

6. Right-click the website name and select Add Reference. Select Browse and then find your Anthem.dll.

You should have a solution setup very similar to what appears in Figure 12-1.

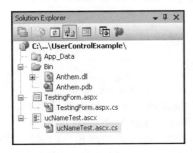

Figure 12-1. *Solution files*

Building the User Control

The first task is to build the user control itself. The primary purpose of the control is to display a textbox and a button. When the user clicks the button, we'll display the textbox value back to the user. Pretty technical work, but it's a start (sarcasm passes quickly here).

Ultimately, when we're done, we should have results similar to what you see in Figure 12-2.

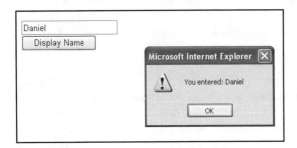

Figure 12-2. *The example user control in action*

The textbox and HTML button have been dropped into the control page, and subsequently the control was dropped onto TestingForm.aspx. Let's build that part now:

1. Switch to the ucNameText.aspx page. You'll want to be in design view of the .aspx file.

2. Drop a standard TextBox and an HTML Button onto the page and modify the HTML properties of these controls as follows:

```
<asp:TextBox ID="txtName" runat="server"></asp:TextBox>
<br />
<input id="btnDisplay" type="button" value="Display Name" />
```

Now that you've successfully added your primary controls to the user control, it would be awesome if they actually accomplished something. For the sake of simplicity, we'll have the button fire off an event that will pop up an alert with our entered information. Remain in the HTML view of the ucNameTest page and add the following script to the page so that the entire HTML reads as follows:

```
<%@ Control Language="C#" AutoEventWireup="true"
 CodeFile="ucNameTest.ascx.cs" Inherits="ucNameTest" %>
<script type="text/javascript">
function ButtonClicked()
{
    var txtbox= document.getElementById("txtName");
    alert("You entered: "  + txtbox.value);
}
</script>

<div id="divBuyButton">
  <asp:TextBox ID="txtName" runat="server"></asp:TextBox>
  <br />
  <input id="btnDisplay" type="button" value="Display Name" runat="server" />
</div>
```

As you glance through the code, you've undoubtedly become incredibly impressed by its superb complexity. OK, so maybe not. We have a JavaScript function called ButtonClicked() patiently waiting for an onclick event so that it can promptly render the alert box. However, the onclick event has yet to be implemented. Typically, we would throw an onclick="ButtonClicked();" into the HTML as an attribute for the button. However, we'll accomplish that in the Page_Load event on the server side. It's not the best practice for a simple click, but we'll get to the reasoning behind it momentarily.

Switch to the ucNameTest.ascx.cs and drill down into the Page_Load() function. Add the following code to your startup routine:

```
Anthem.Manager.Register(this);

if(!Page.IsPostBack)
{
    btnDisplay.Attributes["onclick"] = "javascript:return ButtonClicked();";
}
```

You'll recall from previous chapters that a call must be made to register this control as an Ajax-aware component. The click event should fire off the ButtonClicked() JavaScript function as a result of this assignment. Your user control code should be similar to the following:

```
using System;
using System.Data;
using System.Configuration;
using System.Collections;
using System.Web;
using System.Web.Security;
```

```
using System.Web.UI;
using System.Web.UI.WebControls;
using System.Web.UI.WebControls.WebParts;
using System.Web.UI.HtmlControls;

public partial class ucNameTest : System.Web.UI.UserControl
{
    protected void Page_Load(object sender, EventArgs e)
    {
        Anthem.Manager.Register(this);

        if (!Page.IsPostBack)
        {
            btnDisplay.Attributes["onclick"] = "javascript:return ButtonClicked();";
        }


    }
}
```

The user control is now finished. However, we can't test the functionality until it has been placed on an ASP.NET page.

1. Switch back to the TestingForm.aspx page (in design view).

2. Drag and drop your user control from the Solution Explorer onto the page.

By this point, your form should appear as shown in Figure 12-3.

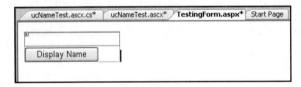

Figure 12-3. *TestingForm.aspx complete with user control*

Finally, we're presented with our user control, visible textbox and button included. Enter some text in the textbox and click the button. You'll notice immediately the conspicuous lack of an alert box. Instead, you'll find that the page has generated yet another error (as indicated by the JavaScript error icon at the bottom left of the screen in Figure 12-4).

Figure 12-4. *Page error*

Double-click the error icon to reveal the details of the error, as illustrated in Figure 12-5.

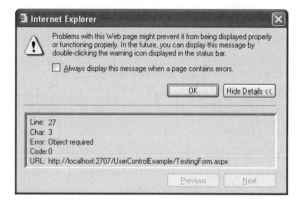

Figure 12-5. *Error details*

ClientID

This brings us to our first caveat of Ajax-enabled user controls. It's not particular to Ajax controls, but ASP.NET user controls in general. Our message indicates that something on the page is missing. In fact, it is our attempt at reading the control's textbox that has generated the error. If you bring up the source for the HTML by clicking View Source, you'll see an interesting problem concerning user controls on an ASP.NET page. Give particular attention to the portion of the page where the textbox and button have been rendered:

```
<div id="divBuyButton">
  <input name="UcNameTest1$txtName" type="text" id="UcNameTest1_txtName" />
  <br />
  <input name="UcNameTest1$btnDisplay" type="button"
         id="UcNameTest1_btnDisplay" value="Display Name"
         onclick="javascript:return ButtonClicked();" />
</div>
```

Interesting. The id properties of our controls have been renamed to UcNameTest1_txtName and UcNameTest1_btnDisplay, respectively. The ClientID property has been prefixed to the controls ID.

MSDN AND THE CLIENTID

All user controls will have their ID property modified at runtime. Refer to the MSDN site for more information: http://msdn.microsoft.com/library/default.asp?url=/library/en-us/cpref/html/ frlrfsystemwebuicontrolclassclientidtopic.asp.

This causes an error when the JavaScript `ButtonClicked()` function attempts to read the contents of the textbox with the following:

```
var txtbox= document.getElementById("txtName");
```

This is because our `ElementID` is no longer `txtName`. However, the repair for such a situation is easily implemented.

We first must pass the control's `ClientID` at runtime to the JavaScript function. In the `Page_Load` of the user control, modify your attribute assignment as shown:

```
btnDisplay.Attributes["onclick"] =
  "javascript:return ButtonClicked('"+ this.ClientID + "');";
```

When the control is initially compiled, the `ClientID` will be made available for use. Now that we've obtained the proper value, we'll need to modify the JavaScript's `ButtonClicked()` function to appropriate that passed-in value and utilize it as necessary:

```
function ButtonClicked(ClientID)
{
    var txtbox= document.getElementById(ClientID + "_txtName");
    alert("You entered: "  + txtbox.value);
}
```

The value is passed into and prefixed to the textbox ID. Notice also that the underscore must be added as well; otherwise, you'll be left with an `ElementID` of `ucNameTest1txtName` and you'll still be met with the same object-required issue. After you have modified the relevant script, run the application again. Finally, the results from Figure 12-2 have been realized.

Summarizing what you've garnered so far, concerning Ajax user controls:

- Always remember to register the user control with the `Anthem.Manager`.

- The `ClientID` is always prefixed to your `ElementID`s at runtime. You must account for this when attempting to locate them within the DOM.

Google Suggest Control

Now that a pattern for user control implementation has been established, it's a convenient time to realize the aforementioned request to have the Suggest clone rolled out as an ASP.NET user control.

To simplify things, let's create a separate solution for our new control:

1. Start a new instance of Visual Studio and select New ➤ WebSite.

2. Name your site **SuggestControlExample** and click OK.

3. Right-click the site name, and select Add New item ➤ Web User Control. Name your control ucSuggestControl.ascx and then click Open.

4. Rename Default.aspx to TestingForm.aspx.

5. Add the Anthem.dll file as in the previous example.

Your Solution Explorer should now resemble Figure 12-6.

Figure 12-6. *Solution Explorer for the Suggest clone control*

Once again, our shell is built, and it's time to fill in the forms to get this control off the ground and flying.

In a separate instance of Visual Studio, open up the Google Suggest clone project from the previous chapter. We'll be copying and pasting from that project to save time. After the clone project has loaded successfully, begin adding the runtime requirement to the appropriate control; in ucSuggestControl.aspx.cs add the Anthem registration to the Page_Load of the control:

```
Anthem.Manager.Register(this);
```

Now we'll add the appropriate functionality to the user control. Switch over to the Google Suggest clone project and open the HTML view of the SearchPage.aspx file. Select and copy everything in the <script></script> block **ONLY**. Do not grab any of the HTML-specific script. We're adding this to an ASP.NET user control, and those tags will produce undesirable results. Paste the JavaScript into your ucSuggestControl.aspx form. We will need our textbox and button, so we'll add the necessary HTML to the area following the closing </script>.

Let's first take a look at the finished .aspx file, shown here in Listing 12-1, so that you'll have a concept of what changes will need to be made to the client-side markup.

Listing 12-1. *The Modified ucSuggestControl.aspx*

```
<%@ Control Language="C#" AutoEventWireup="true"
 CodeFile="ucSuggestControl.ascx.cs" Inherits="ucSuggestControl" %>
<style type="text/css"> .mouseOut{ background: #ccccff; color: #0000000; }
.mouseOver{ background: #FFFAFA; color: #0000000; }
</style>

<script type="text/javascript">
var ClientID;

function ShowDiv(divid)
{
    if (document.layers) document.layers[divid].visibility="show";
    else document.getElementById(divid).style.visibility="visible";
}
```

```
function HideDiv(divid)
{
    if (document.layers) document.layers[divid].visibility="hide";
    else document.getElementById(divid).style.visibility="hidden";
}

function BodyLoad()
{
    HideDiv(ClientID + "searchresults");

    // Set focus to the input box
    var findtextbox = document.getElementById(ClientID + "keyword");
    findtextbox.focus();
}

function ClearResults()
{
    // Remove existing rows in results table
    var resultsdiv = document.getElementById(ClientID + "searchresults");
    var counter = resultsdiv.childNodes.length;
    for (var i = counter -1; i >= 0; i--)
    {
        resultsdiv.removeChild(resultsdiv.childNodes[i]);
    }
}

function LoadResults(searchterm)
{
    if (searchterm.length == 0)
    {
        // If the input box is empty, let's dump all the rows from
        // the results table
        ClearResults();
        HideDiv(ClientID + "searchresults");
        return;
    }

    // Fetch results from server side
    // This is our actual Ajax call
    Anthem_InvokeControlMethod(
        "<%= ClientID %>",
        'RetrieveRows',
        [searchterm],
        LoadResultsCallback);
}
```

```
function LoadResultsCallback(result)
{
    // The XmlHttpRequest will return to this function.
    ShowDiv(ClientID + "searchresults");
    ClearResults();

    // Callback results from Ajax call.
    // We'll assign the inbound DataTable
    // to the items variable
    var items = result.value;

    var count = items.Rows.length;

    // We'll create a table object in the DOM
    var divResults = document.getElementById(ClientID + "searchresults");
    var tblTable = document.createElement("table");
    var tablebody = document.createElement("tbody");
    var tablerow, tablecell, tablenode;

    // Loop through each of the rows in the DataTable
    for (var i = 0; i < count; i++)
    {
        var currenttext = items.Rows[i].Name;

        // We'll create each table row and append it to the
        // table body
        tablerow = document.createElement("tr");
        tablecell = document.createElement("td");
        // Build the cell attributes and functions
        tablecell.onmouseover = function(){this.className='mouseOver';};
        tablecell.onmouseout = function(){this.className='mouseOut';};
        tablecell.setAttribute("border", "0");
        tablecell.onclick = function(){ReplaceInput(this);};
        tablenode = document.createTextNode(currenttext);
        tablecell.appendChild(tablenode);
        tablerow.appendChild(tablecell);
        tablebody.appendChild(tablerow);
    }

    // Add the table body to the table
    tblTable.appendChild(tablebody);
    // Add the table to the div tag
    divResults.appendChild(tblTable);
}
```

```
function ReplaceInput(tablecell)
{
    // Swap Input box value with the value selected by
    // the user's mouse click
    var inputbox = document.getElementById(ClientID + "keyword");
    inputbox.value = tablecell.firstChild.nodeValue;
    ClearResults();
    HideDiv(ClientID + "searchresults");
}
</script>
```

```
<strong>Search:</strong>
<input name="keyword" onkeyup="LoadResults(this.value)"
       id="keyword" runat="server" style="WIDTH:500px" />
<div align="left" class="box" id="searchresults" runat="server"
    style="WIDTH:500px;BACKGROUND-COLOR:#ccccff">
</div>
```

One of the first modifications made to this sample versus the code in the previous chapter is that we have declared a global variable in the JavaScript where we'll park the ClientID for use in our various DOM lookups:

```
<script type="text/javascript">
var ClientID;
```

You'll see later how we populate that variable for use on the client side. The ShowDiv() and HideDiv() functions remain unchanged. The BodyLoad() function does have some minor changes as we begin to implement the ClientID requirement:

```
HideDiv(ClientID + "searchresults");
```

The ability to set the focus to the textbox has been altered as well:

```
var findtextbox = document.getElementById(ClientID + "keyword");
findtextbox.focus();
```

It's not until we hit the LoadResults() function that we start to see another Ajax control caveat:

```
Anthem_InvokeControlMethod(
  "<%= ClientID %>",
  'RetrieveRows',
  [searchterm],
  LoadResultsCallback);
```

Because our user control will be affected by the introduction of the ClientID prefix, we must account for that when calling our server-side function. Our Anthem library will accept that inline ClientID as an overloaded parameter, allowing our traffic the proper navigational aid.

Aside from the various ClientID additions to the ElementID locators, our final client-side change is nothing more than adding runat='server' and an ID assignment to the textbox and

HTML button. This will allow the two controls the opportunity to render with the respective ClientID prefixes when they're sent out to the user's browser.

Moving on to the server-side code within ucSuggestControl.ascx.cs, we find only a few minor changes as well:

```
using System;
using System.Data;
using System.Configuration;
using System.Collections;
using System.Web;
using System.Web.Security;
using System.Web.UI;
using System.Web.UI.WebControls;
using System.Web.UI.WebControls.WebParts;
using System.Web.UI.HtmlControls;
using System.Data.SqlClient;

public partial class ucSuggestControl : System.Web.UI.UserControl
{
    protected void Page_Load(object sender, EventArgs e)
    {
        Anthem.Manager.Register(this);
    }

    [Anthem.Method]
    public DataTable RetrieveRows(string searchterm)
    {
        SqlConnection conn = new SqlConnection("Data
         Source=(local);Initial Catalog=AdventureWorks;
         Integrated Security=SSPI");
        DataTable dtReturn = new DataTable();

        conn.Open();
        SqlCommand cmd = new SqlCommand("SELECT TOP 10 Name FROM Sales.Store ➥
WHERE Name LIKE @searchterm ORDER BY Name", conn);
        SqlParameter param = new SqlParameter();
        param.ParameterName = "@searchterm";
        searchterm.Trim().Replace("'", "''");
        searchterm += "%";
        param.Value = searchterm;
        cmd.Parameters.Add(param);

        SqlDataAdapter adpt = new SqlDataAdapter(cmd);
        adpt.Fill(dtReturn);
        conn.Close();
```

```
    // Send the DataTable back to the CallBack function
    return dtReturn;
}


protected override void OnInit(EventArgs e)
{
    base.OnInit(e);

    string jcode = "<script language=\"javascript\"
     type=\"text/javascript\">ClientID = '" + this.ClientID +
     "_" + "';BodyLoad();</script>";

    Page.ClientScript.RegisterStartupScript(typeof
    (Page),"suggest_control",  jcode);
}
}
```

The control is registered with the `Anthem.Manager`, as is typical with our other examples:

```
Anthem.Manager.Register(this);
```

And our Anthem method, `RetrieveRows()`, remains unchanged. There is some interesting code in the `OnInit()` call, however. In this function, we are building some JavaScript that will be called and established on HTML startup. What essentially will happen is that when the page is rendered, we will have an active JavaScript function call. Viewing the source for the page reveals that, indeed, our dynamic script has been rendered:

```
<script language="javascript" type="text/javascript">
  ClientID = 'UcSuggestControl1_';BodyLoad();</script>
```

If you'll recall from a few pages prior, we knew that we would be populating our client-side `ClientID` global variable from somewhere. The preceding code accomplishes this goal. We assign that variable and subsequently call the `BodyLoad()` function. Some minor housekeeping duties are dealt with, and our page loads as anticipated.

On the parent page, we simply drag and drop our user control onto the page.

Switching to design view, we'll modify the `Testingform.aspx` page to present a slightly more informative interface to the user. However, the functionality is unchanged:

```
<%@ Page Language="C#" AutoEventWireup="true"
 CodeFile="TestingForm.aspx.cs" Inherits="_Default" %>

<%@ Register Src="ucSuggestControl.ascx" TagName="ucSuggestControl"
 TagPrefix="uc1" %>

<!DOCTYPE html PUBLIC "-//W3C//DTD XHTML 1.0 Transitional//EN"
 "http://www.w3.org/TR/xhtml1/DTD/xhtml1-transitional.dtd">
```

```html
<html xmlns="http://www.w3.org/1999/xhtml" >
  <head runat="server">
    <title>Untitled Page</title>
  </head>
  <body>
    <form id="form1" runat="server">
      <table border="1">
        <tbody>
          <tr>
            <td valign="top">
              <strong>Welcome to the Search Page!</strong>
            </td>
            <td valign="top">
              <uc1:ucSuggestControl ID="UcSuggestControl2" runat="server" />
            </td>
          </tr>
        </tbody>
      </table>
    </form>
  </body>
</html>
```

Compiling and running our application should now give birth to the ultimate user interface, as shown in Figure 12-7.

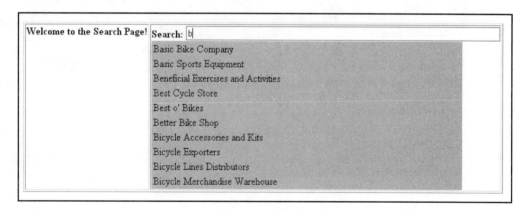

Figure 12-7. *TestingForm.aspx complete with working user control*

Summary

In this chapter, we've explored the various caveats to implementing user controls. Some key elements to remember:

- Always register your controls with the Ajax library!

- Don't forget to account for `ClientID`.

- Calls to the control's server-side code must include the `ClientID`.

- You can append dynamic JavaScript code at runtime from the server side.

A majority of the Ajax developers that I have had the pleasure of discussing this technology with will resoundingly agree that a majority of their work is done within the confines of web user controls. Mastering the design, coding, and provisions of this tool will go a long way when building truly interactive HTML interfaces for the web.

In the next chapter, we'll take a look at a few "out-of-the-box" controls that our library (and many others) can interact with. You may find it hard to go back to the standard .NET user controls after having a taste of the dynamic!

CHAPTER 13

■ ■ ■

Ajax and Mapping

One of the more popular Ajax-enabled applications on the web is the *map-enabled utility site*. Commonly referred to as *mash-ups*, these applications are typically a combination of various technologies all rolled into one useful tool. Microsoft's Virtual Earth (VE) application is one such application that has become a central tool to many of the mash-ups on the web. At its core, the VE library provides a scrollable Ajax map that can be dropped onto a web page seamlessly, as shown in Figure 13-1.

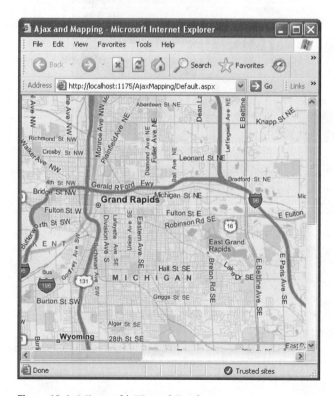

Figure 13-1. *Microsoft's Virtual Earth*

Virtual Earth is much more than just a draggable map. You can insert pushpins at designated points on the map and create layovers for various user-interaction tasks. A growing number of such applications are appearing almost daily on the web. One such application that I've found to be an interesting implementation of the Virtual Earth engine is Fresh Logic Studios' Atlas mapping site (not to be confused with the Atlas engine by Microsoft); it is an excellent example of what can be done with the Virtual Earth library, as Figure 13-2 demonstrates. They've created a site that has the map as its base technology and mashed up other tools on top of the VE.

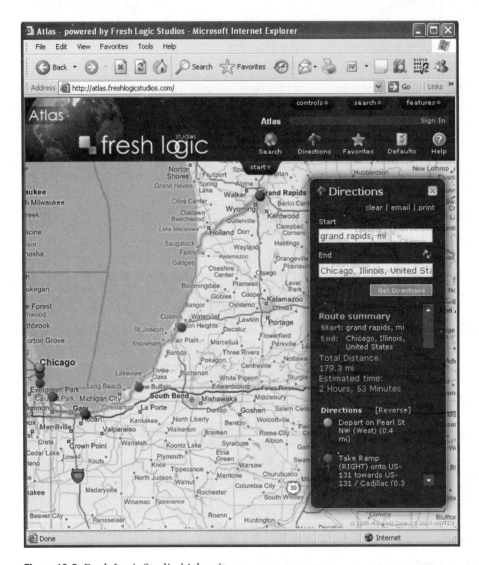

Figure 13-2. *Fresh Logic Studios' Atlas site*

For this chapter, I'll show you how to create a Virtual Earth mash-up. We'll be using the standard VE library files, available for free from Microsoft by searching for "Virtual Earth SDK" on the download site at http://www.microsoft.com/downloads; these files are also part of the sample application for this chapter.

The site that we will be building will combine Ajax, Virtual Earth, and Yahoo's traffic RSS feed. I should also credit Peter A. Bromberg, PhD, for his awesome article and VS 2003 application that mirrors the one we will be developing in this chapter. You can find them at Peter's blog: http://petesbloggerama.blogspot.com.

Using VE as a base for the page, we'll dynamically add pushpins of various traffic reports to the map. Yahoo has made a traffic RSS feed available to the public that includes not only a description of the event, but also longitude and latitude locators as well. We'll discuss the feed in more detail as well as the Virtual Earth library, but for now let's take a look at what the application can do and the associated solution and source code.

Ajax Traffic

In our application, the page will display a VE map centered on a hard-coded ZIP code (more on this in a moment), and pushpins will appear for various traffic delays that are near the aforementioned ZIP code, as you see in Figure 13-3.

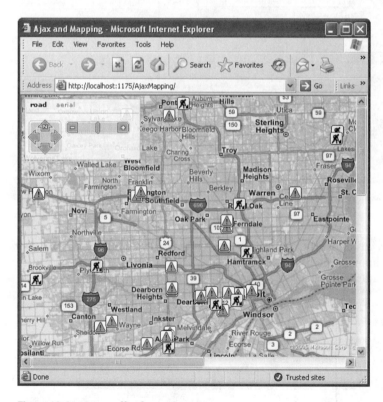

Figure 13-3. *Ajax traffic demonstration*

There are a few things worth noting concerning our application. As you can see, we have various traffic incidents in the Detroit area. You'll also notice that we have a variety of push-pins that have been applied to the map. Those are actually custom pushpins that did not come with the SDK. You'll see later how to add your own custom pushpins as well. Also notice that we have a floating toolbar that is home to our zoom controls. One other thing to note about the site is that each pushpin has a mouseover event that will render a pop-up containing details of the traffic report, as shown in Figure 13-4.

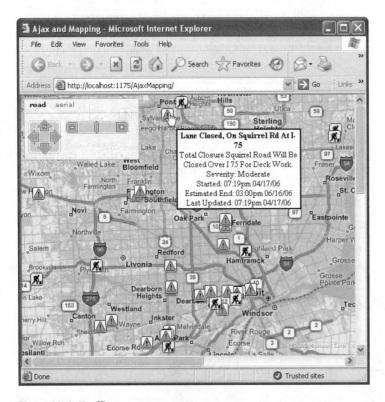

Figure 13-4. *Traffic pop-up*

You could, of course, customize the application (and I hope that you do) to center on your own hometown with the appropriate traffic for your area.

So let's open the solution and take a look at the file list, displayed in Figure 13-5.

Figure 13-5. *Ajax traffic solution*

We should first discuss the various files in brief:

- Anthem.dll: Ajax class library

- *Pin images*: Pushpins for the map

- Default.aspx: Our only web page and home to the map

- Web.Config: Standard Web.Config file

I've separated the custom pushpins out into their own directory. Each of the pushpins, illustrated in Figures 13-6 through 13-9, represents the category or severity of the traffic report.

Figure 13-6. *dude.gif—construction zone*

Figure 13-7. *minor.gif—minor traffic incident*

Figure 13-8. *moderate.gif—moderate traffic incident*

Figure 13-9. *major.gif—major traffic incident*

As I've said, you can modify these in a graphics editor of your choice, and they'll still work as planned.

Default.aspx

Now that we've taken a brief look at the overall structure of the application, let's take a look at the HTML and C# code for Default.aspx.

```
<%@ Page Language="C#" AutoEventWireup="true"
CodeFile="Default.aspx.cs" Inherits="_Default" %>

<!DOCTYPE html PUBLIC "-//W3C//DTD XHTML 1.0 Transitional//EN"
 "http://www.w3.org/TR/xhtml1/DTD/xhtml1-transitional.dtd">

<html xmlns="http://www.w3.org/1999/xhtml" >
  <head runat="server">
    <title>Ajax and Mapping</title>
```

```
<link href="http://dev.virtualearth.net/standard/v2/MapControl.css"
      type="text/css" rel="stylesheet" />
<script src="http://dev.virtualearth.net/standard/v2/MapControl.js"
        type="text/javascript"></script>

<style type="text/css" media="screen">
  #popup
  {
  POSITION:absolute;VISIBILITY:hidden;Z-INDEX:199;
  }

  .pinConstruction
  {
  cursor:pointer;text-decoration:none;
  z-index:5;
  }

  .pinMinor
  {
  cursor:pointer;text-decoration:none;
  z-index:5;
  }

  .pinModerate
  {
  cursor:pointer;text-decoration:none;
  z-index:5;
  }

  .pinMajor
  {
  cursor:pointer;text-decoration:none;
  z-index:5;
  }

</style>

<script type="text/javascript" language="javascript">
  var map = null;
  var myPanel;

  function OnPageLoad()
  {
    // Latitude and longitude have been hard-coded
    var params = new Object();
    params.latitude = 42.42;
    params.longitude = -83.02;
```

```
    params.zoomlevel = 10;
    params.mapstyle = Msn.VE.MapStyle.Road;
    params.showScaleBar = false;
    params.showDashboard = true;
    params.dashboardSize = Msn.VE.DashboardSize.Normal;
    params.dashboardX = 5;
    params.dashboardY = 5;
    map =
      new Msn.VE.MapControl(document.getElementById("myMap"),
        params);
    map.Init()
    PopulateMap();
}

function PopulateMap()
{
  // ZIP code has been hard-coded
  var zip = "48067";
  var mapmiles = 5;
  var mapseverity = 0;

  Anthem_InvokePageMethod(
      'PopulateMap', [zip, mapmiles, mapseverity], CallBack);
}

function CallBack(result)
{
  var table = result.value;
  var title = '';
  var description = '';
  var severity = '';

  var popstr = "";
  var newPushpin = null;
  var categry = '';

  for(var i=0;i<table.Rows.length;i++)
  {
    description = table.Rows[i].description ;
    description = replaceAll(description, ",", "<br>");
    severity = table.Rows[i].severity;
  title = table.Rows[i].title;
  category = table.Rows[i].category;
  severity = severity.replace(/^\s*|\s*$/g,"");
  category = category.replace(/^\s*|\s*$/g,"");
```

```
description = escape(description);
title = escape(title);

switch(category)
{
  case "Construction":
    var message = '<div><img src=\"pins/dude.gif\"';
      message +=  'onmouseover=\"popup(\'' + title + '\',\''
      message += description + '\','+ table.Rows[i].latitude
      message += ', ' + table.Rows[i].longitude
      message += ')\"; ONMOUSEOUT=\"closePopup()\"; />';
      message += '</div>';
    map.AddPushpin('pin' + i, table.Rows[i].latitude,
     table.Rows[i].longitude, 20, 20, 'pinConstruction', message);
    break;

  case "Incident":
    switch(severity)
    {
      case "Minor":
        var message = '<div><img src=\"pins/minor.gif\"';
          message +=  'onmouseover=\"popup(\'' + title + '\',\''
          message += description + '\','+ table.Rows[i].latitude
          message += ', ' + table.Rows[i].longitude
          message += ')\"; ONMOUSEOUT=\"closePopup()\"; />';
          message += '</div>';

        map.AddPushpin('pin' + i, table.Rows[i].latitude,
         table.Rows[i].longitude, 88, 34, 'pinMinor', message);
        break;

      case "Moderate":
        var message = '<div><img src=\"pins/moderate.gif\"';
          message += 'onmouseover=\"popup(\'' + title + '\',\''
          message += description + '\','+ table.Rows[i].latitude
          message += ', ' + table.Rows[i].longitude
          message += ')\"; ONMOUSEOUT=\"closePopup()\"; />';
          message += '</div>';

        map.AddPushpin('pin' + i, table.Rows[i].latitude,
         table.Rows[i].longitude, 88, 34, 'pinModerate', message);
        break;
```

```
            case "Major":
              var message = '<div><img src=\"pins/major.gif\"';
                message +=  'onmouseover=\"popup(\'' + title + '\',\''
                message += description + '\','+  table.Rows[i].latitude
                message += ', ' + table.Rows[i].longitude
                message += ')\"; ONMOUSEOUT=\"closePopup()\"; />';
                message += '</div>';

                map.AddPushpin('pin' + i, table.Rows[i].latitude,
                 table.Rows[i].longitude, 88, 34, 'pinMajor', message);
                break;
          }
        }
      }
    }

    function replaceAll( str, from, to )
    {
      var newindex = str.indexOf( from );
      while ( newindex > -1 )
      {
        str = str.replace( from, to );
        newindex = str.indexOf( from );
      }
      return str;
    }
  </script>
</head>

<body onload="OnPageLoad();">
  <form id="form1" runat="server">
    <div id="myMap" style="WIDTH: 600px; HEIGHT: 400px;
      OVERFLOW:hidden;"></div>
  <div id="popup"></div>
  </form>


  <script type="text/javascript">
    offX = -20;
    offY = 15;
    var popupStyle;
    var varY = -999;
    // Browser check variables
    var ns4 = document.layers;
    var ns6 = document.getElementById&&!document.all;
    var ie4 = document.all;
    var iex = (document.all);
```

```
if (ns4)
{
  popupStyle = document.popup;
}
else if (ns6)
{
popupStyle = document.getElementById("popup").style;
}
else if (ie4)
{
popupStyle = document.all.popup.style;
}

if(ns4)
{
document.captureEvents(Event.MOUSEMOVE);
}
else
{
popupStyle.visibility = "visible";
popupStyle.display = "none";
}

function popup(title, text, latit, longit)
{

  text = unescape(text);
  title = unescape(title);
  title = "<strong>" + title + "</strong><br>";

  var popHTML = "<TABLE  WIDTH=200 BORDER=1 BORDERCOLOR=black
   CELLPADDING=1 CELLSPACING=0 BGCOLOR=white";
  popHTML += "><TR><TD ALIGN=center><FONT COLOR=black SIZE=2>" +
   title + text + "</FONT></TD></TR></TABLE>";

  var left = map.GetX(longit);
  var top = map.GetY(latit);
  popupStyle.left = left + offX;
  popupStyle.top = top + offY;

  if(ns4)
  {
    popupStyle.document.write(popHTML);
    popupStyle.document.close();
    popupStyle.visibility = "visible"
  }
```

```
    if(ns6)
    {
      document.getElementById("popup").innerHTML = popHTML;
      popupStyle.display = '';
    }
    if(ie4)
    {
      document.all("popup").innerHTML = popHTML;
      popupStyle.display = '';
    }
  }

  function closePopup()
  {

    varY = -999;

    if(ns4)
    {
      popupStyle.visibility = "hidden";
    }
    else if (ns6||ie4)
    {
      popupStyle.display = "none";
    }
  }
</script>
</body>
</html>
```

Default.aspx.cs

Here's the code-behind file:

```
using System;
using System.Data;
using System.Configuration;
using System.Web;
using System.Web.Security;
using System.Web.UI;
using System.Web.UI.WebControls;
using System.Web.UI.WebControls.WebParts;
using System.Web.UI.HtmlControls;
```

```csharp
public partial class _Default : System.Web.UI.Page
{
  protected void Page_Load(object sender, EventArgs e)
  {
    Anthem.Manager.Register(this);
  }

  [Anthem.Method]
  public DataTable PopulateMap(string zipCode, int miles, int severity)
  {

    string urlpart1 = "http://maps.yahoo.com/traffic.rss?csz=";
    string urlpart2 = "&mag=";
    string urlpart3 = "&minsev=";
    DataTable returnDataTable = new DataTable();

    // Make the call and do map
    DataSet ds = new DataSet();
    string urlComplete = urlpart1 + zipCode + urlpart2 + miles.ToString()
     + urlpart3 + severity.ToString();

    ds.ReadXml(urlComplete);
    DataTable rsstbl = ds.Tables[2];

    returnDataTable.Columns.Add("latitude");
    returnDataTable.Columns.Add("longitude");
    returnDataTable.Columns.Add("title");
    returnDataTable.Columns.Add("description");
    returnDataTable.Columns.Add("severity");
    returnDataTable.Columns.Add("category");

    DataRow buildrow = null;
    foreach (DataRow row in rsstbl.Rows)
    {
      buildrow = returnDataTable.NewRow();
      buildrow["title"] = row["title"];
      buildrow["description"] = row["description"];
      buildrow["severity"] = row["severity"];
      buildrow["category"] = row["category"];

      string[] foundrow = row["link"].ToString().Split('&');
      foreach (string strPoints in foundrow)
      {
        if (strPoints.IndexOf("mlt=") > -1)
        {
          string[] strLat = strPoints.Split('=');
          buildrow["latitude"] = strLat[1];
        }
```

```
    if (strPoints.IndexOf("mln=") > -1)
    {
      string[] strLon = strPoints.Split('=');
      buildrow["longitude"] = strLon[1];
    }
  }
  returnDataTable.Rows.Add(buildrow);
}
return returnDataTable;
}
}
```

There really isn't much to the page, so it won't take long to dissect the application. As I stated earlier in the chapter, this application is a mash-up of three technologies, Virtual Earth, Yahoo's traffic feed, and Ajax.

Microsoft's Virtual Earth

One of the first things that I feel I should mention about this particular tool is that it is free **ONLY** if you use it for noncommercial purposes. If you use it for any for-profit purpose, you will need to use the commercial install instead. In our current example, we'll be using the free version of the control. You can find the appropriate MSDN information for it at `http://msdn.microsoft.com/library/default.asp?url=/library/en-us/VEMCSDK/HTML/Introduction.asp`.

Once you've opted for the appropriate license, you'll notice that Virtual Earth is really just a few files that you'll reference from your client-side application. As you can see from the first few lines of the `.aspx` code, we establish the VE control references right from the start:

```
<link href="http://dev.virtualearth.net/standard/v2/MapControl.css"
 type="text/css" rel="stylesheet" />
<script src="http://dev.virtualearth.net/standard/v2/MapControl.js"
 type="text/javascript"></script>
```

After setting script locations, using the map is rather simple. To render a viable map, we must accomplish a few things:

- Instantiate and assign the maps parameters.

- Create an instance of the map, with those parameters.

- Add pushpins (if desired).

First and foremost, we must create a new instance of the map. We accomplish this as shown:

```
map = new Msn.VE.MapControl(document.getElementById("myMap"), params);
```

The constructor accepts the placement element (our `div` container) as well as a detailed list of settings, as parameters prior to rendering your requested area:

- *Latitude*

- *Longitude*

- *Zoom level*: 1 (country level) to 19 (street level)
- *Map style*: r—road, h—hybrid, and a—aerial. `Msn.VE.MapStyle` enumerations available, as well
- *showScaleBar*: A scaled comparison bar
- *showDashboard*: The control panel for the map
- *dashboardSize*: Normal or small
- *dashboardX*: Left location of the dashboard
- *dashboardY*: Top location of the dashboard

As most of those listed are self-explanatory, only map style needs a bit more of an explanation.

Map Styles

Each of the map styles provides a unique perspective, so you'll need to choose what is appropriate for your application.

Road View

Selecting r for this particular parameter will render a standard road map view, as shown in Figure 13-10.

Figure 13-10. *Road view*

Hybrid View

Selecting h will produce the aerial view with labels, as you see in Figure 13-11.

Figure 13-11. *Hybrid view*

Aerial View

An a setting for map style will render a map similar to the hybrid, but without the labels, as shown in Figure 13-12.

Figure 13-12. *Aerial view*

Pushpins

The only other mapping component that we have yet to discuss is the Virtual Earth pushpin. Figure 13-4 demonstrated the pushpin pop-up that we have access to, out of the box. Creating a pushpin requires only one method:

```
map.AddPushpin('pin' + i, table.Rows[i].latitude,
  table.Rows[i].longitude, 88, 34, 'pinMajor', message);
```

Here's the constructor for the pushpin:

```
AddPushpin(id, latitude, longitude, width, height, css class, innerHTML, Z-index)
```

- id: A unique ID for the pushpin

- latitude: Global location on the map to place the pushpin

- longitude: Global location on the map to place the pushpin

- width: Width of the pushpin

- height: Height of the pushpin

- css class: Class name of the CSS style to inherit

- innerHTML: HTML text for the mouseover pop-up

- Z-index: The Z-index of the pushpin

I've created a few CSS classes for each of the individual pushpins, but they all have the same contents. You could, of course, reduce them down to one and use that as the class parameter for the pushpin. I've spread them out for the sake of customization and readability. If you're not interested in pop-ups in your own Virtual Earth map, you'll make heavy use of the style blocks, perhaps assigning your own images to the background-image property. For now, the styles appear as shown:

```
.pinConstruction
{
cursor:pointer;text-decoration:none;
z-index:5;
}
.pinMinor
{
cursor:pointer;text-decoration:none;
z-index:5;
}
.pinModerate
{
cursor:pointer;text-decoration:none;
z-index:5;
}
.pinMajor
{
cursor:pointer;text-decoration:none;
z-index:5;
}
```

Now that we've examined the style sheets for pushpins, the actual creation and placement of those items simply involve retrieving the dynamic data (our traffic data), building the HTML for the pushpin, and adding them to the map, which you'll see in the "Using the Feed" section.

And this brings us to our second major technology of the mash-up, the Yahoo traffic feed.

Yahoo Traffic Feed

The kind folks at Yahoo have made available a rather intricate RSS feed, capable of accepting a variety of request parameters and returning any registered traffic reports for the given area. I should note, however, that not all cities are supported. The best thing you could do is just plug in some parameters and try it out. Also, Yahoo relies on the submission of reports from the appropriate Department of Transportation, and occasionally there may be things unreported. For instance, as I was driving home recently, I came across a construction zone, yet the Yahoo RSS feed showed nothing for my area. So if you're going to use the feed for retail purposes, be aware that it's not always spot-on. But it's a cool tool to use and worthy of deep scrutiny.

Fortunately for all you RSS addicts, the feed is RSS 2.0 conformant. That's good news for those of you building and implementing your own aggregators, as you'll be able to seamlessly integrate this feed.

Calling the feed can be as simple as pasting the URL into your browser and viewing the results. For instance, a feed of Detroit, Michigan, can be obtained by pasting the following URL into the address bar and letting Yahoo work its magic: http://api.local.yahoo.com/MapsService/rss/trafficData.xml?appid=YahooDemo&city=Detroit&state=Michigan.

Let's take a look at the feed that comes back from Yahoo, and then we will discuss the request parameters and response elements:

```
<?xml version="1.0" encoding="UTF-8"?>
<rss xmlns:geo="http://www.w3.org/2003/01/geo/wgs84_pos#" version="2.0">
<channel>
<title>Yahoo! Traffic Alerts</title>
<link>http://maps.yahoo.com</link>
<language>en</language>
<description>Traffic Alerts</description>
<copyright>Copyright (c) 2005 Yahoo! Inc. All rights reserved.</copyright>
<lastBuildDate>Tue, 21 Feb 2006 13:39:08 -0800</lastBuildDate>
<image>
<url>http://us.i1.yimg.com/us.yimg.com/i/us/nt/b/rss/rss_search.gif</url>
<title>Yahoo! Maps</title>
<link>http://maps.yahoo.com</link>
<width>142</width>
<height>18</height>
</image>
<item>
<title>Object on Roadway</title>
<link>http://img.maps.yahoo.com/mapimage?MAPDATA=
A3yNBed6wXWyUygjgNR64Ey8tpikQJ7Tr.w_72S_uZO2TXZQh
BIPCCtZdEUyHQp62zZ8za6IlWspuj1TooX05Aqep9JPK6E3Z3
6Pc7V6v5KMSrM7DXxhaCBffkwmuA5oxi2_.vpu423r1eYCAAK
VEra.C.c20GNu9ra9fYO-</link>
<description>DEBRIS ON ROAD; USE CAUTION; ON LEFT
 SIDE OF RAMP   STAY RIGHT   FIBERGLASS INSULATION
IS PARTIALLY BLOCKING THE RAMP.</description>
<geo:lat>42.487840</geo:lat>
<geo:long>-83.045690</geo:long>
```

```
<guid isPermaLink="false">http://img.maps.yahoo.com/mapimage?
MAPDATA=A3yNBed6wXWyUygjgNR64Ey8tpikQJ7Tr.w_72S_uZO2TXZQhBIPC
CtZdEUyHQp62zZ8za6IlWspuj1TooXO5Aqep9JPK6E3Z36Pc7V6v5KMSrM7DX
xhaCBffkwmuA5oxi2_.vpu423r1eYCAAKVEra.C.c2OGNu9ra9fYO-</guid>
<pubDate>Tue, 21 Feb 2006 13:05:41 -0800</pubDate>
</item>
</channel>
</rss>
<!-- ws02.search.re2.yahoo.com compressed/chunked Tue Feb 21 13:42:40 PST 2006 -->
```

What? Only one incident in the entire city of Detroit? OK, so maybe I deleted a few (or 15) for the sake of brevity. But the structure is the same, and you'll be able to understand the concept being presented here.

To get this feed, you'll notice that I supplied the RSS address with a few selective parameters:

```
appid=YahooDemo&city=Detroit&state=Michigan
```

The input parameters are key to getting the traffic for the region that you're interested in. Yahoo has been gracious enough to supply a pretty detailed list of the requisite items, provided here in Table 13-1.

Table 13-1. *Yahoo RSS Request Parameters*

Parameter	Data Type	Description
appid	String	Application ID of your site. Any unique ID that you specify.
latitude	Float (–90 to 90)	The latitude of the location.
longitude	Float	The longitude of the location.
street	String	The street name of the location—unit number optional.
city	String	The city name of the location.
zip	Int (int-int)	Five-digit ZIP code or five-digit plus four-digit extension. City and state will be ignored if they don't match the ZIP code specified.
location	Free text	Allows you to enter complete location information in various formats, as previously shown: city, state city, state, zip zip street, city, state street, city, state, zip street, zip If you supply any information in this field, it will take priority over any of the other individual location fields.
severity	Int (1 to 5)	The smallest severity level to return (1 is minor, 5 is severe).
zoom	Int (1 to 12)	Zoom level (similar to the map) indicating area to capture events for. A 1 would be street level, and 12 gathers country level. If you provide a radius parameter, Yahoo will ignore this parameter.

Parameter	Data Type	Description
radius	Float	The area in miles that Yahoo should provide traffic data for.
include_map	Binary	This parameter is always 1. Yahoo will always generate a map.
image_type	PNG or GIF	PNG is the default image format, but GIFs are available.
image_height	Int (10 to 2000)	Height of the image returned in pixels. Default is 500.
image_width	Int (10 to 2000)	Width of the image returned in pixels. Default is 620.

Once you're armed with the proper parameters, you can start to play around with the RSS service a little more.

A few notes about the various parameters:

- appid is anything that you want it to be. It should be unique across your multiple applications.

- If you use the location parameter, be aware that anything you provide in the other indicators (state, ZIP, street, etc.) will be overridden by the data contained within the location text. Usage is pretty simple: http://api.local.yahoo.com/MapsService/rss/trafficData.xml?appid=YahooDemo&location=Hollywood,%20California.

The XML elements of the response text have been annotated well by Yahoo, as you would expect.

Yahoo Response Elements

Tables 13-2 and 13-3 show the response elements contained in the RSS feed.

Table 13-2. *Top-level Element*

Element	Description
rss	Topmost element of the feed. Yahoo's traffic feed conforms to RSS 2.0 specs.

Example:

```
<rss xmlns:geo="http://www.w3.org/2003/01/geo/wgs84_pos#" version="2.0">
```

The rss element contains a channel element as its child element. The channel element contains child elements as described in Table 13-3.

Table 13-3. *Channel Elements*

Element	Description
title	Feed title.
link	The Yahoo map URL.
language	Language of the supplied traffic alert (English—en).
description	The feed description ("Traffic Alerts").
copyright	The Yahoo default copyright for the feed.
lastBuildDate	Date of last update for the report location.
image	The identification image for the feed. Typically, this is the Yahoo logo. We'll discuss the image element and its child elements in a moment.
item	An individual traffic report. We'll discuss the item element momentarily.

Here's an example:

```
<channel>
<title>Yahoo! Traffic Alerts</title>
<link>http://maps.yahoo.com</link>
<language>en</language>
<description>Traffic Alerts</description>
<copyright>Copyright (c) 2005 Yahoo! Inc. All rights reserved.</copyright>
<lastBuildDate>Tue, 21 Feb 2006 13:39:08 -0800</lastBuildDate>
<image>
...more about this, later.
</image>
<item>
...we'll discuss this in a moment.
</item>
</channel>
```

Image Elements

The image element describes the icon or graphic associated with the feed. Most likely it will be the Yahoo Search logo, because we are using the Yahoo Search engine to obtain the results. (I'm guessing on the association. I don't work at Yahoo, and they don't exactly say, but it sure seems obvious.) In the preceding XML result, if we copy and paste the image URL location, we should see the graphic shown in Figure 13-13.

Figure 13-13. *Image element*

The image element has the structure outlined in Table 13-4.

Table 13-4. *Image Elements*

Element	Description
url	Web address of the image
title	The title of the site that the feed is referring to
link	URL of the site that the feed is referring to
width	Width of the image in pixels
height	Height of the image in pixels

Here's an example:

```
<image>
<url>http://us.i1.yimg.com/us.yimg.com/i/us/nt/b/rss/rss_search.gif</url>
<title>Yahoo! Maps</title>
<link>http://maps.yahoo.com</link>
<width>142</width>
<height>18</height>
</image>
```

Item Elements

The channel element contains one final element block, which is encapsulated within <item> tags. item elements are the actual reports that we're after, and the tags are pretty much what would we have come to expect so far, as you can see in Table 13-5.

Table 13-5. *Item Elements*

Element	Description
title	The title of the alert.
link	The address of the available map for the alert. This will always be available.
description	The details of the traffic report.
geo:lat	The latitude of the report.
geo:long	The longitude of the report.
guid	The Yahoo-generated identifier for the report.
pubDate	Date and time of the traffic incident.

Here's an example:

```
<item>
<title>Object on Roadway</title>
<link>http://img.maps.yahoo.com/mapimage?MAPDATA=A3yNBed6wXWyUygjgNR64Ey8tpikQJ7Tr
.W_72S_uZO2TXZQhBIPCCtZdEUyHQp62zZ8za6IlWspuj1TooXO5Aqep9JPK6E3Z36Pc7V6v5KMSrM7DXxha
CBffkwmuA5oxi2_.vpu423r1eYCAAKVEra.C.c2OGNu9ra9fYO-</link>
<description>DEBRIS ON ROAD; USE CAUTION; ON LEFT SIDE OF RAMP  STAY RIGHT
FIBERGLASS INSULATION  IS PARTIALLY BLOCKING THE RAMP.</description>
```

```
<geo:lat>42.487840</geo:lat>
<geo:long>-83.045690</geo:long>
<guid isPermaLink="false">http://img.maps.yahoo.com/mapimage?MAPDATA=A3yNBed6wXWyU
ygjgNR64Ey8tpikQJ7Tr.w_72S_uZO2TXZQhBIPCCtZdEUyHQp62zZ8za6IlWspuj1TooXO5Aqep9JPK6E3Z
36Pc7V6v5KMSrM7DXxhaCBffkwmuA5oxi2_.vpu423r1eYCAAKVEra.C.c2OGNu9ra9fYO-</guid>
<pubDate>Tue, 21 Feb 2006 13:05:41 -0800</pubDate>
</item>
```

Using the Feed

So now that you have a pretty good grasp on what it is that Yahoo can do for you, let's take a look at how we bring this feed into the application and ultimately parse the data for the map. Here we will discuss the method from which we will draw our pushpin locations that will represent various traffic reports across the area. We handle the Ajax-enabled call to retrieve a data table in PopulateMap:

```
function PopulateMap()
{
  // ZIP code has been hard-coded
  var zip = "48067";
  var mapmiles = 5;
  var mapseverity = 0;

  Anthem_InvokePageMethod('PopulateMap',[zip, mapmiles, mapseverity], CallBack);

}
```

As you can see, we're hard-coding the ZIP code for the map that we wish to retrieve. We could just as easily provide a textbox interface for this element, but for simplicity's sake, we'll just hard-code it. We then provide a radius of coverage that we'd like to see returned as well as the severity level of the reports being generated. We'll ask for zero, which means we'll receive all the results for the area we've requested.

We then make the call to the Ajax method, providing CallBack as the callback function.

Server Side

On the server side of things, we communicate with Yahoo, providing the requisite parameters and building a DataTable that we'll pass back to the client for parsing:

```
[Anthem.Method]
public DataTable PopulateMap(string zipCode, int miles, int severity)
{
  string urlpart1 = "http://maps.yahoo.com/traffic.rss?csz=";
  string urlpart2 = "&mag=";
  string urlpart3 = "&minsev=";
  DataTable returnDataTable = new DataTable();
```

```
// Make the call and do map
DataSet ds = new DataSet();
string urlComplete = urlpart1 + zipCode + urlpart2 + miles.ToString()
  + urlpart3 + severity.ToString();

ds.ReadXml(urlComplete);
DataTable rsstbl = ds.Tables[2];

returnDataTable.Columns.Add("latitude");
returnDataTable.Columns.Add("longitude");
returnDataTable.Columns.Add("title");
returnDataTable.Columns.Add("description");
returnDataTable.Columns.Add("severity");
returnDataTable.Columns.Add("category");

DataRow buildrow = null;
foreach (DataRow row in rsstbl.Rows)
{
  buildrow = returnDataTable.NewRow();
  buildrow["title"] = row["title"];
  buildrow["description"] = row["description"];
  buildrow["severity"] = row["severity"];
  buildrow["category"] = row["category"];

  string[] foundrow = row["link"].ToString().Split('&');
  foreach (string strPoints in foundrow)
  {
    if (strPoints.IndexOf("mlt=") > -1)
    {
      string[] strLat = strPoints.Split('=');
      buildrow["latitude"] = strLat[1];
    }

    if (strPoints.IndexOf("mln=") > -1)
    {
      string[] strLon = strPoints.Split('=');
      buildrow["longitude"] = strLon[1];
    }
  }
  returnDataTable.Rows.Add(buildrow);
}
return returnDataTable;
}
```

Client Side

Back on the client side of things, as you've seen before, our callback method waits patiently for the traffic table to return for parsing. After parsing the table and adding pushpins with the map.AddPushpin() method, we exit the process and wait for the next user interaction:

```
function CallBack(result)
{
  var table = result.value;
  var title = '';
  var description = '';
  var severity = '';

  var popstr = "";
  var newPushpin = null;
  var categry = '';

  for(var i=0;i<table.Rows.length;i++)
  {
    description = table.Rows[i].description ;
    description = replaceAll(description, ",", "<br>");
    severity = table.Rows[i].severity;
    title = table.Rows[i].title;
    category = table.Rows[i].category;
    severity = severity.replace(/^\s*|\s*$/g,"");
    category = category.replace(/^\s*|\s*$/g,"");

    description = escape(description);
    title = escape(title);
    switch(category)
    {
      case "Construction":
        var message = '<div><img src=\"pins/dude.gif\"';
          message += 'onmouseover=\"popup(\'' + title + '\',\'';
          message += description + '\','+ table.Rows[i].latitude ;
          message += ', ' + table.Rows[i].longitude ;
          message += ')\"; ONMOUSEOUT=\"closePopup()\"; />';
          message += '</div>';
        map.AddPushpin('pin' + i, table.Rows[i].latitude,
          table.Rows[i].longitude, 20, 20, 'pinConstruction', message);
        break;

      case "Incident":
        switch(severity)
        {
          case "Minor":
            var message = '<div><img src=\"pins/minor.gif\"';
```

```
      message +=  'onmouseover=\"popup(\'' + title + '\',\''
      message += description + '\','+ table.Rows[i].latitude
      message += ', ' + table.Rows[i].longitude
      message += ')\"; ONMOUSEOUT=\"closePopup()\"; />';
      message += '</div>';

    map.AddPushpin('pin' + i, table.Rows[i].latitude,
      table.Rows[i].longitude, 88, 34, 'pinMinor', message);
    break;

  case "Moderate":
    var message = '<div><img src=\"pins/moderate.gif\"';
      message +=  'onmouseover=\"popup(\'' + title + '\',\''
      message += description + '\','+ table.Rows[i].latitude
      message += ', ' + table.Rows[i].longitude
      message += ')\"; ONMOUSEOUT=\"closePopup()\"; />';
      message += '</div>';

    map.AddPushpin('pin' + i, table.Rows[i].latitude,
      table.Rows[i].longitude, 88, 34, 'pinModerate', message);
    break;

  case "Major":
    var message = '<div><img src=\"pins/major.gif\"';
      message +=  'onmouseover=\"popup(\'' + title + '\',\''
      message += description + '\','+ table.Rows[i].latitude
      message += ', ' + table.Rows[i].longitude
      message += ')\"; ONMOUSEOUT=\"closePopup()\"; />';
      message += '</div>';

    map.AddPushpin('pin' + i, table.Rows[i].latitude,
      table.Rows[i].longitude, 88, 34, 'pinMajor', message);
    break;
    }
   }
  }
 }
}
```

Depending on the severity of the traffic incident, a corresponding set of parameters is generated for the AddPushpin() method. We supply the latitude and longitude as you would expect, and we also provide the generated message. Our message is built upon the idea that we'll be using a custom div and a nested pin image as the pushpin, rather than just a static image. Because of this, we'll be able to generate a pop-up of the incident details as shown earlier in Figure 13-4. The popup method is called in the onmouseover event, as shown previously. The popup code itself is a pretty easy read:

```
<div id="popup"></div>
<script type="text/javascript">
  offX = -20;
  offY = 15;
  var popupStyle;
  var varY = -999;
  // Browser check variables
  var ns4=document.layers;
  var ns6=document.getElementById&&!document.all;
  var ie4=document.all;
  var iex = (document.all);

  if (ns4)
  {
    popupStyle = document.popup;
  }
  else if (ns6)
  {
    popupStyle = document.getElementById("popup").style;
  }
  else if (ie4)
  {
    popupStyle = document.all.popup.style;
  }

  if(ns4)
  {
    document.captureEvents(Event.MOUSEMOVE);
  }
  else
  {
    popupStyle.visibility = "visible";
    popupStyle.display = "none";
  }

  function popup(title, text, latit, longit)
  {
    text = unescape(text);
    title = unescape(title);
    title = "<strong>" + title + "</strong><br>";

    var popHTML = "<TABLE  WIDTH=200 BORDER=1 BORDERCOLOR=black
      CELLPADDING=1 CELLSPACING=0 BGCOLOR=white";
    popHTML += "><TR><TD ALIGN=center><FONT COLOR=black SIZE=2>" +
      title + text + "</FONT></TD></TR></TABLE>";
```

```
    var left = map.GetX(longit);
    var top = map.GetY(latit);
    popupStyle.left = left + offX;
    popupStyle.top = top + offY;

    if(ns4)
    {
      popupStyle.document.write(popHTML);
      popupStyle.document.close(),
      popupStyle.visibility = "visible"
    }

    if(ns6)
    {
      document.getElementById("popup").innerHTML = popHTML;
      popupStyle.display = '';
    }

    if(ie4)
    {
      document.all("popup").innerHTML = popHTML;
      popupStyle.display = '';
    }
  }

  function closePopup()
  {

    varY = -999;

    if(ns4)
    {
      popupStyle.visibility = "hidden";
    }
    else if (ns6||ie4)
    {
      popupStyle.display = "none";
    }
  }
}
</script>
```

We're able to supply the popup function parameters, based on information that we've retrieved from the Yahoo feed:

```
function popup(title, text, latit, longit)
```

The popup function builds and compiles the innerHTML that we'll push out to the empty <div> block that we have statically assigned to the body of the page:

```
<div id="popup"></div>
```

Our popup function basically turns on the visibility of the floating <div>, and our traffic details are proudly displayed to the user.

And that's it! We've successfully completed the full cycle of the map application.

Summary

Combining Ajax with other various online tools, whether they be dynamic mapping, RSS feeds, or image providers, can be truly powerful, with a huge impact on site appreciation. Ajax-enabled applications, as you've seen here, can be so much more than just simple dynamic textbox updating. It's easy to get excited when you see how easy it is to mash up your own applications.

In the next few chapters, you'll see how Ajax can be used, not as a mash-up component, but as an integral part of application frameworks as well. We'll build an Ajax Web Part for ASP.NET 2.0 as we begin to take advantage of the unique, new tools that version 2.0 has given us.

■ ■ ■

Ajax and Web Parts

Recently, I attended the 2006 Tech Trends event featuring Keith Brophy. Each year, Keith not only discusses his perception of the coming future, but also grades himself on his previous year's forecast.

This year he fared well on his previous assessments, despite the reluctance on his part to grant himself a high grade for anything. During the course of his predictions for 2006 and beyond, he mentioned some very key points about the course of web technology that I'm sure you've probably also taken note of. The web as we know it is changing. We have the tools, bandwidth, and resources to do things now that were unheard of 5 years ago. And we're beginning to see a shift away from what the technology has become and have begun to concentrate on how we will use the technology. And as Keith said in his annual speech, the web is becoming more about connecting people. The ability to connect systems, machines, and devices isn't really a challenge anymore. However, building a site that represents a meaningful collection of personal, relevant data is slowly emerging as the next Internet boom.

It seems that nearly everyone has a MySpace (http://www.myspace.com) account (except me), and one of the reasons for its success is that it connects people with an interface that is a personalized reflection of the member. When you visit a MySpace site, you quickly get a feel for the personality of the member from the various parts of the page.

Commonly known as *portal sites*, these web applications tend to dissect the page into various sections of grouped data. You might find a weather box detailing the forecast for the member's hometown or a collection of blogs that they frequent. Some portal sites have streaming stock quote parts as well as multimedia players, all separated into their own windows or spaces on the page. The really cool sites allow you to choose from an assortment of these components to plug into the site, giving it a truly personalized environment.

One such site, Microsoft's My MSN, gathers information from your Passport profile and then applies such settings as your location to various web components on the web page. When you visit your site, you'll find the weather for your area, possible traffic maps for the surrounding city, and local news as well.

IN THE AREA?

If you're in the Midwest, I'd encourage you to attend Keith's forecast. You'll come away with an encouraging and hopeful feel for what technology has in store for us in the coming years. Details are generally available at http://www.glimawest.org.

MICROSOFT AND MY MSN

If you have a Microsoft Passport account, check out your customizable web portal at http://my.msn.com.

As you can see in Figure 14-1, the portal is made up of various parts. In a single page, I have access to the information that I would have generally had to visit quite a few pages to get. More and more, we begin to see community sites evolving to a similar methodology of information modularization.

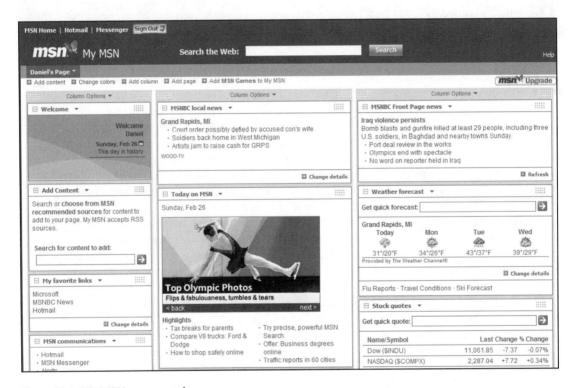

Figure 14-1. *My MSN page portal*

Another product that has run with the notion of building sites with manipulative components is DotNetNuke. This product thrives because of its ease of use and the ability to add custom modules to the page. I use the product for my personal site (shown in Figure 14-2) and find it to be an extremely intuitive product.

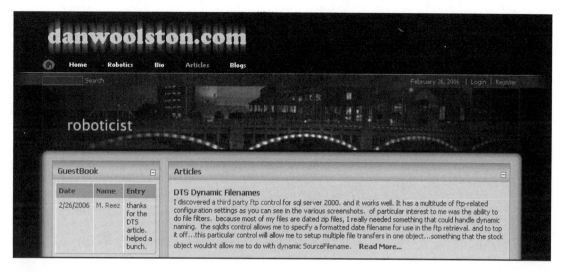

Figure 14-2. *My DotNetNuke site with modules*

ASP.NET 2.0 brings one important ingredient to these portal sites that is an essential building block: *Web Parts.* Web Parts have been around, relatively speaking, for quite some time. They are a direct descendant of the SharePoint Server 2003 Web Part. This component allows web developers to build customizable parts that not only represent unique information, but also allow users to rearrange the page to their own liking, as shown in Figure 14-3.

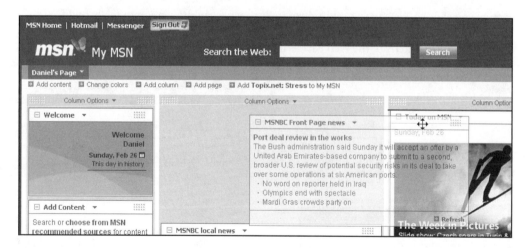

Figure 14-3. *Drag-and-drop Web Parts*

This chapter will introduce not only Web Parts, but also how to throw some Ajax into the mix. We'll build a rather simple web interface with a couple Web Parts that we'll be able to drag around on the page and drop into our designated areas.

Web Parts

So what exactly is a Web Part? As we've seen, it is a modular component that is capable of customization, themes, and relocation. In Visual Studio 2005, creating a Web Part can be as simple as dragging a server control into a Web Part Zone. You're free to build custom user controls and implement them as Web Parts, as well.

The toolbox provides a ton of out-of-the-box functionality for us, with some preexisting components, shown in Figure 14-4, that we'll use in the coming example.

Figure 14-4. *Web Parts toolset*

As you can see, we have a multitude of tools that we can draw upon to really build dynamic portal sites. However, before we begin the sample application, we should probably begin with the hierarchy of the Web Part as it relates to the page.

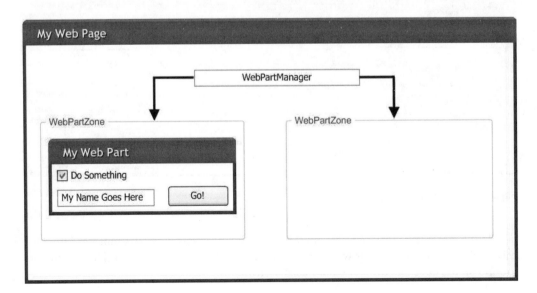

Figure 14-5. *Web Parts hierarchy*

Figure 14-5 illustrates the idea that a Web Part is not the only component on the page when it's put into use. For us to have that functionality, we must first drag one, and only one, WebPartManager control out onto the page. This control is responsible for managing the various Web Parts on the page and, as I've stated, you can only have one per page.

Another condition that we must consider is that Web Parts must have a place to live. You can't just drop them onto the page. You'll need to take advantage of the WebPartZone containers. You can have one to many of these controls on the page, placing them where you'd like to have a Web Part presence. And of course, you have the Web Part. You can easily create a Web Part by dragging a server control onto a WebPartZone. Visual Studio will create a GenericWebPart control for you. However, dragging multiple controls onto the zone will simply create more Web Parts.

If you want to create a multicontrol Web Part, you'll need to create a Web User Control (which we'll be doing soon). For the most part, I would recommend to you that you not use the GenericWebPart and instead choose to implement the IWebPart interface. You'll see a performance boost as well as some more advanced properties.

The best way for you to really learn the process of assembling these components is to simply build it by example.

Ajax and Web Parts Sample Application

First and foremost, let's discuss what the application will do. Figure 14-6 illustrates the layout and general functionality.

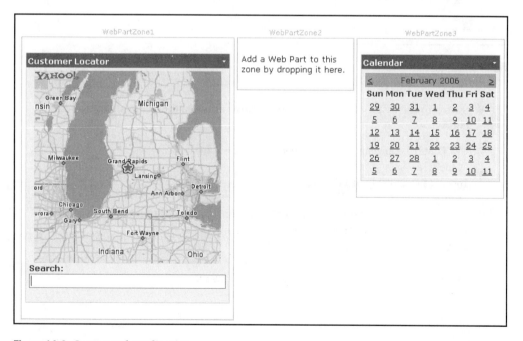

Figure 14-6. *Our portal application*

You can see that we have three WebPartZones from which we can drag and drop our two individual Web Parts out onto an ASP.NET page. When we type in the Search box, a drop-down list appears as we type (look familiar?), and when we click the store location, a new map is retrieved and displayed above the search box. The calendar, however, does nothing. Well, it does give us the date, so technically it's doing *something*.

So without further delay, let's build the example application.

1. Open Visual Studio and create a new WebSite project, naming it "Portal".

2. Add the Anthem reference, as you have before.

3. Create a controls folder, naming it controls.

4. Add a Web User Control to the controls folder, naming that ucCustomerLocator.ascx.

5. Don't delete Default.aspx. We'll be using that as the host for our user control.

Your solution should now look like Figure 14-7.

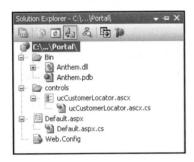

Figure 14-7. *Current solution files*

6. Switch to the .aspx view of ucCustomerLocator and add the following to your HTML code view:

```
<%@ Control Language="C#" AutoEventWireup="true"
 CodeFile="ucCustomerLocator.ascx.cs"
Inherits="controls_ucCustomerLocator" %>
<style type="text/css">
    .mouseOut{ background: #ccccff; color: #0000000; }
    .mouseOver{ background: #FFFAFA; color: #0000000; }
</style>

<script type="text/javascript" language="javascript">
var ClientID = "";
```

```
function ShowDiv(divid)
{
   if (document.layers) document.layers[divid].visibility="show";
   else document.getElementById(divid).style.visibility="visible";
}

function HideDiv(divid)
{
   if (document.layers) document.layers[divid].visibility="hide";
   else document.getElementById(divid).style.visibility="hidden";
}

function BodyStart()
{
   // Populate a customer map
   StarterMap();

   HideDiv(ClientID + "searchresults");

   // Set focus to the input box
   var findtextbox = document.getElementById(ClientID + "keyword");
   findtextbox.focus();
}

function ClearResults()
{
   // Remove existing rows in results table
   var resultsdiv = document.getElementById(ClientID + "searchresults");
   var counter = resultsdiv.childNodes.length;
   for (var i = counter -1; i >= 0; i--)
   {
      resultsdiv.removeChild(resultsdiv.childNodes[i]);
   }
}

function LoadResults(searchterm)
{
   if (searchterm.length == 0)
   {
      // If the input box is empty let's dump all the rows
      // from the results table
      ClearResults();
      HideDiv(ClientID + "searchresults");
      return;
   }
```

```
    // Fetch results from server side.
    // This is our actual Ajax call
    Anthem_InvokeControlMethod(
            "<%= ClientID %>" ,
            'RetrieveRows',
            [searchterm],
            LoadResultsCallback);
}

function LoadResultsCallback(result)
{
    // The XmlHttpRequest will return to this function.
    ShowDiv(ClientID + "searchresults");
    ClearResults();

    // Callback results from Ajax call.
    // We'll assign the inbound DataTable
    // to the items variable
    var items = result.value;

    var count = items.Rows.length;

    // We'll create a table object in the DOM
    var divResults = document.getElementById(ClientID + "searchresults");
    var tblTable = document.createElement("table");
    var tablebody = document.createElement("tbody");
    var tablerow, tablecell, tablenode;

    // Loop through each of the rows in the DataTable
    for (var i = 0; i < count; i++)
    {
        var zip = items.Rows[i].PostalCode;
        var currenttext = items.Rows[i].Name + ": " + items.Rows[i].State;

        // We'll create each table row and append it to the
        // table body
        tablerow = document.createElement("tr");
        tablecell = document.createElement("td");
        // build the cell attributes and functions
        tablecell.onmouseover = function(){this.className='mouseOver';};
        tablecell.onmouseout = function(){this.className='mouseOut';};
        tablecell.setAttribute("border", "0");

        // Let's store the ZIP code in the ID field of the table cell
        // so that we can simply pass the table cell on the click event.
        tablecell.ID = zip;
```

```
        tablecell.onclick =  function(){ReplaceInput(this);};
        tablenode = document.createTextNode(currenttext);
        tablecell.appendChild(tablenode);
        tablerow.appendChild(tablecell);
        tablebody.appendChild(tablerow);
    }
    // Add the table body to the table
    tblTable.appendChild(tablebody);
    // add the table to the div tag
    divResults.appendChild(tblTable);
}

function ReplaceInput(tablecell)
{
    // Grab the ZIP code out of the table cell's ID field.
    var zipcode = tablecell.ID;

    // Save the ZIP code in a hidden control for retrieval
    var hidField = document.getElementById(ClientID + "hidZipCode")
    hidField.value = zipcode;

    Anthem_InvokeControlMethod(
        "<%= ClientID %>",
        'GetMapUrl',
        [zipcode],
        displayMap);
        // Replace textbox value with the assembled text.
        var inputbox = document.getElementById(ClientID + "keyword");
        inputbox.value = tablecell.firstChild.nodeValue;
        ClearResults();
        HideDiv(ClientID + "searchresults");
}

function displayMap(results)
{
    document.getElementById(ClientID + "divStoreMap").innerHTML =
    results.value;
}

function StarterMap()
{
    var zip ="";
```

```
    // Let's grab any existing ZIP code from the hidden field.
    var hidZipCode = document.getElementById(ClientID + "hidZipCode").value;
    if(hidZipCode.length > 0)
    {
       zip = hidZipCode;
    }
    else
    {
       zip = '49503';
    }
    // GetMapUrl
    Anthem_InvokeControlMethod(
       "<%= ClientID %>",
       'GetMapUrl',
       [zip],
       displayMap);
}

</script>

<div id="divStoreMap" runat="server"></div>
<strong>Search:</strong><br />
<input name="keyword" onkeyup="LoadResults(this.value)" id="keyword"
       runat="server" style="WIDTH:310px" autocomplete="off" />
<div class="box" id="searchresults" runat="server"
     style="WIDTH:310px;BACKGROUND-COLOR:#ccccff">
</div>
<input id="hidZipCode" type="hidden" runat="server" />
```

7. And now switch over to the C# code view and add the following code:

```
using System;
using System.Data;
using System.Configuration;
using System.Collections;
using System.Web;
using System.Web.Security;
using System.Web.UI;
using System.Web.UI.WebControls;
using System.Web.UI.WebControls.WebParts;
using System.Web.UI.HtmlControls;
using System.Data.SqlClient;
using System.Xml;
using System.Text;
```

```
public partial class controls_ucCustomerLocator :
 System.Web.UI.UserControl, IWebPart
{

    protected string _title = "";
    public string Title
    {
        get { return _title; }
        set { _title = value; }
    }

    private string _subtitle = "";
    public string Subtitle
    {
        get { return _subtitle; }
        set { _subtitle = value; }
    }

    private string _titleurl = "";
    public string TitleUrl
    {
        get { return _titleurl; }
        set { _titleurl = value; }
    }

    private string _catalogIconImageUrl = "";
    public string CatalogIconImageUrl
    {
        get { return _catalogIconImageUrl; }
        set { _catalogIconImageUrl = value; }
    }

    protected string _description = "";
    public string Description
    {
        get { return _description; }
        set { _description = value; }
    }

    private string _titleIconImageUrl = "";
    public string TitleIconImageUrl
    {
        get { return _titleIconImageUrl; }
        set { _titleIconImageUrl = value; }
    }
```

```
protected void Page_Load(object sender, EventArgs e)
{
    Anthem.Manager.Register(this);
    string jcode = "<script language=\"javascript\"
    type=\"text/javascript\">ClientID = '" + this.ClientID + "_" +
    "';BodyStart();</script>";

    this.Page.ClientScript.RegisterStartupScript(typeof(Page),
    "customer_control", jcode);
}

[Anthem.Method]
public string GetMapUrl(string zipcode)
{

    string strMap = "http://api.local.yahoo.com/MapsService/V1/
     mapImage?appid=YahooMap&image_height=300&image_width=300&
     zoom=12&zip=" + zipcode;
    StringBuilder sb = new StringBuilder();
    XmlTextReader xr = null;

    xr = new XmlTextReader(strMap);
    sb.Append("<center><img src='");
    while (xr.Read())
    {
        if (xr.NodeType == XmlNodeType.Element && xr.Name == "Result")
        {
            sb.Append(xr.ReadString());
        }

    }
    sb.Append("' /></center>");
    return sb.ToString();
}


[Anthem.Method]
public DataTable RetrieveRows(string searchterm)
{
    SqlConnection conn = new SqlConnection("Data Source=(local);
    Initial Catalog=AdventureWorks;Integrated Security=SSPI");
    DataTable dtReturn = new DataTable();
    string sqlquery = "SELECT TOP 10 Sales.Store.Name,
    Person.Address.PostalCode, Person.StateProvince.Name AS State
    FROM Sales.Store";
```

```
sqlquery += " JOIN Sales.CustomerAddress ON Sales.Store.CustomerID =
Sales.CustomerAddress.CustomerID";
sqlquery += " JOIN Person.Address ON Person.Address.AddressID =
Sales.CustomerAddress.AddressID";
sqlquery += " JOIN Person.StateProvince ON
Person.StateProvince.StateProvinceID = Person.Address.StateProvinceID";
sqlquery += " WHERE Person.Address.StateProvinceID IN
(SELECT StateProvinceID FROM Person.StateProvince";
sqlquery += " WHERE Person.StateProvince.CountryRegionCode = 'US')
AND Sales.Store.Name LIKE @searchterm ORDER BY Name";

conn.Open();
// Go get the top 10 company names from Northwind that are like
// user's search criteria
SqlCommand cmd = new SqlCommand(sqlquery, conn);
SqlParameter param = new SqlParameter();
param.ParameterName = "@searchterm";
searchterm.Trim().Replace("'", "''");
searchterm += "%";
param.Value = searchterm;
cmd.Parameters.Add(param);

SqlDataAdapter adpt = new SqlDataAdapter(cmd);
adpt.Fill(dtReturn);
conn.Close();

// Send the DataTable back to the CallBack function
return dtReturn;
    }
}
```

8. We now have our user control ready for action. Save the project and let's build the Web Part shell.

9. Switch to the Design View of Default.aspx and then drag a WebPartManager control onto the form.

10. Add a 3-by-1 table to the form, as shown in Figure 14-8.

11. We now need a place for our Web Parts to reside, so drag a WebPartZone into each of the table cells. Your form should now look like Figure 14-9.

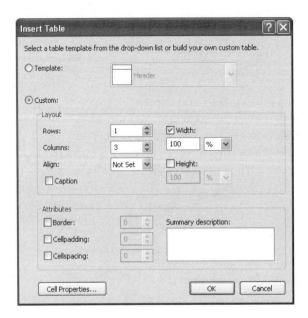

Figure 14-8. *Adding a table*

Figure 14-9. *Web Zones ready and waiting*

12. Before jumping into the Ajax user control, first drag a simple calendar server control onto an empty `WebPartZone`.

13. Now run the application. You'll be prompted to add a `Web.config`. Choose OK and continue.

Your page should appear as shown in Figure 14-10.

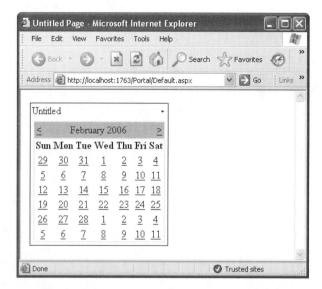

Figure 14-10. *Calendar Web Part*

Notice something strange? Or a few things, perhaps? First, the calendar can't be relocated. Second, the other WebPartZones aren't visible. And finally, the title for the calendar says "Untitled".

When you first implement the WebPartManager, it sets its DisplayMode property to BrowseDisplayMode, which will restrict the movement of the page's Web Parts.

14. We need to add the following line of code to the Page_Load event to have drag and drop:

```
this.WebPartManager1.DisplayMode = WebPartManager.DesignDisplayMode;
```

One more housekeeping task and we'll be done with the calendar control. We should change the title of the control to something a little more elegant than "Untitled". But isn't the calendar a server control and therefore doesn't have the title attribute? Yes! You are totally correct. However, when we dropped the control onto the WebPartZone, Visual Studio was kind enough to wrap the control as a GenericWebPart, and we therefore have a title property now. Switch over to the HTML source view and find the control.

15. Modify the Web Part so that it has the title as shown:

```
<asp:Calendar ID="Calendar1" runat="server" title="Calendar"></asp:Calendar>
```

16. Now run the application again. You should see that the calendar control is titled and draggable, as shown in Figure 14-11.

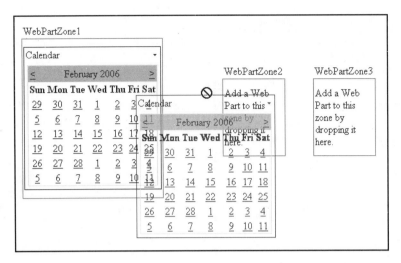

Figure 14-11. *Calendar control complete*

Now drag the user control from the `controls` folder out into a `WebPartZone`. Modify your HTML in much the same way as the previous calendar control adjustment, in which you added a title to the control:

```
<uc1:ucCustomerLocator ID="UcCustomerLocator1"
                       runat="server" title="Customer Locator" />
```

Now when you run the application, you'll have the total, and nearly complete, application available, as shown in Figure 14-12.

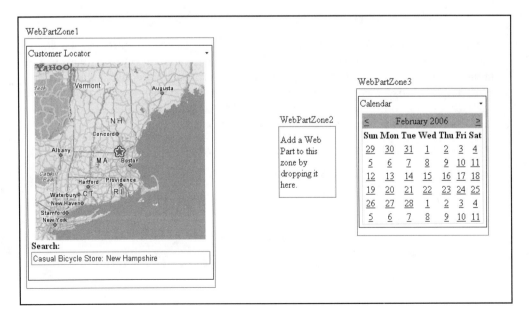

Figure 14-12. *Almost there*

While it is functional, it is in need of some serious alignment and color.

17. Add the following `valign` statement to each table cell:

```
<td valign="top">
```

That will bring our `WebPartZones` to the top of the page, in a more uniform alignment. Let's add some color to the `WebPartZones` now.

Each `WebPartZone` has the ability to apply color schemes to its own content. In the top-right corner of the `WebPartZone`, you'll find a small arrow. Clicking that will open the formatting window, as shown in Figure 14-13.

Figure 14-13. *Formatting the WebPartZone*

You'll also notice that your HTML code has grown considerably, to reflect the formatted values. You're free to modify the values to further customize the zone as you see fit. Let's take a quick glance through the HTML and C# code for the Web Part page, and then we'll discuss the user control:

```
<%@ Page Language="C#" AutoEventWireup="true"
 CodeFile="Default.aspx.cs" Inherits="_Default" %>

<%@ Register Src="controls/ucCustomerLocator.ascx"
 TagName="ucCustomerLocator" TagPrefix="uc2" %>
<!DOCTYPE html PUBLIC "-//W3C//DTD XHTML 1.0 Transitional//EN"
  "http://www.w3.org/TR/xhtml1/DTD/xhtml1-transitional.dtd">
<html xmlns="http://www.w3.org/1999/xhtml" >
  <head runat="server">
    <title>Ajax Web Parts</title>
  </head>
  <body>
    <form id="form1" runat="server">
      <div>
        <asp:WebPartManager ID="WebPartManager1" runat="server">
        </asp:WebPartManager>
        <br />
```

```
<table style="width: 100%">
  <tr>
    <td valign="top">
      <asp:WebPartZone ID="WebPartZone1" runat="server"
           BorderColor="#CCCCCC" Font-Names="Verdana" Padding="6">
        <PartChromeStyle BackColor="#F7F6F3" BorderColor="#E2DED6"
                         Font-Names="Verdana" ForeColor="White" />
        <MenuLabelHoverStyle ForeColor="#E2DED6" />
        <EmptyZoneTextStyle Font-Size="0.8em" />
        <MenuLabelStyle ForeColor="White" />
        <MenuVerbHoverStyle BackColor="#F7F6F3" BorderColor="#CCCCCC"
          BorderStyle="Solid" BorderWidth="1px" ForeColor="#333333" />
        <HeaderStyle Font-Size="0.7em" ForeColor="#CCCCCC"
                    HorizontalAlign="Center" />
        <ZoneTemplate>
          <uc2:ucCustomerLocator ID="UcCustomerLocator1"
                                 runat="server" title="Customer Locator" />
        </ZoneTemplate>
        <MenuVerbStyle BorderColor="#5D7B9D" BorderStyle="Solid"
                    BorderWidth="1px" ForeColor="White" />
        <PartStyle Font-Size="0.8em" ForeColor="#333333" />
        <TitleBarVerbStyle Font-Size="0.6em" Font-Underline="False"
                    ForeColor="White" />
        <MenuPopupStyle BackColor="#5D7B9D" BorderColor="#CCCCCC"
            BorderWidth="1px" Font-Names="Verdana"  Font-Size="0.6em" />
        <PartTitleStyle BackColor="#5D7B9D" Font-Bold="True"
                    Font-Size="0.8em" ForeColor="White" />
      </asp:WebPartZone>
    </td>

    <td valign="top">
      <asp:WebPartZone ID="WebPartZone2" runat="server"
           BorderColor="#CCCCCC" Font-Names="Verdana" Padding="6">
        <PartChromeStyle BackColor="#F7F6F3" BorderColor="#E2DED6"
                         Font-Names="Verdana" ForeColor="White" />
        <MenuLabelHoverStyle ForeColor="#E2DED6" />
        <EmptyZoneTextStyle Font-Size="0.8em" />
        <MenuLabelStyle ForeColor="White" />
        <MenuVerbHoverStyle BackColor="#F7F6F3" BorderColor="#CCCCCC"
            BorderStyle="Solid" BorderWidth="1px" ForeColor="#333333" />
        <HeaderStyle Font-Size="0.7em" ForeColor="#CCCCCC"
                    HorizontalAlign="Center" />
        <MenuVerbStyle BorderColor="#5D7B9D" BorderStyle="Solid"
                    BorderWidth="1px" ForeColor="White" />
        <PartStyle Font-Size="0.8em" ForeColor="#333333" />
```

```
                <TitleBarVerbStyle Font-Size="0.6em" Font-Underline="False"
                            ForeColor="White" />
                <MenuPopupStyle BackColor="#5D7B9D" BorderColor="#CCCCCC"
                    BorderWidth="1px" Font-Names="Verdana" Font-Size="0.6em" />
                <PartTitleStyle BackColor="#5D7B9D" Font-Bold="True"
                            Font-Size="0.8em" ForeColor="White" />
            </asp:WebPartZone>
        </td>

        <td valign="top">
            <asp:WebPartZone ID="WebPartZone3" runat="server"
                BorderColor="#CCCCCC" Font-Names="Verdana" Padding="6">
                <PartChromeStyle BackColor="#F7F6F3" BorderColor="#E2DED6"
                            Font-Names="Verdana" ForeColor="White" />
                <MenuLabelHoverStyle ForeColor="#E2DED6" />
                <EmptyZoneTextStyle Font-Size="0.8em" />
                <MenuLabelStyle ForeColor="White" />
                <MenuVerbHoverStyle BackColor="#F7F6F3" BorderColor="#CCCCCC"
                    BorderStyle="Solid" BorderWidth="1px" ForeColor="#333333" />
                <HeaderStyle Font-Size="0.7em" ForeColor="#CCCCCC"
                            HorizontalAlign="Center" />
                <MenuVerbStyle BorderColor="#5D7B9D" BorderStyle="Solid"
                            BorderWidth="1px" ForeColor="White" />
                <PartStyle Font-Size="0.8em" ForeColor="#333333" />
                <TitleBarVerbStyle Font-Size="0.6em" Font-Underline="False"
                            ForeColor="White" />
                <MenuPopupStyle BackColor="#5D7B9D" BorderColor="#CCCCCC"
                    BorderWidth="1px" Font-Names="Verdana" Font-Size="0.6em" />
                <PartTitleStyle BackColor="#5D7B9D" Font-Bold="True"
                            Font-Size="0.8em" ForeColor="White" />
                <ZoneTemplate>
                    <asp:Calendar ID="Calendar1" runat="server" title="Calendar">
                    </asp:Calendar>
                </ZoneTemplate>
            </asp:WebPartZone>
        </td>
      </tr>
    </table>
      
    </div>
  </form>
</body>
</html>
```

> ### WEB PARTS AND SECURITY
>
> Web Parts will only work for an authenticated user. Currently, our solution has the `Web.Config` set for Windows authentication:
>
> `<authentication mode="Windows"/>`
>
> As you roll your application out to a web-facing environment, you'll want to remember to implement Forms authentication or another method of authentication prior to allowing users access to the page.

The server-side code is fairly minimal:

```
using System;
using System.Data;
using System.Configuration;
using System.Web;
using System.Web.Security;
using System.Web.UI;
using System.Web.UI.WebControls;
using System.Web.UI.WebControls.WebParts;
using System.Web.UI.HtmlControls;

public partial class _Default : System.Web.UI.Page
{
    protected void Page_Load(object sender, EventArgs e)
    {
        // Allow Web Parts to be moved
        this.WebPartManager1.DisplayMode = WebPartManager.DesignDisplayMode;
    }
}
```

Now that we have the application up and running, let's dissect the user control a little more so that you can better understand its mechanics.

ucCustomerLocator

The user control is a collection of previous sample applications from within this book. We're obviously using the type-ahead control from earlier, as shown in Figure 14-14.

The Ajax functionality for this control is unchanged, despite the fact that we're operating from within the confines of an ASP.NET 2.0 Web Part. We still register the control in the same fashion:

```
Anthem.Manager.Register(this);
```

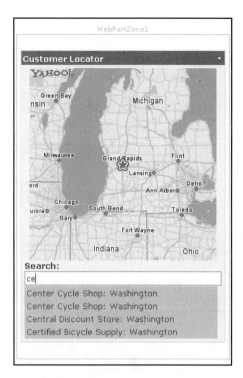

Figure 14-14. *Ajax type-ahead control*

The calling and callback functions are the same:

```
function LoadResults(searchterm)
{
    if (searchterm.length == 0)
    {
        // If the input box is empty, let's dump all the rows
        // from the results table
        ClearResults();
        HideDiv(ClientID + "searchresults");
        return;
    }

    // Fetch results from server side.
    // This is our actual Ajax call
    Anthem_InvokeControlMethod(
        "<%= ClientID %>" ,
        'RetrieveRows',
        [searchterm],
        LoadResultsCallback);
}
```

```
function LoadResultsCallback(result)
{
    // The XmlHttpRequest will return to this function.
    ShowDiv(ClientID + "searchresults");
    ClearResults();

    // Callback results from Ajax call.
    // We'll assign the inbound DataTable
    // to the items variable
    var items = result.value;

    var count = items.Rows.length;

    // We'll create a table object in the DOM
    var divResults = document.getElementById(ClientID + "searchresults");
    var tblTable = document.createElement("table");
    var tablebody = document.createElement("tbody");
    var tablerow, tablecell, tablenode;

    // Loop through each of the rows in the DataTable
    for (var i = 0; i < count; i++)
    {
        var zip = items.Rows[i].PostalCode;
        var currenttext = items.Rows[i].Name + ": " + items.Rows[i].State;

        // We'll create each table row and append it to the
        // table body
        tablerow = document.createElement("tr");
        tablecell = document.createElement("td");
        // Build the cell attributes and functions
        tablecell.onmouseover = function(){this.className='mouseOver';};
        tablecell.onmouseout = function(){this.className='mouseOut';};
        tablecell.setAttribute("border", "0");

        // Let's store the ZIP code in the ID field of the table cell
        // so that we can simply pass the table cell on the click event.
        tablecell.ID = zip;

        tablecell.onclick =  function(){ReplaceInput(this);};
        tablenode = document.createTextNode(currenttext);
        tablecell.appendChild(tablenode);
        tablerow.appendChild(tablecell);
        tablebody.appendChild(tablerow);
    }
    // Add the table body to the table
    tblTable.appendChild(tablebody);
    // Add the table to the div tag
    divResults.appendChild(tblTable);
}
```

However, this is where the similarity to the other controls ends.

As I stated earlier, you can choose to let Visual Studio 2005 wrap your controls within a GenericWebPart shell, or you could (and should) implement the IWebPart interface. As this is an interface, there are some elements that we must implement, if we want the application to compile:

```
protected string _title = "";
public string Title
{
    get { return _title; }
    set { _title = value; }
}

private string _subtitle = "";
public string Subtitle
{
    get { return _subtitle; }
    set { _subtitle = value; }
}

private string _titleurl = "";
public string TitleUrl
{
    get { return _titleurl; }
    set { _titleurl = value; }
}

private string _catalogIconImageUrl = "";
public string CatalogIconImageUrl
{
    get { return _catalogIconImageUrl; }
    set { _catalogIconImageUrl = value; }
}

protected string _description = "";
public string Description
{
    get { return _description; }
    set { _description = value; }
}

private string _titleIconImageUrl = "";
public string TitleIconImageUrl
{
    get { return _titleIconImageUrl; }
    set { _titleIconImageUrl = value; }
}
```

I'm kind of lazy and chose to not assign any default values. You're welcome to change that for experimentation on the sample application.

Tracking ZIP Codes

One of the tasks that we're completing in this application is the storage and retrieval of the ZIP code data returned to us from the AdventureWorks store table. We preserve the ZIP code across state, in a hidden field for use in postback processes:

```
function ReplaceInput(tablecell)
{
    // Grab the ZIP code out of the table cell's ID field.
    var zipcode = tablecell.ID;

    // Save the ZIP code in a hidden control for retrieval
    var hidField = document.getElementById(ClientID + "hidZipCode")
    hidField.value = zipcode;


    ...
}
```

One quick note about the hidden field trick: if you don't make the input control a runat="server" tag, bad things will happen to your code. Bad things like it won't actually store the value in session state, and you'll spend hours trying to figure out why your data is getting dumped. Not that I'm speaking from experience. OK, maybe I am.

So why do we need the ZIP code anyway? We use it to retrieve a static map from Yahoo!, so that our user can visually see the location of the store. The implementation is pretty simple, and I'm sure that you'll want to improve the interface should you choose to make it your own.

Yahoo! Static Maps

Retrieving the static map is similar to the traffic RSS feed from Chapter 13, in that we have a URL that we can retrieve XML results from. For example, our application uses the ZIP code as a parameter for the retrieval of the result set:

```
[Anthem.Method]
public string GetMapUrl(string zipcode)
{

    string strMap = "http://api.local.yahoo.com/MapsService/V1/
     mapImage?appid=YahooMap&image_height=300&image_width=300&
     zoom=12&zip=" + zipcode;
    StringBuilder sb = new StringBuilder();
    XmlTextReader xr = null;

    xr = new XmlTextReader(strMap);
    sb.Append("<center><img src='");
    while (xr.Read())
```

```
    {
        if (xr.NodeType == XmlNodeType.Element && xr.Name == "Result")
        {
            sb.Append(xr.ReadString());
        }
    }
    sb.Append("' /></center>");
    return sb.ToString();
}
```

The preceding example uses an `XmlTextReader`, rather than a DataSet, simply because the data coming back is only a single element, and the DataSet is unnecessary. Posting the following query with a sample ZIP code:

```
http://api.local.yahoo.com/MapsService/V1/mapImage?appid=YahooStoreMap& zip=49503
```

will return the following XML result:

```
<?xml version="1.0" encoding="UTF-8" ?>
<Result xmlns:xsi="http://www.w3.org/2001/XMLSchema-instance">
        http://img.maps.yahoo.com/mapimage?MAPDATA=hTHOf.d6wXUn
        UhXVdSFI9ynSPSo3vLZOWF_UOxu9MEOwThcmuFJcliVoP6AA7CDj_26
        aWlwzrxaZ.CteFRqqson2ny53cENWvzbsLztBRIaFMHU-</Result>
- <!-- ws02.search.re2.yahoo.com compressed/chunked Mon
        Feb 27 18:03:35 PST 2006
  -->
```

The `Result` element's inner text is actually a URL for the image map that Yahoo! has waiting for you. If you cut and paste the URL into a browser, Yahoo! will render the map for you, as shown in Figure 14-15.

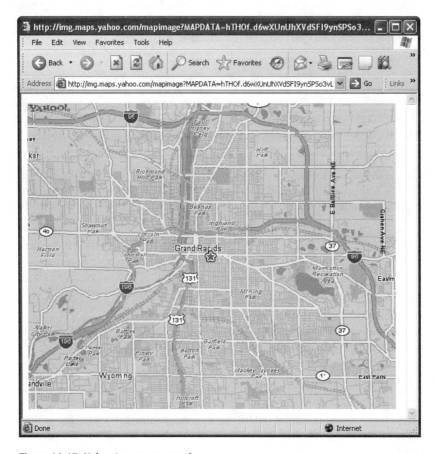

Figure 14-15. *Yahoo! map returned*

The parameters for the Yahoo! service are very similar to the traffic RSS feed, as listed in Table 14-1.

Table 14-1. *Yahoo Map Request Parameters*

Parameter	Data Type	Description
appid	string	Application ID of your site. Any unique ID that you specify.
street	string	The street name of the location—unit number optional.
city	string	The city name of the location.
state	string	The US state. Spelled out or the two-letter abbreviation.
zip	int (int-int)	Five-digit ZIP code or five-digit ZIP code plus four-digit extension. City and state will be ignored if they don't match the ZIP code specified.

Parameter	Data Type	Description
location	Free text	Allows you to enter complete location information in various formats: city, state city, state, ZIP ZIP street, city, state street, city, state, ZIP street, ZIP If you supply any information in this field, it will take priority over any of the other individual location fields.
latitude	float (–90 to 90)	The latitude of the location.
longitude	float	The longitude of the location.
image_type	PNG or GIF	The default returned map format is PNG.
image_height	int (10 to 2000)	Height of the image returned in pixels. Default is 500.
image_width	int (10 to 2000)	Width of the image returned in pixels. Default is 620.
zoom	int (1 to 12)	Zoom level (similar to the map) indicating area to capture events for. A 1 would be street level, and 12 gathers country level. If you provide a radius parameter, Yahoo! will ignore this parameter.
radius	float	The area in miles that Yahoo! should provide traffic data for.
output	string	The format for the result string. By default, you'll receive XML. However, serialized PHP is available.

Building the Map

Once we've retrieved the established URL from Yahoo, we build the appropriate HTML on the server side of the Ajax call and return the string back to the client for binding to the innerHTML of the div tag:

```
sb.Append("<center><img src='");
while (xr.Read())
{
    if (xr.NodeType == XmlNodeType.Element && xr.Name == "Result")
    {
        sb.Append(xr.ReadString());
    }


}
sb.Append("' /></center>");
```

This will allow us to create an <img> tag on the fly with the map embedded within.

As the user selects new customers, we'll start the process over and retrieve a fresh new map.

One key process that we must keep in mind is the possibility of a postback wiping out the current image. We'll need to reload the control with the saved ZIP code. As you already know, dynamically manipulating the tags with Ajax can do some nasty things to the current

ViewState. The server-side and client-side versions of the state will vary greatly if we make any changes, so a postback in our situation could create some headaches. So we store the ZIP code as previously described and retrieve it on return trips:

```
function StarterMap()
{
    var zip ="";

    // Let's grab any existing ZIP code from the hidden field.
    var hidZipCode = document.getElementById(ClientID + "hidZipCode").value;
    if(hidZipCode.length > 0)
    {
        zip = hidZipCode;
    }
    else
    {
        zip = '49503';
    }
    // GetMapUrl
    Anthem_InvokeControlMethod(
      "<%= ClientID %>",
      'GetMapUrl',
      [zip],
      displayMap);
}
```

Summary

ASP.NET 2.0 Web Parts are an incredible tool for up-and-coming websites. Portal technology will continue to evolve as the community embraces the toolset. It's reassuring to know that we'll still be able to throw some Ajax into the mix since Ajax Web Parts are still, at their heart, user controls.

In the next few chapters, we'll shift away from the sample applications and begin to look at security, performance, and debugging of Ajax applications. A lot of the topics that we'll discuss are applicable to all ASP.NET 2.0 applications and will be worth reading about even if you're not concerned with the role that Ajax will play in those areas.

PART 4

■ ■ ■

Security and Performance

In this part, we will shift away from the coding and take a cursory look at Ajax security and performance. Having really cool, dynamic web applications is a true blessing, but at what cost? Are Ajax applications secure? Does all of that user interaction tax the web servers to the brink of collapse? I'll address these issues and more in the coming chapters.

CHAPTER 15

■ ■ ■

Ajax and ASP.NET Security

It seems that whenever any kind of technology becomes mainstream, one of the first concerns to emerge from public discussion is security. And rightly so. Given the plethora of media coverage that we've seen lately on the subject of corporate hacks and misplaced and stolen personal data, we should definitely devote some time to the concept of protecting our sites. Security should always be a consideration for every developer as they code their applications, regardless of where the program runs. All too often, securing the application is an afterthought to the development process rather than a dedicated part of the cycle. How many times have you heard, "Well, the application is done, now how do we lock it down?" This is certainly a dangerous way to build and publish software.

With Ajax in the spotlight, certain questions have surfaced:

Is Ajax a secure method of transferring data to and from server-side resources?

How can I take advantage of the .NET Framework's built-in security tools?

These are good questions to ask, and we'll look at them in this chapter.

Ajax As a Secure Platform

Let's address the first issue. Is Ajax a secure platform from which we can safely make asynchronous calls? Well, let's think about this for a minute. Joe Developer creates a web page with various Ajax calls to the server side. Joe deploys that page to his hosted account for public access. An anonymous user comes along, loads the page, and Joe's server delivers the initial page to the user's browser. They perform some asynchronous actions, accessing and updating a database on Joe's host. Is this a "trusted" situation? Well, the short answer is, it depends. When you think about an Ajax method being executed, you have to dive deeper into the process than just that. The action of committing an asynchronous call to the server side of things boils down to the implementation of the XmlHttpRequest object (in most situations), and what essentially is the XmlHttpRequest? A request/response data transfer model that still operates within the same zone as the hosting page.

Obviously, there is more to this story. For an Ajax call to be considered a trusted operation, it must call back to the same domain as it was issued from. So you may have some issues accessing www.nusoftsolutions.com resources if your page was delivered from www.danwoolston.com. The origin needs to match the destination. In this book, we work from the localhost environment and, as you may know, that falls within the computer's Trusted Sites zone. Let's take a quick look at a sample application that tests this situation. I've built a simple .aspx page and uploaded it to a hosted site that I use to test web-facing application code. The site has nothing more than a few HTML buttons tied to various events, as shown in Figure 15-1.

Figure 15-1. *Simple security application*

The back-end code performs only two actions. In the event that the server-side button is clicked, an Ajax call is made to the server side and another call is made to the Yahoo! maps service. The resulting data is simply posted with an alert box. If the client-side button is clicked, JavaScript will make the call to Yahoo! and, again, post the information with an alert box. The HTML and C# code is pretty straightforward, as you can see in Listings 15-1 and 15-2.

Listing 15-1. *HTML Code*

```
<%@ Page Language="C#" AutoEventWireup="true"
 CodeFile="Default.aspx.cs" Inherits="_Default" %>

<!DOCTYPE html PUBLIC "-//W3C//DTD XHTML 1.0 Transitional//EN"
  "http://www.w3.org/TR/xhtml1/DTD/xhtml1-transitional.dtd">

<html xmlns="http://www.w3.org/1999/xhtml" >
  <head runat="server">
    <title>Untitled Page</title>
  </head>
  <body>
    <script type="text/javascript" language="javascript">
    var xmlhttp = false;

    function getHTTPRequestObject()
    {
        try
        {
            // Try legacy object first
            xmlhttp = new ActiveXObject("Msxml2.XMLHTTP");
        }
```

```
        catch(e)
        {
            try
            {
                // Try IE implementation now
                xmlhttp = new ActiveXObject("Microsoft.XMLHTTP");
            }
            catch(E)
            {
                xmlhttp = false;
            }
        }
        if(!xmlhttp && typeof XMLHttpRequest!= 'undefined')
        {
            // We must be using a Mozilla-based browser
            // so create a native request object now
            xmlhttp = new XMLHttpRequest();
        }
}

function trimString (str)
{
    str = this != window? this : str;
    return str.replace(/^\s+/g, '').replace(/\s+$/g, '');
}

function ClientSideCall()
{
    getHTTPRequestObject();

    if(xmlhttp)
    {
        xmlhttp.open("GET",
          "http://api.local.yahoo.com/MapsService/V1
          /mapImage?appid=YahooMap&zip=49503", true);

        xmlhttp.onreadystatechange = function()
        {
            if(xmlhttp.readyState == 4)
            {
                var textresponse = xmlhttp.responseText;
                alert(textresponse);
            }
        }
        xmlhttp.send(null);
    }
}
```

```
    function ServerSideCall()
    {
        var response = Anthem_InvokePageMethod('GetSomeXML', []);
        alert(response.value);
    }
    </script>

    <form id="form1" runat="server">
      <div>
        Retrieve From Server Side:
        <input id="Button1" type="button" value="Go Get It!"
              onclick="ServerSideCall();"/>
        <br />
        <br />
        Retrieve From Client Side: 
        <input id="Button2" type="button" value="Fetch Me Some XML Jeeves."
              onclick="ClientSideCall();"/>
      </div>
    </form>
  </body>
</html>
```

Listing 15-2. *C# Code*

```
using System;
using System.Data;
using System.Configuration;
using System.Web;
using System.Web.Security;
using System.Web.UI;
using System.Web.UI.WebControls;
using System.Web.UI.WebControls.WebParts;
using System.Web.UI.HtmlControls;
using System.Text;
using System.Xml;

public partial class _Default : System.Web.UI.Page
{
    protected void Page_Load(object sender, EventArgs e)
    {
        Anthem.Manager.Register(this);
    }

    [Anthem.Method]
    public string GetSomeXML()
```

```
    {
        string strMap = "http://api.local.yahoo.com
/MapsService/V1/mapImage?appid=YahooMap&
image_height=300&image_width=300&zoom=12&zip=49503";

        StringBuilder sb = new StringBuilder();
        XmlTextReader xr = null;

        xr = new XmlTextReader(strMap);
        while (xr.Read())
        {
            if (xr.NodeType == XmlNodeType.Element && xr.Name == "Result")
            {
                sb.Append(xr.ReadString());
            }
        }

        return sb.ToString();
    }
}
```

The HTML code has the usual XmlHttpRequest object-creation code and the corresponding event handlers. You can plainly see the GET request that the JavaScript will attempt to make:

```
xmlhttp.open("GET","http://api.local.yahoo.com/MapsService/V1/mapImage?
appid=YahooMap&zip=49503", true);
```

I click the server-side button and an alert box greets me with the expected data, as shown in Figure 15-2.

Figure 15-2. *Server-side result*

However, when I click the client-side button, I'm met with something quite different, as shown in Figure 15-3.

This time I've received a permissions error as I try to access something that is outside of the security zone. I can get a more detailed error message by bringing up Firefox and using the JavaScript Console to view the error in detail, as shown in Figure 15-4.

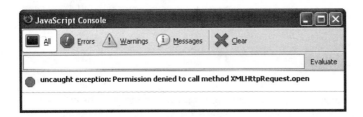

Figure 15-3. *Client-side result*

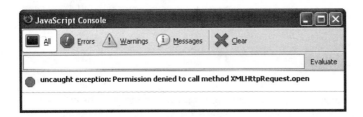

Figure 15-4. *Firefox JavaScript console message*

I've attempted to access an outside resource, and consequently the code has crashed. More and more, I'm finding that Ajax developers are avoiding the client-side resource calls in favor of server-side access. And for good reason, as you now know.

So that you understand that JavaScript external web access can create some security issues, let's turn our attention to server-side security. And for us, that will mean ASP.NET 2.0's Forms Authentication model. Because Ajax operates within the confines of page-level security, we really don't need to worry about the individual calls made by our library. So long as we've implemented the framework protection, we'll be safe within our calls. Obviously, standards of input validation to avoid injection attacks still apply. But I'd like to focus on Forms Authentication for the remainder of this chapter. If you already have a decent comprehension of this particular topic, you may be best served by casually browsing the chapter.

ASP.NET 2.0 Security

In the .NET world, there are three methods of user authentication:

- Passport Authentication

- Windows Authentication

- Forms Authentication

Windows Authentication, as you may have already realized, is what we've used up to this point. If you check the Web.Config files of the various sample applications, you'll find this to be true:

```
<authentication mode="Windows"/>
```

However, this does us little good when we're delivering our application via a web-facing site.

Passport Authentication is a centralized service provided by Microsoft and will require registration with MS. So for our purposes, we'll be using Forms Authentication.

Forms Authentication

When you set your authentication mode to Forms, you are telling the client browser that the user must clear a login page prior to accessing any resources on the website. ASP.NET 2.0 introduces some enhancements to the Forms model, but let's take a look at the basic functionality first.

Setting Up a Site for Authentication

As you can imagine, the authentication mode begins with the Web.Config file. Out of the box, Visual Studio 2005 provides a Windows Authentication provider. To modify that, we can make adjustments to the file, as shown in Listing 15-3.

Listing 15-3. *Forms Authentication in Web.Config*

```xml
<?xml version="1.0"?>
<configuration xmlns="http://schemas.microsoft.com/.NetConfiguration/v2.0">
  <appSettings/>
  <connectionStrings/>
  <system.web>
    <compilation debug="true"/>
    <authentication mode="Forms">
      <forms name=".ASPXAUTH"
             loginUrl="Default.aspx"
             defaultUrl="Default.aspx"
             protection="All" />
    </authentication>
    <authorization>
      <deny users="?" />
    </authorization>
  </system.web>
</configuration>
```

SOMETHING NEW!

On occasion, the user may end up back at the login page without having first visited a protected page. Therefore, a ReturnUrl will not be embedded as a page parameter for the login page. In ASP.NET 1.x, we had a
hard-coded Default.aspx where the user was sent in this situation. However, that's not always efficient or
applicable. With ASP.NET 2.0, we have the ability to declaratively set this page with the defaultUrl attribute. After a user successfully authenticates, they'll be redirected to this appointed page.

We first set the authentication mode to Forms and then modify the attributes of the
<forms> element:

- name: The authentication cookie name

- loginUrl: The login page for any protected pages

- defaultUrl: The URL to go to if no ReturnUrl is specified following a successful login

- protection: The protection level of the authentication cookie

Also note that in the Web.Config we have an <authorization> block as well. Within this
block we can accomplish a multitude of security tasks:

- <deny users>: Self-explanatory. An assignment of ? indicates that the page should deny
  all anonymous users. Assigning * would deny **ALL** users.

- <allow users>: ? and * assignments as in the preceding entry.

With the restricted Web.Config that we've examined, we now have a site that is restricted
to authenticated users. Validating the incoming user mandates that we successfully authenti-
cate with Forms Authentication. With ASP.NET 2.0, we now find that we have a new process
by which to implement Forms Authentication. The new Membership Provider Model gives the
developer (and site admins) a tremendous amount of flexibility when it comes to maintaining
authenticated user accounts. We'll not be digging too deeply into the Membership API for
now, so we'll simply use the tools that Visual Studio 2005 supplies for us to manage the website. Before we can do that, we need to build a site to manage.

1. Open Visual Studio 2005 and create a new WebSite project, naming it FormsApp.

2. After the site has been created, add another web page to the project, and accept the
   Default2.aspx name.

3. Right-click the project name and select Add New Item ➤ Web Configuration File.

4. Modify the Web.Config as shown in Listing 15-3 earlier.

5. Save your project.

Your solution should appear as shown in Figure 15-5.

Figure 15-5. *FormsApp files*

Visual Studio 2005 provides a variety of various authentication tools that we can take advantage of, as shown in Figure 15-6.

Figure 15-6. *ASP.NET 2.0 login controls*

We'll use a majority of these tools within our sample application.

Login Status

On `Default.aspx`, drag a LoginStatus control onto your page, as shown in Figure 15-7.

Figure 15-7. *LoginStatus control*

The text in the panel of the control is displayed based on the login status of the current user. Should the user log in or log out, you have the opportunity to modify the message that they see. We'll leave the default messages alone for now.

Add a few line breaks to the web page, making room for another control below the status control.

CreateUserWizard

Because we're asking for user information, it would sure be swell if the anonymous member had the means by which to register for an account. That's where our CreateUserWizard control comes into play. Drag one of these bad boys out onto the page, below the status control, as shown in Figure 15-8.

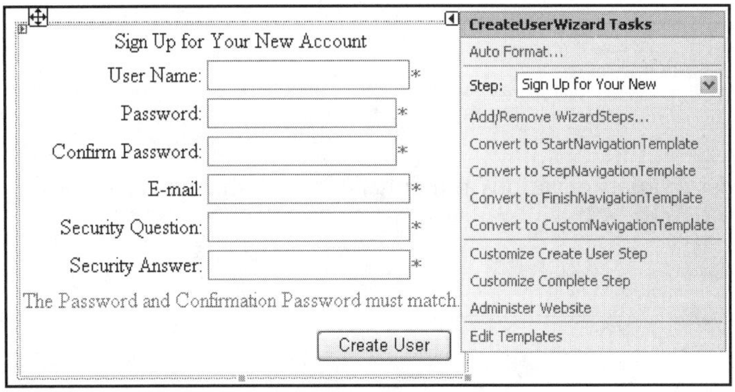

Figure 15-8. *CreateUserWizard control*

For now, let's just accept the defaults on this control. You can always visit it later to experiment with the formatting options.

So far we have a control to indicate our login status and a means by which a new user can register for an account. However, we do not have anything in place to accommodate returning members as they attempt to log in to the site. We could build back-end server-side code that would issue the authentication ticket based on user credentials. Or we could simply drag another control on the page. We'll opt for the latter.

Login Control

Out-of-the-box solutions are incredible time savers. And the Login control is no different. Typically, we would have to spend hours building redundant login processes. ASP.NET 2.0, fortunately, has come to the rescue.

The Login control is simple to use and adheres to what public perception maintains that a login control should be.

Drag a Login control onto your page, as shown in Figure 15-9. Accept the defaults and move on to the next step.

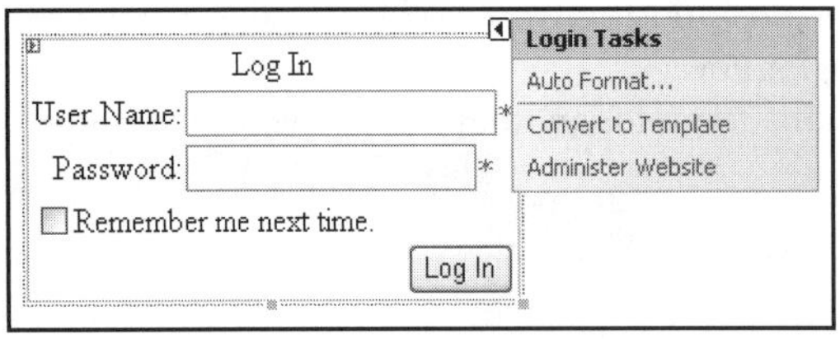

Figure 15-9. *Login control*

We've now built the basic structure for our site's login process. It wouldn't be a bad idea, at this point, to throw in at least a few user roles and accounts. We'll do that with the Website Administration Tool (WAT). However, first we should discuss roles and accounts briefly before we start drilling down into the WAT.

Roles

User roles, when enabled, simply dictate what abilities a logged-in user may or may not have. You might have an Admin role with supreme site administration powers. At the opposite end of the spectrum, you might create a role called Newbies for the new users to your site, allowing them basic access to resources. You will enable site limitations based on access rules that you'll build with the WAT.

We should take a deeper look at these user/role-administration tools in the WAT. In the menu bar of Visual Studio, there should be a menu header for Website. Clicking that will reveal a set of further options; of interest to us is ASP.NET Configuration. After a moment of configuration, you'll be met with the main interface, as shown in Figure 15-10.

Figure 15-10. *WAT interface*

We're interested in the Security screen, so click the Security hyperlink.

As I mentioned before, the WAT tool allows us to manage users, roles, and access. You can see the three categories in Figure 15-11.

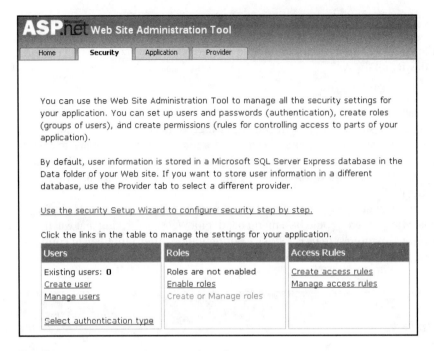

Figure 15-11. *Security maintenance interface*

Creating a Role

Let's create an initial role structure for our site, prior to adding any users. We'll create just one for now, so that you can see the technology in use. You can always visit the WAT at a later time for experimentation.

We will simply create an Admin role for now. Click the Enable roles hyperlink in the Roles panel.

After a moment, roles-based security will be enabled. You'll need to add individual role accounts now. Click the Create or Manage roles hyperlink.

As I'm sure you'll notice, there really isn't much to this particular option, as shown in Figure 15-12.

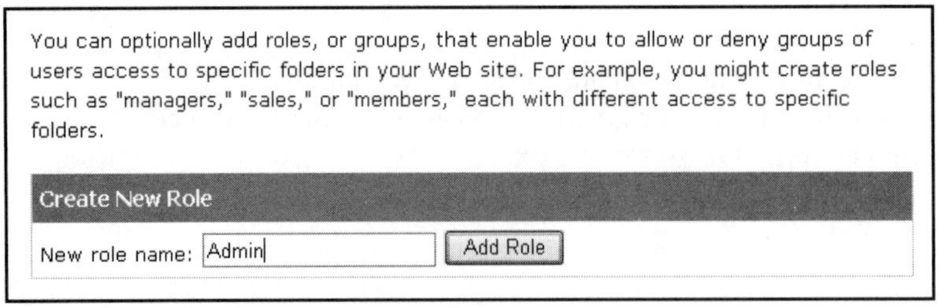

You can optionally add roles, or groups, that enable you to allow or deny groups of users access to specific folders in your Web site. For example, you might create roles such as "managers," "sales," or "members," each with different access to specific folders.

Create New Role

New role name: Admin   [Add Role]

Figure 15-12. *Role account maintenance*

After having created our new role, the WAT will now present us with yet another maintenance panel, as shown as Figure 15-13.

Figure 15-13. *Role accounts with user maintenance*

Within this newfound panel, we'll be able to add users to the listed roles. However, we
need to add a user account in order to take advantage of this feature.

Creating a User Account

Click the Security tab at the top to return to the main account form. Click the Create user
hyperlink in the Users panel.

We're presented with the typical, generic, user-data model, as shown in Figure 15-14. This
particular form should look real familiar. It is identical to the CreateUserWizard control on our
form!

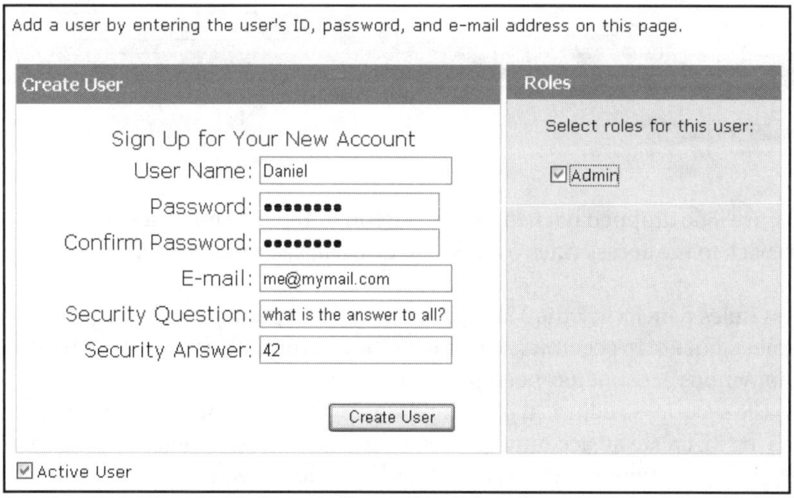

Figure 15-14. *Creating a user account*

Create an account and then select the only available role (Admin). Save the account.

You'll be given a positive response screen, if you have entered valid and complete data.

Once again, click the Security tab to return to the maintenance screen. Because we're interested in visiting all of the options on this screen, we should create some access rules as well.

Creating Access Rules

Click the Create access rules hyperlink in the Access Rules panel.

We're now dropped into the access rules page, as shown in Figure 15-15. This is a pretty self-explanatory page. Based on the directory listing to the left, we can restrict or allow set role access to those particular resources. For now we'll just simply allow the Admin role access to the entire site.

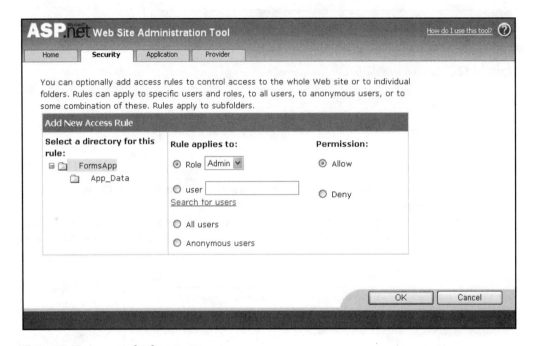

Figure 15-15. *Access rules form*

After clicking OK, we'll be dropped back to the security-maintenance form. It would be good for us to return back to the access rules page, so that we can see what the WAT just did for us.

Within the Access Rules panel, click the Manage access rules hyperlink.

As you would expect, our Admin account is listed with the appropriate access granted. Also note that the anonymous account has been preset for us, as shown in Figure 15-16.

We now have a basic security structure in place, and we also have a sample login page that will enable the user to log in, create an account, and see their login status. To really appreciate the fact that we're restricting anonymous access and allowing credentialed users through, let's utilize Default2.aspx as our members only page to test the security model.

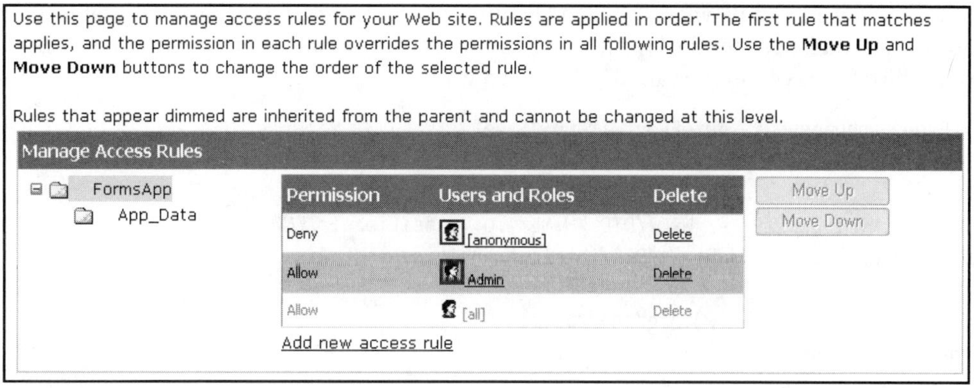
Use this page to manage access rules for your Web site. Rules are applied in order. The first rule that matches applies, and the permission in each rule overrides the permissions in all following rules. Use the Move Up and Move Down buttons to change the order of the selected rule.
Rules that appear dimmed are inherited from the parent and cannot be changed at this level.
Manage Access Rules
FormsApp
App_Data
Permission
Users and Roles
Delete
Move Up
Move Down
Deny
[anonymous]
Delete
Allow
Admin
Delete
Allow
[all]
Delete
Add new access rule

Figure 15-16. *Manage access rules form*

Testing the Security

We'll add a hyperlink on the login page to `Default2.aspx` and tidy up the login page.

Drag a Hyperlink Server control on to `Default.aspx` and set its `NavigateUrl` property to `Default2.aspx`. Change the `Text` property to Enter Members Only section.

To clean up the form a bit, let's add the CreateUserWizard and Login controls to a table, as shown in Figure 15-17.

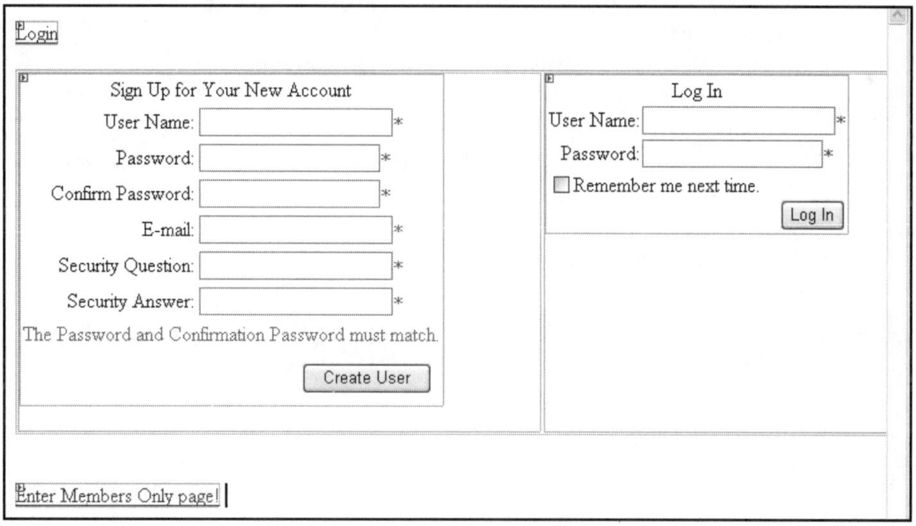
Login
Sign Up for Your New Account
User Name:
Password:
Confirm Password:
E-mail:
Security Question:
Security Answer:
The Password and Confirmation Password must match.
Create User
Log In
User Name:
Password:
Remember me next time.
Log In
Enter Members Only page!

Figure 15-17. *Our finished sample application*

To give you an idea of what is going on behind the scenes, let's take a look at the table formatting that you'll need for the layout, as well as the default settings that Visual Studio 2005 has supplied for us within the various security controls:

```
<%@ Page Language="C#" AutoEventWireup="true"
 CodeFile="Default.aspx.cs" Inherits="_Default" %>

<!DOCTYPE html PUBLIC "-//W3C//DTD XHTML 1.0 Transitional//EN"
 "http://www.w3.org/TR/xhtml1/DTD/xhtml1-transitional.dtd">

<html xmlns="http://www.w3.org/1999/xhtml" >
  <head runat="server">
    <title>Untitled Page</title>
  </head>
  <body>
    <form id="form1" runat="server">
      <div>
        <asp:LoginStatus ID="LoginStatus1" runat="server" />
        <br />
        <br />

        <table width="100%">
          <tr>
            <td valign="top">
              <asp:CreateUserWizard ID="CreateUserWizard1" runat="server">
                <WizardSteps>
                  <asp:CreateUserWizardStep ID="CreateUserWizardStep1"
                                            runat="server">
                  </asp:CreateUserWizardStep>
                  <asp:CompleteWizardStep ID="CompleteWizardStep1" runat="server">
                  </asp:CompleteWizardStep>
                </WizardSteps>
              </asp:CreateUserWizard>
            </td>
            <td valign="top">
              <asp:Login ID="Login1" runat="server"></asp:Login>
            </td>
          </tr>
        </table>
      </div>

      <br />
      <br />
      <asp:HyperLink ID="HyperLink1" runat="server" NavigateUrl="Default2.aspx">
        Enter Members Only page!</asp:HyperLink>
    </form>
  </body>
</html>
```

Before we run the application, jump over to Default2.aspx and add some text to the form, as shown in Figure 15-18. It's not spectacular, but it is enough to let us know after the click event that we have arrived somewhere else.

Figure 15-18. *Default2.aspx sample page*

The time has come! Let's run the application!

When the page loads, don't enter any information. Instead, while you're still an anonymous user, click the Members Only hyperlink at the bottom of the page. Notice where you ended up? That's right! Back at the login page, as expected.

Enter the login information from the account you created earlier and click Log In.

Wait a minute! How is it that we're already on the members only page? Well, when we first attempted to access the members only section, as an anonymous user, we were rejected and sent back to the login page. Consequently, the ReturnURL parameter of the page was set to Default2.aspx. Stop and restart the application. We now have an empty URL parameter list. Now log in again. You'll notice that the Login Status control has changed to reflect the new log out ability.

This wraps up our brief discussion and usage of the few select login controls that we've implemented. However, I'd still like to discuss two outstanding issues that I've seen pop up on the web concerning Ajax and Forms Authentication as well as the ability to use a custom SQL Server database in lieu of the stock express provider.

Ajax on Protected Login Pages

One question that I've been asked recently concerned the ability of Ajax to function on a login page where Forms Authentication is hard at work: would an Ajax call work in this circumstance? Rather than build an application, step by step, to demonstrate this, I'll just describe the sample page that I wrote to illustrate the question.

In addition to the form that we built previously, I used an HTML button that calls a JavaScript function CallAjax(), as shown in Figure 15-19.

Figure 15-19. *Ajax calling button*

The HTML code for the button event is typical of what we've done so far:

```
<script type="text/javascript" language="javascript">
function CallAjax()
{
    Anthem_InvokePageMethod('SayHello', [], AjaxCallBack);
}

function AjaxCallBack(result)
{
    alert(result.value);
}
</script>

...

Call Ajax: <input id="Button1" type="button" value="Go!" onclick="CallAjax();"/>
<br />
```

On the server side, I simply register my page and generate a simple Ajax method for passing back some generic data:

```
using System;
using System.Data;
using System.Configuration;
using System.Web;
using System.Web.Security;
using System.Web.UI;
using System.Web.UI.WebControls;
using System.Web.UI.WebControls.WebParts;
using System.Web.UI.HtmlControls;

public partial class _Default : System.Web.UI.Page
{
    protected void Page_Load(object sender, EventArgs e)
    {
        Anthem.Manager.Register(this);
    }

    [Anthem.Method]
    public string SayHello()
    {
        return "Hello There!";
    }
}
```

When I run the application and click the Go! button, I quickly receive the anticipated alert box. This happens because the Ajax call that is rendered on the login page is open for anonymous usage as it was delivered as such. You'll want to keep this in mind, should you want to use an Ajax-enabled tool on any login/anonymous page. Generally speaking, if the anonymous user can see it, they can use it.

Forms Authentication and SQL Server

Finally, I'd like to address the issue that you will certainly face with Forms Authentication and SQL Server databases. It's nice that Visual Studio 2005 has the built-in express provider, but this is not feasible for web deployment to an enterprise or hosted service. Setting up the provider model to reference a custom SQL Server database can be a daunting task. Fortunately for you (and me), my technical reviewer, Nick McCollum, has done the investigative work for us and was kind enough to write a short article on customizing the provider model to access any SQL Server database. He was also generous in allowing me to include the article in its entirety in this chapter.

Using ASP.NET 2.0 Membership with a SQL Server Database of Your Choice

by Nick McCollum
http://blogs.sagestone.net/nmccollum/

The membership features in ASP.NET 2.0 provide a great way to include Forms Authentication and role-based security in your web application. However, the default settings are less than desirable when creating an enterprise application. The machine.config file installed by the .NET 2.0 Framework contains default SQL Server provider settings for membership, roles, and profiles. When you run the ASP.NET Configuration tool from within Visual Studio 2005, these default settings result in the creation of a local SQL Server Express database within the App_Data folder of your website to store the membership, role, and profile information.

While this option is functional, it is definitely not ideal. It would be much better if you could specify the database used to store this information. The good news is that you can make this happen by taking advantage of a utility program included with Visual Studio 2005 along with some minor modifications to your Web.Config file.

This first step in hosting the membership data in a SQL Server database of your choice is to run the Aspnet_regsql.exe tool located in the drive:\WINDOWS\Microsoft.NET\Framework\versionNumber folder. Simply walk through this wizard to install the tables and stored procedures needed to host membership, roles, and profiles on the database of your choice.

Once you have configured your database to support membership, load the Web.Config file for your website into the editor in Visual Studio 2005. Add a connection string for your database to the connectionStrings section of your Web.Config file.

```
<CONNECTIONSTRINGS>
<ADD name="MySqlServer" connectionString="Data Source=.\SQLEXPRESS;
    Database=MembershipTest;User Id=Membership_User;Password=p@ssw0rd;" />
</CONNECTIONSTRINGS>
```

Once you have added your connection string, add the following provider sections to the system.web section of your Web.Config file:

```
<SYSTEM.WEB>
  <MEMBERSHIP>
    <PROVIDERS>
      <ADD name="MySqlMembershipProvider"
           type="System.Web.Security.SqlMembershipProvider,
             System.Web, Version=2.0.0.0, Culture=neutral,
             PublicKeyToken=b03f5f7f11d50a3a"
           connectionStringName="MySqlServer"
           enablePasswordRetrieval="false"
           enablePasswordReset="true"
           requiresQuestionAndAnswer="true"
           applicationName="/"
           requiresUniqueEmail="false"
           passwordFormat="Hashed"
           maxInvalidPasswordAttempts="5"
           minRequiredPasswordLength="7"
           minRequiredNonalphanumericCharacters="1"
           passwordAttemptWindow="10"
           passwordStrengthRegularExpression="" />
    </PROVIDERS>
  </MEMBERSHIP>
  <PROFILE>
    <PROVIDERS>
      <ADD name="MySqlProfileProvider"
           type="System.Web.Profile.SqlProfileProvider,
             System.Web, Version=2.0.0.0, Culture=neutral,
             PublicKeyToken=b03f5f7f11d50a3a"
           connectionStringName="MySqlServer"
           applicationName="/" />
    </PROVIDERS>
  </PROFILE>
  <ROLEMANAGER>
    <PROVIDERS>
      <ADD name="MySqlRoleProvider"
           type="System.Web.Security.SqlRoleProvider,
             System.Web, Version=2.0.0.0, Culture=neutral,
             PublicKeyToken=b03f5f7f11d50a3a"
           connectionStringName="MySqlServer"
           applicationName="/" />
    </PROVIDERS>
  </ROLEMANAGER>
</SYSTEM.WEB>
```

These settings are basically copies of the entries found in the `machine.config` file with two minor changes. First, the names have been changed. The default names are `AspNetSqlMembershipProvider`, `AspNetSqlProfileProvider`, and `AspNetSqlRoleProvider`. If you attempt to use one of these names without using the remove syntax in your `Web.Config` file first, you will receive an error. I found it much simpler to just change the names of the providers.

The second change you need to make to the provider entries is to update the `connectionStringName` attribute to point to the connection string entry in the `Web.Config` file that you created earlier. Once you have made these changes, save your `Web.Config` file. You are now ready to run the ASP.NET Configuration tool found under the Website menu in Visual Studio 2005.

Launch the ASP.NET Configuration tool and click the Provider tab to access the provider settings. Click the Select a different provider for each feature (advanced) link. You should see your new membership provider entry under the Membership Provider section and your new role provider under the Role Provider section. Note that the profile provider is not managed using this tool. Click the radio button next to each of your new providers and click the Test link to verify that the membership and role features can access your database. Close the configuration tool.

You are now ready to begin developing the security features required by your application using the membership features of ASP.NET 2.0 with the SQL Server database of your choice.

Summary

In this chapter, I have hopefully dispelled one of the foremost misconceptions concerning Ajax and security, that separate provisions must be made for an Ajax application. As you've seen, by adhering to recognized .NET security standards, we are able to maintain the same level of protection that typical ASP.NET processes enjoy. The .NET 2.0 Framework has been kind enough to provide us with an exemplary set of security components that we can readily implement with our dynamic web applications.

In the next chapter, we'll shift our focus towards site performance and the availability of monitoring tools for an Ajax application.

CHAPTER 16

Performance

I'm sure that by now you have come to realize that the dynamic user experience of an Ajax-enabled site is just one of the compelling reasons for choosing to implement this dynamic toolset. However, a postbackless environment is secondary to the benefits that we reap from bandwidth that is dramatically reduced by continuous user interaction. On a typical web page, the user is presented with an assortment of controls, text, and images. Usually, the point of the page is to allow the user and site owner a portal of interaction with each other. The means by which this communication takes place is the gathering or selecting of information and taking appropriate actions based on the interaction process.

On a retail site, products may be listed for customers to browse, select, and purchase. They might do this by clicking a "Buy It" button and adding the product to a virtual shopping cart. A common model for this style of interaction on a straightforward web page is to present a page to a user's browser and wait for the user to trigger some form of event on the page. When such an event occurs, a majority of the page is sent back to the server side, values are compared with their originals, and actions are put into place based on that returned information. Accordingly, the server generates an entirely new copy of the page that is sent back to the user as a representation of the actions that the user has just initiated.

As you can imagine, this constant swapping of full (or nearly full) postback pages can be taxing on the server when scaled up to a multitude of simultaneous users. Now imagine that we generate a page that has Ajax controls that allow the customer to interact with server-side resources. With Ajax, rather than a full-blown postback, we send only a minor request and receive a minor response. Now imagine this model scaled out to a few thousand users. You can begin to see the performance benefits that can be reaped by just a few key Ajax controls.

In this chapter, we'll take a look at postback statistics and how they relate to Ajax data package sizes. We'll also examine the benefits of JSON versus XML with a real-world example. Finally, we'll take a look at some key JavaScript concepts that may help to optimize our processes.

Monitoring Tools

Obviously, if we're going to track any type of site statistics, we're going to need an application in place to monitor our activities. Most developers and server admins find themselves really monitoring two distinct and important processes: server usage and application events. As you would expect, monitoring the events triggered by your website involves debugging through Visual Studio. For that I refer you to Chapter 17. Server usage, however, involves a few external tools that we'll examine here.

Server Monitoring

There are a variety of third-party tools out on the market for monitoring IIS server state and system usage. However, some of these tools are overkill for the basic questions that we tend to ask:

- Does our application kill the server?

- Is the server overwhelmed by requests?

- How many applications do we have running on that thing?

These are all-important questions that developers should certainly consider while coding applications that they will be deploying to production environments.

Server Monitoring with perfmon

One tool in particular that I find myself using quite a bit is Microsoft's Performance Monitor (perfmon), shown in Figure 16-1. It's free and a relatively simple application to set up and monitor.

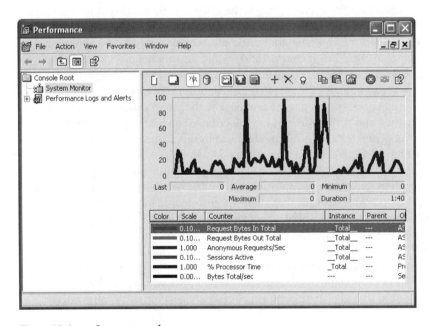

Figure 16-1. *perfmon at work*

To quickly start perfmon, you'll click Start ➤ Run, enter **perfmon** as shown in Figure 16-2, and click OK.

perfmon can monitor system resources, but it's also quite adept at monitoring ASP.NET applications. As you can see in Figure 16-1 earlier, I have a few counters hard at work, monitoring the activity of the system as well as any ASP.NET applications that I might have running at the time. Adding a counter to this screen is as easy as clicking the plus button and then choosing from the multitude of available, ready-made counters that Microsoft has built into the tool, as you can see in Figure 16-3.

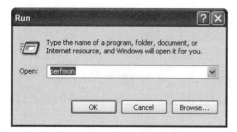

Figure 16-2. *Starting perfmon*

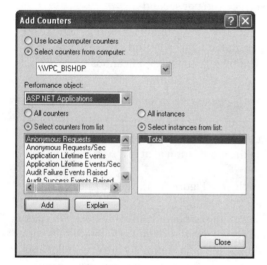

Figure 16-3. *Adding counters to perfmon*

Some of the more useful counters for perfmon:

- ASP.NET counters:

    - *Application Restart*: As the name implies, this monitors how many times your application has been restarted during the life of the server. Obviously, if the application has an excessive number of restarts, an alarm should be raised and investigations should ensue.

    - *Requests Queued*: Tracks the number of users that are waiting in line for resources. If this becomes proportionate to the client load, it indicates that the server has reached its concurrency limit.

    - *Requests Rejected*: This is the bad number. The system can't handle the load and people are getting the "503 Server Busy" error. Sometimes this is the last thing that new users will ever see of your site, because they may never return.

    - *Worker Processes Running*: It is as the name implies. Monitoring this will give you an idea of what IIS is processing at any given time.

- ASP.NET application counters:

  - *Anonymous Requests*: Total number of requests that are using anonymous authentication

  - *Errors Total*: Total number of errors during execution of the HTTP requests

  - *Request Bytes In Total*: Total byte size of all requests

  - *Request Bytes Out Total*: Total byte size of all responses sent back to the client

  - *Requests Total*: Total number of requests since the service was started

  - *Requests/Sec*: Total number of requests received per second

There are many more counters that you can add; I've only listed the ones that I find to be useful. I encourage you to experiment with the perfmon tool. It's free and simple to use, and the information that you get from it may help to optimize your web applications.

Server Monitoring with Fiddler

I want to also discuss another performance monitoring tool that I find myself using on nearly every web project that I'm involved in. Microsoft's Fiddler is another free offering that you'll find yourself using quite a bit as well. You can find the application at http://www.fiddlertool.com.

Like perfmon, Fiddler's interface is rather simple (see Figure 16-4), yet the underlying toolset is incredibly useful.

Fiddler is a traffic-monitoring tool that allows you to see not only the HTTP session calls, but also the underlying HTML data that is pushed across the wire. If you're having issues with your application and not sure where to turn for diagnostic help, definitely fire up Fiddler and examine the data streams first. You may be surprised to find that the data being sent to and from the server is not quite what you had in mind.

As requests process on your system, they'll be displayed within Fiddler's HTTP Sessions window. The left panel will display each streaming page hit and the appropriate session information:

- *Session ID*: Generated by Fiddler, for tracking purposes

- *HTTP Request Result*: 200—Successfully found

- *Host*: Hostname of the server that you sent the request to

- *URL*: Path and file that you've asked for

- *Body*: Size, in bytes, of the Response body

- *Caching*: Listing of page caching, if any

- *Content-Type*: What was sent across the wire (text, image, or script)

- *User Defined*: Text that you can set via scripting

As you can see in Figure 16-5, the panel to the right in Fiddler presents a variety of tabs, by which you can view the request/response results in unique ways. If you're only interested in the raw text that was sent and received, you could click the Raw button.

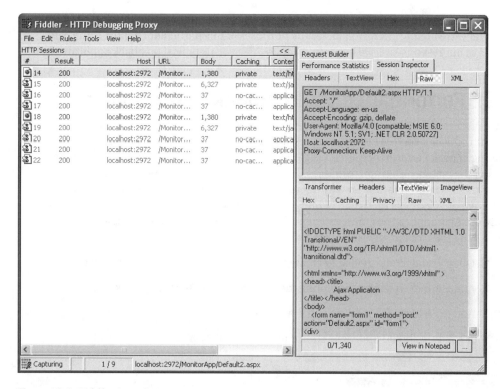

Figure 16-4. *Fiddler interface*

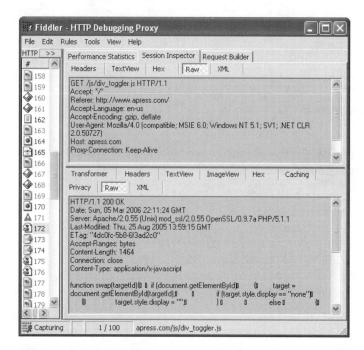

Figure 16-5. *Raw response view*

The tool has an incredible range of possibilities for something offered as free to the public. What we're mainly interested in, for the purposes of this particular chapter, is the byte counts of our responses as we begin to compare Ajax versus typical postback applications.

Ajax Performance vs. Postback Performance

As we discussed earlier, the dynamic user interface is really just a sideshow to the main event of bandwidth and server load efficiency. A large numer of popular web sites have web servers running at peak performance streaming HTML out to the user's computers that are barely moving the meters on system resources. Typically, most client computers spend a majority of their time in a 90% idle state. So why not offload some of the site's workload to the user's PC? This is where Ajax steps up to bat, helping to move those processing cycles elsewhere. But, really, are Ajax applications more efficient than postbacks? Let's build a sample application and see the stats for ourselves. To start with, do the following:

1. Open Visual Studio 2005 and create a new WebSite project, naming it `MonitorApp`.

2. Add another web form, accepting the default name of `Default2.aspx`.

3. Add the `Anthem.dll` reference to the project.

Your solution should appear as shown in Figure 16-6.

Figure 16-6. *Sample application structure*

Now it's time to work on the code. You should modify your `Default.aspx` HTML code to reflect the following, which is the typical postback page:

```
<%@ Page Language="C#" AutoEventWireup="true"
 CodeFile="Default.aspx.cs" Inherits="_Default" %>

<!DOCTYPE html PUBLIC "-//W3C//DTD XHTML 1.0 Transitional//EN"
 "http://www.w3.org/TR/xhtml1/DTD/xhtml1-transitional.dtd">

<html xmlns="http://www.w3.org/1999/xhtml" >
<head runat="server">
    <title>Postback Page</title>
</head>
```

```
<body>
    <form id="form1" runat="server">
        <div>
         Enter Your First Name:
         <asp:TextBox ID="TextBox1" runat="server"></asp:TextBox>
         <asp:Button ID="Button1" runat="server" Text="Go!"
           OnClick="Button1_Click" />
        </div>
        <div id="divResults" runat="server"></div>
    </form>
</body>
</html>
```

Your server-side C# code for Default.aspx.cs is as follows:

```
using System;
using System.Data;
using System.Configuration;
using System.Web;
using System.Web.Security;
using System.Web.UI;
using System.Web.UI.WebControls;
using System.Web.UI.WebControls.WebParts;
using System.Web.UI.HtmlControls;

public partial class _Default : System.Web.UI.Page
{
    protected void Page_Load(object sender, EventArgs e)
    {

    }
    protected void Button1_Click(object sender, EventArgs e)
    {
        this.divResults.InnerHtml = "Hello " + this.TextBox1.Text;
    }
}
```

Switch over to Default2.aspx's HTML view and modify it as well. This is our Ajax version:

```
<%@ Page Language="C#" AutoEventWireup="true"
CodeFile="Default2.aspx.cs" Inherits="Default2" %>

<!DOCTYPE html PUBLIC "-//W3C//DTD XHTML 1.0 Transitional//EN"
"http://www.w3.org/TR/xhtml1/DTD/xhtml1-transitional.dtd">

<html xmlns="http://www.w3.org/1999/xhtml" >
<head runat="server">
    <title>Ajax Applicaton</title>
</head>
```

```html
<body>
    <form id="form1" runat="server">
    <script type="text/javascript">
        function SayHello()
        {
            Anthem_InvokePageMethod('GetMessage',
            [document.getElementById("TextBox1").value],
            HelloCallBack);
        }
        function HelloCallBack(result)
        {
            document.getElementById("divResults").innerHTML = result.value;
        }
    </script>
    <div>
        Enter Your First Name:
        <asp:TextBox ID="TextBox1" runat="server"></asp:TextBox>
        <input id="Button1" type="button" value="Go!" onclick="SayHello();" />
    </div>
    <div id="divResults"></div>
    </form>
</body>
</html>
```

Finally, we need the C# side of things for Default2.aspx.cs:

```csharp
using System;
using System.Data;
using System.Configuration;
using System.Collections;
using System.Web;
using System.Web.Security;
using System.Web.UI;
using System.Web.UI.WebControls;
using System.Web.UI.WebControls.WebParts;
using System.Web.UI.HtmlControls;

public partial class Default2 : System.Web.UI.Page
{
    protected void Page_Load(object sender, EventArgs e)
    {
        Anthem.Manager.Register(this);
    }

    [Anthem.Method]
    public string GetMessage(string NameIn)
    {
        return "Hello " + NameIn;
    }
}
```

As `Default.aspx` is a typical postback page, we have a textbox for user input and a button for triggering the response event. After the user enters their name, we will prefix a "Hello" string to the textbox value and return that to the client browser, binding it to a `div` tag's `innerHTML` property.

Keeping consistent with the functionality of the postback page, I've built the Ajax version of the page with nearly identical browser functionality. However, an Ajax call is made to the server side, and the "Hello" string is concatenated and returned for display on the browser, without postback.

Comparing the Performance

Now that we've built the two pages for comparison, how do the response stats fare? Well, before we run the application, let's start Fiddler and watch the responses received for each of the two pages.

Evaluating the Postback Version

Let's start with the postback version. Set `Default.aspx` as the startup page by right-clicking the filename in the Solution Explorer and choosing Set As Start Page, as shown in Figure 16-7.

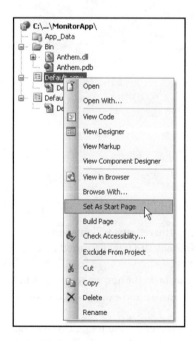

Figure 16-7. *Switching between startup pages*

Before we run the application, let's clear out any existing sessions in Fiddler. This will give us a clean slate from which to work.

To do so, start Fiddler, right-click the Sessions window, and choose Remove ➤ All Sessions, as shown in Figure 16-8.

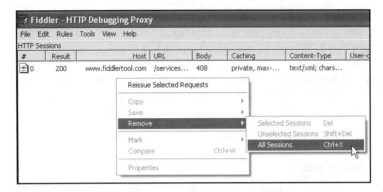

Figure 16-8. *Removing sessions from Fiddler*

Now start the MonitorApp site in Visual Studio 2005. After a moment, you'll be met with the rather simple page you see in Figure 16-9.

Figure 16-9. *The postback sample application*

Enter your name and click the Go! button. After a moment, the request will arrive at the server, and the server will process the string message and post back the newly formed text within a div tag underneath the textbox (see Figure 16-10).

We're not really interested so much in the GUI results of our task. Rather, we're curious to know what the postback transfer size was. Let's switch over to Fiddler and examine the session data, shown in Figure 16-11.

The first session is our initial request that was made to the server for the page. The second session is the postback event for our page and contains the data that we're looking to track. We can see that the page successfully loaded and has a result of 200. We can also see that the postback data size is 928 bytes.

Also, if you click the XML button on the bottom pane of the Session Inspector, you'll have an opportunity to see the page in its XML DOM format once it has been assembled and posted back, as shown in Figure 16-12.

Figure 16-10. *Results of postback*

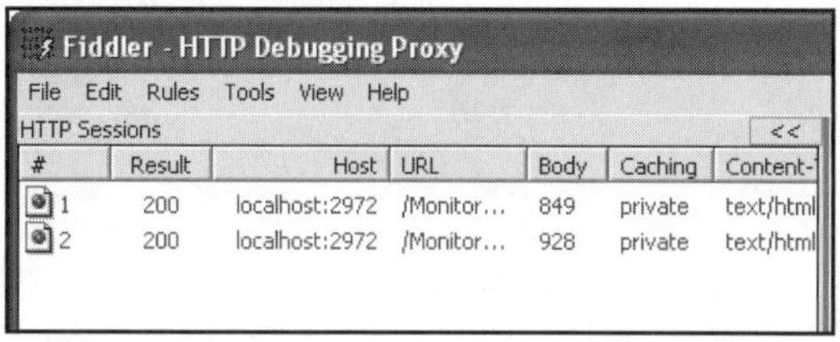

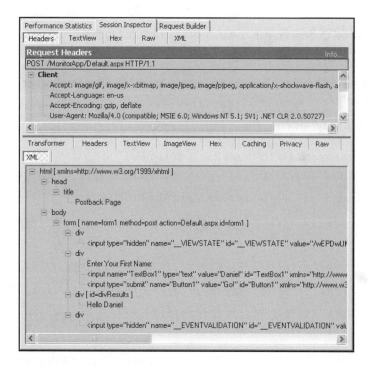

Figure 16-11. *Fiddler results of postback process*

Figure 16-12. *XML DOM view of the results page*

Evaluating the Ajax Version

So now that we've evaluated the postback version of the page, let's turn our attention to the Ajax version.

Right-click Default2.aspx in Solution Explorer and set the page as the default startup page. Now run the application.

The page interface is nearly identical to that of Default.aspx, which is what we intended. It would be rather unscientific of us to compare the two if they were drastically different. One thing that you will immediately notice is that the Ajax page has an initial deliverable size that is larger than the postback version. And that would make sense. We have JavaScript and Ajax code that will be delivered to the client's browser, thus making the deliverable quite a bit larger. But we're not really investigating page size at the moment. What is of interest to us is the postback process.

Enter your name (use the same name as the previous example) and click the Go! button.

After a moment, you'll see that the div tag is populated in a similar fashion to the previous demonstration, without the postback, of course.

So now we switch back to Fiddler and find that our Ajax process has come in with a significantly lower byte size, as shown in Figure 16-13.

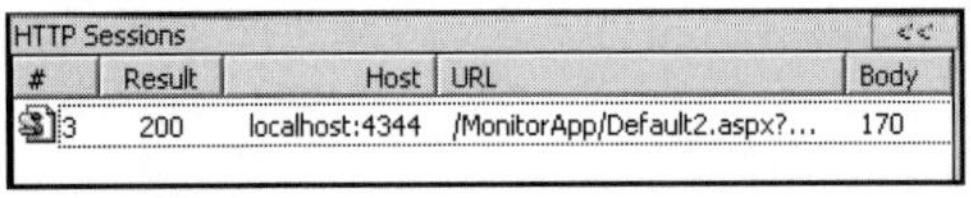

Figure 16-13. *Ajax return results*

What an incredible difference! Our Ajax result comes in at a miniscule 170 bytes. Surely there must be some missing data? Well let's look at the Session Inspector and examine the data that was sent back (see Figure 16-14).

We can see in the Raw display of the data that our request was served and the appropriate JSON text was built and returned:

{"value":"Hello Dan","error":null,"viewState":
 "/wEPDwUJMjgzMDgzOTgzZGTLq1Av3FIca2e7GHnQ7SgWchp48w==",
"eventValidation":"/wEWAgLQ9d6fDgLsObLrBv2iW1FteAsT8w2JLmBQx3Po/AEC"
}

which leads to an excellent question. Is JSON a performing alternative to XML?

Figure 16-14. *Ajax return data*

Comparing JSON and XML

Since we're already on a performance-monitoring roll, let's go ahead and sample some data.

In the current solution, right-click the project name and add another web form. Accept the Default3.aspx name.

Modify the HTML code so that it appears as shown:

```
<%@ Page Language="C#" AutoEventWireup="true"
 CodeFile="Default3.aspx.cs" Inherits="Default3" %>

<!DOCTYPE html PUBLIC "-//W3C//DTD XHTML 1.0 Transitional//EN"
 "http://www.w3.org/TR/xhtml1/DTD/xhtml1-transitional.dtd">

<html xmlns="http://www.w3.org/1999/xhtml" >
<head id="Head1" runat="server">
    <title>JSON Reader</title>
</head>
<script type="text/javascript" language="javascript">
var xmlhttp = false;
```

```
getHTTPRequestObject();

function getHTTPRequestObject()
{
    try
    {
        // Try legacy object first
        xmlhttp = new ActiveXObject("Msxml2.XMLHTTP");
    }
    catch(e)
    {
        try
        {
            // Try IE implementation now
            xmlhttp = new ActiveXObject("Microsoft.XMLHTTP");
        }
        catch(E)
        {
            xmlhttp = false;
        }
    }
    if(!xmlhttp && typeof XMLHttpRequest!= 'undefined')
    {
        // We must be using a mozilla-based browser
        // so create a native request object now
        xmlhttp = new XMLHttpRequest();
    }
}

function callback()
{
        if(xmlhttp.readyState == 4)
        {
            if(xmlhttp.status == 200)
            {
              var response = xmlhttp.responseText;
              var finddiv = document.getElementById("divResponse");
              finddiv.innerHTML = response;
            }
        }
}
```

```
function btnClick()
{
    // Retrieve the JSON text from the local file.
    xmlhttp.open("GET", "JSON.txt", true);
    xmlhttp.onreadystatechange = callback;
    xmlhttp.send(null);
}
</script>

<body>
    <form id="form1" runat="server">
        <input id="btnGetJSON" type="button" value="Get JSON"
          onclick="btnClick();" />
        <div id="divResponse"></div>
    </form>
</body>
</html>
```

We don't have any code on the server side, so the .cs file should remain as the default:

```
using System;
using System.Data;
using System.Configuration;
using System.Collections;
using System.Web;
using System.Web.Security;
using System.Web.UI;
using System.Web.UI.WebControls;
using System.Web.UI.WebControls.WebParts;
using System.Web.UI.HtmlControls;
public partial class Default3 : System.Web.UI.Page
{
    protected void Page_Load(object sender, EventArgs e)
    {

    }
}
```

Now we need to add a JSON file. Right-click the project name and this time choose to add a text file instead, named JSON.txt, as shown in Figure 16-15.

Within the JSON.txt file, add the following text:

```
{"Results":{"computer":[{"Manufacturer":"Dell","Model":"Latitude","Price":"1650"},
{"Manufacturer":"Dell","Model":"Inspiron","Price":"1850"}]}
}
```

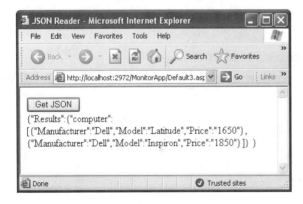

Figure 16-15. *Adding the text file for JSON*

You can always copy and paste the text from the downloaded sample application, if you're worried about syntax errors. Now save your work.

Set `Default3.aspx` as the startup page and run the application.

Press the button to retrieve the JSON text. You'll find that we're not processing the incoming file at all, as you can see in Figure 16-16.

Figure 16-16. *JSON page results*

We're simply dumping the raw file out to the `innerHTML` of the `div` tag. Because we're interested in the transfer size and not the client-side processing, let's take a look at what Fiddler has monitored (see Figure 16-17).

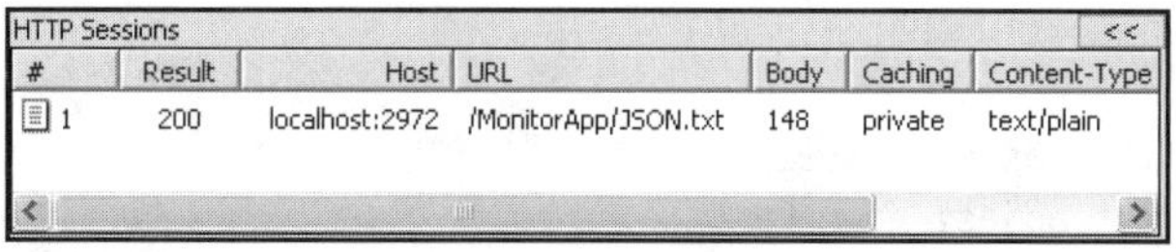

Figure 16-17. *JSON return stats*

So you can see that the JSON file has come across the wire with a 148 byte payload. Now let's see how well the XML file will fare.

In our current project, add yet another web form, accepting Default4.aspx as the page name.

Modify the HTML code to reflect the following:

```
<%@ Page Language="C#" AutoEventWireup="true"
 CodeFile="Default4.aspx.cs" Inherits="Default4" %>

<!DOCTYPE html PUBLIC "-//W3C//DTD XHTML 1.0 Transitional//EN"
 "http://www.w3.org/TR/xhtml1/DTD/xhtml1-transitional.dtd">

<html xmlns="http://www.w3.org/1999/xhtml" >
<head id="Head1" runat="server">
    <title>XML Reader</title>
</head>
<script type="text/javascript" language="javascript">
var xmlhttp = false;

getHTTPRequestObject();

function getHTTPRequestObject()
{
    try
    {
        // Try legacy object first
        xmlhttp = new ActiveXObject("Msxml2.XMLHTTP");
    }
    catch(e)
    {
        try
        {
            // Try IE implementation now
            xmlhttp = new ActiveXObject("Microsoft.XMLHTTP");
        }
        catch(E)
        {
            xmlhttp = false;
        }
    }
```

```
    if(!xmlhttp && typeof XMLHttpRequest!= 'undefined')
    {
        // We must be using a mozilla-based browser
        // so create a native request object now
        xmlhttp = new XMLHttpRequest();
    }
}

function callback()
{
        if(xmlhttp.readyState == 4)
        {
            if(xmlhttp.status == 200)
            {
                var textresponse = xmlhttp.responseText;
                var finddiv = document.getElementById("divResponse");
                finddiv.innerText = textresponse;
            }
        }
}

function btnClick()
{
    xmlhttp.open("GET", "XMLFile.xml", true);
    xmlhttp.onreadystatechange = callback;
    xmlhttp.send(null);
}
</script>

<body>
    <form id="form1" runat="server">
        <input id="btnGetXML" type="button" value="Get XML" onclick="btnClick();" />
        <div id="divResponse"></div>
    </form>
</body>
</html>
```

Again, the .cs code file is the default:

```
using System;
using System.Data;
using System.Configuration;
using System.Collections;
using System.Web;
using System.Web.Security;
using System.Web.UI;
using System.Web.UI.WebControls;
using System.Web.UI.WebControls.WebParts;
using System.Web.UI.HtmlControls;
```

```
public partial class Default4 : System.Web.UI.Page
{
    protected void Page_Load(object sender, EventArgs e)
    {

    }
}
```

If we want to test this page, we're obviously going to need an XML file. Right-click the project name and add a new item again. This time select XML File in the list of options and accept the default filename, as shown in Figure 16-18.

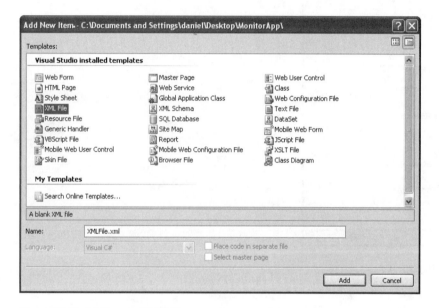

Figure 16-18. *Adding an XML file to project*

You'll want to add the following to the XML file and then save your work:

```
<?xml version="1.0" encoding="utf-8" ?>
<Results>
    <computer>
        <Manufacturer>Dell</Manufacturer>
        <Model>Latitude</Model>
        <Price>1650</Price>
    </computer>
    <computer>
        <Manufacturer>Dell</Manufacturer>
        <Model>Inspiron</Model>
        <Price>1850</Price>
    </computer>
</Results>
```

The XML file, when compared to the JSON file, is the same format with identical content. I've eliminated any attributes or other fields that do not show up in the competing file structure. So how does it perform?

As before, set `Default4.aspx` as the startup page, run the application, and click the Get XML button.

The results are dumped out to the `div` tag without any form of client-side parsing, as you see in Figure 16-19.

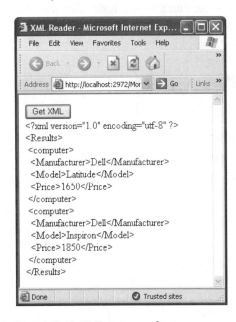

Figure 16-19. *XML page results*

So the moment of truth! We switch to Fiddler and find the stats shown in Figure 16-20.

Figure 16-20. *XML transfer stats*

The XML file has weighed in with a hefty 290 bytes—nearly double that of the JSON file size!

So what am I saying here? Am I calling for the end of XML? Certainly not. XML is a powerful tool when used appropriately. But if your only interest is passing data back to the client side for generic parsing, why not parse it into JSON format and let JavaScript's eval() function do the work for you? It's a lighter payload than XML, which in turn lightens the load on your network resources.

■Note If you're receiving XML data from another source, it would not be beneficial to parse that data into JSON format. The CPU cycles that you would use to parse the XML to JSON would outweigh any benefit that you might reap in the transfer phase. However, if you're retrieving or generating generic data and find that you must choose between XML and JSON, it may be in your best interest to use JSON format instead.

Our Findings

So, what have we found? Figures 16-21 and 16-22 present a summary of our findings.

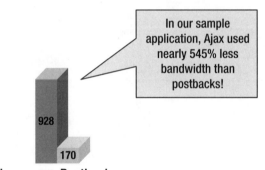

Figure 16-21. *Ajax versus postback*

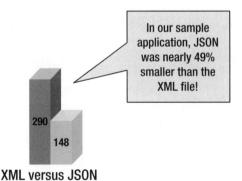

Figure 16-22. *XML versus JSON*

Obviously, Ajax is the hands-down winner on this performance test.

In appropriate situations, XML is a necessary file format, but I encourage you to keep JSON in the back of your mind and use it whenever it seems plausible. It has a lower footprint, and JavaScript loves it.

Summary

In this chapter, we've discussed the performance benefit that is inherently built into the Ajax methodology. The dynamic user interface is certainly a selling point, but what really seals the deal is the fact that Ajax is just so much faster and easier on the server. And if you're really looking for optimized transfer, keep JSON in the back of your mind. With a 49% savings on bandwidth, it can hardly be ignored.

In the next chapter, we'll discuss debugging and how it applies to Ajax. We'll take a look at the Ajax debug options as well as some debugging tools for the browser.

CHAPTER 17

■■■

Debugging Your Application

If you're one of those rare developers who writes flawless code and will never need to debug it, I invite you to skip this chapter and move on to Chapter 18. However, if like most developers you find yourself debugging code from time to time, this chapter is for you; I'll use this discussion to show you a few debugging techniques that may make your Ajax development a little less strenuous. We'll look at some new functionality introduced with Visual Studio 2005 as well as some third-party tools for debugging.

Deep-level debugging is something that we always dread. Occasionally, we'll have the simple variables named incorrectly or the notorious missing semicolon. But what steps do we take when things really go wrong? What does Microsoft provide for us to make this part of development easier?

With the release of Visual Studio 2005, Microsoft has revamped its debugging toolset and introduced some new functionality that we as developers can put to use immediately and with little learning curve. Some of the newest enhancements that we'll examine are

- Edit and Continue debugging

- Visualizers

- Enhanced DataTips

- Just My Code debugging

I would also like to spend a little more time demonstrating two previously mentioned tools that I find indispensable for Ajax development:

- Microsoft's Fiddler

- Microsoft's Developer Toolbar

With the combination of Visual Studio 2005, Fiddler, and the Developer Toolbar, you'll have a powerhouse of debugging tools at hand to help you solve any problem your code may throw your way.

Visual Studio 2005

In this section, you'll learn about the debugging tools that come with Visual Studio 2005 and how they help with debugging Ajax applications.

Edit and Continue

It seems that Microsoft has heard the pleas of many C# developers. For those of us who came
to the language from Visual Basic, one of the things that we've really missed was the ability to
pause the application at runtime, make some changes, and then continue where we left off.
Finally, VS 2005 has given us that option. If you haven't had a chance to use this functionality,
you'll find it to be an incredible tool for debugging.

To enable Edit and Continue functionality, you'll want to ensure that the proper option
has been checked under Tools ➤ Options ➤ Debugging, as shown in Figure 17-1.

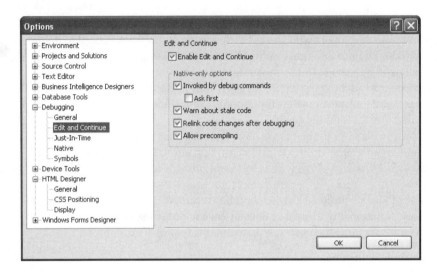

Figure 17-1. *Edit and Continue options*

To use Edit and Continue, we'll need to set some breakpoints within the code. That will
enable us to reach Break mode.

While you're in Break mode, make changes to your code, then proceed with the application by pressing F5 or clicking Continue in the Debug menu options.

There are some limitations to Edit and Continue, however. Microsoft has provided a list
of things that you **cannot** do while in debug mode:

- Change the current active or other active statements. Active statements include the
  current statement or any statements in the call stack that were called to get to the current statement.

- Change global symbols including adding a new type, adding methods to a type, changing a signature for the type, and adding fields, properties, or events for a type.

- Change attributes.

- Change using directives.

- Remove or change local variables. You can, however, add local variables.

- Add a foreach, lock, or using statement around the current statement.

There are other restrictions, and I encourage you to check with Microsoft for a complete list of them all at `http://msdn2.microsoft.com/en-us/library/ms164927(VS.80).aspx`.

Using Visualizers

For Ajax and web developers, one of the most exciting additions to Visual Studio 2005 is the introduction of visualizers. How many times have you had to drill down into a DataSet just to find a value for one of the columns? It takes an exhaustive amount of effort and time just to find a simple value. Wouldn't it be great if you could have a more representational display of the DataSet's current data? That is where visualizers step in. You'll find the visualizer icon (a magnifying glass) if you hover over a value that is visualizer friendly, as you see in Figure 17-2.

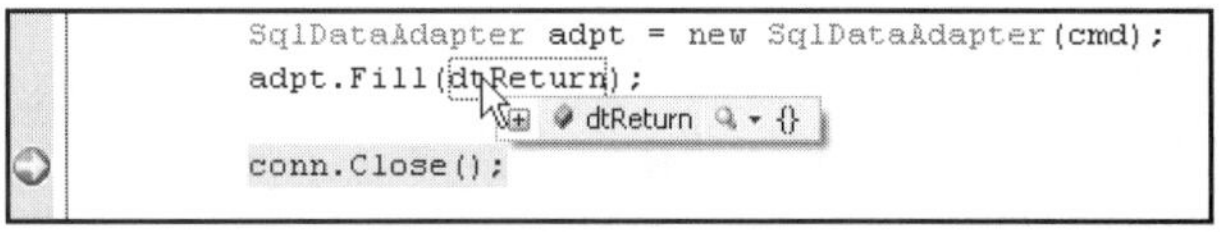

Figure 17-2. *The visualizer icon*

If you click the drop-down next to the magnifying glass, you'll find a list of possible compatible visualizers for the data type that you're hovering over, as shown in Figure 17-3.

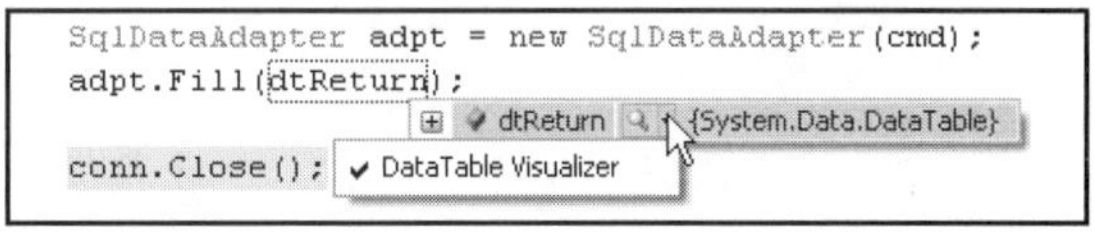

Figure 17-3. *DataTable Visualizer*

Clicking on the DataTable Visualizer brings up a really cool display of the current data, as Figure 17-4 illustrates.

Looking at the DataTable Visualizer, we have a better representation of the table results. Rather than having to drill down into the data type in the Locals window, we can use the simpler visualizer window for quick results. As a web developer, one of my favorite visualizers is the HTML Visualizer. Recall from our portal application that we had a section of code that retrieved a static map from Yahoo:

```
string strMapURL = sb.ToString();
string strHTML = "<center><img src='" + strMapURL + "' /></center>";
```

If I run this code and hover over `strHTML` after it has been assigned a value, I'll have a few other visualizers at my disposal (see Figure 17-5).

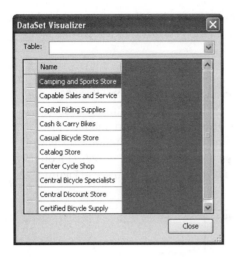

Figure 17-4. *DataTable in a presentable state*

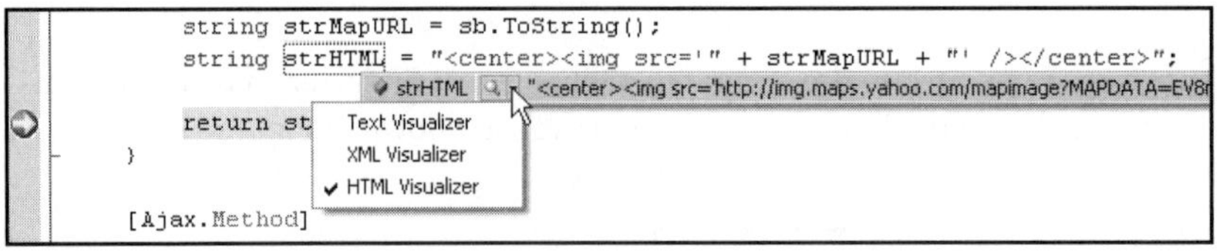

```
        string strMapURL = sb.ToString();
        string strHTML = "<center><img src='" + strMapURL + "' /></center>";
```
```
                        ⊘ strHTML  🔍 ▾  "<center><img src='http://img.maps.yahoo.com/mapimage?MAPDATA=EV8r
        return st         Text Visualizer
    }                     XML Visualizer
                        ✔ HTML Visualizer

    [Ajax.Method]
```

Figure 17-5. *More visualizer options for our data type*

Note that the URL for the image that is built at this stage of the function is rather large and therefore pushes the rest of the HTML way off the visible IDE, rendering the DataTip practically useless for debugging. However, the list of visualizers grants me one option in particular that is awesome for HTML work: my favorite, the HTML Visualizer!

When I click the HTML Visualizer, I'm given a browser-based representation of my string, as shown in Figure 17-6.

The expression that is currently being rendered is shown at the top with the HTML display in the Value box. This is a very useful tool for web developers, especially when you throw tables and positioning into the mix.

It is possible to build your own visualizer from scratch, although that topic is beyond the scope of this book. If you happen to build one for JSON, feel free to send it my way, as I'm sure that many of us will find a need for one.

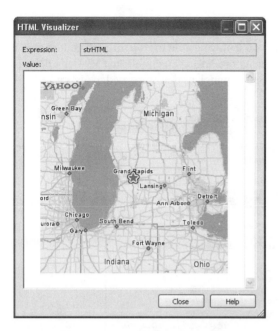

Figure 17-6. *HTML representation of data*

Enhanced DataTips

One of the things that you'll notice in the pop-up DataTips that we've discussed is that the information tends to be more useful than the standard mouseover tooltip. If the object that you're hovered over is a complex data type, you'll find a plus sign next to the variable name that indicates that you can drill down into the various properties of that object from the DataTip itself (see Figure 17-7).

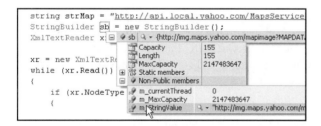

Figure 17-7. *Enhanced DataTips*

Our mouseover debugging duties are a little more efficient thanks to the new DataTips.

Just My Code Debugging

Enabling Just My Code debugging means that you'll only be able to step through code that you have written, and system-generated calls will be ignored. You can enable Just My Code debugging in the Tools ➤ Options ➤ Debugging ➤ General panel, as demonstrated in Figure 17-8.

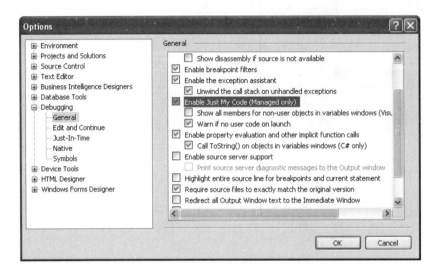

Figure 17-8. *Enabling Just My Code debugging*

If you'd like to step through all calls, system or otherwise, you would disable this functionality.

Third-party Tools

We've discussed the new and improved toolset that Microsoft has given us with Visual Studio 2005, but there are some third-party tools available on the web, for free, that we can also take advantage of. Now I say "third party," but in fact, they're both Microsoft products. However, they run outside of the Visual Studio 2005 environment, so I consider them to be third party.

Fiddler

We've used this tool a bit already in Chapter 16. And it's worth mentioning again, when taken in the context of a debugging chapter. I've become so accustomed to using it that I now find it an indispensable tool for identifying transfer errors and optimizations in my debugging cycle of development. Fortunately for us it is, as mentioned before, an entirely **FREE** product (http://www.fiddlertool.com). And free is always a good price to pay.

As you saw in Chapter 16, monitoring HTTP traffic and the corresponding transferred data is a simple click away. You should understand a little more about the background process involved when you run the tool.

When Fiddler is started, it wedges itself into the system and establishes itself as a proxy for Windows Internet Services (WinInet). WinInet, as you may already know, is the HTTP layer that Windows will draw its traffic from. Fiddler parks itself right there in the process as a system proxy. If you start Fiddler and then open a browser, you'll find in Tools ➤ Internet Options ➤ Connections ➤ Lan Settings ➤ Advanced that indeed a proxy is set (see Figure 17-9).

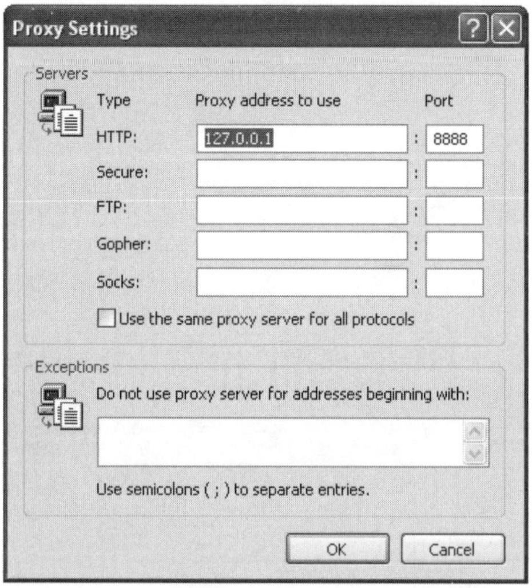

Figure 17-9. *Fiddler as a proxy*

With Fiddler set as the intercepting proxy, all traffic to the browser will flow through it first, as shown in Figure 17-10.

With Fiddler intercepting HTTP traffic, we're now able to monitor the incoming and outgoing request/response packages. We've already taken a pretty good look at traffic monitoring earlier, so I really want to concentrate on a debugging capability that I've overlooked until now. Fiddler has the ability to step through HTTP transactions by first enabling breakpoints and then moving through each traffic process.

Let's take a look at a sample Fiddler debugging session by stepping through a working site. First start Fiddler and open a browser window. Visit Microsoft.com inside of your browser. You'll see a pretty good request/response flow run through Fiddler, as shown in Figure 17-11.

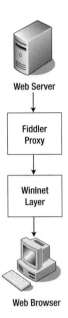

Figure 17-10. *HTTP traffic path*

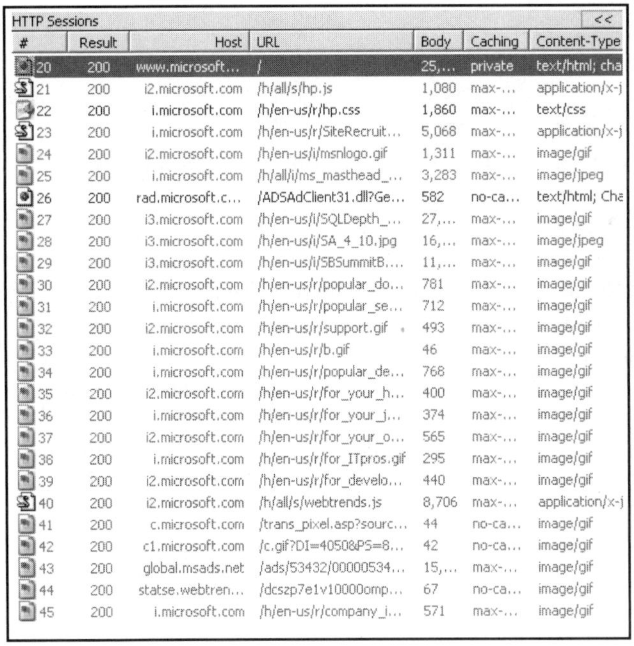

#	Result	Host	URL	Body	Caching	Content-Type
20	200	www.microsoft...	/	25,...	private	text/html; cha
21	200	i2.microsoft.com	/h/all/s/hp.js	1,080	max-...	application/x-j
22	200	i.microsoft.com	/h/en-us/r/hp.css	1,860	max-...	text/css
23	200	i.microsoft.com	/h/en-us/r/SiteRecruit...	5,068	max-...	application/x-j
24	200	i2.microsoft.com	/h/en-us/i/msnlogo.gif	1,311	max-...	image/gif
25	200	i.microsoft.com	/h/all/i/ms_masthead_...	3,283	max-...	image/jpeg
26	200	rad.microsoft.c...	/ADSAdClient31.dll?Ge...	582	no-ca...	text/html; Cha
27	200	i3.microsoft.com	/h/en-us/i/SQLDepth_...	27,...	max-...	image/gif
28	200	i3.microsoft.com	/h/en-us/i/SA_4_10.jpg	16,...	max-...	image/jpeg
29	200	i3.microsoft.com	/h/en-us/i/SBSummitB....	11,...	max-...	image/gif
30	200	i2.microsoft.com	/h/en-us/r/popular_do...	781	max-...	image/gif
31	200	i.microsoft.com	/h/en-us/r/popular_se...	712	max-...	image/gif
32	200	i2.microsoft.com	/h/en-us/r/support.gif	493	max-...	image/gif
33	200	i.microsoft.com	/h/en-us/r/b.gif	46	max-...	image/gif
34	200	i.microsoft.com	/h/en-us/r/popular_de...	768	max-...	image/gif
35	200	i2.microsoft.com	/h/en-us/r/for_your_h...	400	max-...	image/gif
36	200	i.microsoft.com	/h/en-us/r/for_your_j...	374	max-...	image/gif
37	200	i2.microsoft.com	/h/en-us/r/for_your_o...	565	max-...	image/gif
38	200	i.microsoft.com	/h/en-us/r/for_ITpros.gif	295	max-...	image/gif
39	200	i2.microsoft.com	/h/en-us/r/for_develo...	440	max-...	image/gif
40	200	i2.microsoft.com	/h/all/s/webtrends.js	8,706	max-...	application/x-j
41	200	c.microsoft.com	/trans_pixel.asp?sourc...	44	no-ca...	image/gif
42	200	c1.microsoft.com	/c.gif?DI=4050&PS=8...	42	no-ca...	image/gif
43	200	global.msads.net	/ads/53432/00000534...	15,...	max-...	image/gif
44	200	statse.webtren...	/dcszp7e1v10000omp...	67	no-ca...	image/gif
45	200	i.microsoft.com	/h/en-us/r/company_i...	571	max-...	image/gif

Figure 17-11. *Fiddler traffic for Microsoft.com*

If we want to see each of the steps on an individual basis, as they load, we'll need to first turn on the breakpoint system within Fiddler. We find that option under Rules ➤ Automatic Breakpoints, as shown in Figure 17-12.

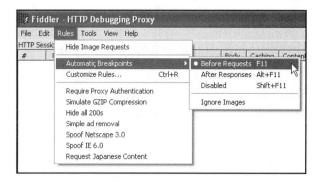

Figure 17-12. *Turning on Fiddler breakpoints*

For the purposes of this demonstration, I would recommend leaving Ignore Images checked, as some sites could make for tedious debugging if you're forced to step through all of the site's graphics. After enabling breakpoints, right-click the HTTP Sessions window and remove all current sessions from the view. With an empty slate on Fiddler, switch back to your browser and visit Microsoft.com again. You'll immediately notice that the page fails to paint and that the Fiddler taskbar is flashing. You've already hit your first breakpoint! If you click the session, you'll notice a different set of options, as shown in Figure 17-13.

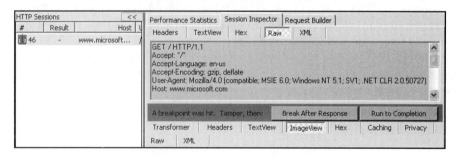

Figure 17-13. *Fiddler breakpoint hit*

We can choose either Break After Response, which will execute the current session and then stop, or Run To Completion, which will execute the current session and move on to the next (if any) session in the request cycle.

You can begin to see how the debugging power of Fiddler will really let you drill down into every aspect of your web requests and their corresponding responses.

Don't forget that you can also flip through the various tabbed data views for a variety of output methods appropriate to your current request or response.

Custom Inspectors

It is possible to extend the functionality of Fiddler with custom Session Inspectors. Sure the XML, TextView, and other tabs are good at getting to the data, but maybe your situation is a bit different, and you'd like to build your own representation of the data. It's completely possible.

While I'm not going to cover that particular topic in the context of the current chapter, I will show one particular inspector that Michael Schwarz put together for his Ajax.NET library that I've used on occasion and found to be quite handy. After downloading the DLL from his site at `http://weblogs.asp.net/mschwarz`, I drop the `.dll` file into the `inspectors` directory within Fiddler's install path at `C:\Program Files\Fiddler\Inspectors`.

When I restart the application, I now have an Ajax.NET Session Inspector parked right next to the XML tab, waiting for me to put it to work. If I visit a site that uses an XML-based Ajax library, I should be able to see some information come through my inspector, as Figure 17-14 demonstrates.

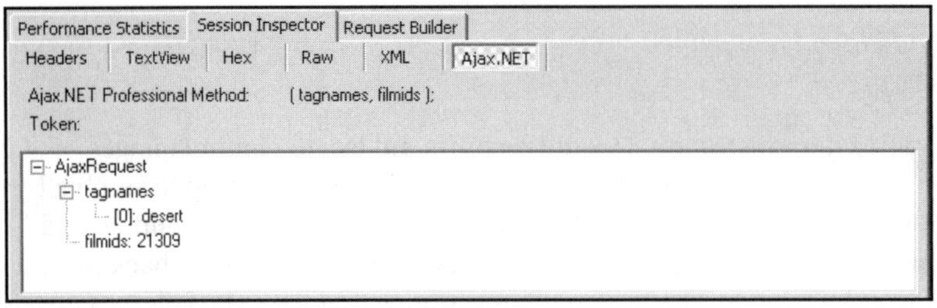

Figure 17-14. *Custom Ajax Fiddler inspector*

As we see in the Ajax.NET Session Inspector, the information relayed on the Ajax call in particular is displayed in an easy-to-read and easy-to-debug format. I encourage you to visit Michael Schwartz's blog and try the inspector for yourself.

Microsoft's Fiddler really comes in handy when you're debugging missing pages, content, or general Ajax issues. I can't encourage you enough to at least give the application a try. It's free and takes a relatively short amount of time to ramp up on.

Microsoft's Developer Toolbar

Yet another free tool that Microsoft has put out for developers that I've found to be incredibly useful is the Developer Toolbar. It's a fairly low-tech application, but it sure packs a punch. There's been many a time when I've actually forgotten that I have the thing and have spent a considerable amount of time in Notepad, viewing source for a page attempting to diagnose a broken Ajax call, only to find that the element was named incorrectly. Using the Developer Toolbar, I could have simply clicked the page element and viewed all of the properties for the corresponding item and quickly realized my error.

We've covered a portion of the functionality of this component in Chapter 6, but I want to reemphasize its importance in the world of debugging. Let's face it. A majority of the web pages that we build tend to have a ton of components on the page. Unless you work for Google and have one textbox and a button, chances are pretty good that your web pages are filled with various HTML and server-side controls. Keeping track of the IDs, properties, and values can be a daunting task. Fortunately, the Developer Toolbar steps in and helps make sense of the page structure. But there is much more to the toolbar than just identifying items in the Document Object Model. The product can not only find and highlight page items, but will also let you disable IE settings, control images, use the layover ruler for pixel-perfect measurements and placement, and even resize the browser window to typical resolution sizes for testing and evaluation.

The Toolbar

After installing the toolbar, you'll find it to be a very small and unassuming little piece of software, as you can see in Figure 17-15.

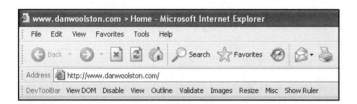

Figure 17-15. *Developer Toolbar installed*

View DOM

As the name implies, the View DOM button will present a variety of options, all of which are geared towards helping you identify page items within the DOM (see Figure 17-16).

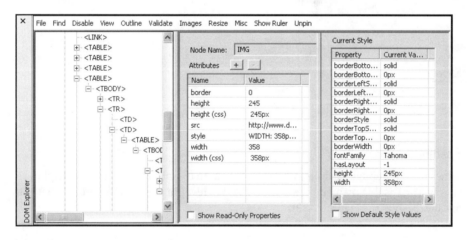

Figure 17-16. *View DOM panels*

The three panels presented upon clicking View DOM represent the tree-view display of the Document Object Model, the properties for the individual element, and a corresponding style panel with all of the appropriate CSS tags that you would expect to find for the selected element.

You could use the tree view as a search tool, clicking the plus signs to drill down into the nested elements. However, if you're searching for an individual element, this can be time consuming, frustrating, and downright irritating. If you can already see the page item displayed but want to find the element properties for the item itself, wouldn't it be great if you could just click the element and have the toolbar find the thing in the DOM for you? As you can see in Figure 17-17, such functionality has been built into the Developer Toolbar and is just a click away.

Figure 17-17. *Select Element by Click setting*

Once you enable the Select Element by Click option, whenever you click a page item, you'll be directed to the DOM location, properties, and style in the toolbar. If you can't see the element, but you know some of the element properties, you could use the Find Element selection that pops up the window shown in Figure 17-18, allowing you to find the item by searching for it.

Figure 17-18. *Searching for node items*

Disable IE settings

There are times in your debugging cycles when you'll want to disable some of Internet Explorer's various features. The Disable menu item will drop down to reveal a few of those settings that you can dynamically disable (see Figure 17-19).

Figure 17-19. *Disabling options*

Most of the Disable choices are self-explanatory, so I'll not go into too much detail. I will say that the selections represent various user-browser situations that you may want to test your site in. For instance, it's quite possible that you'll encounter a percentage of site users who will have cookies disabled or blocked. Disabling them here will give you a head start on working around the block. From an Ajax standpoint, you'll want to select Disable Script to view the user experience for your Ajax-less site. When you disable something from the Developer Toolbar, you'll want to remember to reenable it before exiting the product. Otherwise, you may find yourself debugging an application problem that doesn't exist, because you forgot to turn a feature back on. Not that I'm speaking from experience or anything like that. OK, maybe once or twice.

Outline

If you're really big into using HTML table elements, you'll find the Outline menu options, shown in Figure 17-20, to be indispensable. This feature will highlight a variety of items, but I find the table work to be most beneficial.

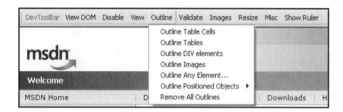

Figure 17-20. *Outlining page items*

When you select the desired page node to outline, you'll see a visual cue, as shown in Figure 17-21.

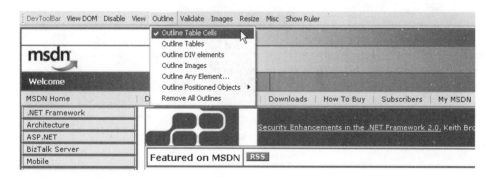

Figure 17-21. *Table cells outlined*

Validate

If you'd like to see how your site holds up to various W3C standards, you can run the current page through the W3C validator engine by selecting the particular standard that you wish to validate, as shown in Figure 17-22.

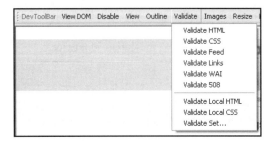

Figure 17-22. *Page validation selections*

Images

As you would expect, the Images menu selection will make available a few image-related options. For instance, if you wanted to overlay image size and dimensions on top of each page image, you would select the settings from this menu drop-down, as shown in Figure 17-23.

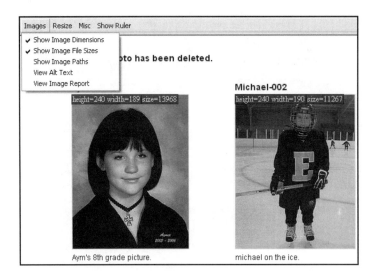

Figure 17-23. *Image properties displayed*

Another interesting ability that is provided for us is the View Image Report item, which compiles a complete listing of all page images, as well as the assigned properties for each of the individual pictures. This can be beneficial when you're trying to optimize page size and you'd like to cut corners wherever possible.

Figure 17-24 shows a portion of a sample image report that I generated from my Flickr page.

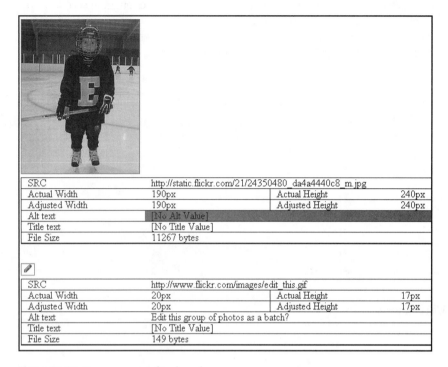

SRC	http://static.flickr.com/21/24350480_da4a4440c8_m.jpg		
Actual Width	190px	Actual Height	240px
Adjusted Width	190px	Adjusted Height	240px
Alt text	[No Alt Value]		
Title text	[No Title Value]		
File Size	11267 bytes		
SRC	http://www.flickr.com/images/edit_this.gif		
Actual Width	20px	Actual Height	17px
Adjusted Width	20px	Adjusted Height	17px
Alt text	Edit this group of photos as a batch?		
Title text	[No Title Value]		
File Size	149 bytes		

Figure 17-24. *Image report displayed*

As you can see from my report, I have some work to do, in that I failed to provide an alt value for my image. On a web-facing project, I'd want to make sure that I have this information provided to accommodate a larger user audience.

Resize

The Resize options resize the browser window to reflect possible user screen resolutions, as listed in Figure 17-25.

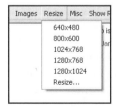

Figure 17-25. *Browser resizing*

Misc

As the name implies, the Misc menu is for miscellaneous tasks. When debugging certain web applications, you may have a need to continuously clear the browser cache or clear out any cookies that you may have dropped in. This will give you a shortcut to those tasks. There are also a few page links here for the W3C, CSS, and Internet Explorer blog pages, as you can see in Figure 17-26.

Figure 17-26. *Miscellaneous tasks*

Show Ruler

If you're in need for precision element placement, Show Ruler is the tool for you. It is a bit tricky to use at first. The menu that pops up, shown in Figure 17-27, gives you a few choices from which to construct your rulers.

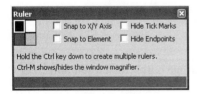

Figure 17-27. *Ruler selections*

You'll immediately notice something peculiar when you first click the Show Ruler button: there is a serious lack of ruler. That's because you need to draw one on the page!

For the ruler that you see in Figure 17-28, I first selected the color black from the palette in the upper-left corner of the ruler window. All I need to do is draw the ruler where I'd like to have detailed measurements available.

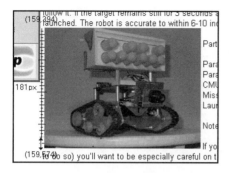

Figure 17-28. *Ruler placed at the side of the image*

You can see that the appropriate pixel coordinates are located at each end of the ruler. You can add more rulers to the same page by simply holding the Ctrl key and drawing the new ruler where you'd like. Another cool feature that we're given is the magnifying glass tool, available by using the Ctrl+M key combo to turn it on and off. This will give us a zoomed-in view of any area on the page, as Figure 17-29 demonstrates.

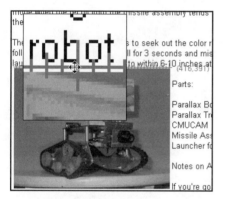

Figure 17-29. *Ruler zoom turned on*

Summary

I've covered Fiddler and the Developer Toolbar in detail in this chapter because I really feel that for Ajax debugging, these two tools will become incredibly beneficial to most web developers. They're a quick download away, and for a price of, well, **FREE**, it's worth giving them a shot.

Debugging in Visual Studio 2005 has become so intuitive that I often wonder how we ever wrote applications without the tools that we'll soon become accustomed to in our new IDE. I'm sure that improvements could be made here and there, but if you're ever frustrated with the current debugging toolset, reinstall Visual Basic 6.0 and relive some legacy debugging pain. You'll quickly sing the praises of Visual Studio 2005 debugging techniques.

In the next chapter, we'll transition from debugging our applications to testing. We'll examine some simple load testing, and you'll learn the answer to the question, "Can you test an Ajax application with current testing software?" I think you'll be pleasantly surprised.

CHAPTER 18

■ ■ ■

Ajax and Site Testing

A while ago, I attended a technology presentation that centered primarily on Atlas web development. About halfway through the demo, one of the attendees chimed in with his opinion of Atlas and Ajax in general. It seems that any time you gather a herd of geeks together for a product demonstration, there always seems to be that one token naysayer. This particular doubting Thomas expressed his concern that Ajax applications couldn't possibly scale well, given that so many visits occur across the wire for dynamic page updates. In his defense (somewhat), we understand by now that it is possible to write an Ajax application that will perform poorly.

When we discussed the type-ahead textboxes, we decided that it would indeed be a poor practice to query the database on every key-up event. In this particular situation, the scalability of the application could suffer. However, speaking from personal experience, it is possible (and easy) to build an application that scales up by adhering to the various recommendations found throughout this book.

In the previous chapter, we took a detailed look at how we could use Fiddler to monitor dynamic content and watch the meters on our web application traffic. And that's a good practice to get into, but we need to take a look at the larger, web-facing, side of things. How will our server react to multiple site users? At what point will the application begin to turn people away as it fails to deliver pages as requested? To answer these questions, we need to stress test the web application. And we should address the concerns of the naysayer who would claim that our application couldn't possibly scale to a decent user load.

Stress Test Tools

Stress testing the web application means that we'll need to utilize a traffic-generating program. With the new Visual Studio 2005 applications rolling out into production, we'll soon be seeing the Team System test tools as the primary weapon of choice. Unfortunately, as I write this, the Team System product is very much in beta. The 180-day demo that I attempted to fire up had a less-than-desirable outcome. To be fair to Microsoft, I was attempting to install to a Virtual PC image, and many of the developers whom I've talked to who have tried the same have had similar results. One of the drawbacks of working with beta software is that sometimes things just don't go your way, as you can see in Figure 18-1.

I'm sure that once the product is released in its finished form, it will stabilize and install correctly.

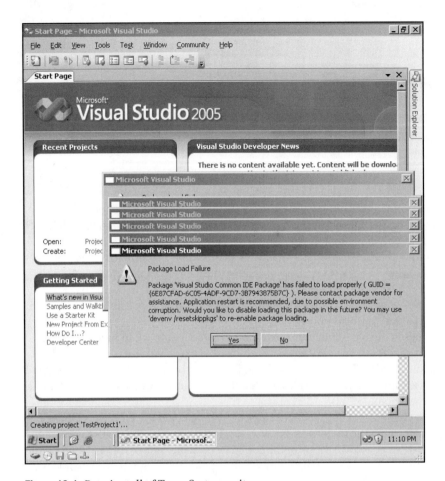

Figure 18-1. *Beta install of Team System suite*

For the purposes of this book, I wanted to use a tool that a majority of the readers will likely have access to. I've opted to skip third-party tools in favor of something that you may already have or could download for free. Microsoft's Web Application Stress Tool (WAST) is an excellent tool for stress/capacity testing, and we'll use that for our testing environment.

Because this utility is free, it will give everyone a chance to do some capacity testing regardless of their Visual Studio installation.

You can download this stand-alone application at http://www.microsoft.com/technet/archive/itsolutions/intranet/downloads/webstres.mspx?mfr=true.

The interface for WAST is pretty low key, as can be seen in Figure 18-2.

The program comes with a pregenerated test case that you can use as a guideline for what the application can do. In this chapter, however, we'll be recording a live session for playback by WAST. Before we get to that point, we'll need an application to test.

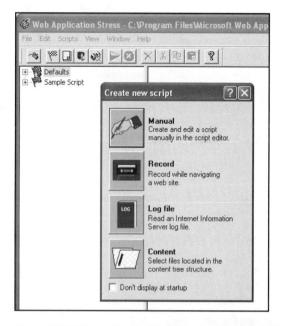

Figure 18-2. *Microsoft's Web Application Stress Tool*

Creating the Application to Test

If you recall from Chapter 16, we had an application with a postback page and an Ajax page that accomplished the same simple task. For the stress/capacity test of this chapter, we'll make use of this application, because we're interested in doing a comparative view of Ajax versus postback in a high-traffic environment. Rather than running the application from Visual Studio 2005, we'll be deploying the project to IIS.

Open the Chapter 16 sample application, MonitorApp, in Visual Studio 2005. You should have a Solution Explorer list of files as shown in Figure 18-3.

Now that you have the files loaded and ready, right-click the project name and select Publish Web Site.

You'll need to click the ellipses button next to the Target Location textbox so that you can choose the appropriate IIS options, as shown in Figure 18-4.

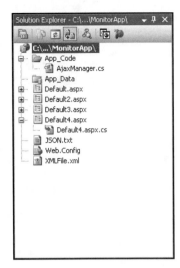

Figure 18-3. *The MonitorApp application, revisited*

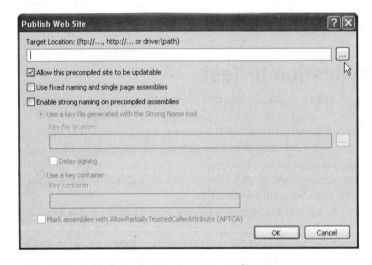

Figure 18-4. *Publishing the MonitorApp application*

After clicking the ellipses button, click the Local IIS button to display a treeview of your local IIS installation, as shown in Figure 18-5.

You'll need to click the Create New Web Application button in the upper-right corner and then name the application. I've chosen StressTest as you can see in Figure 18-5. Click Open and then OK when you return to the Publish Web Site window. The application will now build and deploy to IIS.

We can test the application by firing up Internet Explorer and visiting the first comparison page at http://localhost/StressTest/default.aspx, as shown in Figure 18-6.

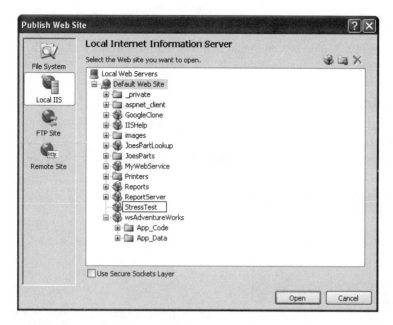

Figure 18-5. *Setting up our IIS application*

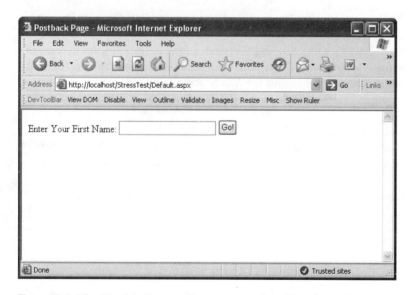

Figure 18-6. *The MonitorApp application up and waiting for action*

As a reminder:

- `http://localhost/StressTest/Default.aspx` is the postback page.

- `http://localhost/StressTest/Default2.aspx` is the Ajax page.

Using the Test Suite

Now that we have an application out on IIS waiting for us, let's gather some data with WAST. We'll start by testing the postback page before testing the Ajax version.

Testing the Postback Page

First of all, close Visual Studio 2005. We no longer need it. Now start WAST, if you haven't already, and click the Record button on the wizard form.

We'll be met with more options. For now, leave them all unchecked, as shown in Figure 18-7.

Figure 18-7. *Recording options*

Click Next, and you'll be warned that you're about to begin recording. Click Finish.

A browser window will pop up. Here you'll need to enter the URL for the postback page on the browser address bar. After a moment the page will load, and you'll be ready for user input.

For consistency in testing, enter only three names, clicking Go! after each entry. This will give us three page refreshes to compare against the Ajax process.

After you've run through three postbacks, switch back to the WAST window and click Stop Recording.

We'll now see our three user entry sessions listed on the right, as shown in Figure 18-8.

Now that we have a fully interactive test session to work with, we need to let WAST run with it. We'll accept the default script settings and simply click the Run Script button in the menu bar.

WAST will now begin the process of stress testing the application, as shown in Figure 18-9.

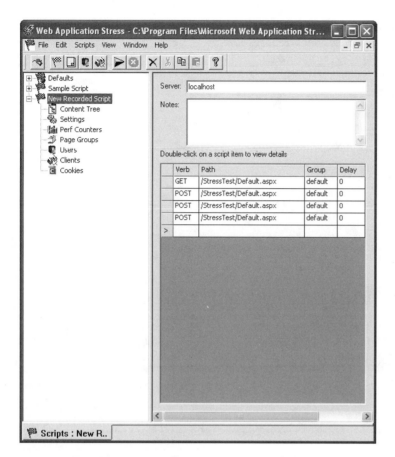

Figure 18-8. *Test session recorded*

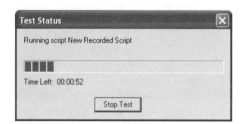

Figure 18-9. *Stress testing in session*

After the test runs, click View ➤ Reports. We'll find that the application has generated a decent set of test data for our single concurrent session:

```
Overview
================================================================================
Report name:              5/17/2006 9:40:02 PM
Run on:                   5/17/2006 9:40:02 PM
Run length:               00:01:00

Web Application Stress Tool Version:1.1.293.1

Number of test clients:   1

Number of hits:           58421
Requests per Second:      973.78

Socket Statistics
--------------------------------------------------------------------------------
Socket Connects:          58422
Total Bytes Sent (in KB): 30309.05
Bytes Sent Rate (in KB/s): 505.20
Total Bytes Recv (in KB): 70301.89
Bytes Recv Rate (in KB/s): 1171.82

Socket Errors
--------------------------------------------------------------------------------
Connect:                  0
Send:                     0
Recv:                     0
Timeouts:                 0

RDS Results
--------------------------------------------------------------------------------
Successful Queries:       0


Script Settings
================================================================================
Server:                   localhost
Number of threads:        1

Test length:              00:01:00
Warmup:                   00:00:00
Cooldown:                 00:00:00

Use Random Delay:         No
```

```
Follow Redirects:          Yes
Max Redirect Depth:        15


Clients used in test
==============================================================================
localhost

Clients not used in test
==============================================================================


Result Codes
Code      Description                  Count
==============================================================================
200       OK                           58421


Page Summary
Page                       Hits    TTFB Avg  TTLB Avg  Auth   Query
==============================================================================
GET /stresstest/default.aspx   14606   0.01      0.01      No     No
POST /stresstest/default.aspx  14605   0.05      0.07      No     No
POST /stresstest/default.aspx  14605   0.06      0.08      No     No
POST /stresstest/default.aspx  14605   0.06      0.10      No     No
```

Our test was run for one minute, and the web server received 58,421 hits against it. It performed beautifully, with a result code of 200 for all 58,421 requests. Not bad for my puny laptop. Let's crank up the concurrent sessions to 100 and see how our application fares:

```
Overview
==============================================================================
Report name:          5/17/2006 9:36:55 PM
Run on:               5/17/2006 9:36:55 PM
Run length:           00:01:00

Web Application Stress Tool Version:1.1.293.1

Number of test clients:     1

Number of hits:             52977
Requests per Second:        883.08
```

```
Socket Statistics
--------------------------------------------------------------------------------
Socket Connects:            53112
Total Bytes Sent (in KB):   27521.33
Bytes Sent Rate (in KB/s):  458.76
Total Bytes Recv (in KB):   63933.91
Bytes Recv Rate (in KB/s):  1065.73

Socket Errors
--------------------------------------------------------------------------------
Connect:                    0
Send:                       40
Recv:                       0
Timeouts:                   0

RDS Results
--------------------------------------------------------------------------------
Successful Queries:         0


Script Settings
================================================================================
Server:                     localhost
Number of threads:          100

Test length:                00:01:00
Warmup:                     00:00:00
Cooldown:                   00:00:00

Use Random Delay:           No

Follow Redirects:           Yes
Max Redirect Depth:         15


Clients used in test
================================================================================
localhost

Clients not used in test
================================================================================
```

```
Result Codes
Code      Description                    Count
===============================================================================
200       OK                             52717
403       Forbidden                      122
NA        HTTP result code not given     138
```

```
Page Summary
Page                         Hits    TTFB Avg  TTLB Avg  Auth    Query
===============================================================================
GET /stresstest/default.aspx  13275   104.85    105.04    No      No
POST /stresstest/default.aspx 13255   101.73    102.22    No      No
POST /stresstest/default.aspx 13236   98.58     99.13     No      No
POST /stresstest/default.aspx 13211   96.42     97.13     No      No
```

We've dropped some traffic by running with a larger load. A whopping half percent of our traffic was turned away as a result of the increased concurrency.

Let's try our Ajax application now and see whether the application will perform better or worse than the postback process.

Testing the Ajax Page

Close the report window and click the New Script button on the menu bar, as shown in Figure 18-10.

Figure 18-10. *Adding a new script*

Choose to record as you did before, ignore the record options, and click Next. Click Finish to start recording. This time we're testing the Ajax page, so enter http://localhost/ StressTest/Default2.aspx in the address bar of the new browser window.

Again, we'll be entering three names, as demonstrated in Figure 18-11, clicking Go! after each entry.

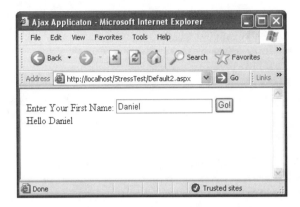

Figure 18-11. *Our stress test application in action*

It's interesting to watch the header information stream through the WAST interface as the Ajax actions take place:

```
GET /StressTest/Default2.aspx?Ajax_Script=true
Accept: */*
Referer: http://localhost/StressTest/Default2.aspx
Accept-Language: en-us
Accept-Encoding: gzip, deflate
User-Agent: Mozilla/4.0 (compatible; MSIE 6.0;
Windows NT 5.1; SV1; .NET CLR 2.0.50727;
.NET CLR 1.1.4322)
Host: localhost


POST /StressTest/Default2.aspx?Ajax_CallBack=true
Accept: */*
Content-Type: application/x-www-form-urlencoded;
charset=utf-8
Referer: http://localhost/StressTest/Default2.aspx
Accept-Language: en-u
Accept-Encoding: gzip, deflate
User-Agent: Mozilla/4.0 (compatible; MSIE 6.0;
Windows NT 5.1; SV1; .NET CLR 2.0.50727;
.NET CLR 1.1.4322)
Host: localhost
Content-Length: 292
Pragma: no-cache
```

We can see that, yes, WAST is picking up the dynamic Ajax calls as well.

After you've finished your three-name session, switch back to the WAST GUI and click Stop Recording, as shown in Figure 18-12.

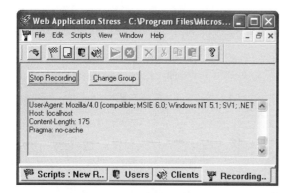

Figure 18-12. *WAST recording window*

You'll need to run the script now by clicking the Run Script button on the menu bar. The test will now run for one minute.

When it's finished, view the corresponding report as you did previously:

```
Overview
================================================================================
Report name:              5/17/2006 11:21:35 PM
Run on:                   5/17/2006 11:21:35 PM
Run length:               00:01:00

Web Application Stress Tool Version:1.1.293.1

Number of test clients:   1

Number of hits:           47679
Requests per Second:      794.51

Socket Statistics
--------------------------------------------------------------------------------
Socket Connects:          47679
Total Bytes Sent (in KB): 27436.27
Bytes Sent Rate (in KB/s): 457.19
Total Bytes Recv (in KB): 39659.07
Bytes Recv Rate (in KB/s): 660.86

Socket Errors
--------------------------------------------------------------------------------
Connect:                  0
Send:                     0
Recv:                     0
Timeouts:                 0
```

```
RDS Results
-------------------------------------------------------------------------------
Successful Queries:          0


Script Settings
===============================================================================
Server:                 localhost
Number of threads:      1

Test length:            00:01:00
Warmup:                 00:00:00
Cooldown:               00:00:00

Use Random Delay:       No

Follow Redirects:       Yes
Max Redirect Depth:     15


Clients used in test
===============================================================================
localhost

Clients not used in test
===============================================================================


Result Codes
Code      Description                Count
===============================================================================
200       OK                         47679


Page Summary
Page                      Hits     TTFB Avg  TTLB Avg  Auth    Query
===============================================================================
GET /stresstest/default2.aspx  11920    0.03      0.04      No      No
POST /stresstest/default2.aspx 11920    0.39      0.44      No      No
POST /stresstest/default2.aspx 11920    0.32      0.36      No      No
POST /stresstest/default2.aspx 11919    0.30      0.35      No      No
```

And, here again, let's add some load to the test by increasing the concurrency to 100 threads:

```
Overview
================================================================================
Report name:            5/17/2006 11:25:06 PM
Run on:                 5/17/2006 11:25:06 PM
Run length:             00:01:01

Web Application Stress Tool Version:1.1.293.1

Number of test clients:     1

Number of hits:         43180
Requests per Second:    719.54

Socket Statistics
--------------------------------------------------------------------------------
Socket Connects:        43282
Total Bytes Sent (in KB):   24889.45
Bytes Sent Rate (in KB/s):  414.75
Total Bytes Recv (in KB):   36234.93
Bytes Recv Rate (in KB/s):  603.81

Socket Errors
--------------------------------------------------------------------------------
Connect:                0
Send:                   7
Recv:                   0
Timeouts:               0

RDS Results
--------------------------------------------------------------------------------
Successful Queries:     0


Script Settings
================================================================================
Server:                 localhost
Number of threads:      100

Test length:            00:01:00
Warmup:                 00:00:00
Cooldown:               00:00:00

Use Random Delay:       No

Follow Redirects:       Yes
Max Redirect Depth:     15
```

```
Clients used in test
==============================================================================
localhost

Clients not used in test
==============================================================================


Result Codes
Code       Description                        Count
==============================================================================
200        OK                                 42874
403        Forbidden                          129
NA         HTTP result code not given         177


Page Summary
Page                          Hits      TTFB Avg  TTLB Avg  Auth    Query
==============================================================================
GET /stresstest/default2.aspx  10827    125.60    126.16    No      No
POST /stresstest/defaull2.aspx 10807    123.31    124.18    No      No
POST /stresstest/default2.aspx 10785    123.24    123.76    No      No
POST /stresstest/default2.aspx 10761    120.98    122.04    No      No
```

We have some interesting statistics from this Ajax-enabled test run. Notice that the Ajax application, under load, will begin to fail at 100 concurrent sessions (on my IIS machine) in much the same fashion as the typical postback page process did before. The failure rate is parallel as well, running at approximately one-half percent of total hits involved. When you stop and think about this for a moment, you begin to realize that the Ajax application is still involved in a client-to-server transaction, and therefore the same traffic sessions still exist. The two biggest differences, however, are the "Total Bytes Received" size as well as the fact that the Ajax application functionality was performed without interruption to the user's page experience. So our application is scaling as we would expect. However, we're benefiting from a lower bandwidth expense, and our site users will enjoy the added usability.

Another interesting item to note is the individual call data. Expand the Page Data folder as shown in Figure 18-13.

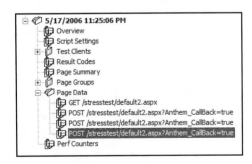

Figure 18-13. *WAST reports view*

Click the last POST statement to view the details:

```
Page Results
================================================================================
URI:                         POST /stresstest/default2.aspx?Anthem_CallBack=true
Hit Count:                   10761

Result Codes
Code      Description                   Count
--------------------------------------------------------------------------------
200       OK                            10679
403       Forbidden                     31
NA        HTTP result code not given    51

Time to first byte (in milliseconds)
--------------------------------------------------------------------------------
Average:                     120.98
Min:                         0.16
25th Percentile:             1.35
50th Percentile:             18.91
75th Percentile:             224.59
Max:                         2034.32

Time to last byte (in milliseconds)
--------------------------------------------------------------------------------
Average:                     122.04
Min:                         0.90
25th Percentile:             1.46
50th Percentile:             19.38
75th Percentile:             226.45
Max:                         2034.34

Downloaded Content Length (in bytes)
--------------------------------------------------------------------------------
Min:                         0
25th Percentile:             170
50th Percentile:             170
75th Percentile:             170
Max:                         4056

Socket Statistics
--------------------------------------------------------------------------------
Socket connects:             10788
Total Bytes Sent (in KB):    7332.47
Bytes Sent Rate (in KB/s):   122.19
Total Bytes Recv (in KB):    5894.80
Bytes Recv Rate (in KB/s):   98.23
```

```
Socket Errors
----------------------------------------------------------------------------
Connect:                    0
Send:                       0
Recv:                       0
Timeouts:                   0

Successful Authentications:   0

Successful RDS Queries:       0
```

You can see that our Ajax callbacks are coming in at a trivial 98K package size. That's so much better than the 300K receive rate of the postback page from the earlier test.

Summary

The dynamic page was able to process with lower bandwidth per request than our old-school postback page. Obviously, Ajax applications, when written correctly, scale just fine. Based on the limited testing that we've done in this chapter, we can see the enterprise benefit of implementing Ajax technology within web content. Of course, you'll want to run stress testing on a much larger Ajax application to really get a feel for the overall statistics.

In the next chapter, we'll discuss best practices as they relate to the world of Ajax development. Knowing when you should and should not use Ajax has become a hot topic on the web lately. We'll take a look at a few situations concerning both sides of the debate as we continue down this path of creating efficient and stable Ajax applications.

CHAPTER 19

Ajax Usability

I remember when Macromedia Flash began to flood the web, appearing on numerous personal pages at first and then transitioning into the corporate world. It seemed that every web developer on the planet wanted to make their mark with some fancy Flash presentation, rollover, or menus. I realize that you might be thinking, "Well, I didn't jump on the Flash bandwagon." But I'm sure that we would agree that when a new technology hits the web, it typically does so in floods. I wouldn't necessarily call them fads, either. Saying that something is a fad implies that the thing has come and gone. With many of the so-called technology fads, the implementation would surge, plateau, and see moderate and controlled usage afterward. For instance, when JavaScript first appeared as a weapon of the browser war, developers would use the scripting language just for the sake of using it. After a few years, architects and administrators began to establish some control and best practices surrounding the usage of JavaScript.

Ajax, as you would expect, seems to be following the same pattern. As more developers begin to grasp the technology, they seek out ways in which to use their newfound tool. Often, the library is put to good use; however, many have managed to overuse and wield it unwittingly.

Throughout the book, I've mentioned various tidbits of information that should help you in making the right Ajax decisions. But we're now at the point where we need to consider the Ajax world in a sort of best practices frame of mind. Before we begin that conversation, I want to make it abundantly clear that I am **NOT** establishing any global standards here. I simply want to convey to you a few things that I've come across, on the web and in my development projects, that seem to make sense to me. Some of the issues that I address may become nonissues as the Ajax libraries evolve and mutate over the next few years.

The Back Button

It is highly likely that in your Ajax web applications you will break the Back button. What exactly is a broken Back button and how does it happen? Well, let's take a look.

When you visit an Ajax-enabled application, you modify the current session when you add or delete content on the current page. Essentially, the server side loses track of what it is that you're doing out there on the client side, and so it simply invalidates the call. For instance, at Microsoft's Windows Live site (http://www.live.com), an Ajaxed site, I log in and modify some of the Web Parts as you see in Figure 19-1.

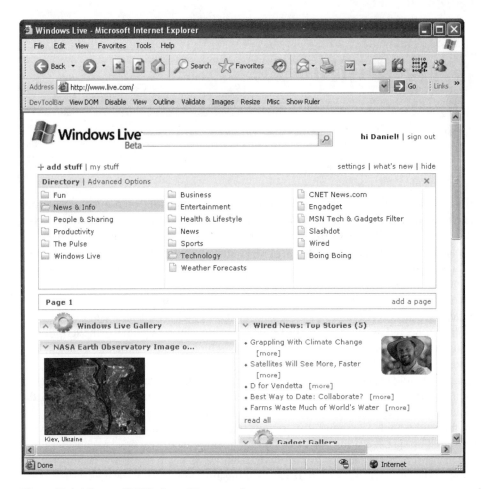

Figure 19-1. *Microsoft's Windows Live portal*

One of the things that I really like about the Windows Live site is the fact that it's a step in the right direction for Web 2.0. It's customizable and extendable; however, it does step out of a few paradigms for common web tasks. Most users don't understand that they can drag and drop Web Parts around on the screen. Will that catch on? Probably. As the popularity of the technology grows, so will the user adoption. I've heard a few web designers call it an "accidental technology" because people generally won't know about it unless they inadvertently move a part. That's generally followed by a "Wow, I didn't know I could do that" type of response—similar to the response that we as developers had when we first saw Ajax in action.

As we have discussed, Ajax destroys the Back button. For example, the Microsoft Windows Live site, shown in Figure 19-1, obliterates the ability to use the button. When I modify my portal content and click the Back button, I'm greeted by the page shown in Figure 19-2.

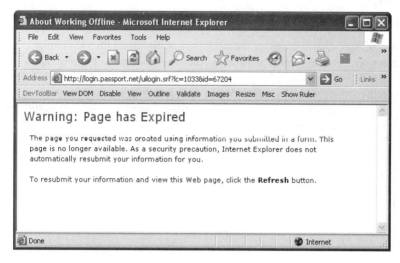

Figure 19-2. *Broken Back button*

Many Ajax developers will tell you that this is just an acceptable trade-off for the cool factor of dynamic content ability. My personal thought on this is that the Back button is there for what? To allow users to surf back to their previous page. While it's not likely that the button will be repaired by Ajax libraries anytime soon, we can minimize the damage that it imposes. If the user needs a way to get back to a previous page within the website, it's easy enough to store page visits as you surf within your site and provide an on-page link to the previous page. Many sites use this functionality within breadcrumb-style navigation. One such site that incorporates this well is the Spout site (`http://www.spout.com`). This online film community site has a ton of Ajax under the hood, and the back functionality is provided via logical breadcrumb navigation, as you see in Figure 19-3.

Figure 19-3. *Breadcrumb navigation*

While they may not be a full replacement for the Back button, on-page navigational aids can boost the usability of the site. When you're pushing industry-established paradigms, you'll want to make it easier on everyone involved.

Ajax Menus

There has been an influx of Ajax-enabled navigation menus popping up on the web lately. Based on user interaction, the Ajax implementation dynamically retrieves a set of page links and builds this into a page-level menu control.

One such site that I have come across when Googling Ajax dynamic menus is Betfair (`http://www.betfair.com`), an online betting portal. This site uses Ajax to dynamically build the navigational menu system, as shown in Figure 19-4.

Figure 19-4. *Betfair's Ajax-style navigation*

The primary problem that I have with this type of menu system is that search engines are going to have a very difficult time spidering the site. Without a set of linked URLs compiled into the page, there is a good chance that nested pages will never be found by the world.

Ajax Type-Aheads

Let's face it, type-ahead search boxes are really cool. Google Suggest (`http://www.google.com/webhp?complete=1&hl=en`) has them. Spout has one too. And we've even had a chance to build one for ourselves. However, if used improperly, type-ahead search boxes can become a scalable nightmare. There are a few issues that you'll need to address when constructing them. First and foremost is the level of usage that the particular search box will endure. If the type-ahead is central to your site's content retrieval, you may find the scalability to be somewhat limited. For instance, in the Google Suggest clone that we constructed, we would retrieve search results on the key-up event of the control. Here's the HTML:

```
<input name="keyword" onkeyup="LoadResults(this.value)" style="WIDTH:500px" />
```

And now the JavaScript:

```
function LoadResults(searchterm)
{
    if (searchterm.length == 0)
    {
        // If the input box is empty, let's dump all the rows from the results table
        ClearResults();
        HideDiv("searchresults");
        return;
    }

    // Fetch results from server side.
    // This is our actual Ajax call
    Anthem_InvokePageMethod('RetrieveRows', [searchterm], LoadResultsCallback);
}
```

Every time a single user types a key, a hit is made to the database. This is not necessarily the best strategy for this style of global searching. However, there are a few things that you can do to optimize this process.

First, don't search on the key-up event. I would recommend instead a JavaScript timeout that would periodically check the current textbox value to see whether it has changed since the previous search. If it has, then make the call to the database. This can drastically cut down on the amount of web server and database traffic.

Finally, you should store the current search results to maintain a viable set of previous data in memory. Let's say the user types the film name "Star Wars" on the Spout site. As the user types, new search results are given for each iteration of the key entry, as shown in Figure 19-5.

Figure 19-5. *Spout type-ahead film search*

The type-ahead functionality builds the search results as the user types, recommending possible matches for the current term. Each retrieval and modification of the results table, however, represents a unique trip to and from the database. And here's an interesting situation: what do we do if the user hits the Backspace key? Do we make another trip to the database with the new search term? Or do we recognize that the Backspace key has been pressed and simply return the stored result set from the previous retrieval process? As you can imagine, having the previous result set in memory can save us a trip to the database. Sure, it's just one hit, but scale that out to a few thousand simultaneous users, and I'm sure that you can see the benefit.

Bookmarking

For sites that have content generated on the fly with Ajax-enabled search, you'll lose the ability to bookmark that particular page with the retrieved results as you've found them.

This can pose a problem if a user wants to recommend your site to a friend. The URL that they have in their browser window will not retrieve the same results. Often it will return the user's friend to the search page, but without any of the same data that the first user had found. Can you circumvent that? No...not really. I've spoken to a few web developers, and the general consensus is that for search results that tend to be the focus of the site (i.e., film results, flight schedules, retail products), they recommend using a postback to the result site. This way, you'll have a page that can be bookmarked and forwarded. One successful usage of this concept is, again, Spout's film-searching methodology. The search mechanism is Ajaxed, all the way. But when the user clicks the desired film that they wish to see more detail on, they're whisked away to a results page, shown in Figure 19-6.

If you look closely at Figure 19-6, you'll notice that the URL of the page reflects the contents of the page. Spout is using URL rewriting to enable a web address that can be easily added to the user's Favorites folders or sent to a friend. Therefore, anyone visiting `http://www.spout.com/films/BladeRunner/3585/default.aspx` will receive the same search results as the next guy.

You'll need to evaluate for yourself how important the bookmark is for your site's dynamic data. Keep in mind that if you want repeat business, you'll need to make it easy for users to hit the pages that matter.

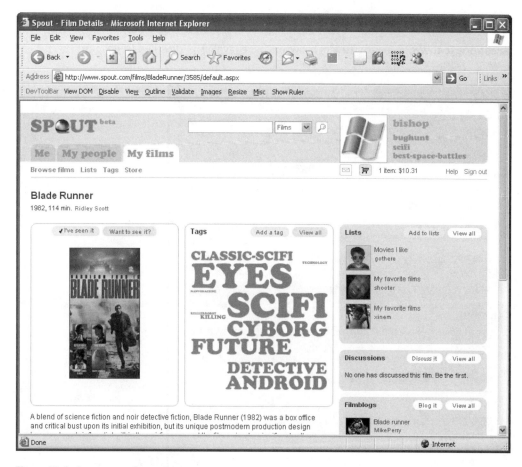

Figure 19-6. *Spout search result page*

Connected Controls

If you have a dynamic control on your site that modifies content that another control consumes, you'll need to ensure that the two are connected. For instance, if you have a control that allows the user to add an item to their shopping cart, you'll want to make sure that if you have another cart-listing control on the page it is updated to reflect the new information. Generally, this is a situation in which you may need to steer away from Ajax functionality. I've only seen a few sites where this has worked in a beneficial and logical manner. More often than not, the other control is simply not updated, and the user has to refresh the page to see the new changes.

Disabled JavaScript

According to the W3C, nearly 10% of browsers have JavaScript disabled (see Figure 19-7).

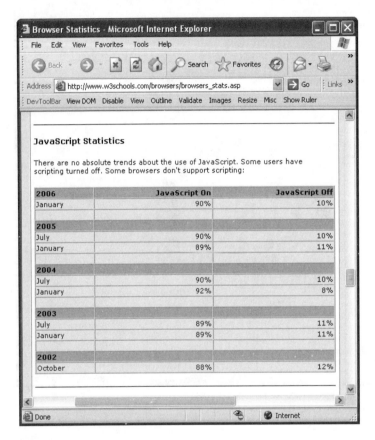

Figure 19-7. *W3C statistics*

So you've written this really cool Ajax site, and recently you've begun to receive a flood of e-mail from your users stating the site is trashed and nothing seems to load. An investigation reveals that the common denominator is that they have disabled JavaScript, and you haven't provided a graceful handling of this scenario. Yes, it will add to the development overhead, but would you agree that accommodating 10% of all potential customers/users is reason enough to modify your pages to sniff out the disabled script? I've seen a few methodologies concerning graceful degradation. Some sites simply inform the user that they must have JavaScript enabled in order to use the site. Meanwhile, some sites, like the one shown in Figure 19-8, just choose to do nothing.

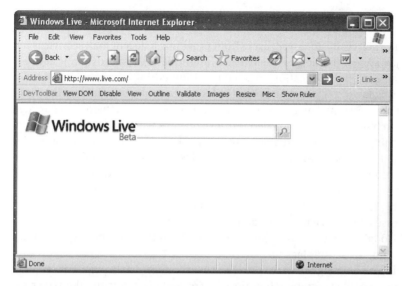

Figure 19-8. *Windows Live's nonhandling of disabled JavaScript*

As you can see in Figure 19-8, Microsoft's Windows Live is lacking a graceful exit strategy for disabled JavaScript. Now granted, the whole point of the site is dynamic Ajax-style content, and scripting is an absolute necessity. However, there's nothing on the page to indicate that. Just a misaligned textbox and a big empty space where the page probably should be. Some developers are willing to just live with whatever the site renders when the scripting language has been nixed. That's a decision that you'll need to make for yourself. My personal opinion is that a 10% share of the web is a rather large portion of the web to simply ignore, or worse yet, have them think that your site is broken simply because you've chosen to not degrade gracefully.

Page Shifting

I've mentioned this in an earlier chapter, but I want to reiterate that I find it rude and obtrusive if the page moves things around as a result of a dynamic callback process. It's one thing to reposition page content because I've asked for new data or I've physically relocated a Web Part, but if you have a portion of the page that auto-refreshes and consequently moves the page while I'm trying to view it, it makes me want to delete your bookmark and never ping that URL again. I'm just picky that way. If you've ever been on a busy train, reading a magazine, and had somebody bump into the pages as you're reading them, you'll understand.

This is a personal pet peeve of mine, but I mention it to warn you that if you mess with the user experience without the user's permission, bad things may happen. I've seen this rear its ugly head, predominantly with banner ads. One example I'm thinking of, in particular, is a popular sports-related website that has a huge banner that displays on the page load and has a timeout value set to collapse the ad to a smaller size after a moment or two. Unfortunately, they always seem to shrink the ad at the exact moment that I start to read the page content. The content slides up, forcing me to lose my place on the page and start over. If you need to reposition content, wait until the user has triggered an event and then proceed.

Dynamic Feedback

One of the things that Gmail really does well, aside from providing a decent mail service, is its implementation of Ajax-style technology. The site has a multitude of various dynamic activities that I can trigger and receive notification on screen that something is happening. All too often I find Ajax sites that have really cool functionality built into some really interesting Ajax-enabled controls that have no visual means of informing the user that an activity is occurring. If I post a comment to a blog via an Ajax-enabled textbox and click Submit, I'm a little discouraged if I don't see anything happen immediately. If the network happens to be running slowly at the time of my post, it may take a minute or two for the Ajax process to run full cycle; meanwhile I'm sitting at the computer wondering, "Did the comment make it through?"

If the site doesn't provide some form of visual cue indicating that, yes indeed, an action has occurred and we're right on top of it, then I find myself wondering if the site is broken or disabled. Gmail addresses this with a pop-up loading-style box in the corner of the browser, letting me know that Google is on top of my request and that I should relax and wait a minute while they set things right. Many sites lack this.

Visual cues should also be assigned to data that has been changed on a page. For example, on the previous Ajax-enabled comment box, once I've posted my comment, the server side stores that and forwards the new set of comments to the browser for dynamic display. It would be nice to have some form of feedback on the comments list indicating that the content has recently been modified. I've mentioned the Yellow Fade Technique before and feel that I should mention it again, as I find it to be incredibly beneficial for just such a task as this. It's never a bad thing to include the user when it comes to providing proper feedback to interactive usage.

Visible Source

Unless you scramble your JavaScript, you should be aware that your script will be out there for the world to see. If you have sensitive corporate data built into the client side, be aware that the world is watching. As we've discussed in Chapter 4, it's a good idea to separate your logic and presentation layers. With ASP.NET 2.0's ability to precompile the site, this vulnerability/weakness should disappear, providing that developers use it accordingly.

Page Paradigms

If you have made a conscientious decision that your site will break the barriers of all user interaction paradigms, this paragraph is not for you. For the rest of us, we must maintain a clear head when it comes to determining what to Ajax and what not to Ajax. There are activities and events that our users will trigger that necessitate a postback versus a dynamic page update. For instance, if I'm filling out a form for site membership, I expect that I'll click a Submit button and be notified of the results (see Figure 19-9).

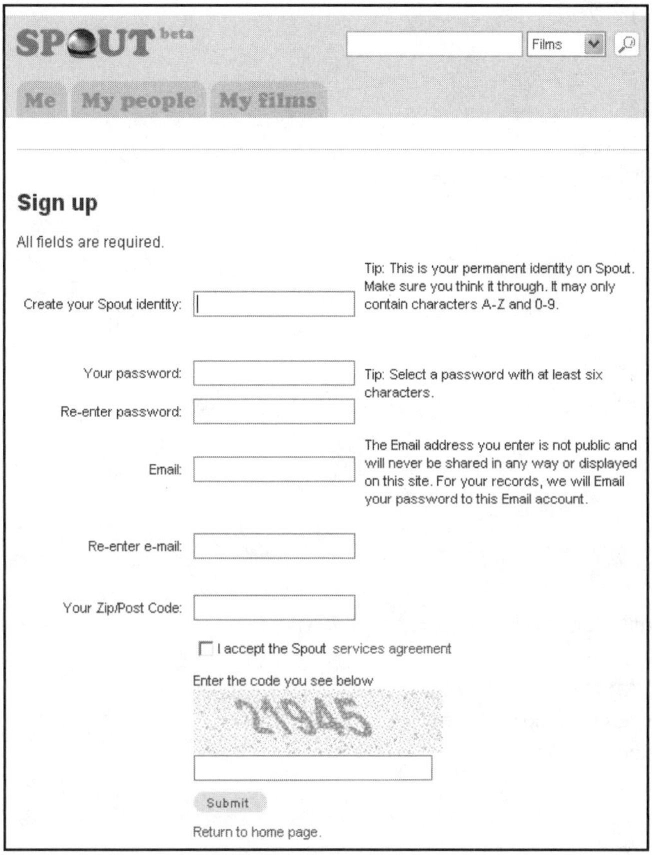

Figure 19-9. *Spout's signup page*

There are definitive situations where you'll find that it is just logical to do a postback rather than an Ajax call, simply because you can. Chances are, if the interaction just doesn't feel right, then you've probably tried to push a round Ajax peg into a square postback hole.

Universal Specifications

Let's talk about the universal specifications for Ajax technology. There are none. How's that for a short discussion? OK seriously, we really have no governing set of laws that dictate how Ajax should or should not be handled. Let me reintroduce you to the XmlHttpRequest construction routine (you should be able to write this in your sleep by now):

```
function getHTTPRequestObject()
{
    try
    {
        // Try legacy object first
        xmlhttp = new ActiveXObject("Msxml2.XMLHTTP");
    }
    catch(e)
    {
        try
        {
            // Try IE implementation now
            xmlhttp = new ActiveXObject("Microsoft.XMLHTTP");
        }
        catch(E)
        {
            xmlhttp = false;
        }
    }
    if(!xmlhttp && typeof XMLHttpRequest!= 'undefined')
    {
        // We must be using a Mozilla-based browser
        // so create a native request object now
        xmlhttp = new XMLHttpRequest();
    }
}
```

If a governing body of standards existed, we sure would be able to shrink the preceding code down to something as simple as the following:

```
xmlhttp = new ActiveXObject("StandardXMLHTTP");
```

But we don't have that luxury. We have XML standards and CSS guidelines, but nothing that dictates how the dynamic technology should be moderated. I don't really see this changing anytime soon. Until that time comes, you'll need to continue building your applications with cross-browser code support.

Session Variables

If you're using a library that supports session state variables in the Ajax calls, use it only as needed. It is a nice ability to have, but unless you have a real need to use the control values, you may be better off just sticking to input parameters rather than posting an Ajax call with a huge page state included. You'll maintain the cool factor of the postbackless page update; however, your bandwidth will reap zero rewards for your Ajaxed page. Only use the state when needed.

Summary

In this short, yet important, chapter, we've discussed the idea that developers should always ask themselves whether or not Ajax is the right tool for the job. I'm obviously 100% on the side that believes that Ajax is an awesome and exciting technology to build with. But I'm also of the persuasion that discretion is a key ingredient to building a successful dynamic user interface. I'm sure that you'll run across sites that will have you immediately thinking, "Wow...this is really Ajaxed to death." And, I'm equally as sure that you will find sites out there where an Ajax user control would make perfect sense. Now that you've had a solid grounding in building an Ajax-enabled site, perhaps you can send those sites in need of some Ajax love a business card and a sales proposal and help spread the frenzy that Ajax implementation has become.

We've come full circle with third-party Ajax controls and have reached that point where we are forced to ask the question, "Is Ajax the tool of the future, and how does Microsoft's Atlas play into the context of Ajax development?" In the next and final chapter, we will take a quick look at Atlas and discuss how it stands up against Ajax technology as a whole.

PART 5

Moving Forward

In this last section, we'll gaze into our magic Ajax crystal ball and seek a glimpse of the future. As you've undoubtedly realized by now, web technology moves quickly. It keeps a maddening pace and waits for no one. We either keep up or quickly fall behind. So that we might not only keep up, but also perhaps gain a little ground, let's grab a sneak peak of the race ahead. The final chapter presents a "possible" view of the future for .NET web developers, and that future is Atlas.

CHAPTER 20

■■■

Atlas

It would be an injustice to discuss Ajax and the .NET 2.0 Framework without covering Microsoft's Atlas product to some degree. I've come to realize that many developers feel that Atlas is something revolutionary and mysterious based on the hype that Microsoft has pumped into the public realm. At the 2005 PDC conference, Microsoft officially launched the beta product and later the production-ready release at the 2006 Mix06 conference in Las Vegas. During Bill Gates' keynote address, he gave the go-ahead for developers to use the Atlas library on live sites. He was also kind enough to remind everybody that Microsoft basically invented "Ajax" back in 1997 with their DHTML scripting platform and that Atlas is the next generation of that initial technology. In fact, Microsoft's Outlook Web Access, shown in Figure 20-1, has long been considered one of the first mainstream Ajax applications out on the web.

Figure 20-1. *Microsoft's OWA application*

I'm inclined to believe that the Atlas library is pretty cool. But mysterious and revolutionary? Not so much. What the Microsoft team has done is build an encapsulated Ajax-style tool that takes advantage of the .NET 2.0 Framework. I would almost say that the ASP.NET 2.0 release itself is much more extraordinary than the release of the Atlas library.

Now don't get me wrong. Despite my initial assessment, I do like Atlas, but I think you should understand that it is simply a Microsoft version of the Ajax library that you've seen throughout this book. It is an excellent out-of-the-box solution for Microsoft developers, and as the crew at MySpace (`http://www.myspace.com`) claim:

> ...we started out with a few Ajax libraries, we spent about two months playing around with it, but Microsoft Atlas in like two evenings with two developers working for two or three hours, they were able to use that library to completely convert it to the Microsoft Atlas framework.
>
> Atlas is a complete ecosystem, it's more than just Ajax libraries, it's the consistency into your development cycle.

There's no denying that Atlas is a force to be contended with, and as such we should definitely take a cursory look at this technology. In this final chapter, I'd like to take an overall look at the product and demonstrate it with a sample application or two. There are some very interesting controls made available to us, and we'll give them due process.

What Atlas Is

The Atlas library is more than just dynamic web controls and packaged scripting. In a sense, it has become a complete framework solution. According to Microsoft:

> The primary goal of "Atlas" is to integrate client script features with the features of ASP.NET on the server to provide a comprehensive development platform.

OK, I can buy that. The one key term that they use, and accurately so, is "integrate." The backbone of the Atlas library is its ability to seamlessly integrate ASP.NET functionality with the client-side browser.

Some of the more prevalent key features of Atlas are as follows:

- *Automatic browser compatibility*: I don't know about you, but this is huge for me. Having developed solutions that must maintain consistency when ported to Firefox, Safari, and others, I can confidently claim that (for me) this is quite possibly the biggest and most useful feature so far.

- *Object-oriented API in JavaScript*: OOP on the client side is really nothing new for Ajax developers. The library that we've worked with is quite similar in syntax to what Microsoft has built for us. I appreciate that the API is wrapped and available.

- *Desktop similarities*: The Atlas controls provide an interactive experience, similar to Windows desktop functionality. Drag-and-drop behavior in a client browser is fascinating when you compare it to the web of four or five years ago.

- *Declarative model*: The Atlas controls have declarative scripting, similar to those of other ASP.NET controls. You'll see this in action shortly.

- *Client layers*: A variety of scripting layers provide framework capabilities to ASP.NET web applications.

If you're anything like me, features are nice to read about, but I would much rather see the thing in action. So let's get right to it. We'll download Atlas and take a look at the file structure that Microsoft provides.

Downloading Atlas

You'll want to head over to `http://atlas.asp.net` if you want to download the latest and greatest build of Atlas. Follow the download links until you get to the actual file download form. As of this writing, the file(s) are located at `http://atlas.asp.net/default.aspx?tabid=47&subtabid=471`.

You'll be redirected to the Microsoft download form, wherein lives the Download button. Clicking said button will retrieve `AtlasSetup.msi`. After downloading the installer, go ahead and run the utility.

You'll eventually be prompted to install the Visual Studio Atlas template, as shown in Figure 20-2.

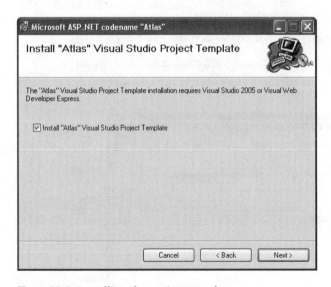

Figure 20-2. *Installing the project template*

You definitely want to install the template. It'll save you some time when it comes to constructing an Atlas application. After ensuring that the option to install the template is checked, continue through the install, accepting defaults as you go. I would strongly recommend including the .asbx web services bridge extension when asked.

After the install has completed, click Start ➤ All Programs ➤ Microsoft ASP.NET Atlas ➤ Atlas ➤ Atlas Assembly and Script Library to see the installation.

Examining the Atlas Files

You'll find that a few JavaScript files have been created for us in the ScriptLibrary folder. These are the heart of the Atlas library and will be available to use through the Atlas framework:

- AtlasRuntime.js: This is the basic script that you can use to enable Atlas features. It's a bare-bones script file that you'll implement when you need minimal Atlas capabilities. For instance, if you want to access a web service from JavaScript, this is the script for you.

- Atlas.js: This is the full-deal file. It includes the Atlas runtime and full-feature pack. When you add an Atlas ScriptManager, you'll get this guy by default.

- AtlasCompat.js: This script provides cross-browser compatibility for Atlas features.

- AtlasCompat2.js: This script also provides cross-browser compatibility for Atlas features.

- AtlasFX.js: If you're building gadgets in a hosted environment, you'll be using this script. It has the same content as the Atlas.js file, but is lacking the AtlasRuntime.js coding.

- AtlasUIDragDrop.js: This script provides drag-and-drop functionality.

- AtlasUIGlitz.js: This script provides user interface special effects.

- AtlasUIMap.js: This script provides virtual mapping functionality.

- AtlasWebParts.js: This script provides web parts functionality.

- GadgetRuntime.js: This runtime script is used by Microsoft and MSN.

An Atlas template for Visual Studio 2005 has also been created for us, as shown in Figure 20-3.

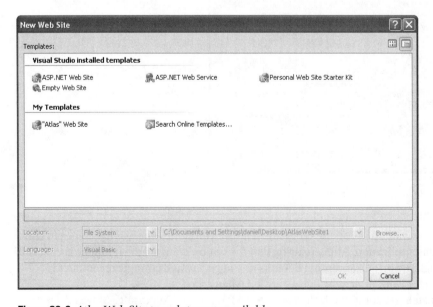

Figure 20-3. *Atlas Web Site template now available*

Let's take a look at just a few of the Atlas controls that we'll inherit from the freshly installed framework and work through a few sample applications.

Using Atlas for the First Time

Our first application will take advantage of the Atlas UpdatePanel. Similar to MagicAjax.NET's AjaxPanel (http://www.magicajax.net), the UpdatePanel will allow you to encapsulate Ajax functionality for controls that are nested within its bounds, as shown in Figure 20-4.

Figure 20-4. *Atlas UpdatePanel*

This, in my opinion, will be the most popular of all Atlas controls, in that it will allow developers to add Ajax functionality to preexisting ASP.NET pages without a huge amount of additional code. To demonstrate, we'll first create a simple lookup web page and then add the Atlas capabilities after the fact.

The Non-Atlas Application

Let's first create a new WebSite project with our brand new template, naming the site AtlasSample, as shown in Figure 20-5.

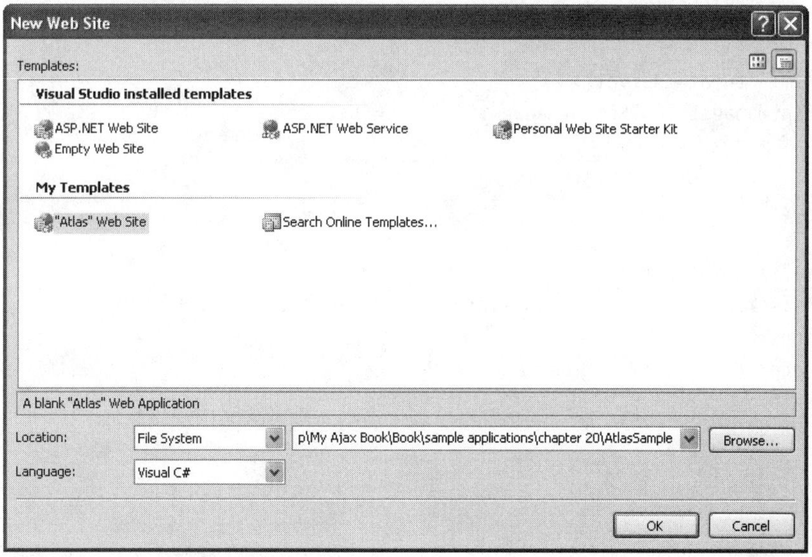

Figure 20-5. *Starting a new site*

Once the project has opened, you'll notice that the Atlas template adds a few files to the project by default, as you see in Figure 20-6.

Figure 20-6. *Atlas default files*

Atlas.dll, as you would expect, provides our Ajax functionality in much the same way that the Anthem library did for our previous applications. The readme.txt and eula.rtf are Microsoft-generated documents with links, info, and licensing agreement. You can delete them at will.

If you look within Default.aspx, you'll find some more pregenerated code:

```
<%@ Page Language="C#" AutoEventWireup="true"
  CodeFile="Default.aspx.cs" Inherits="_Default" %>

<!DOCTYPE html PUBLIC "-//W3C//DTD XHTML 1.1//EN"
  "http://www.w3.org/TR/xhtml11/DTD/xhtml11.dtd">
<html xmlns="http://www.w3.org/1999/xhtml">
  <head runat="server">
    <title>Atlas Sample Page</title>
  </head>
  <body>
    <form id="form1" runat="server">
      <atlas:ScriptManager ID="ScriptManager1" runat="server" />
      <div>
      </div>
    </form>

    <script type="text/xml-script">
      <page xmlns:script="http://schemas.microsoft.com/xml-script/2005">
        <references>
        </references>
        <components>
        </components>
      </page>
    </script>
  </body>
</html>
```

The Atlas template was kind enough to drop the <atlas:ScriptManager> tag onto the page for us. The ScriptManager is the brains of the page body. It is the liaison between the client JavaScript code and the ASP.NET implementation of Atlas. The ScriptManager has a default reference to the Atlas.js file that I described earlier and, more importantly, every ASP.NET page that desires to work the Atlas magic must include the <atlas:ScriptManager> tag. We'll come back to this control in a few pages. For now, let's continue building the non-Atlas version of the application.

Adding the DropDownList

Drag a DropDownList control onto Default.aspx, as shown in Figure 20-7.

Figure 20-7. *Adding DropDownList to the page*

Select Choose Data Source. We'll be connecting to the AdventureWorks data, as we have in previous examples.

You'll need to add a new data source, when asked to select the data source. On the drop-down for Select a Data Source, select New Data Source, and the source selection window will pop up as shown in Figure 20-8.

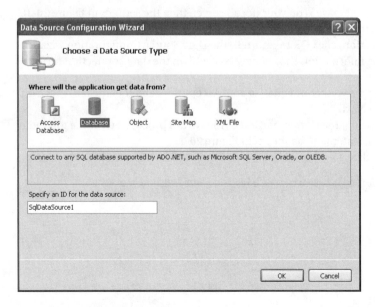

Figure 20-8. *Adding the database as our data source*

We'll select Database as the source and also accept the default SqlDataSource1 for the ID. Click OK to move on.

You'll be prompted to choose a connection, as shown in Figure 20-9, and you'll want to click the New Connection button (if you have the AdventureWorks connection still available from previous examples, you'll want to use that).

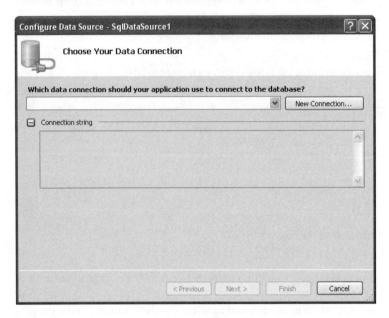

Figure 20-9. *Adding a new connection to the data source*

If your AdventureWorks database is on your (local) server, then the settings in Figure 20-10 will be quite similar to the connection settings that you'll choose as well.

After testing the connection, click OK to return to the Data Source Configuration wizard. Your new connection string information should now be listed on the data connection form. Click Next to move along.

You'll be prompted to save your connection string. Accept the default name and move on to the next form by clicking Next.

We've now arrived at the data-selection portion of the wizard process. Select the top radio button to add a custom SQL statement, as shown in Figure 20-11.

After clicking Next, we'll be given the chance to add our custom SQL string:

```
SELECT DISTINCT * FROM person.stateprovince WHERE countryregioncode = 'US'
```

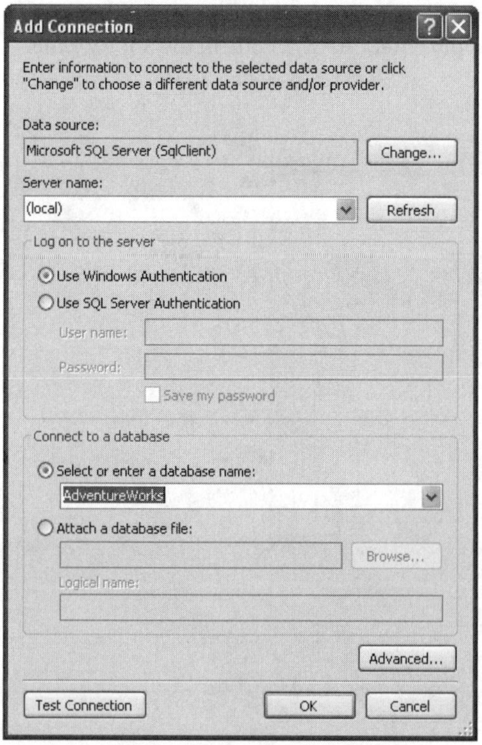

Figure 20-10. *Connection settings*

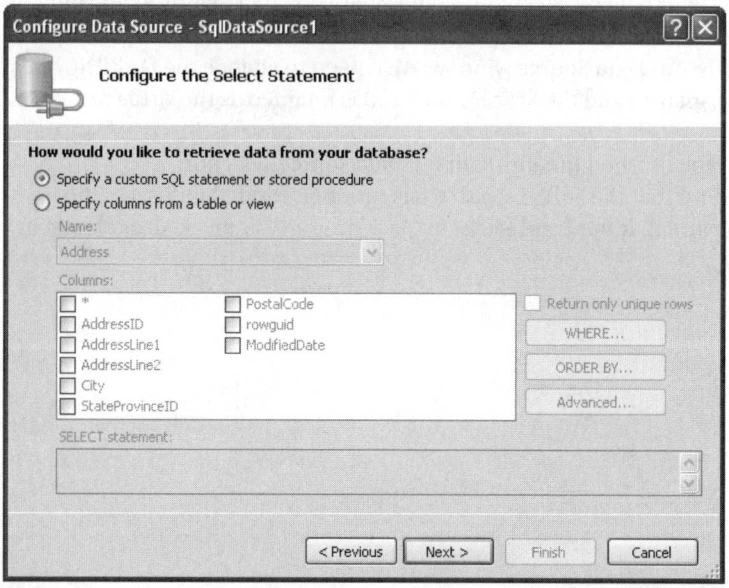

Figure 20-11. *Adding the Select statement*

Our DropDownList is only interested in a read-only set of data, so there's no need to worry about the INSERT, UPDATE, or DELETE queries. We simply enter our SQL code in the appropriate window, as shown in Figure 20-12, and click Next.

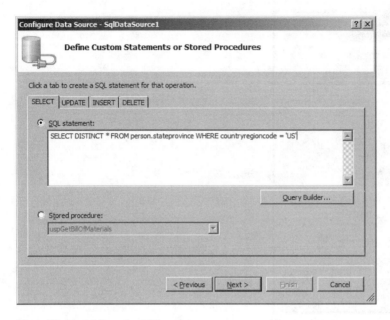

Figure 20-12. *Adding the SQL code*

Go ahead and preview your data by clicking Test Query, as shown in Figure 20-13, and then click Finish.

We'll be brought back to our Data Source window. We'll need to change the DropDownList values so that the Name is displayed and the StateProvinceID is retained as the Value property, as shown in Figure 20-14.

After clicking OK, we'll be finished (finally) with our data source selection.

Back on the page, we find that the SqlDataSource has now been added for us. On the DropDownList options, ensure that the EnableAutoPostBack property is checked, as shown in Figure 20-15.

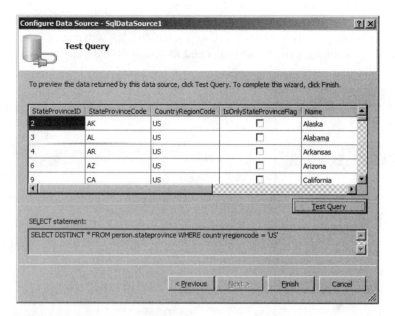

Figure 20-13. *Testing our SQL query*

Figure 20-14. *Setting data fields on the DropDownList*

Figure 20-15. *Enabling postback for the DropDownList*

Before we move on with the application, let's go ahead and run what we have so far. Click the play button (labeled Start Debugging) and accept the Web.Config additions. The web page should display a DropDownList with a set of regional data when opened, as shown in Figure 20-16.

Figure 20-16. *Atlas sample first run*

Stop debugging after you've tested the application.

Adding the Grid View

The first half of the application is complete. The remaining half is fairly quick and straightforward. Now that we have a state lookup control, let's add a GridView to the page that will provide more detail for our selection process.

Drag a GridView control onto the page just below the DropDownList, as shown in Figure 20-17.

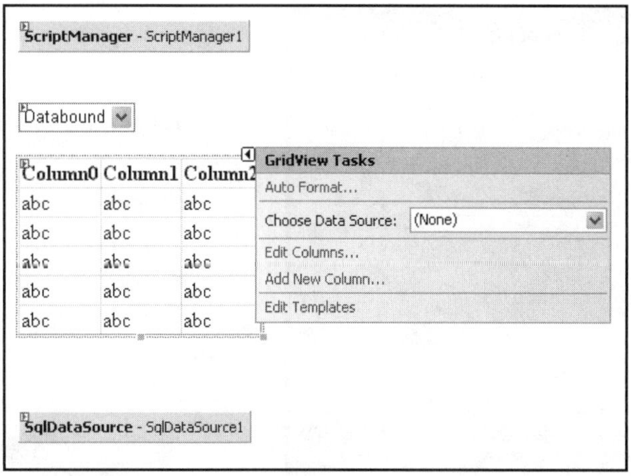

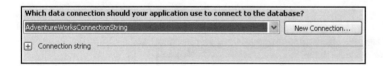

Figure 20-17. *Adding the GridView control*

With the GridView now on the page, click the drop-down for Choose Data Source and select New Data Source. We'll be following much the same process we used for the DropDownList as we configure this data source.

Select Database and accept SqlDataSource2 as the ID for the source. Click OK to continue.

We will be able to reuse our previously configured connection string, so find the previously saved connection information on the drop-down, as shown in Figure 20-18, and click Next.

Which data connection should your application use to connect to the database?

AdventureWorksConnectionString   [v]   [New Connection...]

[+] Connection string

Figure 20-18. *Adding the existing connection*

Once again, we'll be declaring our own custom SQL string, so we'll select the appropriate option, as shown in Figure 20-19.

After clicking Next, we'll now need to add the actual SQL string to the wizard:

```
SELECT Sales.Store.CustomerID,
Sales.Store.Name,
Person.Address.PostalCode,
Person.StateProvince.Name AS State
FROM Sales.Store join Sales.CustomerAddress
ON Sales.Store.CustomerID = Sales.CustomerAddress.CustomerID
JOIN Person.Address ON
Person.Address.AddressID = Sales.CustomerAddress.AddressID
JOIN Person.StateProvince ON
Person.StateProvince.StateProvinceID = Person.Address.StateProvinceID
WHERE Person.Address.StateProvinceID = @stateid
```

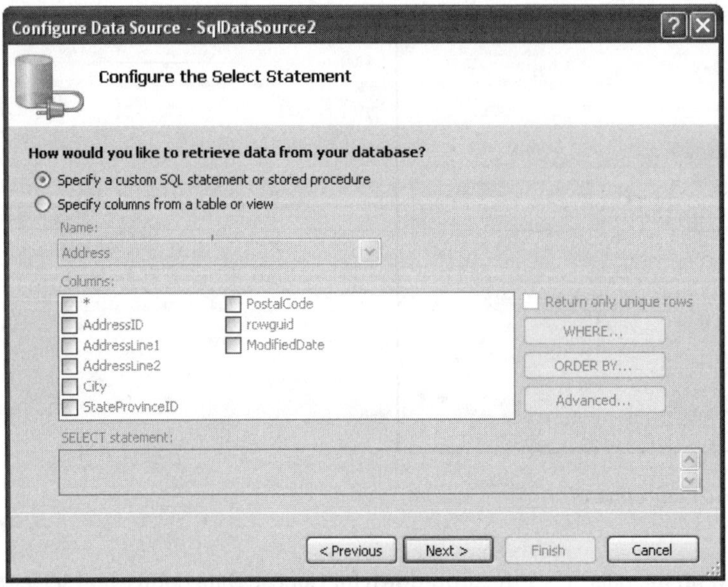

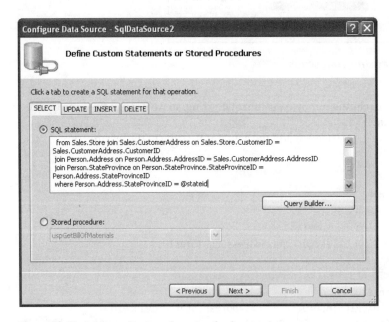

Figure 20-19. *Adding our own SQL statement*

We're not interested in doing any kind of updates on the GridView, so we'll not concern ourselves with the UPDATE, INSERT, and DELETE tabs.

We add the preceding SQL code to the statement box, as shown in Figure 20-20, and click Next.

Figure 20-20. *Adding the store location lookup script*

One of the coolest features that Visual Studio 2005 has brought to the table is its simple data-binding setup. Because our SQL statement relies upon an input parameter for successful operation, Visual Studio now gives us an opportunity to declare where that parameter will come from. We'll use the data value field from the DropDownList as the provider for the parameter, as shown in Figure 20-21.

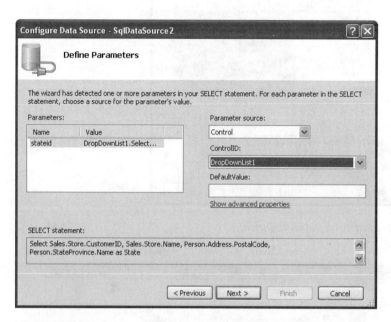

Figure 20-21. *Adding the DropDownList as the input parameter*

After adding the DropDownList information, click Next to continue the process. Test your query, as shown in Figure 20-22, and click Finish when done.

When we click Finish, the IDE will ask us whether we want to refresh the schema for the control, as shown in Figure 20-23.

Click Yes to refresh the grid and keys as requested.

We'll be dropped back to the web page, and the grid will be modified to reflect the SQL query columns.

Let's go ahead and enable paging and sorting by checking off the appropriate checkboxes on the GridView options as shown in Figure 20-24.

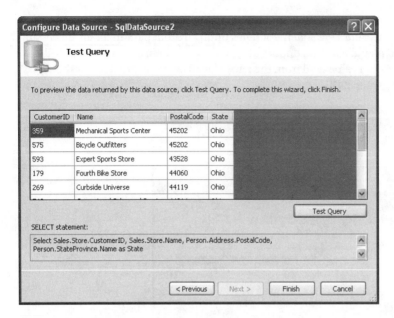

Figure 20-22. *Testing and completing the data source*

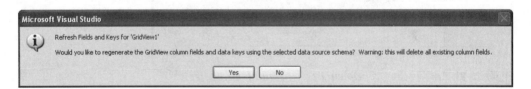

Figure 20-23. *Refreshing GridView fields*

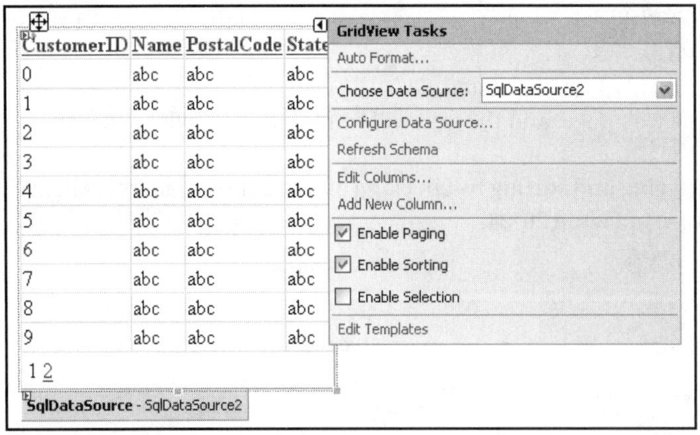

Figure 20-24. *Enabling paging and sorting*

The non-Atlas portion of the application is now complete and ready to run. We expect that we'll be able to select a state and then have the corresponding store locations for that state returned to us, as shown in Figure 20-25.

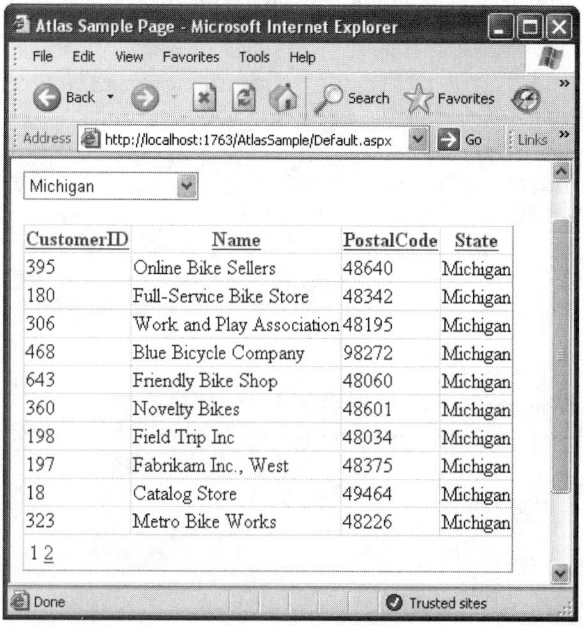

Figure 20-25. *Non-Ajax store lookup in action*

As you click around on the column headings, you'll find that the sorting works flawlessly. Clicking the page numbers at the bottom reveals that pagination is off to a good start as well. There's only one problem with this application: it's using crummy old postbacks! Let's dig out our Atlas tools and fix that.

The Atlas Version

The Atlas UpdatePanel allows us to indicate to the server that information contained within its scripted boundaries is subject to Ajax-like activities.

The client-side template for the control looks something like the following:

```
<atlas:UpdatePanel runat="server" ID="atlasPanel1">
  <ContentTemplate>

  </ContentTemplate>
  <Triggers>
    <atlas:ControlEventTrigger />
    <atlas:ControlValueTrigger />
  </Triggers>
</atlas:UpdatePanel>
```

The ContentTemplate tags will contain the controls that we wish to have dynamically updated. The triggers are just that; they indicate the action that must take place for the Ajax activity to be triggered. You'll see these in action in a moment.

If we want to add Ajax functionality to the current page, we'll need to relocate the Grid-View and specify a trigger. Your new Default.aspx page should appear as shown:

```
<%@ Page Language="C#" AutoEventWireup="true"
 CodeFile="Default.aspx.cs" Inherits="_Default" %>

<!DOCTYPE html PUBLIC "-//W3C//DTD XHTML 1.1//EN"
 "http://www.w3.org/TR/xhtml11/DTD/xhtml11.dtd">
<html xmlns="http://www.w3.org/1999/xhtml">
  <head runat="server">
    <title>Atlas Sample Page</title>
  </head>
  <body>
    <form id="form1" runat="server">
      <atlas:ScriptManager ID="ScriptManager1"
                           runat="server" EnablePartialRendering="true" />
      <br />
      <br />
      <div>
        <asp:DropDownList ID="DropDownList1"
                          runat="server" AutoPostBack="True"
                          DataSourceID="SqlDataSource1"
                          DataTextField="Name"
                          DataValueField="StateProvinceID">
        </asp:DropDownList><br />
        <br />
        <atlas:UpdatePanel runat="server" ID="atlasPanel1">
          <ContentTemplate>
            <asp:GridView ID="GridView1" runat="server"
                          AllowPaging="True" AllowSorting="True"
                          AutoGenerateColumns="False"
                          DataKeyNames="CustomerID"
                          DataSourceID="SqlDataSource2">
              <Columns>
                <asp:BoundField DataField="CustomerID"
                                HeaderText="CustomerID"
                                ReadOnly="True"
                                SortExpression="CustomerID" />
                <asp:BoundField DataField="Name"
                                HeaderText="Name"
                                SortExpression="Name" />
                <asp:BoundField DataField="PostalCode"
                                HeaderText="PostalCode"
                                SortExpression="PostalCode" />
```

```
                    <asp:BoundField DataField="State"
                                    HeaderText="State"
                                    SortExpression="State" />
            </Columns>
          </asp:GridView>
        </ContentTemplate>
        <Triggers>
          <atlas:ControlEventTrigger ControlID="DropDownList1"
                                     EventName="SelectedIndexChanged" />
        </Triggers>
      </atlas:UpdatePanel>

      <asp:SqlDataSource ID="SqlDataSource2" runat="server"
          ConnectionString=
            "<%$ ConnectionStrings:AdventureWorksConnectionString %>"
          SelectCommand="SELECT Sales.Store.CustomerID,
            Sales.Store.Name, Person.Address.PostalCode,
            Person.StateProvince.Name AS State
            FROM Sales.Store JOIN Sales.CustomerAddress ON
            Sales.Store.CustomerID =
            Sales.CustomerAddress.CustomerID
            JOIN Person.Address ON Person.Address.AddressID =
            Sales.CustomerAddress.AddressID
            JOIN Person.StateProvince ON
            Person.StateProvince.StateProvinceID =
            Person.Address.StateProvinceID
            WHERE Person.Address.StateProvinceID = @stateid">
        <SelectParameters>
          <asp:ControlParameter ControlID="DropDownList1"
                                Name="stateid" PropertyName="SelectedValue" />
        </SelectParameters>
      </asp:SqlDataSource>
      <br />
      <br />
      <br />
      <asp:SqlDataSource ID="SqlDataSource1" runat="server"
          ConnectionString=
            "<%$ ConnectionStrings:AdventureWorksConnectionString %>"
          SelectCommand="SELECT DISTINCT * FROM
            Person.StateProvince WHERE CountryRegionCode = 'US'">
      </asp:SqlDataSource>
      <br />
    </div>
  </form>
```

```
        <script type="text/xml-script">
          <page xmlns:script="http://schemas.microsoft.com/xml-script/2005">
            <references>
            </references>
            <components>
            </components>
          </page>
        </script>
    </body>
</html>
```

One of the first things that I should point out is the modified ScriptManager code:

```
<atlas:ScriptManager ID="ScriptManager1"
                     runat="server" EnablePartialRendering="true" />
```

In order to use the UpdatePanel, we'll need to enable partial page rendering. This lets the server know that this page will have an updatable region, and our UpdatePanel is that required region. As you look through the code, you'll see that we have our GridView parked in the ContentTemplate and the DropDownList's SelectedIndexChanged event has been declared as a trigger for the UpdatePanel:

```
<atlas:UpdatePanel runat="server" ID="atlasPanel1">
    <ContentTemplate>
      <asp:GridView ID="GridView1" runat="server"
                    AllowPaging="True" AllowSorting="True"
                    AutoGenerateColumns="False"
                    DataKeyNames="CustomerID"
                    DataSourceID="SqlDataSource2">
                (column stuff goes here. . . )
      </asp:GridView>
    </ContentTemplate>
    <Triggers>
      <atlas:ControlEventTrigger ControlID="DropDownList1"
                                 EventName="SelectedIndexChanged" />
    </Triggers>
</atlas:UpdatePanel>
```

Now when we run the application, we find that the application has indeed been made postbackless, with all of the aforementioned functionality still intact.

The UpdatePanel is a simple yet powerful Atlas control, and I anticipate that it will see a significant amount of use in the coming years. For updating current non-Ajax pages to the wonderful world of dynamic page content, it's an awesome tool to have.

One of the other more significant Atlas capabilities that I'd like to show you is the AutoCompleteBehavior class.

AutoCompleteBehavior Class

The AutoCompleteBehavior class, as you would expect, provides text completion functionality similar to the Google Suggest clone that we assembled in Chapter 11. One major difference between the Atlas version and the Ajax version is the amount of code involved. Because Atlas has much of its capabilities encapsulated within the framework, we need only provide basic information for our application to perform the autocomplete.

There are, of course, more caveats involved with the class as compared to the Ajax version. For instance, the Atlas class makes heavy use of web services as the data provider for the control. With Ajax, we could choose our own destiny. If you're not a big fan of web services, this is probably not the control for you.

Before we take a look at the properties and methods of the class, let's first see the autocomplete in action. To start, open the Atlas UpdatePanel solution from the previous demonstration.

As I mentioned earlier, we'll need a web service for the AutoCompleteBehavior class to communicate with. Right-click the project name and choose Add New Item.

You'll want to add a web service, as shown in Figure 20-26.

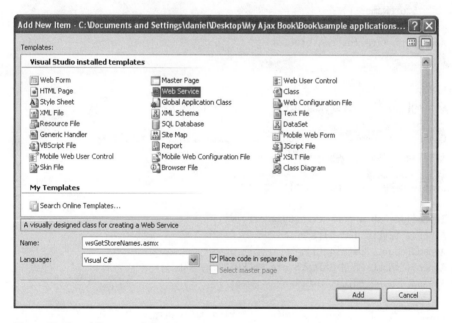

Figure 20-26. *Adding a web service*

Name your web service file wsGetStoreNames.asmx and click Add.

Modify wsGetStoreNames.cs to reflect the following data-retrieval code:

```
using System;
using System.Web;
using System.Data;
using System.Collections;
using System.Web.Services;
using System.Web.Services.Protocols;
using System.Data.SqlClient;


/// <summary>
/// Summary description for wsGetStoreNames
/// </summary>
[WebService(Namespace = "http://tempuri.org/")]
[WebServiceBinding(ConformsTo = WsiProfiles.BasicProfile1_1)]
public class wsGetStoreNames : System.Web.Services.WebService {

    public wsGetStoreNames ()
    {
        // Add stuff here for constructor
    }

    [WebMethod]
    public string[] GetNames(string prefixText, int count)
    {
        SqlConnection conn = new SqlConnection("Data Source=(local); ➥
            Initial Catalog=AdventureWorks; Integrated Security=SSPI");

        DataTable dtReturn = new DataTable();

        StringBuilder sb = new StringBuilder();
        sb.Append("SELECT TOP ");
        sb.Append(count.ToString());
        sb.Append(" Name FROM Sales.Store WHERE Name LIKE");
        sb.Append(" @searchterm ORDER BY Name");

        SqlCommand cmd = new SqlCommand(sb.ToString(), conn);
        SqlParameter param = new SqlParameter();
        param.ParameterName = "@searchterm";
        prefixText.Trim().Replace("'", "''");
        prefixText += "%";
        param.Value = prefixText;
        cmd.Parameters.Add(param);
        SqlDataAdapter adpt = new SqlDataAdapter(cmd);
        adpt.Fill(dtReturn);

        conn.Close();
```

```
        string[] strReturn = new string[dtReturn.Rows.Count];
        for(int i = 0; i < dtReturn.Rows.Count; i++)
        {
            strReturn[i] = (string)dtReturn.Rows[i]["Name"];
        }

        return strReturn;
    }
}
```

We now have our data provider all squared away, so let's add another page to access the service. Right-click the project name and select Add New Item. Add a web form and accept the name Default2.aspx. Click Add to finish.

Your project files should be similar to those shown in Figure 20-27.

Figure 20-27. *Atlas project files*

Modify the Default2.aspx code as follows:

```
<%@ Page Language="C#" AutoEventWireup="true"
  CodeFile="Default2.aspx.cs" Inherits="Default2" %>

<!DOCTYPE html PUBLIC "-//W3C//DTD XHTML 1.0 Transitional//EN"
"http://www.w3.org/TR/xhtml1/DTD/xhtml1-transitional.dtd">

<html xmlns="http://www.w3.org/1999/xhtml" >
  <head runat="server">
    <title>Untitled Page</title>
    <atlas:ScriptManager ID="atlasSM" runat="server">
    </atlas:ScriptManager>
  </head>
```

```
<body>
  <form id="form1" runat="server">
    <div>
      <input id="TextBox1" type="text" style="width: 240px" />
    </div>
  </form>
  <script type="text/xml-script">
    <pagexmlns:script="http://schemas.microsoft.com/xml-script/2005">
      <components>
        <textBox id="TextBox1">
          <behaviors>
            <autoComplete serviceURL="wsGetStoreNames.asmx"
                          serviceMethod="GetNames"
                          minimumPrefixLength="1"
                          completionSetCount="8"
                          completionInterval="200" />
          </behaviors>
        </textBox>
      </components>
    </page>
  </script>
</body>
</html>
```

Believe it or not, that's all we need for the autocomplete to work. When we run the application, we find that, indeed, we have autocompletion on our textbox, as shown in Figure 20-28.

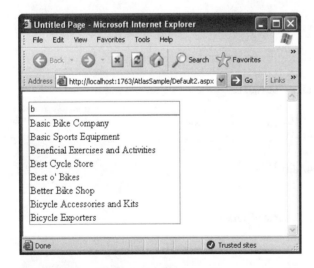

Figure 20-28. *Atlas autocomplete at work*

Atlas has given us something "out-of-the-box" that previously we had to write quite a bit of code to develop. But wait! Before we look at the properties, we should take a look at an option that the AutoCompleteBehavior provides for a rather cool effect for the type-ahead drop-down box.

We need to modify the code slightly:

```
<%@ Page Language="C#" AutoEventWireup="true"
  CodeFile="Default2.aspx.cs" Inherits="Default2" %>

<!DOCTYPE html PUBLIC "-//W3C//DTD XHTML 1.0 Transitional//EN"
  "http://www.w3.org/TR/xhtml1/DTD/xhtml1-transitional.dtd">

<html xmlns="http://www.w3.org/1999/xhtml" >
  <head runat="server">
    <title>Untitled Page</title>
    <atlas:ScriptManager ID="atlasSM" runat="server">
    </atlas:ScriptManager>
  </head>
  <body>
    <form id="form1" runat="server">
      <div>
        <input id="TextBox1" type="text" style="width: 240px" />
        <div id="transpDrop"
             style="opacity:0.8;
                    filter:alpha(opacity=85)">
        </div>
        <p>Daniel Woolston is a software developer
        from the Grand Rapids, Michigan, area.
        He's currently working with Nusoft Solutions,
        a Microsoft Gold Partner, on an Ajax.Net
        implementation for an upcoming site release.
        Daniel's software journey began in the late
        1980s with the infamous Sinclair ZX80.</p>
      </div>
    </form>
    <script type="text/xml-script">
      <page xmlns:script="http://schemas.microsoft.com/xml-script/2005">
        <components>
          <textBox id="TextBox1">
            <behaviors>
              <autoComplete completionList="transpDrop"
                            serviceURL="wsGetStoreNames.asmx"
                            serviceMethod="GetNames"
                            minimumPrefixLength="1"
                            completionSetCount="8"
                            completionInterval="200" />
```

```
                  </behaviors>
               </textBox>
            </components>
         </page>
      </script>
   </body>
</html>
```

I've added a `<div>` tag with some custom properties that allow the drop-down list to appear as transparent. I've also added another property to the `<autoComplete>` tag to point to the appropriate `<div>` tag.

When we run the application, we're presented with a really cool visual effect on the drop-down, as shown in Figure 20-29.

Figure 20-29. *Transparent drop-down list*

Now that you've seen what the `AutoCompleteBehavior` class can do, we should also examine the set of properties that we were declaring on our web page:

- `completionInterval`: The amount of time to wait between drop-down updates

- `completionList`: The page HTML element (our div tag) to use as the drop-down box

- `completionSetCount`: The set number of rows that you want in the drop-down

- `id`: The unique identifier for the component lookup

- `minimumPrefixLength`: The minimum number of characters that the box must have before the process begins

- `serviceMethod`: The method name for the completion-text retrieval on the web service

- `serviceURL`: URL of the web service that you're attaching to for your autocomplete data

- `dataContext`: Data source for data binding

- `propertyChanged`: Event handler to call for `propertyChanged` event

As you can see from the list, as compared to the actual code that we implemented, we're not using all of the properties, and that's fine. I encourage you to experiment with the control and drop-down CSS styling. You'll find that the new `AutoCompleteBehavior` class is a powerful new addition to the ASP.NET 2.0 world.

Summary

The Atlas library is very much a beta product and will continue to evolve for quite some time. Microsoft has made a serious commitment to leveraging Ajax against web technology, seeking to take the lead in dynamic site generation. Given the level of support in the development community for the various third-party Ajax libraries, I imagine that we'll continue to see great innovation on that front as well. Do I prefer one over the other? No, not really. I really believe that Ajax and Atlas have the same goal in mind, but with a different approach. To call them competitors would be a taunting statement, one that I hope will spur both parties to continue innovating and pushing the limits of the web.

I encourage you to continue monitoring the various Atlas and Ajax sites, keeping abreast of new changes, enhancements, and discoveries. It truly is an exciting time to be deeply involved with Ajax development!

Index

Find it faster at http://superindex.apress.com/

Find it faster at http://superindex.apress.com/

You Need the Companion eBook

Your purchase of this book entitles you to buy the companion PDF-version eBook for only $10. Take the weightless companion with you anywhere.

We believe this Apress title will prove so indispensable that you'll want to carry it with you everywhere, which is why we are offering the companion eBook (in PDF format) for $10 to customers who purchase this book now. Convenient and fully searchable, the PDF version of any content-rich, page-heavy Apress book makes a valuable addition to your programming library. You can easily find and copy code—or perform examples by quickly toggling between instructions and the application. Even simultaneously tackling a donut, diet soda, and complex code becomes simplified with hands-free eBooks!

Once you purchase your book, getting the $10 companion eBook is simple:

❶ Visit **www.apress.com/promo/tendollars/**.

❷ Complete a basic registration form to receive a randomly generated question about this title.

❸ Answer the question correctly in 60 seconds, and you will receive a promotional code to redeem for the $10.00 eBook.

2560 Ninth Street • Suite 219 • Berkeley, CA 94710

eBookshop

THE EXPERT'S VOICE™

Offer valid through 1/07.